Innovative Psychotherapy Techniques in Child and Adolescent Therapy

Innovative Psychotherapy Techniques in Child and Adolescent Therapy

Second Edition

Edited by
Charles E. Schaefer

John Wiley & Sons, Inc.

New York • Chichester • Weinheim • Brisbane • Singapore • Toronto

Copyright © 1999 by John Wiley & Sons, Inc. All rights reserved.

Published simultaneously in Canada.

Library of Congress Cataloging-in-Publication Data:

Innovative psychotherapy techniques in child and adolescent therapy /
    edited by Charles E. Schaefer. — 2nd ed.
            p.   cm.
        Includes indexes.
        Rev. ed. of: Innovative interventions in child and adolescent
    therapy / edited by Charles E. Schaefer. c1988.
        ISBN 0-471-24404-X (cloth : alk. paper)
        1. Child psychotherapy.   2. Adolescent psychotherapy.
    I. Schaefer, Charles E.
        [DNLM: 1. Psychotherapy—in infancy & childhood.
    2. Psychotherapy—in adolescence.   3. Psychotherapy—methods.
    WS350.2 I584 1999]
    RJ504.I57   1999
    618.92'8914—dc21
    DNLM/DLC
    for Library of Congress   98-55167

Printed in the United States of America.

10 9 8 7 6 5 4 3 2 1

To Annabelle

Editor

Charles E. Schaefer, PhD
Professor of Psychology
Fairleigh Dickinson University
Teaneck, New Jersey

Contributors

Louis L. Aymard, PhD
Arnold-Severn Center
Annapolis, Maryland

Dene S. Berman, PhD
Clinical Professor of Professional
    Psychology and Associate
Clinical Professor of Medicine
Wright State University
Dayton, Ohio

Timothy P. Culbert, MD
The Alexander Center for Child
    Development and Behavior
HealthSystem Minnesota
Assistant Professor of Clinical
    Pediatrics
University of Minnesota
Bloomington, Minnesota

Jennifer Davis-Berman, PhD
Department of Sociology,
    Anthropology, and
    Social Work
University of Dayton
Dayton, Ohio

Peter W. Dowrick, PhD
Professor of Disability Studies
    and Graduate Studies in
    Psychology
University of Hawaii
Manoa, Hawaii

Tiffany Field, PhD
Touch Research Institute
Department of Pediatrics
University of Miami School
    of Medicine
Miami, Florida
Nova Southeastern
    University
Ft. Lauderdale, Florida

Deanne Ginns-Gruenberg, MA
Director
The Self-Esteem Shop
Royal Oak, Michigan

Richard B. Griffin, PsyD
President of the Virginia
  Hypnosis Society and
  Approved Consultant with
  the American Society of
  Clinical Hypnosis
Hampton, Virginia
Assistant Professor of Psychiatry
Eastern Virginia Medical School
Norfolk, Virginia

Maria Hernandez-Reif, PhD
Director of Research
Touch Research Institute
Department of Pediatrics
University of Miami School
  of Medicine
Miami, Florida

Melissa Johnson, PhD
WakeMed and Wake AHEC
  Pediatrics
Raleigh, North Carolina
Clinical Associate Professor of
  Pediatrics and Clinical
  Assistant Professor of
  Psychiatry
University of North Carolina at
  Chapel Hill School of Medicine

Luciano L'Abate, PhD, ABEPP
Professor Emeritus of Psychology
Georgia State University
Atlanta, Georgia

Stuart M. Leeds, PsyD, DABFE
Juvenile Evaluation and
  Treatment Services: Intensive
  Outpatient Program
Atlantic Behavioral Health
Morristown Memorial Hospital
Morristown, New Jersey

Gerald P. Mallon, DSW
Hunter College School of
  Social Work
New York, New York

Susan G. Nash, BH, BSC, GCE
Research Officer
School of Psychology
University College of North
  Wales
Bangor, Great Britain

Helen Payne, MPhil; PhD
Principal Lecturer
University of Hertfordshire
Hertfordshire, Great Britain

Bart Santen, PhD
De Mark Center for Child and
  Adolescent Psychiatry
Breda, The Netherlands

Dawn C. Wimpory, PhD
Lecturer and Consultant
  Clinical Psychologist
School of Psychology
University College of North
  Wales
Bangor, Great Britain

Arye Zacks, BA
Director of Marketing
The Self-Esteem Shop
Royal Oak, Michigan

Preface

THE ACADEMIC preparation of child therapists has traditionally included courses in major theoretical orientations and applications but not in more specialized child therapy techniques. The goal of this volume is to describe a wide variety of the most promising therapeutic procedures that have been developed for children and adolescents. In this second edition, all of the fourteen chapters are new, with two (Music and Dance Therapy) being revised and updated versions of chapters in the first edition. New sections have been added on wilderness approaches and the therapeutic applications of modern technology.

All of the techniques are nontraditional (unconventional and/or innovative) which means that they are not currently in the mainstream of clinical practice. Thus, they would not be discussed in traditional therapy courses on humanistic, psychodynamic, cognitive-behavioral, or family approaches. They are also not likely to be taught in practicum experiences or clinical internships. By adding nontraditional techniques to their repertoire, practitioners are more likely to find the right tool to solve a client's particular problem.

Quite comprehensive in scope, this sourcebook includes chapters by specialists who have extensive experience with the techniques. The range of specific approaches includes programmed writing, hypnosis, guided imagery, focusing, biofeedback, pet therapy, bibliotherapy, wilderness-challenge therapy, touch therapy, and video self-modeling.

The techniques, which cut across diagnostic categories and theoretical orientations, are classified for ease of reference in this book into four broad categories: Creative Arts, Adventure-Based, Technology-Based, and other techniques.

The emphasis of the chapters is on clinical practice—particularly a detailed description of the nuts-and-bolts of the techniques. The presentation of each procedure follows a common format, in which the historical and theoretical foundations of the technique are first discussed, followed by a step-by-step account of how to carry out the technique, and finally illustrative examples drawn from actual cases are presented. These case examples provide the reader with considerable depth and richness of detail. The procedures have been tested by the authors over many years and have been found to be capable of producing therapeutic change.

A word of caution about the techniques described in this volume: Some of the therapeutic practices are based on extensive empirical validation, while others appear promising but have been successful with only a limited number of cases. Consequently, a number of the techniques described in this book should be viewed with full recognition of the need for more extensive independent replication. It should also be recognized that the procedures contained herein are best used as supplements to more general theoretical orientations. In general, they are meant to be adjunct practices rather than a clinician's primary or sole therapeutic approach. Moreover, an understanding of childhood psychopathology, child development, and personality theory is needed to effectively apply these techniques.

Clinicians and counselors of all theoretical persuasions who have an interest in enhancing their repertoire of skills should find much of value in this book.

It has been a pleasure to organize and edit this second edition. I believe this process broadened my horizons and increased my clinical acumen. I am indebted to the contributors, each a respected clinician in his or her own field, for fostering the development of these innovative practices.

CHARLES E. SCHAEFER

Teaneck, New Jersey

Contents

PART ONE

EXPRESSIVE ARTS TECHNIQUES

CHAPTER 1

Musical Interaction Therapy for Children with Autism

DAWN C. WIMPORY and SUSAN G. NASH

INTRODUCTION

THE SOCIAL interaction deficit in autism has devastating implications for most aspects of development (Wimpory, 1995). This chapter outlines the use of Musical Interaction Therapy in seeking to facilitate social interaction experiences between young children with autism and their caregivers. The use of Musical Interaction Therapy with a wider age range and in a school setting is well established at Sutherland House School in Nottingham.

By the age of 2½, children with autism show impairments in social relationships, particularly in their use of eye contact, turn-taking, and sharing experience; they also show impairments in body language and spoken language, and preoccupations indicating rigidity of thought patterns (*DSM-IV*; American Psychological Association [APA], 1994). ". . . [E]very kind of impairment in autism has links with every other impairment in the syndrome. They all overflow into and pervade each other, and it is indeed the *interaction* between different parts of the syndrome which is most characteristic of autism" (Newson, 1987, p. 36).

3

BACKGROUND

Musical Interaction Therapy was originally developed in Nottingham, UK, by music/drama and teaching staff at Sutherland House School for children with autism (Christie & Wimpory, 1986). It is currently practiced and developed by Speech and Language Therapist, Wendy Prevezer, and Music Therapists, Rhian Saville and Ruth Spencer, working with teaching staff at Sutherland House where it continues to receive the support of developmental psychologists from the Early Years Diagnostic Centre, Professor Elizabeth Newson, and Sutherland House's director, Phil Christie. Musical Interaction Therapy is also practiced and developed by the first author and Music Therapy staff in North Wales where research has validated its efficacy (Wimpory, 1995; Wimpory, Chadwick, & Nash, 1995). Any implementation of Musical Interaction Therapy should take place within an interactive program that focuses on gesture and eye contact as well as the main area addressed by Musical Interaction Therapy, which encourages the development of preverbal conversation skills or social timing.

A brief background to the therapeutic applications of music for children with autism will be presented before a description of Musical Interaction Therapy and how it is implemented. We then hope to illustrate how Musical Interaction Therapy works by presenting two case studies. These are followed by a summary and suggestions for future research.

THERAPEUTIC APPLICATIONS OF MUSIC FOR CHILDREN WITH AUTISM

Children with autism are often reported to be particularly responsive both to music and to music therapy (e.g., Alvin, 1978; Applebaum, Egel, Koegel, & Imhoff, 1979; Benenzon, 1976; DeMyer, 1979; Sloboda, Hermelin, & O'Connor, 1985; Thaut, 1987, 1988). Hypo- or hyper-responsivity to sound is claimed by some to be an inherent feature of these children (e.g., Ornitz & Rivo, 1968, cited in Nelson, Anderson, & Gonzales, 1984). It is possible that the repetitive form and content of most music appeals to children whose difficulties often include (or lead to) obsessive repetitive behavior or fixations on objects that move repetitively. Music appears to soothe and/or to provide stimulation and even background music may enable such children to be more relaxed (Skelly, 1992). Although children with autism seem to be responsive to music, they are reported to have specific difficulties in dealing with temporal perception (Condon, 1975; Evans, 1986; Hermelin & O'Connor, 1970), which could be linked to their early difficulties with communicative interaction. Temporal perception is closely related to rhythmic movement (Nelson et al., 1984) and normal children have much better movement rhythm than do children with autism during music-prompted movement activities (DeMyer, 1979). From the point of view of finding a means of motivating the child with autism and addressing the proposed fundamental deficit in temporal perception, the use of music is very appropriate.

Nelson et al.'s (1984) review of music activities as therapy for children with autism and other pervasive developmental disorders, is based on an understanding of the interaction of the specific disabilities within autism. Nelson et al. make several practical suggestions based on research findings, for tailoring musical input to the exact responses of individual children. For example, they suggest that stimuli of very short duration could be used so that stimuli do not become confused. They also advocate that the therapist attempt to move and speak in synchrony with the child. They suggest that the timing of stimuli could be as important as the quality of the stimulus. "Perhaps learning to control and therefore predict the timing of sounds will improve the child's ability to integrate sequences of sounds" (p. 110).

A review by Wimpory (1995) found that therapies based on developing a relationship between the therapist and the child with autism are the most frequently reported. These tend to be nondirective and are often based on psychodynamic theory. Such therapies generally involve both child and therapist improvising on musical instruments. Results of therapy are usually reported by the therapist in terms of changed quality of relationship between himself or herself and the child. In autism in particular, it is very difficult for advances attained in one setting to become evident in other settings, and subjective reports do not often include comment on any changes apart from those achieved in the therapy setting. Some studies claim considerable change in the child, but qualitative changes can be difficult to quantify and such studies have not been very constructive in guiding the music therapist in any specific method to use with children with autism, nor in explaining what elements of the therapy might be effective.

More recently, the emphasis has been shifting to attempt evaluated studies of detailed interventions. For example, Müller and Warwick (1993) used a traditional experimental design and systematic observations to look at a variety of hypotheses relating to changes in the communication of children with autism and changes in mother-child interaction that were achieved through music therapy. Results showed an increase in turntaking, some increase in musical activity, and a decrease in stereotypic behavior (repetitive and unchanging patterns) during the sessions. This latter finding is in keeping with Nordoff and Robbins' (1971, 1972) work which indicates that stereotyped behavior may be reduced through matching rhythm and loudness and/or vocalizing precisely to the child's playing. Kostka (1993) also found that the arm flapping and body swaying of a 9-year-old boy decreased in regular music classes. Müller and Warwick's work is notable in that it is conducted and reported in a way that allows practitioners to select strategies and predict their effects on their clients. Furthermore, it supports the mother-child interaction with the therapeutic use of live music, rather than limiting the aims of therapy to the therapist-child interaction.

The Role of Musical Interaction Therapy

Musical Interaction Therapy is an approach to therapy for children with autism that parallels those mother-baby interactions that lead to the development of language in the normal child. Musical Interaction Therapy offers enhanced and prolonged experience of preverbal interaction patterns supported by a musician, in response to the difficulties in social reciprocity or timing experienced by children with autism. The use of "support" in this context indicates that the music is part of any interaction in both making meaning more overt, and holding the sequence together. The aim of Musical Interaction Therapy is to elicit and develop whatever sociability the child may have, by the music providing opportunities for the child and familiar adult to tune into each other. In Musical Interaction Therapy, the music is used to form a dialogue that is very important in helping to develop this tuning in. Any social interchange such as a (preverbal) conversation begins with shared focus. The fact that the child with autism is not innately tuned in is a fundamental impairment. Normal infants appear to develop "communicative competence" through experience with adults acting as though they are engaging with them in conversation long before they are completely competent to do so. For example, parents will select their baby's most socially relevant behaviors to imitate, and comment on noises and movements from a wide repertoire as though these are purposeful. This social scaffolding (Bruner, 1983) prepares the child for producing meaningful language. Like normal infants, children with autism also need to experience preverbal conversation before using (verbal or nonverbal) language communicatively. However, their specific disabilities, particularly with nonverbal body language and its timing in communication, mean that caregivers need support to provide this. The handicaps of the baby with autism mean that although his mother tries to communicate with him, he cannot make sense of these early dialogues and so cannot participate. Although children with autism may learn to speak, they do not develop conversation skills in the natural way that other children do. Interventions with young children with autism should focus on the development of conversational skills and on encouraging social development (Phil Christie, Director, Sutherland House; in Wimpory, 1985). Musical Interaction Therapy has a crucial role to play in this respect.

WHAT DOES RESEARCH SHOW ABOUT MUSICAL INTERACTION THERAPY?

Our research has analyzed videorecordings of clinicians and preschoolers with autism during one-to-one play sessions (without music support) to determine how adults facilitate children's active participation in episodes of social engagement. An episode of social engagement was defined as the child looking toward the face of the adult while expressing some other communicative behavior (for example, vocalizing). In confirmation and extension of previous studies (Sigman, Mundy, Sherman, & Ungerer, 1986), adult strategies identified as positive included musical/motoric activities and communicative turns oriented to the child's own focus of attention which included an element of "patterning" such as imitation, playful self-repetition, and social routines. Lap games with action rhymes and singing form a basis for proper intonation and timing when the child learns to speak. Musical Interaction Therapy capitalizes on the effectiveness of these strategies.

The use of Musical Interaction Therapy with the two children whose case studies are presented later has also been evaluated by research (Wimpory, 1995). The first of these was a long-term preschool, single case study (Heather) which compared pre-intervention baseline data with full Musical Interaction Therapy and follow-up assessments almost two years after completion of therapy (Wimpory et al., 1995). Onset of Musical Interaction Therapy was followed by improvements in the child's use of social acknowledgment (the time taken for Heather to acknowledge her mother), eye-contact, and initiations of interactive involvement. At two-year follow up these improvements were maintained and Heather's mother reported that she no longer showed frequent social withdrawal. The generalized emergence of teasing and pretend play during and following Musical Interaction Therapy has not been found in any other evaluated intervention for autism.

The other case study (Sian) attempted to separate out the relative effects of Musical Interaction Therapy's component parts. It found that exposure to full Musical Interaction Therapy was more effective in facilitating child sociability than was either passive exposure to prerecorded Musical Interaction Therapy music or regular supportive visits (without music) to the child's mother from the Musical Interaction Therapy therapist. This conclusion was determined by the frequency of episodes of social engagement between the child (Sian) and her mother during videorecordings at home. The objective measures and developmental perspective of these Musical Interaction Therapy studies (Wimpory, 1995; Wimpory et al., 1995) extend beyond previous research in confirming the therapeutic applications of music employed live within an interactive approach.

OUTLINE OF MUSICAL INTERACTION THERAPY FOR PRACTITIONERS

The model supporting Musical Interaction Therapy is one of normal infant-parent interaction. Caregiver and musician aim to emulate this by focusing on the interactions between the caregiver and the child. This model also serves both to explain and guide the process of therapy over time in that the interaction tends to move from general to specific contributions from both partners (caregiver and child) and becomes increasingly intentional on the child's part. Urwin (1984) argues that the normal infant's "illusion of control" during communication may be essential for language acquisition. The musician starts by supporting or even filling in the roles of caregiver and/or child which initially gives the experience of reciprocity. She moves over time to playing music in general support of the dyad's more genuine interaction as it becomes established and thereby transferable from the Musical Interaction Therapy setting.

CONSTANT THEMES

Three themes can be identified as running throughout Musical Interaction Therapy at any stage of its active process. These are the active roles afforded to the child through the illusion of communicative *control*, the *scaffolding* of the interaction by the caregiver who, along with the child, is afforded varying degrees of a musician's *musical support* in their contribution to the interaction. The musician also provides scaffolding, but does so less over time. These themes will be developed throughout the chapter. Caregivers typically report that children with autism appear more relaxed during activities which involve what research has identified as musical motoric experiences (Wimpory, 1995). These would include playing in water, experiencing music, and rough and tumble play. Music is unique as a medium in that it is timing-based and therefore has the potential to afford support to the difficulties children with autism may have with respect to the timing of reciprocal interactions (Newson, 1984; Wimpory 1995).

DESCRIPTION OF MUSICAL INTERACTION THERAPY

During Musical Interaction Therapy, a caregiver who is familiar to the child (usually a parent with preschool children) attempts to engage with him or her. Their activities and the behavior of each individual is supported by the live music of a therapist. The live accompanying music of Musical Interaction Therapy enhances both the caregiver's behavior, and the child's perception of it. The caregiver and musician can thereby between them construct an experience of (apparent) give and take communication between the caregiver and child. Through this experience the child may ultimately play his or her own communicative role with intentionality. The musician is ready to fill in, support, or enhance either partner's role in the (initially) preverbal discourse so that the participants' experience of it is holistic rather than disjointed as is usually the case with autism.

The experience of the caregiver is that the music appears to make it easier for him or her to "get through" to the child. This may be because the child's perceptions of the caregiver's behavior are enhanced by the musical accompaniment (e.g., the child may find it hard to pick up on the tempo or mood of a spontaneous activity, but the accompanying music makes it more predictable). It may be because the Musical Interaction Therapy accompaniment enables both caregiver and child to feel more relaxed and so less inhibited in their communication with each other. Alternatively it may be that the musician's singing and playing alerts the caregiver to possibilities in communicating with the child of which he or she may have otherwise been unaware. The musician plays to make the adult more potent and to enable the child to notice his or her effect on others so that caregiver and child share the social control over an interactive sequence. Heather's case study (see p. 19) illustrates this. The mother felt herself to be a more active agent as a result of letting her child lead.

What Happens in a Session of Musical Interaction Therapy?

We normally employ videofilm to convey the techniques underlying Musical Interaction Therapy (Wimpory, 1985). For the purposes of this chapter, we have drawn on our own experience of Musical Interaction Therapy with preschoolers and are indebted to Eleri Turner for the use of her report giving a personal view of what it is like to implement Musical Interaction Therapy with children with autism (Turner, 1998). We are also indebted to former colleagues at the Early Years Centre and Sutherland House in compiling the following account for practitioners. Wendy Prevezer's (1998) booklet is perhaps the most practical and detailed of articles concerning Musical Interaction Therapy and we also draw closely on her work. This chapter is focused on preschool children with autism and Musical Interaction Therapy as conducted in the child's home. We would refer the reader to Prevezer for a more comprehensive coverage of how Musical Interaction Therapy can also be used with older or verbal children, in group work and school settings.

Music Therapist

In our experience, the musician needs to have some training in facilitating communication with children but need not necessarily be a trained music therapist. The musician will have to work very closely with the caregiver of the child with autism and initially he or she will probably have to remind the caregiver of the aims of the therapy when caregiver and musician plan each session. The adult may need to be helped with ideas as to how to behave with the child, especially after a history of little interaction. The musician may need to reassure the caregiver that musical ability is not required and that while she builds up confidence, simply echoing what the child does is a start. Musical Interaction Therapy depends on a strong supportive relationship between musician and caregiver, particularly to enable the latter to risk trying out strategies that her instincts dictate, but which may not be part of her usual repertoire with her child, for example, blowing on the child's ear lobe, if the child responds to this, or making repetitive moaning noises that echo those of the child. The therapist needs to be sensitive to the current quality of the interaction (or lack of) between caregiver and child because her main aim is to facilitate that interaction. In addition to supporting the caregiver-child interaction, the therapist will sometimes use music or words during the sessions to suggest how the caregiver might act.

Instruments

These authors are not aware of any research indicating that the use of particular instruments may be more effective than others in Musical Interaction Therapy. It is very likely that different children will respond differently to different instruments and a parent may have some idea of her child's preference. However, it is difficult to obtain any sort of music support for children with autism, and any instrument that does not obstruct the therapist's view of the adult-child pair can be used in addition to the adults' voices. We are currently engaged in research seeking to facilitate interaction without the use of musical instruments. It is unclear at present whether it is possible to compensate for the obvious advantage that a musical instrument affords in supporting the timing of interactions.

Adult Caregiver

The adult caregiver is someone very familiar to the child with whom it is important for the child with autism to develop a relationship. In our North Wales client group, this is usually the mother. A parent will be the person most familiar with the expressions the child uses and ready to capitalize on them and will know the child's preferred routines. To maximize the benefits of Musical Interaction Therapy, the caregiver should spend time with the child between sessions, actively implementing the principles learned in the therapy sessions, even though there will not be the support of the musician. The shared attention which Musical Interaction Therapy is geared toward developing "needs to become a habit in order for quality relationships to develop" (Prevezer, 1998). We have found that the experience of interaction during Musical Interaction Therapy sessions motivates caregivers to continue with the techniques beyond the designated therapy.

Setting

Musical Interaction Therapy as practiced in North Wales, usually takes place in the family home. Familiarity with the setting helps the child and parent to be reasonably relaxed. The home is also the place where the developing relationship will be practiced, so less should be lost than when moving to the home from a different setting. Sessions can more easily use an "open door" policy if they take place at home. When the child can leave the room at will, it heightens the adults' awareness of how intrusive they may be. The adult tries to tune in physically as well as mentally to the child by, for example, lying or sitting on the floor or rocking. This makes her less threatening and more on the child's physical level. The caregiver may feel easier trying out these strategies at home.

When considering the setting, it is important to be aware of the role of toys or other objects. The ultimate aim of Musical Interaction Therapy is genuine social engagement, and the absorption of the child with autism in some toys may prevent social contact, so the use of such items should be kept to a minimum. However, a child's obsessional plaything or behavior may be used by the caregiver to encourage the child to notice an adult prior to social contact or the item may be used to develop shared attention. For example, an object could be placed within the caregiver's clothing or she could hold it to her mouth so that the child must seek contact with the caregiver to retrieve it.

Program

Twice weekly sessions of Musical Interaction Therapy seem to be particularly effective in helping the child toward social engagement. Turner (1998) finds that prior to beginning the very first session it helps to have one session where she tries to make meaningful contact and dialogue with the child through free play. This helps her to get a general impression for the feel of the child and of the pleasure and difficulties in communicating with the child. If the caregiver is embarrassed about "making a fool of herself," the therapist can model behavior during the first visit so that the parent is more ready for another adult to witness what may be perceived as undignified behavior.

At first music may the help child tolerate the presence of the adults. Initial sessions should aim for the child to habituate to the presence of the adults and for both adults to tune in to the child, as well as to develop experience in working together. This is useful for the caregiver as well as the child. Before sessions begin, parent and musician should discuss what they wish to try during the session, how the child is feeling and hence what she is likely to be most responsive to. Possible behavioral problems can be anticipated and a decision made as to how to handle these. As sessions progress, they can decide on the finer details of how they are going to attempt, for example, pauses within particular routines. However, they will always be responsive to the child. For example, when the child is withdrawn, the mother will perform quiet actions, such as stroking the child's hair while singing the sentence "This is how I stroke your hair." The mother matches the level of intrusion to the child's level of tolerance. When the child seems more receptive, the mother may try to make the child anticipate her action: "This is how . . ." and then wait for some response before completing the sentence. Mothers treat their babies as though they mean to communicate. The caregiver in Musical Interaction Therapy acts as though everything the child does is intended as communication.

Eleri Turner (1998) discusses how it is seen as positive when the child seems to be in control over the duration of the session. She describes how every session is conducted within a framework of a hello and goodbye song. When the child becomes more receptive, he or she is encouraged to make a waving gesture for goodbye. Later the child may begin to initiate the end of a session by spontaneously waving a hand and/or singing the goodbye song. Heather (see her case study later) learned to wave when after months of experiencing Musical Interaction Therapy sessions, she came to understand when they were finishing.

Strategies

Lewis, Prevezer, and Spencer (1996) and Prevezer (1998) describe the strategies employed in Musical Interaction Therapy. Prevezer's organization of discussion of these strategies will be followed here: the use of imitation, running commentary and songs, and play routines. Each of these is used to give the child the illusion of communicative control, each helps the caregiver in scaffolding the interaction, and musical support is present throughout. It will be seen how the illusion of control may develop into negotiation of control and how music gives particular support to timing issues.

Imitation

The first consideration is to tune in to the child and find an appropriate starting point, so that the child is interested but not overwhelmed. This is achieved by following the child's lead, for example, by imitating any sounds made by the child and copying the child's actions. In normal interaction, this gives significance to what the baby is doing and is often the basis for turntaking. Prevezer reports that copying obsessive behavior does not tend to encourage stereotyped behaviors. Repeated reflection of the child's behavior often draws the child into acting deliberately so as to be copied, and through physical imitation the child experiences simple turntaking. Imitation is an ongoing part of mother-baby interaction. For example, babbling can be incorporated into a conversational pattern of sound. The child learns that in a conversation, one person talks and the other listens, and then the other talks and is listened to. The caregiver and musician are therefore providing the framework of a dialogue and words may later be slotted into this. Prolonged straightforward imitation is not enough. It is important to be flexible and offer occasional variation to get the beginnings of reciprocity. Some children respond quite well to a bit of give and take, even in the first few sessions (Prevezer, 1998).

Running Commentary

Giving a running commentary is a way of giving importance to what the child is doing. All the elements of music can be employed to achieve the appropriate match for mood or action. The accompaniment may or may not include words but is matched as closely as possible to the child's mood, vocalization, or movement, and it is kept simple. "A cinema pianist or organist accompanying a silent oldie movie, graphically illustrates how I musically imitate their [child with autism and caregiver] rhythmic movements and general mood on my harp" (Turner, 1998). With music support, the mother takes every opportunity to comment on any of the child's vocal utterances by imitating, setting up vocal turntaking patterns or vocalizing simultaneously with the child's utterances. The music thus reflects and highlights the mood, timing, and meaning of the dyad's activities. For example, if the child happens to jump, the mother also jumps and, together with the musician, sings "jump, jump, jump away" with timing appropriate to the actions. As soon as the child stops jumping, the music and singing pauses in anticipation of her next move. The music becomes quieter if the child avoids her mother and more exciting if she approaches her—gradually reaching a crescendo with the climax of dramatic games (such as "tickly under there!"). In this way the child can also learn that he or she can affect somebody by his or her own actions and vocalizations. He can come to understand what it is to leave a gap for somebody else's utterances before vocalizing again and what it is to share pleasure in covocalizing. Again these are rehearsals for part of the blueprint of meaningful use of words. Hence imitation and a running commentary enable the child to act intentionally so as to influence what his play partner or the musician will do. Spontaneous songs, if short, can be part of a running commentary.

Songs and Play Routines

Singing is a common part of mother-baby interactions. It is often accompanied by movement that gives meaning to the song, and through this experience of being handled and sung to, the baby develops social timing. For example, the caregiver may stop singing and wait for a response at the end of each line. If the baby vocalizes during her mother's turn, the caregiver stops the song and thereby stresses the importance of turntaking in vocalization. The baby quickly becomes relatively competent in social timing, so she and her mother have conversations before she acquires words.

Hence songs and play routines provide scaffolding for communication. Vocalization is an enjoyable experience in itself and singing together can give a feeling of bonding. This is part of the relationship the caregiver has with the musician as well as with her child. There are many levels at which a child may participate, and pauses can be introduced in a way that is less threatening than with the use of speech. Singing, unlike speech, enables adults to hold out their words and wait for a child's response. These pauses can be more or less dramatic and can help a child to anticipate points in a routine, creating a shared experience. The child can then begin to play the social games that normal babies find easy. Prevezer (1998) advises "Children with autism may need us to *wait longer* for a sign of their involvement, to be very *responsive* to the smallest flicker of eye contact, movement or sound, and to *cue them in,* helping to build up their anticipation by our facial expressions, getting slower and louder, or an exaggerated gasp."

Prevezer distinguishes between the use of set and flexible action songs. Set songs although less creative, still offer a familiar framework for the child. Within such songs, tempo, volume, pausing, and wording can be varied in response to the child. Short, simple rhymes (e.g., Wind the Bobbin, The Grand Old Duke of York, Incy Wincy Spider) expose the child to sequencing and timing. At the outset, the child may gently be put through the actions so that he or she may experience the meaning of words through his or her own physical experience. The child may come to imitate the mother's sequential actions and indeed may come to initiate a song by use of actions or singing the first word of a song. More flexible action songs are often also appropriate in the first session. These are still usually familiar and repetitive, but their content is more variable. For example, Prevezer describes how these songs can be used to follow a child's action to make a verse (e.g., walking or swaying); offering an action such as jumping to be watched or copied; performing an action on the child, such as patting; offering a co-operative action (e.g., rocking).

Play routines are patterned in the same way as song routines. Physical contact, often rough and tumble, may be involved. Children with autism often tolerate or enjoy repetitive physical activity such as being swung or tickled. The caregiver tries many different ways of drawing the child's attention to her and explores to find those forms of contact that the child can tolerate. It is almost always the case that children will initially only respond to rough and tumble and tickling and a child can become more used to being touched during these sessions. Prevezer (1998) suggests using timing here, as in the song routines, to facilitate opportunities for the child to join in. She suggests building up tension then pausing before a key point so as to allow the child to anticipate. She uses any sign of responsiveness on the child's part as though it is deliberately communicative to give a sense of turntaking. Obsessional interests may be used as the basis for play routines. Eleri Turner (1998) points out that Peek-a-boo games are used to help the child to experience anticipation, sequence, object permanence, and showing or sharing oneself with another person.

These strategies are geared to facilitate flexible development. As is the case with normal development, a certain amount of conditioning is involved and the use of Musical Interaction Therapy sometimes reflects this. For the child who has very restricted communication, the use of pointing as a gesture to indicate everyday needs would be one of the first things to work on. Pointing may enable a child to communicate even before he realizes that objects have names. The child is helped to point to whatever he finds rewarding within the Musical Interaction Therapy session, for example, bubbles. Or, when a child is motivated to want a repeat experience (e.g., blow on your tummy), the mother can negotiate eye contact as part of the deal for continuing. This negotiation does not have to be verbal. By the use of the reward of more blowing, the child may begin to give meaning to the use of eye contact. Silence from both musician and caregiver upon the child's departure and sustained until his or her return can be effective (for reasons accounted for by a behavioral approach).

How Do Sessions Progress?

Turner (1998) reports that rich and varied free play is woven between more structured activity such as lap game songs. Both types of activities are used to support the child at whatever level of social tolerance he or she can endure at any given time and to gently extend the child's experience of communication. At the start of the sessions, she aims to trace the movements and mood of the caregiver-child dyad very closely as the caregiver attempts to recreate normal, very early mother and baby interaction. She may gently direct or suggest to the mother through music or vocal sounds what to do in response to the child. If the child is switching off to the adult, music may be used appropriately to regain the child's attention. Music is used in response to mood *and* to change mood. After about six sessions when the mother has found her bearings, the therapist draws back and the caregiver increasingly becomes the prime enabler, giving the child an illusion of control, enabling the child to participate in this joint enterprise. The mothers report that after a few months of twice weekly sessions, they get so engrossed in interplay with their child that they are not aware of the musician. At this stage, the therapist tends to concentrate less on imitation and focuses more on improvisation that is still based on the dyad.

Sessions are usually assessed informally by the musician and caregiver who discuss what has happened, how they and the child have responded, any changes that may have been apparent, and what new openings might be indicated for the following session.

CASE STUDIES

The following accounts illustrate the practical and theoretical points made earlier and give a feel of how some of the strategies described could be implemented. We also hope to convey how receiving and participating in Musical Interaction Therapy felt to the children's families.

Heather

Heather has classic autism; she was diagnosed by the first author using Newson's (1978) criteria and *DSM-III-R* (American Psychiatric Association [APA], 1987). An independent clinician scored her autism as severe (48) on the Childhood Autism Rating Scale (Schopler, Reichler, & Renner, 1986).

As a baby (the third of four children), Heather was unhappy if cradled in her mother's arms and she would not snuggle up like other babies to breastfeed. Her mother was therefore forced to bottlefeed her and by three or four months Heather would only tolerate this if she was propped in a semi-sitting position facing away from her mother's body. As Heather became older, she never shared her toy play with others, neither by lifting them into someone else's view and vocalizing nor by pointing. She never imitated with the ease and sociability that her baby sister showed. Her mother learned to accept any physical contact from Heather without reciprocating because Heather would pull away if cuddled.

Heather was 3½ years old at the start of her participation in Musical Interaction Therapy. Behavior modification had been successfully employed for obsessional screaming and tantrums 10 months previously. However, Heather remained without gestural or verbal communication and functioned at a learning disabled level.

Heather was filmed during seven months of 20-minute Musical Interaction Therapy sessions twice weekly. Before these sessions started, Heather was filmed on six occasions over a four-month baseline period playing with and without toys with her mother present. After the seven months, Heather continued to receive Musical Interaction Therapy for a further five months, but the sessions with music were not filmed. Her follow-up play-based assessment took place 20 months after all the Musical Interaction Therapy sessions had finished. A teaching film was used by the first author after the baseline period, to introduce Heather's mother to Musical Interaction Therapy (Wimpory, 1985). Play-based assessments were conducted for Heather in her local Child Development Center at the start and end of her seven months of evaluated Musical Interaction Therapy. These measures were used to determine the effect of Musical Interaction Therapy on Heather's sociability, communication, and pretend play skills (absent at the start of Musical Interaction Therapy).

Heather's mother recalls her introduction to Musical Interaction Therapy in the following way:

"The first time I met Miss Eleri Davies (Music Therapist, now Eleri Turner) I didn't believe we would ever be able to get through the wall of autism and discover our own daughter . . . she was almost totally noncommunicative and life was always quite a struggle. . . . Anyway, on this afternoon, I was introduced to Eleri by Dawn Wimpory and after talking to them both I said that I would try the therapy. I have to say that at that time I was very skeptical although by then I would have tried anything.

"The following Monday Eleri turned up with her harp and we went nervously upstairs. The whole weekend we had worried about how Heather would react to the therapy which would mean she would have to participate (which she hadn't done before). The whole thing rested on treating Heather *[communicatively] not as a 3-year-old but going back to babyhood all over again. [Authors' note: Musical Interaction Therapy supports children with autism through preverbal communication. It should not be confused with any form of emotional regression therapy. Like other aspects of our intervention program it focuses on the developmental level the child has reached in the area we are aiming to develop. Thus, Musical Interaction Therapy is practiced alongside more advanced expectations of cognitive and self-help skills together with age-appropriate demands of motor development, and so on.]*

"Eleri settled herself in a corner and began to play. Every action Heather did she played a tune to match and for the first time in her life Heather could be in charge! A frightening experience for me, knowing only too well how self-abusive she could be! The first 10 minutes were spent with Heather jumping about all over the bed and running round the room with me trying to keep up with her. Then a marvelous change came over her. Heather's whole body relaxed and she lay on the bed, snuggled up next to me as I rocked her to the tune of "Twinkle, twinkle, little star." To say I was overwhelmed is an understatement. It was the same intense feeling of wonder and joy as experienced at her birth."

At the time of the early Musical Interaction Therapy sessions, Heather's mother described her experience of them as "hard," tiring, and even embarrassing to begin with. Despite being told to anticipate good and bad sessions, she felt feelings of failure when the latter occurred. However, her overall experience of even the early sessions was positive and she found herself looking forward to them. Musical Interaction Therapy enabled her to have new experiences of Heather. "I never realized before how tense she was because I'd never been that close to her for long like I am in the Musical Interaction Therapy sessions." Heather's mother described her role in the sessions as initially feeling a bit intrusive in contrast to her inevitable wariness with Heather evolved from previous experience. " When I started it was like doing it with someone else's child . . . when your child is autistic the surface things are fine, it's deep down that you don't know them."

Heather's mother recognized that the Music Therapist "looked after me as well as looking after Heather . . . otherwise . . . there would've been tears with my husband in the evening." Despite her initial worries, she found, "I'm in control as much as the Music Therapist is, that's why it's good." Musical Interaction Therapy also enabled Heather's mother to realize that she could continue to respond to Heather at an appropriate communicative level outside of therapeutic sessions, "It's made me think more about how we were treating Heather, that maybe we could've been doing something differently and that was disappointing." This point emphasizes the value of employing this therapy and as soon as possible after diagnosis; no child with autism is too young for Musical Interaction Therapy.

Looking back, Heather's mother describes the outcome of Musical Interaction Therapy as follows: "So from that small beginning Heather (was) allowed to begin again (in terms of communication) without the fear and isolation. Months later Heather still loved her weekly sessions, each session bringing small delights as she continued to improve. She now performs her songs at the drop of a hat—providing we all join in with her, much to everybody's delight. She withdraws from the world about her rarely and never as deeply as before.

"Heather has shown herself to have a strong personality of her own. For the first time, I have come to know my daughter as I know my other children. She is alert, inquisitive, and most of all, loving. If we are playing games, she will join in laughing and clapping with the sheer joy of knowing she understands what is going on around her.

"At the beginning, she advanced only during the therapy session, but with each session the effects lasted longer and longer until at last we have a daughter who can cope with her handicap—who is coping with normal life. From being a tense child, she is now pliable and above all can show feelings of love to all of us. Life now is an adventure rather than a nightmare! It has helped me tremendously as well. I now have confidence to be a mother to Heather and it has given me the ability to ride over the bad times—which are getting rarer—in the knowledge that it's only a hiccup and that tomorrow the sunshine will be out again.

"I know that Musical Interaction Therapy was the best thing we ever did. The joy of a small pair of arms going round your neck and the warmth of that small body against you, together with those big blue eyes looking deep into yours, are so special after years of being pushed away, evaded, and rebuffed . . . Our home is now a place that is filled with sunshine and laughter and not tears and bewilderment."

The practice of Musical Interaction Therapy will vary depending on different children, therapist musicians, caregivers, and contexts. However, Heather's mother's own experience of Musical Interaction Therapy reflects the experience and intentions of her music therapist. Heather's mother reported that "by the end of that last session it felt like there was only Heather and me. It was like coming home."

Videos were taken before and after the start of therapy through good and bad days. Overall, the number of bad days declined and the good increased and became better in quality. Heather's readiness to initiate any social interaction was measured. This was a measure of the time it took before Heather took any social notice of her mother. Heather's avoidance of eye contact, her turntaking, and creative contributions to an interaction were also measured. After Musical Interaction Therapy, improvements were recorded in all these areas. Such improvements would not be expected as part of a developmental pattern of a child with autism. After therapy Heather was obviously much more aware of her mother. At first it was very difficult to play with Heather at all. In the play-based assessment session before therapy she gave eye contact perhaps once or twice in the whole session (nearly two hours). Afterwards, her eye contact was reliable, usually occurring at least once a minute. In the later months she would be looking about every 15 seconds at her mother. Before therapy Heather once managed to start a sequence of turntaking, afterwards she would start a sequence two or three times in a session. This would be turntaking using her voice, body, and eventually words.

After Musical Interaction Therapy, Heather showed an ability to creatively contribute to an interaction (for example, offering a new part of her body to be tickled). Some children with autism can turn take when they know a routine. It is very hard for them to spontaneously make up their own turns. An example from Heather toward the end of the seven-month session involved her mother capitalizing on her obsession with fluff. Heather used to get absorbed in picking bits of fluff from a bedspread that she would then put in her mouth. When she was doing this during a Musical Interaction Therapy session, her mother grabbed her hand and made an exaggerated, disgusted noise "bleurgh!" as she tickled Heather's hand. Heather laughed and did it again and again with her mother joining in, not actively picking up fluff but putting her hand out. The impression from the film clip is that Heather was laughing in anticipation some of the time. Eventually she put both her hands on the bedspread and laughed in apparent anticipation. Her mother repeated "bleurgh" and took hold of and tickled both hands. The music matched the movement throughout, for example, getting louder as the exciting climax of the tickle approached. Another example of Heather taking turns was when Heather approached her mother and put her face right up close, then withdrew. Heather's mother put her face very close to Heather's and blew a raspberry on Heather's mouth and withdrew. Heather then again approached her mother and held her face close to her mother's face. Her mother blew a raspberry noise to add emphasis to the turn.

Heather also showed some pretend play (dry washing up) and teasing behavior (when she knew she was expected to clap hands, she smiled and clapped her tummy instead).

Associated, positive reported developments that were not the specific aim of Musical Interaction Therapy were that Heather became more attached to her siblings and could play with her father in more sophisticated ways. Her co-ordination became better; her behavior at mealtimes improved and, rather than echoed sentences, she used individual words which were useful to her "hiya, up and again" and joining words "Heather wants it."

The examples described came from the Musical Interaction Therapy sessions. During the times without music, Heather's performance followed what she managed in the Musical Interaction Therapy sessions, but just lagged behind. After about a month, Heather began to be able to interact with her mother (albeit briefly) without music support. It would appear that Musical Interaction Therapy made more and more developments possible. After three months of Musical Interaction Therapy, Heather was much happier to stay for the sessions, possibly because she could do the lap games that occurred during the familiar routines. Although she needed to look away often at this stage, she also became able to face her mother and could express pleasure with her voice. After eight months, Heather would not tolerate her little sister going from the room and would want to go with her. Before Musical Interaction Therapy, Heather would not have noticed Katie coming or going.

Sian

A second case study illustrates how Musical Interaction Therapy was used for Sian, a child with classic autism whose principal caregiver, her mother, Anita, was partially deaf, and English was not the family's first language. The application of Musical Interaction Therapy with Sian was designed to look at what components of Musical Interaction Therapy were most effective, separately and in combination. This was to establish that it was not just the social support from another adult that helped the caregiver in her relationship with her child; that any changes could be attributed to live music that was responsive to the child and mother.

Sian was a lively 3½-year-old with autism, rated as "severely autistic" by an independent clinician using the Childhood Autism Rating Scale (Schopler et al., 1986). Although Sian's everyday behavior was at a learning disabled level, she was able to score an average level on the Griffiths Mental Development Scales (Griffiths, 1984). Her family (Indian) were staying in the United Kingdom to complete her father's training as a psychiatrist. Sian's mother had begun to lose her hearing during her pregnancy with Sian's older sister aged 9. Sian was described by her parents as a quiet baby who rarely cried, and who was quite happy to amuse herself for hours ("she didn't like us interfering"). Sian did not enjoy being cuddled and pushed away from her parents, preferring instead to play with blocks. Attempts to engage Sian tended to be one-sided. "We could play with her from our side . . . but she wouldn't try to interact in return." As a baby, Sian did babble to herself but not with communicative intent nor in a turntaking pattern with others. Sian did not use or understand gestures and neither did she display tantruming behavior, which can also fulfill a basic communicative role. By 2 years of age, Sian's frequency and quality of eye contact was diminishing, and her parents reported that she looked at them "as if we were part of an object, she wouldn't look at you for human qualities." By the time she was 3, Sian had withdrawn further socially, showing no interest in adults or children, and her smiles and laughter were more for herself than for other people.

The introduction of Musical Interaction Therapy needed particular care because of Sian's mother's (Anita) selective hearing difficulties. While she could respond relatively well to the music, she found it difficult to hear comments from the supporting professionals advising her how to proceed. Sessions were therefore brief (just 10 to 20 minutes). The clinical psychologist would model and prompt Anita while the Music Therapist supported both Sian and whoever was attempting to engage with her. These sessions were concluded by a discussion of the strategies they had featured (e.g., imitation, particular action rhymes). After six weeks, when Anita was comfortable and confident about her role in Musical Interaction Therapy, sessions lasted for 30 to 60 minutes and proceeded without the clinical psychologist.

In overcoming the very real difficulties of hearing impairment and cultural isolation, Musical Interaction Therapy exploited the sensitivity and willingness of her mother and music therapist to work together in helping Sian. Good relationships between these adults and their advising clinical psychologist were essential. Sian's mother needed support in beginning to come to terms with the loss of her hearing and previous communicative competence while simultaneously offering her daughter the playful, and sometimes joyful, experiences that she needed. Musical Interaction Therapy in this situation clarified that caregivers cannot be expected to play therapeutically with their children with autism unless they feel able to play. Anita's playfulness was released through the support she experienced from the music therapist within and outside of sessions and through a strong counseling relationship with Sian's clinical psychologist that was sustained through the study (established prior to baseline measures). Clinical experience indicates that such counseling alone is not sufficient to effect changes in children with autism. However, without this additional support it would not have been possible for Anita to have facilitated the communicative experiences that Sian needed whilst simultaneously grieving the loss of her hearing and missing her family and community in rural India.

In practice, the strong relationship between Anita and the professionals was essential during the early Musical Interaction Therapy (training) sessions. Anita initially spent much time watching Eleri in a vain attempt to lip read what she should do next. Sian's clinical psychologist asked and then "told" Anita not to look at Eleri but instead to focus on Sian and to trust that Eleri would follow (rather than direct) their activities. The clinical psychologist's role became to guide Anita through tactile means or to show suggested activities (e.g., swaying) as appropriate. Unlike Eleri who had to stay by her harp, the clinical psychologist could move to within sight of Anita while she was playing with Sian. Anita's need for this gradually decreased over the six-week training period and the music therapist became more skilled at communicating with her using mimed signs for familiar routines and so on. They were able to proceed to full Musical Interaction Therapy without the presence of the clinical psychologist. The administration of Musical Interaction Therapy led to gains by all concerned. For example, through the experience of working with Anita's hearing difficulties, both professionals learned to develop and trust in less conventional means of communication.

Early Musical Interaction Therapy sessions with Sian relied upon her mother and the therapist trying out a number of actions (e.g., tickling, swinging Sian's legs up and down, swaying, rolling) and heavily tracing them with music and song to promote contact between Sian and her mother and ascertain what Sian enjoyed. It had been observed that Sian gave some eye contact to her mother when pressing her hand onto her mother's arm as part of a familiar ritual she had spontaneously developed. This ritual was used as a starting point for Musical Interaction Therapy.

Initially, sessions were very much led by the therapist (who suggested songs and actions, and mirrored the mother-child dyad's actions with music) and Sian's mother (who would try out various songs and actions, and imitate Sian both physically and vocally). Sian's role appeared fairly passive, as she wandered around the room, approaching and retreating from her mother. However, both therapist and mother were also quick to utilize any of Sian's behavior by treating it as if it were intentional. For example, if Sian happened to walk around her mother, this acted as a cue for therapist and mother to start singing "round and round," building up to a crescendo in pitch and loudness, the climax occurring as Sian and Anita fell onto the sofa. Similarly, if Sian happened to rub her face, this acted as a cue for singing "wash wash wash your face" (to the tune of Here we go round the mulberry bush), with Anita rubbing Sian's face either with her hands or using Sian's hands on Sian's face or her own face. Thus in initial sessions, little was required of Sian in terms of participation.

During these early sessions, eye contact from Sian was not a condition of continuing the music, although if given it was quickly reinforced by music/tickling, and so on. Most of the songs and actions contained dramatic pauses and the music built up to a climax/pause just prior to an action, thereby emphasizing timing. However, at first, Sian was not expected to participate at these points, and hence the music would often follow her actions rather than waiting for Sian to interject at the correct point (i.e., the music "fell down" when Sian did, rather than expecting Sian to fall down as cued by the music in later sessions).

The design of the study was: baseline; recorded music; musician's visits without music; training for Musical Interaction Therapy (because of Sian's mother's hearing problems); full Musical Interaction Therapy; baseline with Eleri's visits but no music. Recordings from each session were coded for episodes of social engagement and the total number of instances of vocalization and smiling. Full Musical Interaction Therapy led to the greatest change and instances of positive social behaviors became fewer when Musical Interaction Therapy was withdrawn. Success was not due to maternal social support.

Sian's father summarized the experience of his family with Musical Interaction Therapy as follows: "Sian was a very closed and distant child and she hardly communicated emotionally. She did not have a great variety of activities and had a very restricted pattern of behavior. Because we did not get any reaction from her, I and my eldest daughter Sandra became cold too in our response to Sian, though Anita my wife maintained some variety of activity with Sian, but I could see the strain on her.

"When music therapy was introduced, there was a sudden boost in the variety of Anita's response to Sian which soon started to permeate to us as well. Though it was slow, Sian started to respond to the variety . . . I think for Sian and all the rest of us, music therapy was more natural (than behavior or speech therapies) without many restrictions or boundaries. She showed more attention and interest in interacting, sharing, and reacting. With the music in the background, I think my wife, Anita, felt able to express herself and play with Sian, sometimes even without any reaction from her, which is expected in conversation sequence.

"At the end of every hour session, Anita and Sian were surprisingly more relaxed and cheerful. I think it was mutually very complementary too, both emotionally and physically . . . Sian has grown to be a more active and responsive girl."

CONCLUSION

One of the most valuable aspects of Musical Interaction Therapy is that, in addition to the effects of the techniques outlined earlier and the facilitative effects of live music, Musical Interaction Therapy affords a specific time and place where the search for and experience of shared attention and social engagement is given the status it deserves.

Both Sian's and Heather's Musical Interaction Therapy was followed by speech and language therapy and some behavior modification. The developments made possible through Musical Interaction Therapy facilitated the effectiveness of these therapies. It should be emphasized that the sorts of developments enabled through Musical Interaction Therapy do not occur naturally in children with autism, even over a long time—Musical Interaction Therapy is responsible for these developments.

The cases studies presented here have illustrated how Musical Interaction Therapy works in attempting to facilitate social interaction with a child with autism. Musical Interaction Therapy is based on preverbal caregiver-child interaction and uses live music to elicit and develop the child's sociability. Musical Interaction Therapy offered constant musical support throughout sessions designed to help Heather and Sian have the illusion of control by scaffolding their interaction with their caregivers.

Single case study applications of Musical Interaction Therapy, without external controls or comparison groups, can only carry limited implications. However, our preliminary data are suggestive that Musical Interaction Therapy helped both Heather and Sian to develop their sociability. Comparable measures of preschool children with autism in specialist educational provision show high stability over time (Snow, Hertzig, & Shapiro, 1987). Heather's experience particularly reflected successful application of Musical Interaction Therapy. This echoed previous successes with the technique employed in different situations with different staff whilst the first author was working in Nottingham. The qualitative changes in the social interaction skills of these children justifies both our excitement about Musical Interaction Therapy and our continuing attempts to define its essential characteristics. This chapter has taken an academic and clinical perspective in identifying the developmental processes which may occur through the application of Musical Interaction Therapy by sensitive personnel working with preverbal preschoolers with classic autism. We can thereby use Musical Interaction Therapy to elucidate crucial processes which influence the development of social and symbolic functioning. However, Musical Interaction Therapy is not limited to this application alone, Prevezer (1998) identifies Musical Interaction Therapy as a technique that enables her to find out, and pursue, what works with a variety of children with related difficulties. All applications of Musical Interaction Therapy require that there is an atmosphere of spontaneity and a readiness to rely on intuition throughout and beyond the sessions. Furthermore, the process of Musical Interaction Therapy is always geared toward enabling the caregiver-child dyad to move toward a point of balance—between structure and spontaneity, as well as adult/child control (Prevezer, personal communication, August 24, 1998).

As outlined earlier, the essential aspects of Musical Interaction Therapy appear to be that the caregiver is supported by a therapist's live music as she "scaffolds" an interactive experience for the child to whom she affords the "illusion of *communicative* control." Our own theory of autism (Wimpory, 1995) is that proposed social timing difficulties inherent in the child (Newson, 1984) disable the development of preverbal social interaction, thereby inhibiting the development of teasing and other social/symbolic skills. Applications of Musical Interaction Therapy are always socially demanding on the personnel concerned and constraints of the real world mean that there is always room for improvement in how Musical Interaction Therapy is employed and how much change is facilitated in the child. Where Musical Interaction Therapy is successfully applied the interactive patterns are so intrinsically rewarding that they become self-perpetuating even beyond the sessions. This may perhaps approach Frith's recommendation that any successful remedy "would have to be applied at the beginning of the chain of causal events that leads to Autism" (Frith, 1989, p. 184).

Rather than confirm a purely cognitive account of autism, the findings from Musical Interaction Therapy research and practice are more compatible with the interaction-based theoretical perspectives of Hobson (1994a, 1994b), Newson (1984), Wimpory (1995) and Fein, Pennington, Markowitz, Braverman, and Waterhouse (1986). The latter suggest that: "a minimum level of reciprocity may be necessary as a basis for a shared meaning and communicative intent, and social disinterest in autistic children may thus contribute to delays and failures in language and pretend play" (Fein et al., 1986, p. 208).

Preliminary evidence from previous research (Wimpory, 1995) is that Musical Interaction Therapy facilitates playful joint action formats which generalize beyond therapy and possibly serve to facilitate further social/symbolic developments. However, existing studies cannot offer confirmation of a hypothesized deficit in social timing (Newson, 1978, 1987). Further research needs to determine this and the validity and efficacy of Musical Interaction Therapy in this respect. Although the evaluation of Sian's case study gave support to live Musical

Interaction Therapy as opposed to prerecorded audiotapes of the same, it did not conclusively demonstrate that music is an essential component. Research is in progress to evaluate parental use of Interaction Therapy strategies without the support of live music. This strategy could be usefully incorporated into future research using a multiple baseline format with further case studies. However, our clinical experience is that the complete form of Musical Interaction Therapy socially affords an opportunity for caregivers to reach and interact with children with autism in ways usually beyond their previous experience.

ACKNOWLEDGMENTS

The authors would like to thank Heather's and Sian's families, Eleri Turner, and Wendy Prevezer for their contributions. Work on this chapter was partially supported by the Wales Office for Research and Development in Health and Social Care.

A publication list relating to aspects of Musical Interaction Therapy as practiced at Sutherland House Nottingham, may be obtained from the Information Service, Early Years Diagnostic Centre, 272 Longdale Lane, Ravenshead, Nottinghamshire, NG15 9AH, UK.

REFERENCES

Alvin, J. (1978). *Music therapy for the autistic child.* Oxford, England: Oxford University Press.

American Psychiatric Association. (1987). *Diagnostic and statistical manual of mental disorders* (3rd ed., Rev.). Washington, DC: Author.

American Psychiatric Association. (1994). *Diagnostic and statistical manual of mental disorders* (4th ed.). Washington, DC: Author.

Applebaum, E., Egel, A.L., Koegel, R.L., & Imhoff, B. (1979). Measuring musical abilities of autistic children. *Journal of Autism and Developmental Disorders, 9*(3), 279–285.

Benenzon, R.O. (1976). Music therapy in infantile autism. *British Journal of Music Therapy, 7*(2), 10–17.

Bruner, J.S. (1983). *Child's talk: Learning to use language.* Oxford Paperbacks.

Christie, P., & Wimpory, D. (1986). Recent research into the development of communicative competence and its implications for the teaching of autistic children. *Communication, 20*(1), 4–7.

Condon, W.S. (1975). Multiple response to sound in dysfunctional children. *Journal of Autism and Developmental Disorders, 5*(1), 37–56.

DeMyer, M.K. (1979). *Parents and children in autism.* New York: Wiley.

Evans, J.R. (1986). *Dysrhythmia and disorders of learning and behavior.* Springfield, IL: Thomas.

Fein, D., Pennington, B., Markowitz, P., Braverman, M., & Waterhouse, L. (1986). Towards a neuropsychological model of infantile autism: Are the social deficits primary? *Journal of the American Academy of Child Psychiatry, 25*(2), 198–212.

Frith, U. (1989). *Autism: Explaining the enigma.* Oxford, England: Blackwell.

Griffiths, R. (1984). *The abilities of young children.* Bucks, UK: The Test Agency.

Hermelin, B., & O'Connor, N. (1970). *Psychological experiments with autistic children.* Oxford, England: Pergamon Press.

Hobson, R.P. (1994a). *Autism and the development of mind.* Hove, UK: Erlbaum.

Hobson, R.P. (1994b). Perceiving attitudes, conceiving minds. In C. Lewis & P. Mitchell (Eds.), *Children's early understanding of mind: Origins and development.* Hove, UK: Erlbaum.

Kostka, M.J. (1993). A comparison of selected behaviors of a student with autism in special education and regular music classes. *Music Therapy Perspectives, 11*(2), 57–60.

Lewis, R., Prevezer, W., & Spencer, R. (1996). *Musical interaction: An introduction.* Available from Early years Diagnostic Centre, 272 Longdale Lane, Ravenshead, Nottinghamshire, NG15 9AH, UK.

Müller, P., & Warwick, A. (1993). Autistic children and music therapy: The effects of maternal involvement in therapy. In M. Heal & T. Wigram (Eds.), *Music therapy in health and education.* London: Jessica Kingsley.

Nelson, D., Anderson, V., & Gonzales, A. (1984). Music activities as therapy for children with autism and other pervasive developmental disorders. *Journal of Music Therapy, 21*(3), 100–116.

Newson, E. (1978). *Making sense of autism.* Inge Wakehurst Papers, National Autistic Society.

Newson, E. (1984). *The social development of the young autistic child.* National Autistic Society Conference, Bath, UK.

Newson, E. (1987). The education, treatment and handling of autistic children. *Children and Society, 1,* 34–50.

Nordoff, P., & Robbins, C. (1971). *Therapy in music for handicapped children.* London: Victor Gollancz.

Nordoff, P., & Robbins, C. (1972). *Therapy in music for handicapped children.* New York: St. Martin's Press.

Prevezer, W. (1998). *Entering into interaction: Some facts, thoughts and theories about autism, with a focus on practical strategies for enabling communication.* Available from Wendy Prevezer, 50 Collington Street, Beeston, Nottingham, NG9 1FJ, UK.

Schopler, E., Reichler, R., & Renner, B.R. (1986). *The childhood autism scale (CARS) for diagnostic screening and classification of autism.* New York: Irvington.

Sigman, M., Mundy, P., Sherman, T., & Ungerer, J. (1986). Social interactions of autistic, mentally retarded and normal children with their caregivers. *Journal of Child Psychology and Psychiatry, 27*(5), 647–656.

Skelly, A. (1992, September 11). *Establishing the affective mediation of symbolic play in young children.* Developmental Psychology Section Conference, University of Edinburgh, British Psychological Society.

Sloboda, J., Hermelin, B., & O'Connor, N. (1985). An exceptional musical memory. *Music Perception, 3*(2), 155–169.

Snow, M., Hertzig, J., & Shapiro, T. (1987). Rate of development in young autistic children. *American Journal of the Academy of Child and Adolescent Psychiatry, 26*(6), 834–835.

Thaut, M. (1987). Visual versus auditory (musical) stimulus preferences in autistic children: A pilot study. *Journal of Autism and Developmental Disorders, 17*(3), 425–432.

Thaut, M. (1988). Measuring musical responsiveness in autistic children: A comparative analysis of improvised musical tone sequences of autistic, normal, and mentally retarded individuals. *Journal of Autism and Developmental Disorders, 18*(4), 561–571.

Turner, E. (1998). *Communication therapy with music support: A personal view.* Available from Mrs. Eleri Turner, 7 Maes Afallan, Bow Street, Aberystwyth, Ceredigion, UK.

Urwin, C. (1984). Power relations and the emergence of language. In J. Henriques (Ed.), *Changing the subject.* London: Methuen.

Wimpory, D.C. (1985). *Enabling communication in young autistic children* [Videotape]. (Available from Child Development Research Unit, Nottingham University)

Wimpory, D.C. (1995). *Social engagement in preschool children with autism.* Unpublished doctoral thesis, University of Wales, Bangor, Gwynedd, UK.

Wimpory, D.C., Chadwick, P., & Nash, S. (1995). Brief report: Musical interaction therapy for children with autism: An evaluative case study with two year follow-up. *Journal of Autism and Developmental Disorders, 25,* 541–552.

CHAPTER 2

The Use of Dance Movement Therapy with Troubled Youth

HELEN PAYNE

INTRODUCTION

THIS CHAPTER describes a study (Payne, 1987) that used dance movement therapy (DMT) with adolescents who were placed in care and educated in residential schools. These young people were frequently labeled delinquent and had usually been referred to the courts for being out of parental control and had often engaged in antisocial acts. The teenagers were mostly male with an average age of 13 to 15 years.

HISTORICAL BACKGROUND

The *I Ching* links movement and emotion: "Every mood of the heart influences us to movement" (Wilhelm, 1968, p. 124). Bender and Boas (1941), Laban (1951), Bainbridge (1953), Chace (1953), and Rosen (1954) were among the first authors to write on the subject of DMT, the latest of the arts therapies to develop in the United Kingdom. In the United States, the source of most of the literature, the terms *dance therapy, movement therapy,* and *dance/movement therapy* are used interchangeably and the professional association

36

incorporates them all under the term *dance therapy*. In the United Kingdom, DMT appears to be allied more with the other arts therapies, such as art therapy and dramatherapy (Holden, 1980; Sherborne, 1974; Shirley, 1980), than with psychotherapy.

The term *dance movement therapy* has been adopted in the United Kingdom to avoid confusion between dance therapy and movement therapy and to be specific that it is a particular form of movement, namely dance—the creative or expressive movement form. This enables DMT to be consistent with the other arts therapies.

Dance has been part of all cultures since ancient times when Shamanism used dance to heal. Wright (1980), an anthropologist, drew our attention to exorcism ceremonies in Malaysia where dance, particularly trance-dance, serves as both a strategy for healing and a sign of health. She described how dance becomes an integrative force for some societies. Authors in Spencer's source book (1985) analyzed the place of dance in several societies, interpreting the dance as an aspect of ritual behavior which serves a variety of purposes. These aspects of dance form a vital link with present day DMT.

Early DMT literature refers to the goals of physical activity, social interaction, group rhythmic activity, and relationships with others. All of these are valid but can also be accomplished via sports, dance, music, drama, folk dance, and so on. Chace (1953), in one of the earliest reports, claimed DMT was affecting and alleviating the isolation felt by her depressed, psychotic, and schizophrenic patients.

Bartinieff (1971), an American physiotherapist, suggested that dance therapy could be used to help the emotionally disturbed or could be concerned with movement distortions. She stated, "Dance is a non-verbal medium of emotional expression as well as the joy of action through bodily emotions (p. 20)." This implies that the approach can celebrate the client's interest in dance or can use dance as a way of fostering emotional expression.

Other studies and a large amount of literature in the area of movement and special needs have concentrated on the cognitive connections with movement (Cratty, 1979; Frostig, 1967; Kephart, 1971). Condon and Ogston (1966) and Condon (1968) showed how much synchrony there is in everyday encounters, specifically in speech and nonverbal communication. This research relates to the view of dance as an interactive rhythmic encounter (Fraenkel, 1983). There is far less controlled research in the existential approach, which uses humanistic or psychoanalytical theories. That is, the process aspect, rather than the product, is seen to be fundamental to the therapy. The whole area of psychotherapy research has been struggling with the common problem of evaluating the therapy.

Dance movement therapy literature is scant and published studies concentrate, in the main, on effects in relation to body image, perceptual motor development, and affective states such as relief of anxiety. Descriptive accounts cover a range of populations although disturbed adolescents and delinquents are rarely mentioned.

According to Mason (1974), many leading DMT practitioners advocate the value of DMT for special needs groups, such as the autistic, deaf, visually impaired, elderly, minimal brain dysfunctioned, and school phobic. In this literature, many approaches are utilized. The main ones seem to be corrective and existential. The former uses a medical model and has produced some controlled research studies. It is more analytical than the existential approach and evaluates projects in which movements are provided in a programmed way, systematically treating dysfunctional aspects.

THEORETICAL FOUNDATION

A basic principle of DMT is the notion that bodily movement is related to emotion and that by working on the movement level in conjunction with the emotional level there is an immediate response at a feeling level (Bowlby, 1982; Gendlin, 1962a). This provides an opportunity for emotion at a preverbal level to be re-experienced and integrated through the symbolism of dance.

A second basic principle is that by enabling the client to explore and become familiar with an extended and more balanced range of movement, one fosters a greater adaptability in response to the environment.

A description of DMT, to which the author contributed, has been adopted by the Association for Dance Movement Therapy (founded in 1982) and the Standing Committee of the Arts Therapy Professions. It embodies these two fundamental principles:

> Dance Movement Therapy is the use of expressive movement and dance as a vehicle through which the individual can engage in personal integration and growth. It is founded on the principle that there is a relationship between motion and emotion and that by exploring a more varied vocabulary of movement people experience the possibility of becoming more securely balanced yet increasingly spontaneous and adaptable. Through movement and dance each person's inner world becomes tangible, individuals share much of their personal symbolism and in dancing together relationships become visible. The dance movement therapist creates a holding environment in which such feelings can be safely expressed, acknowledged and communicated. (Standing Committee of Arts Therapy Professions, 1987, p. 3)

Both these principles are related to the concept that a person's body is the self and that feelings about the body and the use of it in stillness and in movement are expressive of the person's inner world. This inner world (Wickes, 1968) becomes accessible not only through individual movement and personal symbols, but also in the interaction with the therapist and the group members. Dance movement therapy claims that through the dance or movement structures, relationships emerge manifesting themselves in, for example, the sharing of opposing rhythms, the use of space, willingness to support others or trusting enough to be supported, and leading or following. In this way, DMT can provide for change, awareness, and exploration, as well as being a diagnostic tool. The emphasis is on individual creativity and the personal statement of dance. The making of the movement is a creative process and engages the healthy part of the client in the journey toward individuation (Jung, 1966).

These inherent principles are the same for all populations although different emphases are applicable with different groups. Dance movement therapy has been applied through a broad spectrum of therapeutic activities that encompass, at one extreme, the use of movement and dance, movement structures, games, and relaxation techniques as media for individual psychotherapy, and, at the other, the organization of more informal groupwork or developmental movement work with the elderly or people with physical, social, emotional, or mental handicaps. Specific treatment programs may be undertaken as interventions for a variety of groups and individuals in social, educational, health, and other rehabilitative settings. Thus, it is difficult to find one definition that embraces the details of such varied applications.

There are several references in the literature to the underlying principles in DMT. Darwin (1872/1955) recounted an infinite number of postural changes that are the distinctive aspects of the expression of feeling. Reich (1945), Schilder (1955), and Lowen (1975) all recognized the interrelationship of soma and psyche. The literature on humanistic psychology also makes reference to the body-mind approach and it has been only since its inception that study and treatment approaches have been seriously considered. A German publication by Gunter (1984) referred to the body and dance therapy in humanistic psychiatry. In the United Kingdom, this nonmechanistic, positive approach to exploring the self has had an influence on the development of DMT. The present attention on the body, dance, and fitness has enabled DMT to become more acceptable to the public. In the United States, Feder and Feder (1981) noted the impact humanistic psychology has had on the creative arts therapies (CAT) generally. They also point out the common ground between art, drama, music, and dance movement therapy: First, they all use the creative process; and, second, they all focus on nonverbal media. For DMT, theoretical models are derived from the psychological school of the individual practitioner and that practitioner's philosophy. Some popular models are psychoanalytical (Bernstein, 1971; Siegal, 1984); Jungian (Whitehouse, 1977); Gestalt (Serlin, 1977); and behavioristic and developmental (Bainbridge-Cohen & Mills, 1979; Espenak, 1981). Dance movement therapy theories and Reichian theories may contribute to a more general theory of body psychotherapy. Lewis (1979) and Levy (1988) both suggest the capacity for health in DMT lies in the nonverbal, affective capability for relatedness. Dosamantes-Alperson (1984) claims its restorative power lives in the empathic communication between therapist and client.

Unblocking resistance to growth as subjects hold frozen movement patterns, muscular tensions, or postures enables a greater breadth of feeling expression, perception, and interpersonal relating responses (Reich, 1945). Problems manifested in emotional, social, or behavioral disturbance are invariably reflected in movement range, in abilities to express and communicate emotions, and in choices in thinking and abstracting. The fundamental belief that movement expression is reflective of the inner self gives access to intervention through body-mind interaction and expression, allowing another level of development to be released. One approach found in DMT literature suggests that a change in movement expression will result in a personality or behavioral change (Leventhal, 1980). Another approach stresses that it is the movement activities that are the vehicle for the therapeutic relationship (Delaney, 1973). There seems to be a common dichotomy here that is similar to that found in the other arts therapy literature; that is, whether it is the movement experience or the relationship that is the agent of change.

Gendlin (1962b), an American psychologist, has done much research on the phenomenological experiencing process that has been used in theoretical papers on DMT. He described two levels: the felt body level and the symbolic level. Ornstein (1973) claimed a psychological basis for this distinction, that of right and left brain respectively, but referred to two levels of experience as unique types of human consciousness: the intuitive and the rational. This is a polarity that has some correspondence with concepts such as subjective and objective. It is claimed that we mostly regard the world from an intellectual perspective because our culture exalts the rational-cognitive side and disparages the physical-emotional side (Mahrabian, 1972). Consequently, when we become strongly aroused we respond in either a constricted or a vague way. There is a lack of familiarity with our affective-motor systems, our control over our bodies, and bodily derived emotional responses. Most verbal therapies fail to recognize that the bodily derived felt level of experience must precede the conceptual level if a person is not to remain out of touch with his or her kinesthetic-affective reactions. Verbal therapies emphasize interaction on a cognitive level. DMT in its use of nonverbal physical expression supported by verbal interaction promotes communication of affect and sensation.

Schaefer (1976), in a description of the therapeutic use of child's play, stressed the need for body release action to recreate flexibility lost in former years. Play therapy is noninterpretive and essentially of a nonverbal nature that makes links with DMT. Schaefer highlighted the fact that parents may restrict body movement when the child is between 1 and 3 years of age (for example, by too early toilet training, confinement to playpens, or deprivation of space to creep, toddle, crawl, or climb). Children may develop cramped control to protect themselves from outer pressures and continuous demands. This can affect the whole psychophysical system and could lead to compulsive neurotic character structures. Schaefer pointed out that the latency-age child has a particular need for activity, both motor and muscular, and that this—combined with the cognitive—provides equipment for the acquisition of skills (Kephart, 1971). "Acting up" is a normal part of any schoolage child. "Acting out" is material dispersed through actions making it unavailable for therapy. Schaefer advised not to battle against action patterns but to use them as material, channeling a freedom of action to aid in the discovery of the body-self.

It may not be a prerequisite, as in adult therapy, that the child be aware that it is therapy he or she is engaged in. Indeed, adolescents labeled troubled or troublesome may find it difficult to accept sessions on such a basis. Nicol (1979), in his descriptions of play therapy, confirmed that the child does not need to know he or she is engaged in therapy.

RESEARCH FINDINGS

The recent development of DMT means that there is a dearth of rigorous research in the field. Most of the published writings come from the United States and consist of descriptive and theoretical or case study approaches. There are very few controlled studies evaluating the effectiveness of DMT; it tends to be neglected in clinical or educational psychological literature, although nonverbal behavior has been the focus of attention in psychiatric literature for some time. There has been some contribution from the nonverbal literature to the fields of both dance and DMT (e.g., Davis, 1973; Hunt, 1978; Kestenberg, 1971). Individual DMT practitioners have begun to record their work but there are few systematic and ordered studies, most being merely descriptive and journalistic in style. Most research is limited to outcome studies of one group or one subject pre- and posttest design. Other research has begun to look at the dance movement role (Johnson & Sandel, 1977; Schmais & Felber, 1977).

Although findings have shown favorable therapeutic outcomes in practice, any research to date has been more exploratory than definitive. Most of the case studies, theoretical material, and writings about DMT and special populations have come from the United States, although a few descriptive accounts in the United Kingdom are now appearing (Meekums, 1981; Meier, 1979; Payne, 1979, 1981, 1985; Payne-West, 1984; Penfield, 1978).

Ling (1983), in a related descriptive account, gives the goals of her work in DMT with women prisoners in the United Kingdom as improving self-image and communication, release of tension, and developing a positive regard for the body.

The literature includes several accounts relevant to work with adolescents. For example, Silberman (1973) tells of her experience working with disturbed late adolescent boys in a city prison hospital. She describes the slow process and her frustration when the offenders found themselves back in prison after release, showing her that the work rarely generalized. Sandel (1973) describes a videotape of work with troubled adolescents and young adults at a psychiatric institution. There is no indication of possible benefits or behavioral changes in these descriptions. Hecox, Levine, and Scott (1975) claim dance works well with adolescents in rehabilitation since there are many social motivators and reinforcers for dancing at this age. Apter, Sharir, Tyano, and Wijsenbeck (1978) studied movement therapy with psychotic adolescents and claimed positive outcomes. A description of DMT with children and adolescents by an Italian practitioner, Parteli (1995) illustrates DMT's contribution to the psychic understanding of motor stereotypes in autism and psychosis.

Some research has been concerned with the use of the arts with children and adolescents. Torrance and Torrance (1972) undertook to teach the three Rs to disadvantaged young people through drama, creative writing, and dance. Using the Torrance Tests of Creative Thinking before and after the project, they found statistically significant gains in the ability to produce ideas. This study argues that most remedial programs were not successful because they were based on deficiencies rather than on strengths.

Torrance and Torrance did not define "disadvantaged," nor did they identify children's strengths prior to the program. They did not provide a control group either. However, the study stressed the use of creative possibilities, for example, enjoyment of music, rhythm, and inventive dance; ability to express feelings and emotions; use of gesture and humor; and responsiveness to the concrete and the kinesthetic. The researchers did not articulate what specific effects each of these activities had on the subjects. Possibly more balanced views may have been gained if the young people had been asked for their thoughts.

Hazelton, Price, and Brown (1979), in a British study with learning disabled (mild) secondary school children of 11 to 13 years of age, stated that there was improved reading success and important personality growth with the implementation of psychodrama, creative movement, and remedial arts over several years. This was studied in contrast to remedial reading techniques which were found not to improve reading. The Cattel Personality Questionnaire was used to measure effects. A control group, a psychodrama group, a remedial arts group, and an unstructured movement group were all used. However, they do not say which aspects improved reading success as measured by ITPA, nor which personality aspects changed.

Dunne, Bruggen, and O'Brian (1982) have reported group body therapy approaches with hospitalized adolescents in the United Kingdom that resulted in reduced sexual behavior and violence, increased verbal interaction, and deeper concern for each other. However, the authors do not make their approach clear.

Hilyar et al. (1982) researched the use of physical fitness with young offenders in a program led by skilled counselors. From their study it can be seen that relationship variables were more important in promoting self-esteem and reducing anxiety and depression in the young people than was the activity of the physical training itself.

The present author has selected adolescents for DMT on the basis of high anxiety scores. This is because there is evidence from DMT literature and other sources from delinquency and psychotherapy that these young people are more likely to benefit from therapy.

In a study by Peterson and Cameron (1978), body movement is recommended for preparing high-anxiety adult patients for verbal psychotherapy. They found that patients were more able to control their anxiety as a result of such activity. Rutter, Tizzard, and Whitmore (1970), in discussing delinquency, suggest that only highly anxious adolescents who want help would benefit from psychotherapy. Johnson (1984) claims complex feeling states that created tremendous anxiety could be expressed and explored within the therapeutic relationship using movement and dramatherapy with an 18-year-old male catatonic schizophrenic.

Lesté and Rust (1984), in a British study, explored modern dance training on levels of anxiety in 114 19-year-old college students. Findings showed significant reductions in anxiety for the dance group and not for the other groups of sport or music. The authors concluded that the effects of music and physical exercise alone were less than when combined in dance. The study also found that the more interested the subjects were in dance prior to the program, the more favorable were the effects. This implies that attitude towards dance may dictate the degree to which it, or DMT, can be useful for the client.

There seems to be some evidence, therefore, that DMT could be of benefit to anxious young people with delinquent behaviors, since it incorporates dance and relaxation. In particular, this author's research found that such young people have limited language skills and are often functioning as learning disabled. Dance movement therapy may reduce their anxiety and increase their verbal skills, especially if they have a favorable attitude to dance already. It is the above literature and studies which provide the rationale for using DMT with this population of young people. In a U.S. description by Johnson and Eicher (1990) the addition of dramatic activities that help to structure the session and access images of the adolescent's inner life is proposed. They suggest the two underlying principles for effective techniques with adolescents are (1) decreasing the ambiguity of emotional states and (2) containing aggression.

Lovell (1980) suggested that DMT may be significant for use with adolescents because of the particular body-related issues of puberty, making DMT a modality suited to resolving the body image concerns of adolescents. Examples include supporting the transition from child to adult by exploring the psychosexual issues relating to body image via movement processes; developing an acceptance of the differences between child and adolescent which are intrinsic to the adolescent phase of development; increasing awareness of the psychological and physical changes of adolescence through verbal and nonverbal means; and heightening body awareness through proprioceptive and tactile stimulation.

Brown, McDowell, and Smith (1981) mentioned that dance theory is suitable for adolescents with behavioral problems since there are many social motivations and reinforcers for dancing at these age levels. They reported a study by Merek (1976) which compared a DMT group with a control group receiving verbal therapy for six weeks. Self-concept and movement scales were used, the latter including self-reports and ratings by others. Although results did not differentially support DMT as superior to verbal therapy, both groups showed gains in physical expressions. These findings support the claim that DMT enhances expressive qualities.

Green (1992) suggests DMT is appropriate for adolescents with learning difficulties. More recently, Farr (1997) in a U.S. description of DMT with African American, male, at-risk, adolescents 15 to 19 years of age claims short-term, goal-orientated, problem-solving, psycho-educational approaches to be the best way of working with this population. "DMT, given the physical expressiveness in both nonverbal communication and applied kinaesthetic skills, provides a medium for the high-energy, fast-paced movement styles of Black children" Farr, (1997, p. 188).

THE AUTHOR'S STUDY

The following is a description of a study this author conducted of the perceptions of male adolescents labeled delinquent toward a program of dance movement therapy (DMT).

Of special interest in this research was the aspect of clients' perceptions toward the experience of DMT. The author was unable to discover any literature in this area apart from a few descriptive accounts. For example, Rosen (1957) quoted an essay by a patient on her reactions to dance therapy on an open ward in a psychiatric hospital. Dickinson (1957) mentioned an article (Keleher, 1956) that described a beginning session at a New York psychiatric hospital for small boys. It began:

> They didn't want to dance, they kicked the locked door trying to get out. The psychiatrist persuaded, the dance therapist kept up a rhythmic beat on the drum, but the boys would have none of it. "We want to go home," they shouted, stomping round the room. But feet fell into step with the dance rhythm and the session was on.

The research was pioneering for several reasons. Little research has been undertaken on DMT in the United Kingdom and the author is not aware of any material on clients' perceptions toward DMT or on DMT with adolescents labeled delinquent to date.

Three stages of experimental fieldwork were undertaken: preliminary, pilot, and final. The preliminary fieldwork took place in a community home with education on the premises (CHE) in the Northeast of England. Subjects were 13 to 15 years old, male, and in care. The pilot study, which was based on recommendations made in the preliminary fieldwork, took place in the same setting with another similar group of young people. One theme was selected from the analysis of pilot study results for the final fieldwork, which aimed to discover how the young people, in particular, perceived and experienced the process of DMT.

The final fieldwork was undertaken in Scotland in a different but comparable setting to the pilot study. A DMT intervention program was designed, based on pilot study recommendations and was implemented over a three-month period. Two weekly sessions took place with four volunteer male adolescents. The primary data collection was by semistructured interviews conducted by trained interviewers over the duration of the program and at follow-up.

The limitations of this research must be recognized, hence caution needs to be employed when drawing conclusions. The following are the seven main conclusions drawn from this research:

1. The young people's experience and worldview can be seen to be concerned with a dimension encompassing enjoyment and boredom. Enjoyment was linked to "good" and boredom to "bad." They enjoyed group sessions but not individual sessions when prior to group sessions. They found the latter more embarrassing and felt "stupid."

2. The young people stressed a variety of experience in concrete terms in order to conceptualize DMT. They labeled movement games, dance, exercise, relaxation, and improvisation. They also named apparatus, music, verbalization, and vocalization.

3. To evaluate their experience, the young people contrasted it with their other activities in school, for example, the simplistic comparison of "skive" with "hard work." They judged the therapist's approach to be nondomineering and responsive.

4. A pretreatment interview was found to be unhelpful in preparing this population for DMT.

5. The young people did not perceive the sessions as helping them in the ways outlined by the therapist.

6. The terminology used and the information given prior to sessions to some extent determined the young people's perceptions. It is recommended that the words "dance" and "therapy" be avoided since these and other aspects were an influence on their perceptions.

7. There is a need for researchers involved in arts therapy fieldwork to separate out their investment in the research and their investment in the therapeutic treatment they are also responsible for; hence, supervision was highly recommended.

Many implications can be drawn from these conclusions. For instance, it seems possible to engage such young people's willing cooperation in the DMT if enjoyment, specifically linked to free-flow with weight or overcoming gravity, is perceived as the main outcome. Their particular needs for sensory weight flow movement experiences were perceived as important for engaging their participation. Group work was less threatening than individual work for this age group, especially with a female therapist. Group work could be helpful in building up a therapeutic relationship prior to working individually or in dyads.

The fact that DMT focuses on the body, rhythm, and on movement influences clients' experience of DMT. How clients feel about their bodies and their movements and thus themselves will determine to some degree their responses to DMT. Therefore, research on self-image, body-image, and body concept is valuable, not only in helping to determine the value of DMT but also in the understanding of DMT processes. Clients' perceptions of DMT relate to how they experience it on bodily or sensory levels in addition to intellectual and emotional levels.

It may be that drawing and other projective methods, such as thematic apperception tests, would be better at discovering perceptions from this population. Verbal expression does not reveal enough owing to the limited language abilities of the young people.

Vocalization and verbalization may be a development in the process of DMT or a supportive aspect to the content of DMT for this group. It aided interaction between the therapist and the young people.

In summary, this section introduced DMT from an historical perspective and outlined the principles of DMT as the author understands them together with relevant research. The latter was designed to provide the rationale for using DMT with groups of male adolescents labeled delinquent. Finally, an overview of the author's research was presented. This was an evaluation of the young people's experience of DMT, not a measurement of any resulting outcome or benefits.

THE TECHNIQUE

The approach to DMT employed by the author in her work with troubled young people grew out of a firm grounding in Rudolf von Laban's work (1879–1958) in the field of dance in education

(Laban, 1978). His methods for teaching dance in schools and colleges were adopted in the United Kingdom after World War II, although Dalcroze's eurhythmics had flourished since the 1920s, as had Margaret Morris's movement. Many children in schools had experienced modern educational dance that was child-based and stressed creativity and groupwork. Both primary and secondary schools used the approach. Most primary teachers were given at least a basic understanding of Laban's methods and many physical education teachers studied Laban-based dance for specialist secondary school teaching. In addition, early students of Laban adapted his methods to a variety of situations, including special education (North, 1972; Sherborne, 1974), the health services (Wethered, 1973), and management (Lamb, 1965; Ramsden, 1973). As early as 1948, dance and fundamental movement was introduced into a London psychiatric hospital with the aim to coordinate action and thought (BSPP, 1986).

Despite these beginnings, Laban-based DMT remains a newly emerging profession in the United Kingdom, and even now there are few fulltime posts for therapists. There has been evidence of a steady development in the practice, however, in special education (Payne, 1977, 1979, 1980; Payne-West, 1984), hospitals (Holden, 1980), day centers (Pasch, 1985), prisons (Ling, 1983), and voluntary settings (Meekums, 1986). There are also some therapists who see clients privately (Permain, 1980).

Dance movement therapy and Laban's modern educational dance share several tools; for example, Laban's categorization of movement into body, effort, and space (Laban, 1978). Dance movement therapy uses Laban Movement Analysis (LMA) for assessment and development of movement range (see pp. 46–47). The process of developing insight, interpretation, movement dialogue, relationship building, symbols, and alternative behavioral responses are all aspects of DMT. The client's behavioral or perceptual manifestations are used as thematic material that is then developed within the therapeutic relationship together with an awareness of developmental needs (Leventhal, 1980, 1986). The approach to DMT by the author is founded in humanistic psychology as developed by Rogers (1967), Maslow (1968), and Rowan (1975) in which the "here and now" is experienced in the moment, together with group analysis (Bion, 1961) and as adapted by Willis (1988).

Southgate's (1980) creative energy cycle is used as a guide to the development of sessions. A warm-up period for nurturing and preparation, an energizing time for a release of theme material and movement exploration such as in popular dance forms, and contemporary styles, a core time of the theme being worked with and through (often rhythmically), and finally a quiet recovery period in which calming relaxation, closure, and anticipation of the next session is engendered. Techniques and teaching are not important aspects, but acceptance of the preverbal symbols generated by the young people are important, as is the encouragement of nonverbal communication and movement improvisation. It is often claimed in DMT literature that the range of movement improvisation is important because it is the measure of the flexibility in adaptive functioning, a desirable symptom of health. This is problematic when it is clear that, for example, dancers have a wide movement range yet suffer symptoms of ill health, stress, and depression. It is acknowledged that DMT as delivered by the author may be different from DMT delivered by another practitioner. However, an assertive, engaging, competent approach appears to engender co-operation and rapport for this group of young people.

Themes from the sessions emerge from tasks and activities designed to facilitate responses in communication and an awareness of self with regard to others and the environment. Movement and creative rhythmic structures with music as an accompaniment may form the basis of the sessions as vehicles for the communication of feelings as experienced in the moment. Themes such as "hiding", "trust," and "being stuck" are explored using time, energy, and spatial dimensions—and, where appropriate, visualization, props (such as parachute or stretchy material) and relaxation techniques. Following the movement experience, verbal counseling is also used when necessary.

Both playing and moving are natural media of self-expression, being spontaneous and creative acts; both process and product are revealing and have the important advantage that they provide evidence of feelings and states of mind. The themes that emerge are significant to both client and therapist. A child's feelings and fantasies undergo a process of transformation in the process of DMT. Freedom of self-expression grows with time and trust, and discussion of movement or of therapeutic process is used only if the therapist feels it is appropriate. Sensitivity to the individual is a guiding factor. The therapist is a partner, closely involved, sharing the client's inner world as far as possible. It should not make any difference if the client moves or just sits; it is the client's time and this is made explicit. In line with play therapy, DMT is a method of helping troubled adolescents and adolescents in trouble to help themselves. The dancing, movement structures, and games act as other modes of self-disclosure alongside words and behavior. This gives DMT groups an added dimension not found in verbal groups. The structures are seen as starting points, rather than as finishing points.

Thus the DMT approach employed, while utilizing some psychoanalytic ideas, builds on the humanistic, nondirective method whereby the assumption is that the growth impulse makes mature behavior more satisfying than immature behavior. It grants individuals permission to be themselves; the therapist respects and accepts that self completely, without evaluation or pressure to change. Recognition and clarification of the expressed attitudes is achieved by a reflection of what the client has expressed and by the process of allowing clients the opportunity to be themselves and to learn to know themselves, charting their own courses openly. That is not to say groundrules and boundaries are not important and enforced as required.

Limits are kept to a minimum to make way for smoother progress. Leaving the room, coming back, and leaving again constitute an evasion of the process; therefore, rules are imposed. To emphasize clients' responsibility for the process, it is important that they understand that if they leave it is because they feel bored, angry, or stubborn; however, if they leave they cannot return to that session. Often leaving is expressing a need to meet some sort of anxiety.

There is thus no pressure to bring about change. Any change that is worthwhile is believed to come from within the client if it is to have any lasting effect. Rules are not used as a pressure. For example, swearing could lead to being excluded from the session, but this exclusion is not used in self-directive therapy. The client makes the choice whether to swear or not to swear, although the therapist's position concerning unacceptable behaviors may be clearly stated, for example, disappointment in the client.

The presence of physical aggression does involve the therapist in a rule that calls for authority and judgment. This might appear as partiality to certain members of the group. Axline (1974) recommends that limits be set for physical attacks in group work but that they need only be introduced when the therapist is certain of the imminence of violence.

The author therefore makes four clear rules with these young people: no hurting of themselves, of others, or of property, and remaining in the space for the duration of the session. These are stated at the beginning of the course of sessions and at various times during sessions when they seem necessary. Change in a client's adherence to rules does not mean conformity through some kind of pressure. The therapist attempts to help the clients realize that if they are responsible for themselves, they achieve self-respect and self-confidence enabling them to make their own choices.

The technique used in DMT sessions with young people will be related to the particular training and experience of the Dance Movement Therapist. The following examples were part of a 20-session program for volunteer male adolescents in Scotland. It was held twice-a-week for one hour each session.

The content of the program was deliberately not predictable in order to respond to the themes and developmental needs of the group, although activities and structures were used when relevant to a theme. The content of the sessions developed out of each session and its processes and interactions, rather than being planned prior to the sessions.

A brief outline of possible content, given in retrospect, follows: functional movement activities; moving spontaneously with music or rhythms; moving in a formed way with musical accompaniment; moving alone or with others in a coordinated manner; learning new movements and using ones already known (using particular clients' movement-dance interests); learning more about the body and how to move; floor work; grounding activities; relaxation techniques; whole body movements; discussion of experiences; verbal exchange; self-disclosure; assertive techniques; exercises and movement games to enhance self awareness and awareness of others; interaction and nonverbal communication structures; tension-release tasks; sensation experiences such as jumping, swinging, and stillness; use of apparatus as a stimulus for movement choices;

and cooperation and interaction with others through objects such as ropes, trampette, parachute, and elastic.

The content of the pilot field work included mirroring exercises, relaxation techniques, dancing in the group, improvisation, games involving objects, percussion and music, group movement tasks, role play, nonverbal and verbal exchange structures, and drawing. Themes included "choice versus no choice," arising out of feelings of a lack of control in the subjects' lives; "resistance and motivation," arising from the issue of nonparticipation and participation; "controlled versus controller," which emerged from aspects of power and leadership; and "trust" and "attacker versus defender."

Activities were intended to serve various aims. Some of these were release of energy and tension, expression of preverbal symbols, development of sensitivity toward self and others, peer leadership and sense of autonomy, group cohesion, increase in body awareness, enhanced self-concept, sense of fun and well-being, and development of spontaneity.

Four seemed to be the minimum acceptable number of young people for a group considering the levels of absenteeism found in the pilot study. It was hoped that this number would allow the group to function if one or two members were absent, although it might have caused difficulties for dyads. Any larger a group and the therapist might have found the numbers too great to facilitate a variety of interactions while remaining responsive to both the group and individual needs.

One part of the school's gymnasium was used for final field-work sessions, with benches screening off three-quarters of the space where ropes and mats were to be found. Space influences the content of sessions, as do objects in the space, individual goals, and subjects' responses.

Since DMT does not work on a cause-and-effect mechanism, there are no specific activities which are automatically utilized for any specific goal in a one-to-one correspondence. For one young person, with a personal goal of wishing to say "No" to others, gestures and sounds representing "No" to the client were explored symbolically in the sessions. This was developed into a rhythmic "Saying No" dance and finally into words and phrases incorporated within a movement interaction. In this, the client moved as if he were in a situation with his friends stealing something; he nonverbally enacted his withdrawal from them. His feelings about the situation were explored and the movement was repeated with the new awareness.

As a further illustration, one goal was to work with each boy individually in the group during the first stages of the development of the group. However, Gary could not let himself make contact with the therapist in this way; hence a goal for the next session was to engage Gary within a movement structure. Since he enjoyed testing his physical strength against others and there was a need to ground the group in some floor work, a wheelbarrow race was devised with the therapist partnering Gary.

Group sessions began with a warmup using loosening exercises, often to music the subjects chose, to relax bodily tension and to sensitize the boys to personal body sensations. There was group interaction, such as personal introductions using name games, sounds, gestures, or whole body movement. The therapist encouraged easy peripheral movements and then focused on specific areas of the body where there seemed to be tension. Next, there would be a period of more spontaneous free-form responses, sometimes with music, often in a structure. Here the aim was to enable the boys to discover the movement they liked to do—their own form of self-expression. This section merged into live situational themes such as "being closed versus being open" in sculpting each other, "mood postures," forming interactions with the therapist through structures of movement echoing, and others using touch where appropriate, for example, leaning against each other in twos.

Later, a relaxation section was introduced to help relieve long-term residual tension and the temporary fatigue built up during movement activities. This usually involved a visualization or muscle tension release work and breathing, followed by a gradual transition from relaxation to movement again, and providing for a closure preparation. Sometimes a verbal feedback period was introduced to reinforce any good feelings and closeness, to provide for sharings of feelings, and to relate events in daily lives that connect with what had been experienced in sessions.

1. Time and length of session: _____ Date: _____ Session Number: _____

2. Setting:

3. Population:

4. Props/music used and reasons:

5. Predominant themes (movement and psychodynamic):

   (a) Themes arrived with:

   (b) Themes evolving:

   (c) Themes clients thought of:

6. What was the behavior overall? (Use symbols.)

7. Changes noted:

8. Expressive gestures:

   (a) Verbal: (b) Nonverbal:

9. Goals achieved.

10. Goals for next session:

11. Any other comments:

Figure 2.1 Evaluation Sheet for Dance Movement Therapy Session.

The form shown in Figure 2.1 was designed to aid observation, recording, and evaluation of sessions. In addition, for individual work in particular, movement observation is valuable when diagnosing and when planning and evaluating DMT programs. The observation sheet in Figure 2.2 is one method the author has found useful.

Name: _____

Date: _____

Date of Birth: _____

Contexts

1.

2.

3.

4.

5.

6.

Six 5-minute observations should be made in different contexts, giving a total in each column. From this an indication of the strengths in movement preferences may be derived. The profile is only a guide; it may need to be supported by other observation sheets, for example, behavioral checklists.

Mark 1 when movements are observed in any of the categories

OBSERVATION		1	2	3	4	5	6	TOTAL
Weight	Strong							
	Heavy (no weight)							
	Light							
Space	Direct							
	Meandering							
Time	Vital							
	Sustained							
Flow	Carefree							
	Cautious							
Body	Broad							
Shape	Thin							
Still	Rounded							
or	Twisted							
Moving	Shapeless							

(continued)

Figure 2.2   Example of Movement Observation Sheet.

Mark 1 when movements are observed in any of the categories

OBSERVATION		1	2	3	4	5	6	TOTAL
Body	Rise							
Shaping	Sink							
	Open							
Movements	Close							
	Advance							
	Retreat							
	Symmetry							
	Asymmetry							
Phases	Long							
	Short							
Personal	Wide							
Space	Close							
Gen. Space	Curved							
Pathways	Angled							

Comments on profile

Figure 2.2   *(Continued)*

CASE ILLUSTRATION

This section contains a selection of material relating to one boy, called Paul for the purpose of this study, who participated in the fieldwork. The first selection is a process recording made by the therapist after session 17. This was a group session and introduces Paul as a member of the group, the other members being Brian, George, and John. These notes serve as an example both of the content of a DMT session and of therapeutic issues that can arise.

Therapist's Notes

This was the first time with all four boys together, quite an achievement in itself. I had called the care staff to say that I would be in on Monday at 9:30, asking that a reminder be given to the boys. They were all waiting and when I arrived and entered the room, John remained outside. His teacher said he wanted him to wait there at the end of the session; he had been in trouble again. Brian and George took their shoes off; Paul and John refused. There was some annoyance from Brian about his white socks getting dirty. They all took their coats off eventually too, although George and John worked under them at the beginning, back to front with their hoods up.

We began with reflecting a movement. Brian and Paul chose to work together. A good start was made. George and John sat on chairs and did not move for the first section. I continued to say "change leaders" at intervals. For the second section of the session, my task was to guess who was leading the movement in the group. They enjoyed outwitting me. Brian's movement was very limited and close to his body and he refused to reflect Paul's movement as a follower. They were both up and standing on the bench. Paul began using his hips and hands, pretending to hold a microphone and singing to the music (Madness). Brian withdrew. John took his shoes off and he and George began moving their fingers under their coats, with some tickling of each other, too.

Next we sat in the center on cushions and they were asked to give, in a sentence, a thought on how they perceived their partner. Comments ranged from "he's daft" to "he's great"—all good humoured though, smiles on faces. George thought everyone was great after insulting them. Paul said Brian was no fun. They all wanted to do the warm-up again. I asked them to change partners but they didn't want to. John got up and George did a lot of show-off dancing.

During the next talking phase, Paul said he wanted me to take my clothes off. George wanted to "do a play on how girls and boys wank together" and John supported this idea. I made it quite clear that taking my clothes off was not what I was there for. However, I allowed the fantasy to develop, stressing it was fine to fantasize as these feelings were natural, yet also aware that Paul had been arrested once for indecent exposure. I structured this by saying that they had to stop when told. They enjoyed this game, stopping each time as requested, although I did have to address each of them by name before they stopped.

They then moved as much as they could in 10 seconds. John organized a football game for this, using a shoe bag that was in the room on the floor. The next time, someone else organized a cushion fight for 10 seconds. Once they threw me a cushion and pulled me into the middle. I said "stop" and they froze. I explained I was not going to participate with them. For the next 10 seconds John elected that he was not going to join in as a play-fight had developed. George was particularly overactive, trying to pull Paul and Brian down to the floor. John organized them into a game "the first to hit the deck." George had a shield and sword (made from cushions). Lots of activity ensued. On each stop we talked about what had happened. I made a running commentary for the last one. Fears about injury arose from Brian and George. Brian said he wasn't joining in anymore, or coming again: "It's daft," he said. John replied that he came and he was older. John expressed his anger at Brian for not participating anymore. I said it was their group; they could make it as daft or stupid as they liked, but if others didn't like it they could club together to change it. I had an idea for a group lean but they did not want to do this. Finally, George said he would fall toward me if Paul and I caught him (trust game). Paul tended to throw George at me. George was self-directed, making his fall when he chose rather than passively letting us control him. He collapsed in his center, however, and usually caught himself before we caught him; perhaps the gap was too wide or perhaps he needed to be in complete control. George then had an idea to put coats on back-to-front with their hoods up for 10 seconds.

The head coordinator pushed on the door and interrupted us in one of our talking phases. The boys said we couldn't stop him because he was the head. They did not want to complete journals, but apart from a few resistant individuals at times, they cooperated successfully. More autonomy is evident now.

The boys at times made me feel useless, helpless, rejected, abandoned, messed up, and cruelly treated; precisely the experiences and feelings they found intolerable or intolerable to bear. This reversal of the painful experience seems the key to understanding the inner world of these boys whose outward behavior itself is often a vital message.

Much of their communication is through action rather than words. My responsibility seems to be to protect the groups' integrity from my own ambivalence and maintain it as an internal conception despite disturbing assaults made on it by group members who remained fearful of intimacy and relatedness. My own sense of loneliness and hopelessness was great.

Distressing countertransference feelings were evoked by the group. Judging the effectiveness of these groups by the usual standards of group therapy experience is inappropriate and leads to devaluation of group members, of the therapy, and of the therapist.

Case History

This is Paul's case history abstracted from his file and left deliberately in note form:

Age: 14 years
Sexual Offenses: indecent assault-11/17 May 1983
Admitted CHE: 7/18/83

Social Work Report: 9/28/83
Benefit from masculine environment. He needs to learn control and respect for others, especially women whom I suspect he thought of no consequence, no doubt modeled on his experience with his mother who covered up for him and denied his excesses.

Social Aspect
Inept attempts to make friends.
—Aim to establish friendships.
Friendships short-lived.
—Aim to remove causes of breakdowns.
Imitates peers.
—Aim to eliminate.

His passivity for involving himself in clownish behavior irritates peers, therefore prevents positive social interaction. Gullible and naive, often butt of his peers. Name calling, doesn't realize that he is so ridiculed because of immature behavior. Discussion helped him gain insight into why not particularly popular and encouraged him to think before acts, thus develop his own level of self-control. As yet he shows no real responsibility for self or others.

Problems
10/5/83: Lots of effort from Paul in house decorating.
1/13/84: Good behavior most of week. Therefore senior status. Very pleased. Talkative and sensible at Youth Club.

1/14/84 and 1/15/84: Good behavior over weekend in house.

1/18/84: Admitted theft of cigarets from office. Sanctioned. Quieter moments says he did not do this but self-reports unreliable.

1/26/84: Odd behavior, starry eyes, fixed gaze, snatching at food with teeth.

2/1/84: Banging head off door in toilets. Precipitated by niggling by/to another. Intervention to prevent self-injury.

3/17/84: Paul making efforts of the order requiring gentle coaxing.

Background
5/5/82: Admitted to Observation and Assessment Center after care order (place of safety order) by Juvenile Court, where Paul appeared charged with criminal damage.

Stepfather; natural-mother, never married Paul's father—since the father was dominated by his own mother. Paul has one sister. Mother says can discipline Paul and surprised he was taken into care. Developmental milestones normal, occasionally nocturnal enuresis.

Results of Interview
Child's view: Expressed deep feelings for mother and stated they have very close relationship, not to exclusion of sister. Mother never physically punished him but shouts when he displeases her. He said she was very disappointed with him when he was in trouble recently but also cried bitterly when he was taken away from home.

Stepfather's family bond with Paul: was in care himself from 9 years of age. Paul thinks of him as own father—good relationship. Mother and stepfather married when Paul was 5 years old (1974). Paul uses father's surname. Paul spends much time with grandmother. Gifts from grandmother given to him. Visits from parents who want him home. He is in the Army Cadets and goes to discos.

Care order: "Beyond control of his parents."

Educational psychologist (at 13 years) recommended remedial teaching. Paul has had no involvement with child guidance or psychology services.

Paul is easily led and sees his main weakness as the friends he has. When he goes home he will not see them if he can help it. Wants to join the army.

Presents as anxious and psychometric data suggest, slightly higher-than-average anxiety. Poor social skills, limited self-control and concern for others. Emotionally shallow. Denies problems— only has minor ones. Impulsive.

Functioning at below average ability academically. Not described as established delinquent.

Evaluative Session

The young people volunteering for sessions would always attend an evaluative session in which the therapist made an attempt to diagnose and be receptive to material which could be developed during the program. First, the plan, structure, and ground rules for Paul's evaluative session are noted. A summary of his diagnosis goals and possible content, structures, and methods are then presented.

Place: Resource Room, Education Center, Training School, CHE.

Rules and Structure (i.e., rules prepared by the therapist)

1. Arrive on time outside Resource Room (the space made available for DMT). Make contract with each boy, for example, I will . . . . . . and he will . . . . . . Shoes and socks removed for sessions.
2. Work for 30 minutes individually for several weeks then in dyads with another boy for a few weeks. Finally we will work in a small group for a short while. The whole program will take place for this term only.
3. Confidentiality issue.
4. Journals. Two minutes at end of session to write down things important to you; for example, what good things/bad things happened to you this week, anything about your family, friends, pets, hobbies, ambitions. Anything felt about session or how you feel. Drawing acceptable. Spelling doesn't matter. This is a message system between us and no one else is to see the journals, only you and I. I will give out and collect at the

end of the session then write in a reply comment for next time. We both put our names on the journal.

5. We will aim to work together as a team to try to help you to overcome some of your difficulties.
6. When I say *stop* I expect you to stop and sit down immediately.

SESSION

Equipment: Chairs/tables/crayons/music/large paper/percussion/mats.

Task: Drawing to music on table. Chairs available.

1. Piece of paper each. Add music and give examples of marks.
2. A paper for us to share and repeat.
3. Draw with unusual hand, with mouth, with foot.

Task: Move hand as though drawing to the music on an enormous sheet of paper on whole wall.

Music: Ask for their favorite.

Task: Relaxation: Allow limbs/head to be moved by me—which parts most relaxed?

Aims of Session
1. To establish the beginning of a relationship through contact using a focus outside of self as the transitionary stage.
2. To use what they can do (i.e., the healthy part) as a way of developing confidence.
3. To give some structure within which unusual things are asked of them.
4. To assess any potential areas which could be worked with.

Diagnostic Statement

The following material summarises the therapist's impressions of Paul from the evaluative session.

CONTENT   Tough versus gentle theme
           Reinforcing that to have sexual feelings is okay

GOALS   To make contact
           To develop trusting relationship
           To use movement experience to draw out difficulties

To extend movement range
To reinforce sexuality
To enhance his expression through movement

Procedures of Therapy

Rhythm

Percussion work

Range of feeling—tone music—(Tough and gentle)
Fight and non-fighting theme

Problems/Possible Causes/Areas Needing Change

1. Sexuality—possible—no girl friend—can't express sexual feelings to anyone—who is it safe for him to show sexual feelings towards?
2. Needs confidence building.

Movement Observations

Effort: quick/flexible. Alternatives in time factor.

Shaping: saggital, some opening and closing. Long phrases.

Passive escape in situations not to his liking which leads to anxiety.

Summary of Sessions Following Evaluation

This is included in order to illustrate how issues arose and were developed using DMT techniques over the duration of Paul's individual sessions.

For the first couple of sessions Paul was overeager to attend. Despite later ambivalence at coming, once he was in the room, his eyes sparkled and he seemed motivated to participate.

He worked with movements that developed from low to high, and open, often accompanied by his choice of music, a band called "Madness" which had a strong rhythmic beat. I selected some music with an opposite feeling tone: John Williams' guitar music. We moved together in a mirroring technique from sitting to kneeling to standing to walking. He was less inhibited with the lighter music, displaying considerably more free flow with sustained and flexible movements, beginning to move into spaces further from his body. He was also keen to show his skills of body management in jumps, turning jumps, and strong postures with fists. He described these dances as "fit" and "exciting," made strong eye contact and commented on how good I was and that dance was tiring. He disclosed that he wanted to grab me and kiss me. Discussion focused on who it would be appropriate to show such feelings to and on my role with him.

In a later session, we worked from a rhythmical framework, particularly with stuck, rigid, and bound movement and with relaxation. It was noticed that Paul associated fear with rigidity and verbalized considerably about such situations in his life.

During the following session, we worked with bound movement again. The following notes are from that session and describe perhaps the most significant event in his individual program:

I took his rooted, bound movement and asked him to exaggerate it moving his bones inside the skin of his feet, but without being able to move from the spot. I asked him what this felt like: "A struggle," he replied. I then pulled his hips and asked him to try to move to the next space in front. He pulled away, leant his body forwards, keeping his legs straight and remaining very bound and tight. "How does that feel?" "Good," he said, with lots of smiles—he seemed to enjoy the contact and struggle. We then developed onto hands and knees; his objective was to reach another space, mine to arrest his movement by holding his hips. We made a short phrase of this. I asked whether he had felt this struggle before. He avoided responding at first, asking if he could do "that hip thing" to me. I explained that the idea was for me to give him attention but since it was his initiation I decided to reverse roles. I felt that he was enjoying the contact but had struggled in that role enough. (I felt his fingers on my belly although he held my hips as I had demonstrated.) I wondered if this was appropriate and I decided to change to wrist to wrist contact. Paul said, "No, don't go." I replied, "Let me go—I'm going." "Who was he holding back?"

I asked. "No one," came the reply; then he continued "When coming to this CHE my mother was holding me tightly, she didn't want me to come here but I had to. She got a bit upset." He made this association and seemed able to share it with me at this later stage, perhaps because he was in the more powerful position (the holder back) or at enough of a distance from himself to allow the feeling and words to emerge.

I suggested he move as though he were himself and I would pretend to move as if I were his mother. He became very involved, eventually breaking away saying "I've got to go," and ran in a free run in the general space. I turned saying, "Come back." "No, I've got to go," he exclaimed. I sank down in the space and sadly said that I was unhappy he had to leave. I felt lonely as though he would never return. I hid my head in a low shape. Silence. He did not answer. He was looking at me, then quickly looked away when I made eye contact. I felt his sadness. I moved into a different shape and said, "We'll finish there, how are you feeling?" "Alright," he answered, his eyes going up and watering. I asked him if there was anything else he'd like to say to his mother, placing a cushion in the space. "Yes—but not to a cushion." "Imagine that is her and speak to her," I encouraged. He was not at all happy with this idea. "I know it's not here—it really cracks you up this place." He seemed angry now. He got up and put his shoes on. I explained that this was a safe place to explore such feelings, that our sessions were about working with these difficulties. I reassured him that it was okay to feel sad and angry here. "Of course I'm angry," he exclaimed. He was definitely very angry. He seemed to be projecting strongly that I was his mother holding onto him—perhaps smothering him. The movement and verbal interaction must have brought back hurt feelings from the past when he was removed from home and brought to the CHE. He may also have resented that and have been feeling a sadness at missing his mother, perhaps seeing for the first time that she was dependent in some way on him.

This illustrates how working with movement, that is, beginning with exaggerating a predominant quality and spatial orientation, and adding physical contact and verbal associations, can lead to working with fear, anger, sadness, and so on.

For Paul, the outcome was not only catharsis but more importantly a recognition of his relationship with his mother who was holding him back. His own lack of power (being frozen and rigid) was evident and he was able to experience this at a more conscious level—and particularly at a symbolic level—in his movement. Subsequently, Paul became even more free, quick, and strong in his movement and began to initiate movement in the group. His confidence was evident in other areas of his treatment program and he was promoted to a more senior care facility where peer group responsibility was the main emphasis, each boy being responsible for his own actions in a less authoritarian, controlled environment. This was not necessarily a result of his DMT program.

Dance movement therapy thus helped Paul to develop a trusting relationship with the therapist in which the "holding environment" was facilitated through the use of rhythm and space. Verbalization and quality of movement were utilized when they emerged as significant material for Paul, enabling him to become more aware of aspects of himself and his relationships.

SUMMARY AND CONCLUSIONS

Techniques of DMT have not been validated, and still not enough research has been done in comparable areas to this study to quote any investigations related to adolescents labeled delinquent. Descriptions of work done with a variety of groups show that some benefits may be expected. It is reasonable, therefore, that some value from experience of DMT can also be expected for male adolescents labeled delinquent.

This author supports the description of DMT that was previously presented. In addition, the author regards vocalization, verbalization, and sound as integral to the DMT process and believes that the therapeutic alliance is crucial for effective therapy.

SUGGESTIONS FOR FURTHER RESEARCH

Both the pilot and final fieldwork findings found that verbalization and vocalization were important aspects of the participants' experience of DMT. Future research could be concerned with challenging the assumption that DMT is a nonverbal modality.

Questions about the amount of verbalization that takes place with different therapists working with a similar population could be studied, with reference to whether verbalization is encouraged, used in particular ways, or stems mainly from therapist to client and vice-versa, or arises between clients. Is verbalization due to the population—its attitudes, values, level of development, disorder, intelligence, personality, or anxiety level? Are vocalizations and verbalizations used as a defense? When do they take place: in combination with movement or without it? Is it used mainly at the beginning, the middle, or the end of sessions and what is its content? Classroom interaction techniques could be used, such as the Flanders Scale (1972), to discover whether speech or vocalization was therapist- or client-initiated, and to determine which activities provoke spontaneous sound. Any links between vocal sounds and verbal expression could be explored together with receptive and expressive language ability in relation to movement interaction. Analysis of a videotaped DMT session could be carried out to discover whether verbalization was used in a supportive role or as a primary activity. Exploration could take place as to whether there is more or less verbalization-vocalization in a group, dyad, or individual session. Spontaneous as opposed to formal language could be compared with the movement processes in use. This kind of research would have important implications for DMT practice and training, and for the theory of nonverbal communication generally.

In the field of perceptions, further study comparing the therapist's perceptions with the client's would yield more information on how DMT is understood, and how the different experience of therapist and client could be explained. It would be of interest to monitor clients' experiences over a long term-program and see what similarities and differences emerged.

The following recommendations are offered. They were developed from the issues arising out of the pilot and final fieldwork findings. Some of these may be of use as guidelines for other practitioners attempting an intervention program with troubled or troublesome young people—in particular a program of DMT or another creative arts therapy:

1. Be clear about your aims and objectives and how you plan to implement them.
2. Spend time forming a liaison with the principal or director of the setting and the educational psychologist first, explaining the project and eliciting their prejudices and biases.
3. Give a presentation to all staff, outlining the project and focusing on the need for their full cooperation and support. Do not promise or guarantee anything: There is a tendency for staff to believe the outsider holds a magic formula and will change bad behavior into good overnight. However, explain any benefits that have taken place as a result of previous programs.
4. Give a demonstration session to the young people. From this, volunteers may come forward willing to participate in the project. Limit numbers to between 4 and 6 per group.
5. Be careful about what you tell the young people: The words you use and the information given will be determining factors in the attitude they will present about sessions.
6. Be aware of the institution's philosophy, time management, organizational resistance, and so on. Be sure to adapt your program to fit in with these elements in order to avoid conflict and confusion for staff and young people.

This chapter has introduced the history and background of DMT. It focused on the author's research study with male adolescents labeled delinquent, and used this study to illustrate DMT practice. Consequently, a number of questions were touched on: (1) What is the conceptual/theoretical foundation of DMT? (2) How should DMT/therapy/research be conducted to provide understanding? (3) How can DMT help clients? (4) What do dance movement therapists do?

Dance movement therapy is is now established in the United Kingdom with professional registration and three university validated post graduate training courses. State registration with the Council for Professions Supplementary to Medicine is almost complete. There have also been several PhDs. awarded in the subject and textbooks are beginning to appear by United Kingdom authors. It needs research in order to enable further understanding of its methods and theoretical foundations. However, it is being found to be a powerful process even by those used to verbal or other arts therapies.

REFERENCES

Anderson, W. (Ed.). (1977). *Therapy and the arts.* New York: Harper and Row.

Apter, H., Sharir, I., Tyano, S., & Wijsenbeck, H. (1978). Movement therapy with psychotic adolescents. *British Journal of Medical Psychology, 51*(2), 155–159.

Axline, V. (1974). *Play therapy.* New York: Ballantine Books.

Bainbridge, G.W. (1953). Dance mime: A contribution to treatment in psychiatry. *Journal of Mental Science, 99,* 308–314.

Bainbridge-Cohen, B., & Mills, M. (1979). *Developmental movement therapy.* (Booklet available through Association for Dance Movement Therapy Publications). London.

Bartinieff, I. (1971). *How is the dancing teacher equipped to do dance therapy?* American Dance Therapy Association Monographs 1 and second Annual Proceedings 1967.

Bender, L., & Boas, F. (1941). Creative dance in therapy. *American Journal of Orthopsychiatry,* 235–244.

Bernstein, P. (1971). *Therapy and methods in dance movement therapy.* Dubuque, IA: Kendall/Hunt.

Bion, W. (1961). *Experiences in groups.* London: Tavistock.

Bowlby, T. (1982). *Attachment and loss* (Vol. 1). London: Hogarth Press.

British Society for Projective Psychology. (1986). *Personal communication.*

Brown, G., McDowell, R.L., & Smith, J. (Eds.). (1981). *Educating adolescents with behavioral disorders.* Columbus, OH: Merrill.

Chace, M. (1953). Dance as an adjunct therapy with hospitalized mental patients. *Bulletin of the Menninger Clinic, 17,* 219–221.

Condon, W.S. (1968, October & 1969, November). Linguistic-kinesic research and dance therapy. *Proceedings of the Third and Fourth American Dance Therapy Association Annual Conference* (1968, pp. 21–44; 1969, pp. 21–39). Columbia, MA: ADTA.

Condon, W.S., & Ogston, W. (1966). Sound film analysis of normal and pathological behavior patterns. *Journal of Nervous and Mental Disease, 143,* 338–343.

Cratty, B. (1979). *Perceptual and motor development in infants and young children.* Englewood Cliffs, NJ: Prentice-Hall.

Darwin, C.R. (1955). *The expression of the emotions in man and animals.* New York: Philosophical Library Edition. (Original work published in 1872)

Davis, M. (1973, February). The potential of non-verbal communication research in dance. *C.O.R.D., 5,* 10–27.

Delaney, W. (1973). Working with children. *Proceedings of the Eighth American Dance Therapy Conference.* (pp. 3–15). Columbia, MA: American Dance Therapy Association.

Dickinson, M. (1957). Music as a tool for psychotherapy for children. *Journal of Music Therapy,* 97–104.

Dosamantes-Alperson, E. (1984). Experiential movement psychotherapy. In P. Lewis (Ed.), *Theoretical approaches to dance movement therapy* (Vol. 2, pp. 145–163). Dubuque, IA: Kendall/Hunt.

Dunne, C., Bruggen, P., & O'Brian, C. (1982). Touch and action in group therapy of younger adolescents. *Journal of Adolescence, 5,* 31–38.

Espenak, L. (1981). *Dance therapy: Theory and application.* Springfield, IL: Thomas.

Farr, M. (1997). The role of DMT in treating at-risk, African American adolescents. *Arts in Psychotherapy, 24,* 2, 183–191.

Feder, E., & Feder, B. (1981). *The expressive arts therapies.* Englewood Cliffs, NJ: Prentice-Hall.

Flanders, A. (1972). *Interaction analysis and in-service training. Social Psychology of Teaching.* London: Penguin.

Fraenkel, D.L. (1983). The relationship of empathy in movement to synchrony, echoing and empathy in verbal interactions. *American Journal of Dance Therapy, 6,* 37–48.

Frostig, M. (1967). *Pictures and patterns: The Frostig program for the development of visual perception.* Chicago: Follet.

Gendlin, E. (1962a). *Experiencing and the creation of meaning.* New York: Viking Press.

Gendlin, E. (1962b). Focusing. *Journal of Psychotherapy Research and Practice, 6,* 4–15.

Green, D. (1992, February 18). Moving to the rhythm. *Therapy Weekly, 15*(30), 5.

Gunter, A. (1984). Body ego identity in humanistic psychiatry, dance therapy. *Dynamische Psychiatrie, 17*(4), 339–356.

Hazelton, T., Price, P., & Brown, G. (1979). Psychodrama, creative movement and remedial activities for children with special needs. *Journal of Association of Educational Psychologists, 5*(1), 32–37.

Hecox, B., Levine, E., & Scott, D. (1976). Dance in physical rehabilitation. *Physical Therapy, 56,* 919–924.

Hilyar, J.C., Wilson, D.G., Dillon, C., Cara, L., Jenkins, C., Spencer, W.A., Meadows, M.E., & Booker, W. (1982). Physical fitness training and counselling as treatment for young offenders. *Journal of Counselling and Psychology 3,* 392–403.

Holden, S. (1980). Art and dance combined in therapy. *Inscape, 4,* 1.

Hunt, V. (1978). Movement behaviour: A model for action. *Quest,* 69–91.

Johnson, D.R. (1984). Movement and dramatherapy as representation of the internal world of an eighteen year old, male, catatonic schizophrenic. *Psychiatry, 47*(4), 299–314.

Johnson, D.R., & Eicher, V. (1990). The use of dramatic activity to facilitate DMT with adolescents. *Arts in Psychotherapy, 17,* 157–164.

Johnson, D.R., & Sandel, S. (1977, Fall/Winter). Structural analysis of group movement sessions: Preliminary research. *American Journal of Dance Therapy,* 32–36.

Jung, C.G. (1966). *Two essays on analytical psychology.* Princeton, NJ: Princeton University Press.

Keleher, C.G. (1956, March). Modern dance as mental therapy. *Dance Observer.*

Kephart, A.I. (1971). *The slow learner in the classroom.* Columbus, OH: Merrill.

Kestenberg, J. (1971). Development of young children through bodily movement. *Journal of American Psychoanalytical Association, 1,* 746–764.

Laban, R. (1951). The educational and therapeutic values of dance. In W. Sorrell (Ed.), *The dance has many faces* (pp. 145–159). New York: World.

Laban, R. (1978). *Modern educational dance.* London: MacDonald and Evans.

Lamb, W. (1965). *Posture and gesture: An introduction to the study of physical behaviour.* London: Duckworth.

Lesté, A., & Rust, J. (1984). Effect of dance on anxiety. *Journal of Perceptual and Motor Skills, 58,* 762–772.

Leventhal, M. (1980). Dance therapy as treatment of choice for emotionally disturbed and learning disabled children. *Journal of Physical Education and Recreation, 51,* 7.

Leventhal, M. (1986). Dance movement therapy: Education or therapy? *Association for Dance Movement Therapy Newsletter, 1,* 15.

Levy, F. (1988). *Dance movement therapy: A healing art.* Reston, VA: American Alliance for Health, Recreation, PE and Dance.

Lewis, P. (Ed.). (1979). *Theoretical approaches in dance movement therapy* (Vol. 1). Dubuque, IA: Kendall/Hunt.

Ling, F. (1983). In touch with self: In touch with others. *Prison Services Journal, 51*, 18–20.

Lovell, S.M. (1980). The bodily-felt sense and body image changes in adolescence. In F. Levine (Ed.), *Compendium of presenters* (pp. 34–36). Columbia, MA: American Dance Therapy Association.

Lowen, A. (1975). *Bioenergetics.* London: Conventure.

Mahrabian, M. (1972). *Non-verbal communication.* Chicago: Aldine.

Maslow, A.H. (1968). *Towards a psychology of being.* New York: Van Nostrand.

Mason, K.C. (1974). *Focus on dance VII–Dance therapy.* Washington, DC: American Association of Health, Physical Education and Recreation.

Meekums, B. (1981). Dance your whole being. *Energy and Character,* 45–47.

Meekums, B. (1986, May 12). The light fantastic. *The Guardian,* p. 8.

Meier, W. (1979). Meeting special needs through movement and dance drama. *Therapeutic Education, 7, 1,* 27–33.

Merek, P.A. (1976). Dance therapy with adult day patients. *Dissertation Abstracts International* (University Microfilms No. 76-1/069).

Nicol, A. (1979). Annotation: Psychotherapy in the school. *Journal of Child Psychology and Psychiatry, 28,* 81–86.

North, M. (1972). *Personality assessment through movement.* London: MacDonald and Evans.

Ornstein, R. (1973). *The psychology of consciousness.* New York: Viking.

Parlett, M. (1981). Illuminative evaluation. In P. Reason & J. Rowan (Eds.), *Human inquiry* (pp. 219–225). New York: Wiley.

Parteli, L. (1995). Aesthetic listening: Contributions of DMT to the psychic understanding of motor stereotypes and distortions in autism and psychosis in childhood and adolescence. *Arts in Psychotherapy, 22, 3,* 241–247.

Pasch, J. (1985). Dance with psychiatric patients. *Association for Dance Movement Therapy Newsletter, 1,* 8.

Payne, H.L. (1977). *To examine the value of movement therapy in improving relationships for a number of emotionally disturbed children.* Unpublished doctoral dissertation, Laban Centre, University of London, Goldsmiths College, London.

Payne, H.L. (1979, April). Movement therapy in a special setting. In *Current developments in special education* (pp. 44–52). Proceedings of conference held at the Cambridge Institute of Education, England.

Payne, H.L. (1980). *Body boundary, social adjustment and self actualization: Their relationship in a group of learning disabled children.* Unpublished dissertation. Cambridge Institute of Education, England.

Payne, H.L. (1981). Movement therapy for the special child. *British Journal of Dramatherapy, 4,* 3.

Payne, H.L. (1985). Jumping for Joy. *Changes: Journal of Psychology and Psychotherapy, 3,* 5.

Payne, H.L. (1987). *The perceptions of male adolescents labelled delinquent towards a programme of dance movement therapy.* Unpublished masters thesis, University of Manchester, England.

Payne-West, H.L. (1984, Autumn). Responding with dance. *Maladjustment and Therapeutic Education, 2*(2), 42–57.

Penfield, K. (1978, October 26). To dance is to learn to live again. *Therapy Magazine,* 5.

Permain, R. (1980, January). Grounding and movement. *Energy and Character, 2,* 1.

Peterson, B., & Cameron, C. (1978). Preparing high anxiety patients for psychotherapy through body therapy. *Journal of Contemporary Psychotherapy, 9*(2), 171–177.

Ramsden, P. (1973). *Top team planning.* London: Carsell/Associated Business Programme.

Reich, W. (1945). *Character analysis.* New York: Simon and Schuster.

Rogers, C. (1967). *On becoming a person.* London: Constable.

Rosen, E. (1954, January). Dance as therapy for the mentally ill. *Teachers College Record, 55,* 215–222.

Rosen, E. (1957). *Dance in psychotherapy.* New York: Columbia University, Teachers College, Bureau of Publications.

Rowan, J. (1975, September 11). Exploring the self. *New Behaviour,* 406–409.

Rutter, M.C., Tizzard, J., & Whitmore, K. (1970). *Education, health and behaviour.* London: Longman.

Sandel, S. (1973). Going down to dance. In E. Fulton (Ed.), *Proceedings of the Eighth Annual Conference of the American Dance Therapy Association* (pp. 15–24). Columbia, MA: ADTA.

Schaefer, C. (1976). *Therapeutic use of child's play.* New York: Aronson.

Schilder, P. (1955). *The image and appearance of the human body.* New York: International Universities Press.

Schmais, C., & Felber, D. (1977, Fall). Dance therapy analysis: A method for observing and analyzing a dance therapy group. *American Journal of Dance Therapy,* pp. 18–25.

Serlin, L. (1977). A portrait of Karen: A Gestalt phenomenological approach to movement therapy. *Journal of Contemporary Psychotherapy, 8*(2), 145–153.

Sherborne, V. (1974). Building relationships through movement with children with communication problems. *Inscape, 1,* 10.

Shirley, C. (1980). Art therapy linked with movement. *Inscape, 4,* 1.

Siegal, E.V. (1984). *Dance movement therapy: Mirror of ourselves, the psychoanalytical approach.* New York & London: Human Sciences Press.

Silberman, L. (1973). A dance therapist's experience of working with disturbed adolescent boys in a city prison hospital. In E. Fulton (Ed.), *Proceedings of the Eighth Annual Conference of the American Dance Therapy Association* (pp. 63–76). Columbia, MA: ADTA.

Southgate, J. (1980). *Community and group dynamics.* London: Barefoot Books.

Spencer, P. (Ed.). (1985). *Society and the dance.* Cambridge, MA: Cambridge Press.

Standing Committee of Arts Therapy Professions. (1987). *The arts therapies: A booklet for employers.* Hatfield, England: University of Hertfordshire.

Torrance, E.P., & Torrance, P. (1972). Combining creative problem solving with creative expressive activity in the education of disadvantaged young people. *Journal of Creative Behavior, 6*(1), 1–10.

Wethered, A. (1973). *Drama and movement in therapy.* London: MacDonald and Evans.

Whitehouse, M. (1977). The transference in dance therapy. *American Journal of Dance Therapy, 1*(4), 3–7.

Wickes, F. (1968). *The inner world of childhood.* London: Mentor Books.

Wilhelm, R. (Trans.). (1968). *The I Ching or book of changes.* London: Routledge & Kegan Paul.

Willis, S. (1988). Group-Analytic drama: A therapy for disturbed adolescents. *Group Analysis, 21,* 153–168.

Wright, B. (1980). Dance as the cure: The arts as metaphors for healing in Kelantanese Malay spirit exorcisms. *C.O.R.D. 12*(2), 3–11.

CHAPTER 3

Imagery—A Tool in Child Psychotherapy

INTRODUCTION

GUIDED IMAGERY as a technique for working with children and adolescents in psychotherapy is a powerful and flexible tool that can be integrated into work done in many settings and from a range of perspectives. The historical and theoretical basis of this work contains diverse elements of influence, such as the analytical psychology of Jung, the cognitive behavioral literature, particularly involving systematic desensitization and hypnosis, and studies of children's play, fantasy, and daydreaming capacities.

HISTORICAL BACKGROUND

Ideally, one could trace the use of guided imagery to help children cope with fear, pain, and stress to stories told of heroes vanquishing villains in preliterate societies. In more recent and well-documented years, the importance of the individual's capacity for fantasy and imagination was presented and developed in the work of Jung (1953), in which the power of the unconscious as "an independent, productive activity" (p. 194) was highlighted in terms of its crucial importance in the process of psychotherapy. Jungian analysts such as J. Singer (1973) have provided rich examples of the use of visual images produced by the patient and elaborated by the therapist to increase access to unconscious material in a way that also facilitated active problem solving. During the same period, German therapist Leuner (1969) described the systematic application of what he called "guided affective imagery" in adults, using a set of ten predetermined images designed to represent major life conflicts, an approach he later amplified for use with children (Leuner, Horn, & Klessman, 1983).

While more analytically based therapists were developing these methodologies, behaviorally oriented innovators were finding applications for guided imagery within the practice of hypnotherapy (Hilgard, 1965) and systematic desensitization (Wolpe, 1958) that were soon applied to work with children (D.G. Singer, 1994). J.L. Singer's work (1974, 1975) played a significant role in highlighting the power of children's daydreaming, fantasy, and imagery abilities in applications within play therapy formats. Sherrod and Singer (1984) cite a body of literature that suggests that children who naturally engage in more imaginative play and those whose imaginative tendencies are experimentally heightened enjoy a variety of advantages over less imaginative children. Another dimension was added to this work after the publication of a book of "children's imagination games" (DeMille, 1967/1981). This book was explicitly designed to stimulate children's imaginations, particularly their visual imagery abilities, through the presentation of a series of visualizations of increasing adventuresomeness. A number of similar publications followed, stimulating a continued and widening interest in the use of guided imagery.

Currently, guided imagery is used widely with adults who have a variety of medical illnesses, often as part of a holistic approach to care of patients with life-threatening illnesses including cancer, HIV disease, and cardiac disease. Brigham (1994) describes imagery as "the foundation of multimodal behavioral medicine program" (p. 32). She describes a program in which images related to combating illness and promoting healing are systematically employed with the goals of both assisting patients in coping with their illness and, in some cases, directly affecting the course of the illness itself.

THEORETICAL FOUNDATION

The current clinical use of guided imagery, despite its roots in Jungian analytic tradition, is heavily based on cognitive perspectives that consider its function as a skill, closely related to play skills, through which children can be helped to cope with stresses and to understand conflicts. This perspective is elucidated again by J.L. Singer, who suggested that

> make-believe play predisposition and fantasy tendencies . . . may contribute to a greater range of personal enjoyment, defenses against anxiety and fear, or creativity in a range of social situations . . . if we regard make-believe play and its subsequent development as an "as if" attitude or capacity for fantasy and daydreaming *as a skill* rather than as the outcome of some conflict, we can see this skill as being available within the personality repertory for a great variety of functions. (1973, p. 229)

At the same time, Singer argues some innate tendencies toward this activity, theorizing that "the capacity to generate imagery and to practice imagery and the associated verbal skills of elaboration are simply fundamental capacities with which most human being are 'wired' and which they can develop to varying degrees depending on external circumstances and learning opportunities" (1973, p. 207).

The question of how these capacities develop, and the relative contribution of innate and learned abilities, also underlies debates on this topic in the cognitive-developmental literature. Somewhat different answers are obtained from the Piagetian and the cognitive psychological perspectives, according to an analysis by Dean (1990). Theories and experimental investigation from both of these perspectives focus not on fantasy or imagination-related capacities, but rather on analyses of how children form and manipulate discrete visual mental images and their relationships to the development of children's understanding of related concepts such as geometric properties of shapes (Piaget & Inhelder, 1971). According to Dean, Piagetian research has demonstrated qualitative developmental changes in such imagery skills, in contrast to some cognitive psychologists' hypothesis that "mental imaging processes are innate and independent of developments in spatial knowledge" (Dean, 1990, p. 135). However, the discrepancies between the two viewpoints have not yet been experimentally resolved. More directly related to the clinical use of imagery in children is the assertion by Piaget (1968) that "The image can be conceived as an internalized imitation" (p. 90). This implied that the more familiar a child is with a suggested image, the more likely he or she is to be able to successfully manipulate it.

A helpful set of distinctions of clinical relevance, among images, imaging, and imagination was offered by Sherrod and Singer (1984). They define images as internal representations of sensory data that are then manipulated in the process of imaging and combined in the development of a script in imagination. All of these processes have potential clinical utility; for example, therapeutic uses of guided imagery usually involve the process of imaging, with images that are appropriate for the child, manipulated in a manner at least partially guided by the therapist for a particular purpose.

Another important distinction that needs to be addressed is between guided imagery techniques and hypnosis. Some of the key factors that define hypnosis, such as relaxation and focused attention, clearly overlap with guided imagery. This is very well illustrated by a clinical suggestion from the work of Kohen (1997), who offers the following model for discussing hypnosis for the management of pediatric asthma with families: "Some people call this imagery or visualization, some call it hypnosis, some call it imagination or daydreaming . . . and I don't really care what you call it, because what is really important is that you can learn how to do it pretty fast and that you can use it to help your asthma" (p. 178). The importance of an altered state of consciousness is often mentioned in descriptions of hypnotherapy, but Korn and Johnson's (1983) discussion of altered states of consciousness includes 23 examples of altered states of consciousness occurring in both therapeutic and nontherapeutic settings. They write that "there is great overlap between what is labeled hypnosis and what is labeled otherwise, such as guided imagery" (p. 49). For the purposes of this chapter, the focus will be on approaches where the emphasis is more on the image than on the process; that is, the phenomenon of greatest interest will be in guiding the child to form mental images in order to achieve therapeutic goals, whether or not the therapist utilizes techniques to induce states of deep relaxation, focused attention, and/or altered states of consciousness as a part of this effort. There will be both overlap and some arbitrary choices involved in making this distinction.

D.G. Singer (1993a) has also explored ways of conceptualizing the uses of imagery in therapy with children from the perspective of play therapy. She describes eight therapeutic approaches that employ imagery as a central focus: relaxation therapy, systematic desensitization, cognitive therapy, eidetic imagery therapy, guided affective imagery, mind play, art therapy, and movement and drama therapy. Using these useful categories, this chapter will again draw some boundaries about its subject matter by omitting those techniques that require more physical activity, such as dramatic and art therapies, and those about which there is very little research with children, such as eidetic psychotherapy (Sheikh & Jordan, 1981).

Having drawn these distinctions, it is useful to consider a question asked by Meichenbaum (1978) some years ago, that is, "Why does using imagery in psychotherapy lead to change?" (p. 381). In a discussion of imagery techniques applied to adults, he summarizes his discussion by suggesting that the key processes in imagery-based therapies that lead to change may involve an increase in the client's sense of control, the altered internal dialog around maladaptive behavior that may ensue, and the mental rehearsal of behavioral alternatives that increase the client's coping skills (p. 392). Twenty years later, this continues to be a useful framework with which to consider the mechanisms by which guided imagery techniques help children.

RESEARCH FINDINGS

While there is a great deal of research on the phenomenon of imagery in cognition, the quantity of research on the therapeutic use of guided imagery with children is small. However, there has been some work that highlights its potential and may provide guidance to the practitioner and to future researchers.

Some light has been shed on the developmental aspects of imagery from a purely cognitive perspective that is useful for clinicians in terms of deciding what kinds of imagery might be appropriate for children of different ages. Kosslyn, Margolis, Barrett, Goldknopf, and Daly (1990) looked at various aspects of imagery in children ages 5, 8, and 14 (from advantaged socioeconomic backgrounds). They found that 5-year-olds performed poorly in a task requiring them to mentally manipulate images of letters; additionally, there was a clear age-based difference in speed of imagery formation between the 8- and 14-year-olds, but both groups were quite accurate. Interestingly, the largest age group differences on the various tasks was between the two youngest groups and the two older groups (14-year-olds and adults), in contrast to Piagetian expectations that cognitive changes would lead to greater differences between ages 5 and 8. However, nothing in the results would contradict the possibility of using verbally guided imagery with even younger children.

One example of research that included the clinical use of simple imagery with children is the work of Graziano and Mooney (1980). They successfully used a short-term package of interventions for children with nighttime fearfulness, including imaging pleasant scenes while in a relaxed state and then engaging in self-talk encouraging bravery. The treatment also included tokens for improvements. While the specific contribution of the images was not assessed, the clinical effectiveness of the total treatment package was impressive.

Another study of the treatment of nighttime fears that focused more specifically on the use of imagery was carried out by King, Cranstoun, and Josephs (1989). They focused on "emotive imagery" originally described by Lazarus and Abramovitz (as cited in King et al., 1989) using images specifically chosen to encourage positive affect. Using a multiple baseline design, King et al. assessed the effectiveness of using each of three highly fearful children's favored television characters for their therapy. They constructed anxiety hierarchies, then developed scripts incorporating each child's preferred character into imagery sequences that specifically addressed the child's fears and suggested coping cognitions. Two of the three children showed marked improvement. The child who did not improve significantly had a long history of sleeping with his mother every night; evidence was cited for family systems and separation issues beyond the scope of the intervention. The authors also noted that the imagery procedure was perceived very favorably by children and parents.

The utility of guided imagery in reducing overall anxiety levels in children with chronic illness was explored in a study by Johnson, Whitt, and Martin (1987). This study compared 26 chronically ill and 26 healthy children, with half of each group randomly assigned to receive either an intervention designed to give the children an experience with guided imagery and potentially increase their fantasy capacity, or an attention-control condition. The DeMille book of guided visual fantasies *Put Your Mother on the Ceiling* (1967/ 1981), parent-administered over a two-week period, was used as the intervention. The intervention did yield a significant decrease in anxiety in both the healthy and chronically ill children when compared to the attention-control group. The authors commented that the intervention had advantages for children with chronic illness because it required no physical activity—a frequently used coping mechanism for healthy children—which was particularly helpful when working with children with disorders such as spina bifida and hemophilia, that often limit such activity.

An experiment comparing visual imagery training, progressive muscle relaxation, and nonspecific instructions to relax (Armstrong, Collins, Greene, & Panzironi, 1988), applied to children with test anxiety, yielded complex results when several outcome measures were evaluated. The three groups all decreased on anxiety self-report and on physiological measures. On a fine-motor task, both the imagery and the muscle relaxation groups showed some improvement, while the nonspecific-instruction group worsened. The authors speculated as to why the imagery and relaxation groups did not show more improvement than the group receiving nonspecific instructions, speculating that baseline anxiety levels may not have been as high as those in clinical situations. It may also be relevant that the imagery condition consisted of a 10- to 12-minute visualization of one of three pleasant scenes;

the question of adapting the visualizations to individual children could not be addressed with this design.

The question of what physiologic changes occur in children as a result of mental imagery was further explored by Lee and Olness (1996) in a study of 76 children who were asked to form brief (120 second) mental images of being in a quiet and pleasant place, followed by mentally imaging participation in an exciting favorite sports activity. They found that pulse rates significantly decreased in response to quiet imagery and increased during active imagery. They also found increases in skin temperature throughout the experimental period, as well as decreases in electrodermal activity during active imagery. Although the magnitude of the changes noted were small, they were consistent, and support the notion that with rather minimal guidance, children's imagery experiences can be strong enough to affect their physiologic function.

The specific relationship between pain in children and the therapeutic use of imagery was reviewed by Krueger (1987) over a decade ago. She noted then that both imagery and pain in children were relatively neglected areas of research, that the little work that had been done utilized a hypnotic framework rather than focusing on imagery per se, and that this work tended to involve case studies rather than controlled research. Despite her recommendation that children's imagery as a tool for pain control needed more close study, little further research has appeared in the literature on this or other pediatric applications of imagery techniques.

The notable exception to this statement is the work of Kohen and colleagues (Kohen, 1997; Kohen & Botts, 1987; Kohen & Wynne, 1997) who have applied imagery techniques to a variety of pediatric problems, most notably asthma. Although Kohen's work is often presented as a form of self-hypnosis, Kohen and Wynne (1997) themselves specifically state that they use the concepts of relaxation/mental imagery and self-hypnosis interchangeably. They found these techniques helpful for children in reducing the severity of episodes of wheezing. In work with four children with Tourette Syndrome (Kohen & Botts, 1987), three were able to significantly diminish tics with a combination of relaxation and imagery. The imagery technique was to encourage the children to use their own "pretending" and imagination, and to offer "suggestions to enhance and positively redirect the patient's own images for his benefit" (p. 228).

Kohen and Wynne (1997) also published results of a study of 25 preschool children whose families participated in a seven-session group intervention. The authors noted, "In providing the story-telling, imagery, and relaxation aspects of the Program, we understood as teachers and facilitators that as we helped children to capture and use natural imaginative skills, we were effectively conducting clinical hypnosis training" (p. 171). Pre- and post-intervention assessments of each child yielded significant improvements in a variety of indicators, including physician visits, frequency of asthma episodes, self-rated severity, and parental expectations, though not on pulmonary function test results. The authors also suggest that future research assess the relative importance of each of the various components of the intervention.

THE TECHNIQUE

It should be clear by now that there is no single technique of guided imagery in child therapy, but a range of techniques with common threads. While it is not possible to do justice to all of the ways in which therapists can employ guided imagery with children, a selective review of the most common and readily employed approaches will be presented.

Over 20 years ago a brief paper (Rosenstiel & Scott, 1977) offered some basic, common-sense pointers in the use of imagery with children that are still of value. Therapists were reminded to tailor the imagery scenes to the age of the child, to incorporate "children's naturally occurring imagery" (p. 288), to attend to the child's nonverbal cues to determine how the child is responding to the image, and to ask for verbal reports on how the image is being perceived. These suggestions, based on a review of the existing clinical literature, still have value in a wide range of imagery applications.

Although guided imagery is employed in many settings, it may be helpful to discuss its use in several broad categories of applications that can somewhat arbitrarily be divided into pediatric situations (e.g., pain and illness symptom management) and psychiatric interventions (e.g., children with histories of trauma or abuse, phobias, and other issues.)

Application to Health Care Settings

Imagery can be used to help children cope with the immediate pain of procedures such as suturing or bone marrow aspirations, (Kohen 1986; McGrath, 1990; Ross & Ross, 1988) as well as more chronic pain and anxiety, such as from cancer (LeBaron & Zeltzer, 1985; Pederson & Harbaugh, 1995; Zeltzer & LeBaron, 1986) or migraine headaches (Pederson, 1994). Typically, the therapist (or nurse, physician, child life specialist, or trained parent) works to engage the child in images using familiar, enjoyable themes, utilizing multiple senses, and then guides the child to become as absorbed as possible in the image. In some situations, the image serves partially as an escape and a distractor, as when children are asked to imagine themselves at the beach or engaged in a favorite sport. At other times, the child may need to incorporate the procedure into the imagery, but in a manner that recasts it as more tolerable, such as when a child who is interested in space imagines being captured by aliens who are trying to force him or her to reveal secrets about the starship. At other times, the image may be more abstract, as in the example offered by McGrath (1990) of a child with cancer who "invented 'magic sparklies,' an invisible air to breathe in deeply prior to invasive procedures. The air helped to relax her and lightly numb her skin before medical treatments" (p. 162).

Ross and Ross (1988) present a useful series of guidelines for the appropriate ethical and clinical application of cognitive coping strategies such as guided imagery in medically ill children. Assessing the child's interest in such strategies is obviously important, along with assessing levels of current energy and competence. Less obvious is the value of assessing the child's natural coping tendencies; they point out that for children who tend to use avoidance to cope, some cognitive coping strategies may cause the child to become more upset. (On the other hand, guided imagery may be helpful for some of these children if their need to avoid stress-related cognitions makes them more open to images about being somewhere else.) They also suggest educating the child about the natural tendencies to become absorbed in one activity, thus become less aware of other inputs. They emphasize giving children the choice of several cognitive strategies to further increase their sense of control. Assessing the child's experience with the concept of practice, and explaining that one gets better at coping techniques through practice, is very important if the child is to be using these strategies repeatedly and especially if they will be using them independently. Ross and Ross describe three kinds of "transformative imagery" that can be used to handle pain. The first, *context transformation*, does not ignore the pain, but incorporates it into a fantasy into which it becomes more acceptable. For example, a child having a venipuncture might be assisted to "see himself as a policeman shot in the arm while pursuing criminals, but continuing on bravely despite his injury" (p. 245). The second kind of imagery, *stimulus transformation*, encourages the child to imagine that a procedure or instrument is something else, such as when a piece of radiation therapy equipment becomes a friendly robot. The third strategy, *incompatible imagery*, utilizes images of a pleasant setting, incompatible with pain, imagined in minute and vivid detail. Such images work best, according to these authors, when the child is guided toward an active, participatory fantasy sequence rather than a passive one.

While most of the material available on the use of imagery in childhood illness assumes the presence of a mental health professional, it has been suggested that pediatric nurses already sometimes integrate these techniques into their practice, and could do so to a greater extent with more support and information (Pederson & Harbaugh, 1995). Pederson (1994) also offers advice on helping parents support their children to use imagery and other nonpharmacologic comfort measures.

In adults, imagery techniques are used to directly approach not only symptom management but also actual disease processes (Brigham, 1994; Korn & Johnson, 1983). There appears to be virtually no data on the effectiveness of this application in children (Zeltzer & LeBaron, 1986). However, using imagery to help children manage the complex emotional tasks inherent in the process of dealing with a terminal illness and contemplating their own death has been described with powerful clinical examples by LeBaron and Zeltzer (1985). They emphasize following the child or adolescent's guidance in helping determine their emotional needs, such as autonomy, developing an identity distinct from the patient role, or dealing with the prospect of separation from loved ones. They suggest working with the patient on images that help them articulate these needs, either directly or metaphorically, and report cases where, with motivated patients and a strong therapeutic relationship, major changes in the psychological coping of very sick children and teens were facilitated.

APPLICATIONS TO PSYCHIATRIC AND TRAUMA-RELATED SETTINGS

Guided imagery applied clinically to assist children with psychiatric diagnoses is generally integrated into a broader treatment plan. Guided Affective Imagery (Leuner et al., 1983) is an exception to this rule in that it is conceived of as a complete treatment package with a unified psychoanalytic perspective. It clearly has hypnotic elements. However, the state of relaxation and focus that is suggested serves merely as the setting for the real work, that consists of the introduction of standard motifs which the patient is asked to visualize and then elaborate upon as vividly as possible, reporting continually on what he "observes" to the therapist. The therapist strives to support, elaborate and reflect the patient's images, help the patient confront his anxieties, and "strengthen the mature parts of the ego" (p. 45). The authors state that "An imaginative and emotionally suggestible child will develop an abundance of projective contents, which provide important references to the unconscious emotional life and lead to therapy in the associative procedure" (p. 17). The eight motifs which they recommend for use with children are as follows: the *meadow*, with which each session begins; the *ascent of a mountain*, the *pursuit of the course of a brook, visiting a house*, an *encounter with relatives*, the *observation of the edge of the woods from the meadow*, a *boat*, and a *cave*. These motifs, according to the authors, are both often produced spontaneously and are important psychodynamically; no data are available on their applicability to contemporary American urban children.

A very differently conceptualized therapeutic use of imagery has roots firmly in the behavioral tradition. Lazarus and Abramovitz, as far back as 1962, published descriptions of the effective treatment of phobias by using guided images of, for example, an exciting adventure with a favorite sports car for one child and an interaction with superheroes with another child (as cited in Schaefer & Millman, 1978). They reported presenting the children with detailed and exciting stories about their preferred topics, interweaving the presence of the phobic stimulus, and allowing the child to signal anxiety with a raised finger. They found this approach to be effective in brief (i.e., three session) therapy, to show no relapse in a year of follow-up, and to be effective without the use of a formal relaxation component.

As therapists have used imagery techniques over time, a number of specific ways of employing images have been suggested. Martin and Williams (1990) present a list of ten of these, based on Beck's cognitive therapy of adult depression. These are recommended to provide therapists with a range of options to affect the cognitions that are causing the child difficulties and to expand their coping skills. Some of these, of particular applicability to children, include the following: *time projection*, or imaging a scene in the future, after having gotten though the difficult situation; *substituting a positive image*, or vividly summoning up a preferred, comforting scene while encountering the anxiety-provoking stimulus; *coping models*, where the child images an admired figure, either real or pretend, coping with the stressful situation; and *goal rehearsal*, in which the child images a potentially stressful situation and mentally rehearses how to cope. The therapist may choose to use several of these either sequentially or together, as the child becomes more competent in using imagery techniques to actively manage their cognitions and emotions. D.G. Singer (1994) offers several examples of employing such combinations with children as young as 6 years old who are suffering from anxiety and phobic symptoms as well as depression.

Children who have been impacted by trauma, induced by natural disasters or by human behavior, seem to be particularly appropriate for treatment with imagery techniques. For example, children who have been having frightening dreams can be helped to " . . . visualize a scenario that transforms the frightening content of the dream into something more benign. For example the child might visualize having a magic wand that changes a monster into a positive and friendly figure" (Pearce & Pezzot-Pearce, 1997, p. 275). James (1989) suggests an exercise for use in either individual or group work with traumatized children that she calls "The Elderly Child Remembers" in which the child is asked to imagine being a successful old person who remembers the trauma experienced when young (pp. 173–174). Although she recommends using this technique for actual sociodramatic play, complete with props and costumes, it also can be used in a purely internal manner by having the child visualize himself sharing with another young child what he has learned during his life. This allows the child to gain a sense of psychic distance from the trauma and vividly introduces the idea that such traumas can be mastered as part of the fabric of a many-faceted life, instead of the dominant force controlling it.

Children who have been affected by natural disasters, such as hurricanes or earthquakes, also have often suffered major losses in terms of their sense of safety and control. At the same time, the adults in their lives have also suffered and are less available for support. Joyner (1991) offers a detailed case history of a composite child affected by Hurricane Hugo in which she incorporates a number of imagery techniques. After an assessment to determine which aspects of the hurricane were most overwhelming, and some normalization of the child's and family's responses, she introduces the concept of imagining oneself in a safe and special place. She uses natural, nonthreatening language, illustrating the low-key, almost casual way that such techniques can be suggested to children:

sometimes when things get a little too much for me to handle, I just close my eyes and imagine that I'm somewhere else. I've made a whole place in my head where I can relax and be content.

And when I've been there a few minutes, I open my eyes again, and I feel like I can handle things a little better. (pp. 405–406)

The therapist then describes a special place in appealing detail, then invites the child to do the same, asks for specifics, writes down the child's fantasy, and then reads back to the child what she has described in a soothing manner. Thus the child is assisted, in a directive but respectful way, to draw on her own strengths to actively cope with an extreme experience through cognitive means, while very likely experiencing increased relaxation in the process.

A similar approach to using visualization of a "safe place" has been suggested for use with sexually abused children to support them as they attempt to discuss specific abuse experiences (Lipovsky, 1992). The child is taught simple relaxation techniques, and the therapist provides several sessions of instruction and practice until the child is comfortable with imaging a safe place. Later, when processing actual abuse memories becomes upsetting, the child can take breaks by mentally going to this safe place to become calm and able to refocus on processing the abuse.

USING EXISTING MATERIALS IN IMAGERY THERAPY

In most of these applications of guided imagery, the therapist and/or the child develop their own images tailored to the child's needs and issues. However, there are many situations in which prepared materials can be helpful. The therapist may use these materials to assist parents in providing imagery experiences for their children at home or in medical settings. The role of parents should be of primary importance because the parent knows the child best, is in the majority of cases the most committed to the child's well-being, and is generally most available to the child over time. For most children with well-functioning parents, the parent can not only be a key resource, but in some cases play a direct therapeutic role. One of the therapist's tasks may be assessing the parents' capacity for participating in this role, and then providing them with the support and education they need to maximize their effectiveness. Prepared materials are also of great value when therapists consult with other professionals such as pediatric nurses, child life specialists, or educators who are helping children deal with traumatic or stressful situations but do not consider themselves psychotherapists and prefer more structured or psychoeducational uses of imagery. Therapists themselves may also find some of the carefully worked out and creatively detailed materials available of great assistance in their practice as they explore ways to offer the most rich and effective imagery experiences to children.

The original publication specifically designed to facilitate guided imagery in children, first published in 1955 and later reissued in revised form, is *Put Your Mother on the Ceiling* (DeMille, 1967/1981). DeMille offers specific suggestions for the use of his "imagination games" including the importance of selecting a nondistracting time and place when the child is willing to participate, and developing a signaling system so that the child can indicate that he is ready to go on to the next image or set of images. The images range from very benign and inviting [e.g., a little mouse standing on his head and changing colors (pp. 57–58)] to those more potentially upsetting to some children [e.g., taking parts of one's body and moving them around the room (pp. 78–79)] and would obviously require therapist judgment in their use with individual children. Images are presented in sequence from easier to more difficult; the more difficult images violate the laws of reality more dramatically, and tend to be more abstract. Such sequences might be useful in therapy to teach a very controlled child the skills of creative fantasy to facilitate the child's ability to develop unique images for specific therapeutic purposes. D.G. Singer (1993b) offered a vivid example of exactly this technique. She used the book with a 5-year-old in the midst of an extraordinarily complex divorce situation who was able to grapple much more effectively with difficult and ambivalent emotions after learning that she could both express her feelings through fantasy and also control her imagery so that it would not overwhelm her. Eventually, she was able to progress to the use of Guided Affective Imagery (Leuner et al., 1983), using some of the competencies she had gained with the use of *Put Your Mother on the Ceiling*. Singer comments that the child:

> seemed comfortable playing the mind games. They evoked feelings that she attempted to express in her play, but that frightened her when she did so. She would go only so far and then would use denial of these feelings as she played. In the imagery exercises, however, she was able to unleash her anger at Lillian [her mother], get control of it, and recognize it as being related to the divorce and her fewer contacts with Arthur [her father]. (p. 169)

Another approach is taken by Brett (1988) whose book *Annie Stories* is designed to help children cope with stresses from new babies to divorce, death, and hospitalizations. The book is designed explicitly for use by parents, although therapists are also likely to find it, and its approach, helpful either for their use or for recommendations to parents. The stories are vivid tales about a little girl named Annie; parents are encouraged to make up a new name for the protagonist as needed for their child's gender or interests. The author disavows any particular therapeutic orientation, but she includes a number of positive visualizations incorporated into the stories, which all involve a child successfully overcoming a life challenge through a variety of coping mechanisms. She emphasizes the importance of helping children feel that they are really in the story through vivid descriptions and the use of multiple sensory modalities, and some of the stories explicitly teach visualization techniques as part of the plot.

Another resource for parents and professionals is a series of three books by Garth (1991, 1992, 1994) referred to in the subtitles as both meditations and visualizations. The author advocates their use with children as young as 3 years of age, and notes that she has found it more difficult for children older than 8 to begin to use the visualizations, although children who have already been familiarized with them are able to continue their involvement. The visualizations in this series are uniformly positive and benign in tone, although each book includes the suggested use of the "Worry Tree" image (Garth, 1991, p. 20) which can profitably be utilized in a variety of therapeutic situations. As the child is invited to enter "a garden that is your own special place," the visualization continues:

> I want you to look at the large tree that is outside. This tree is called the Worry Tree. I want you to pin on this tree anything that might worry you-perhaps you have had some arguments at school or maybe you are having difficulty with your school work. This tree will take any worries at all, be it with your friends or your family. This tree accepts anything you care to pin there. (p. 20)

Although these books were originally written for use by parents particularly at bedtime, and also have been employed in preschool classroom situations, they are especially appropriate for hospitalized and chronically ill young children. Child-life specialists may use them preoperatively, during frightening or uncomfortable procedures, with children who are having difficulty sleeping, and those having difficulty tolerating separation when their parents cannot be present (J. Kreimer, personal communication, April 17, 1998). These resources are noteworthy for their graceful and poetic language and images and tend to be quite compelling even for children under a significant amount of stress. Coping-oriented images more closely related to an individual child's difficulty could readily be inserted or integrated into selected visualizations by the therapist to meet the needs of a particular child.

Yet another resource, most likely to be employed directly by parents or to be used by a therapist for ideas to share with parents, is Brown's *No more monsters in the closet: Teaching your children to overcome everyday fears and phobias* (1995). The author, a pediatrician, translates several of the techniques familiar to therapists into parent-friendly language, using the label "Imagination Training" (p. 10). He provides a number of specific suggestions for parents including a list of appropriate favorite places, favorite vehicles with which to imagine traveling to those places, and some of what he calls "Takealong Friends" (pp. 104–105), comforting characters a child can image and use as a support in difficult situations. These are applied to medical, school, and home challenges typically faced by children, and could be expanded with a therapist's help to more severe stresses.

CASE ILLUSTRATIONS

The following cases were selected to illustrate the use of guided imagery in a variety of clinical situations, and with children with differing histories and strengths. Identifying details have been altered.

The Treatment of Child Abuse

Jennifer was 11 when she entered therapy at the request of her adoptive family because of increased irritability, tearfulness, emotional neediness, and sleep difficulties over the past year, combined with veiled references to inappropriate sexual experiences. She had been removed from her biological family at the age of 8 after a long history of social services intervention for child neglect; she and her four sisters were all placed in separate homes, and eventually adopted. Although sexual abuse was suspected, it was never proven, and the adoptive parents found the subject so anxiety-provoking that, though they wanted to support their daughter, they found it virtually impossible to discuss it with her. The child was amenable to therapy, in part because her need for individual attention was so great that she found the therapy situation met those needs, and further because she was highly motivated to sleep better. She readily reported that she lay awake for long periods at night feeling nervous and upset, but she could not articulate why. Over time, as she developed a trusting relationship with the therapist, she slowly revealed increasing amounts of detail about sexual abuse by her grandfather, who lived in the home and was the major male parent figure. It was clear that these memories had always been present, but that she did not feel safe in revealing them because of her difficulty with trust, and because of threats about what would happen if she "told" that had accompanied the abuse. The more information she disclosed, the more sleep troubles she reported. She was able to cooperate with relaxation training in the office, but had difficult applying it at home at night. Therefore, the therapist decided to expand the imagery component of the relaxation technique, and explore ways of facilitating transfer to the child's home.

The child's most powerful, positive interest was in horses, and it was easily established that her preferred visualization involved horses and meadow scenes. Therefore, the therapist presented a fairly lengthy relaxation sequence in the office that first employed progressive relaxation, and then moved to a counting component encouraging deepening relaxation. Woven into the counting sequence was a detailed description of the ideal horse stable, redolent with the sweet smell of hay and the sounds of horses quietly munching their grain and stomping their hooves, in which each number was the number of a stall with a different horse inside. As the guided imagery moved from stall to stall, a vivid description of the horse inside was offered, along with the suggestion that the patient was becoming even more relaxed and content. After 12 stalls were visited, the young rider was invited to select her favorite horse, and the sequence ended with a quiet wander in a beautiful meadow. (The implications of this child victim being in complete control of a powerful but gentle masculine animal were never addressed directly, but seemed to have special resonance.) Jennifer entered nicely into the fantasy, although she did not seem to have entered an altered state, and participated verbally at several points along the way, appeared more relaxed and expressed feeling happier and more comfortable. The entire sequence was recorded on audiotape and given to the child to take home. She was invited to use the tape at home when she was having difficulty going to sleep, awoke at night feeling anxious, or when she felt upset at other times during the day.

In an illustration of how nothing in child psychotherapy ever proceeds completely as planned, Jennifer returned for her next session very pleased with her ability to use the tape to help herself both feel better and go to sleep more easily. With a mischievous grin, she informed the therapist that although it was a terrific tape, the therapist had made a mistake! She had skipped number nine, and in moving from stall to stall had gone directly from horse number eight to horse number ten. This was a source of considerable amusement to Jennifer. As she and the therapist talked about her experience with the tape, it appeared that her attention tended to be even more closely riveted to the sequence as she waited for the mistake. The therapist shared her mirth, and pointed out how nice it was that one could make a big mistake, and still have done something worthwhile. Much discussion then ensued on the general topic of imperfection that was of great significance to this child, with her powerful feelings of having been both rejected and damaged. Although the therapist offered to redo the tape, Jennifer concluded that she liked it the way it was, in no small account, it appeared, because it was such a concrete reminder that both a person and an effort could be imperfect but still valuable. Subsequent to this, Jennifer seemed to have an easier time in sharing more complete accounts of the nature and extent of her abuse, with less disruption of her sleep patterns. It should be noted that even several years later, this child still has some sleep disturbances, and still retains some of the symptoms of post-traumatic stress disorder. She continues to use the tape regularly. These and related interventions were not curative, but were clearly effective in providing symptom relief, facilitating further therapeutic exploration, and increasing her feelings of competence and control.

The Treatment of a Hospitalized Child Victim of Assault

Chuck was an active 7-year-old who lived with his mother and her male companion in a low-income neighborhood where street crime was relatively common. He was an active, somewhat oppositional child, although his mother did not consider him out of the normal range for boys his age. He was playing outside along the street with several other children when a young teenager challenged him over the ownership of the bicycle he was riding. When Chuck refused to surrender the bicycle, a scuffle ensued. The teen was holding a screwdriver, and in the scuffle, Chuck received a small stab wound to his upper back. In the hospital, it became apparent that there was spinal cord involvement, resulting in major weakness on the left side. Thus Chuck was faced with dealing with the trauma of the attack, which he felt strongly had been inflicted on purpose; the stress of hospitalization with limited family presence; the terrifying possibility of being unable to walk; multiple medical procedures; and conflict among extended family members over responsibility for Chuck's safety. In addition, Chuck was not by nature a highly verbal child, he had not had much experience with using words to cope or to solve problems, and the more active, physical coping strategies he was accustomed to employing were not available to him. Yet he was an affectionate little boy who responded to the approach of strange adults with a shy smile, and enjoyed hearing stories, playing board games, and playing with medical equipment. After several days of hospitalization, Chuck's ability to cooperate with seemingly relentless diagnostic procedures, physical therapy, and nursing care began to wear thin. At this point, he was scheduled again for an MRI (magnetic resonance imaging) test, which required him to lie absolutely still for a lengthy period in a very narrow metal tube, listening to loud, unfamiliar, and unpredictable noises. Not surprisingly, this prospect was quite upsetting. Yet his physicians hoped to limit the amount of sedation he was given, because close monitoring of his neurologic functioning was important. In the limited amount of time available before the scheduled test, the therapist sat down with Chuck and made some very direct suggestions about how he might pretend that the MRI machine was a submarine. She and Chuck discussed how in submarines, the submariners had tiny, skinny little beds where they had to lie quite still so that they wouldn't wake up their friends. Because submarines are made of steel, of course, they are very noisy, especially when missiles are being loaded into their containers. (The therapist actually didn't know much about the operation of a real submarine, but fortunately neither did Chuck.) He was able to enter in to this conversation, concrete and sensory in nature as it was, and share in details about how hard the beds were, how dark they were likely to be, and so on, but in a more positive and certainly more interesting context. He thought that he could continue this pretending while in the MRI machine, and actually seemed excited about seeing how much like the pretend submarine experience the test would be. He tolerated it well and afterward was able to relate how much the experience had fit the anticipation and thus helped the pretending.

In this particular case, the use of guided imagery was confined to specific situations like that described above. Work on other issues such as safety, how such events might be prevented in the future, support for the family to help Chuck more effectively, and medical play all were part of the treatment process. However, the use of imagery played an important role in the specific instances where Chuck very much needed to feel in control of himself, and where his ability to do so was important for his medical care.

The Treatment of an Injured Adolescent

Mary was a 16-year-old competitive skier who sustained a ruptured spleen and several fractured ribs, as well as bruising to other abdominal organs, during a training accident. Mary was a bright, intense teenager who had received some counseling in the past related to some mild acting out and depressive tendencies, but who had been doing well in the months prior to the accident. She had great difficulty coping with some of the diagnostic procedures that were necessary, to the point that she would start screaming at the staff even when she was being moved to a stretcher for transport to the radiology suite. Her loss of self-control was very distressing to her, as well as stressful for her parents and the medical staff. She seemed to be a youngster who had particular difficulty tolerating the general loss of control inherent in hospitalization. Although she certainly had great physical courage when ski racing, she was overwhelmed by the discomfort and pain of her injury and its treatment. She also verbalized feeling crushed about being injured doing the thing she loved best, and worrying about missing school and training time.

The therapist encouraged Mary to ventilate her feelings, and then began to ask her about the sensations and perceptions she associated with skiing. She could describe these fairly vividly and with pleasure. She was reminded about the great amount of body control required for her sport, and how she was able to use some of her muscles to maximum effort while at the same time keeping other muscles relaxed or loose. When it was suggested that she could use those same skills to manage her hospitalization experience, she was initially skeptical, but willing to explore this futher. She was able to visualize herself skiing on a favorite mountain with no other people around on a beautiful, sunny day, and review the sensations of tension and relaxation she would be experiencing in this situation. Because she had in the past used the technique of visualization to prepare for a race, this was fairly easy for her. She and the therapist tried to review and anticipate how it would be to use her imagery skills in the situation of discomfort or other stress, and she was able to rehearse both imaging the skiing and checking her muscles to make sure that they were relaxed. The next time a stretcher arrived to transport her to a procedure she was able to shut her eyes and engage in visualization that helped her calmly tolerate the necessary interventions, which also enhanced her feeling of control and improved her general mood and outlook. This effort was shared with her mother, who had always been supportive of Mary's athletic endeavors, and her mother was able to effectively encourage her in her use of imagery techniques to cope with events throughout the hospital day, in the therapist's absence.

The Treatment of a Child with a Chronic, Painful Illness

Ray was 11 when he entered a period of exacerbation of his sickle cell disease, as often happens around the time of puberty, and began to experience frequent hospitalizations for painful crises. His single mother was unable to be present in the hospital very often due to many other family responsibilities, including the care of three other children and aging relatives. To further add to the disappointments in Ray's life, his pediatrician had recommended that he give up some of his favorite activities, particularly baseball and track, because it was felt that strenuous physical activity was contributing to the onset of sickle cell crises.

The pediatric staff noted that Ray appeared sad much of the time, and despite significant doses of narcotic pain medication, appeared tense, uncomfortable, and generally miserable for days. While there was no doubt that his disease was causing real and significant pain, it appeared that anxiety and sadness was adding to his suffering and possibly increasing the need for prolonged narcotic use.

Ray tended to be a relatively nonverbal child, but he enjoyed interacting around such structured activities as board and card games. He was not able to verbalize an internal fantasy life, or talk about his thoughts very much, and for that reason it took the therapist several hospitalizations to begin to make a concerted effort to work with

Ray using guided imagery. This proved to be an underestimate of this child's capacity for learning new coping strategies. When he was invited to try some ways of using his mind to help himself feel better, he was cooperative in generating ideas such as his favorite places to be, and situations that made him happy. He identified the outdoors in general, and track meets in particular, as settings where he was generally happy. He also indicated that he was not afraid of heights or flight, and in fact though it would be fun to be up in the air. Based on this information, he was invited to participate in a guided imagery sequence consisting of flying in a hot air balloon, with vivid descriptions of the sights and sensations he might experience, and then having the balloon slowly descend (with suggestions for feelings of increased relaxation and well-being during the gradual descent) until the balloon landed on the infield of a track meet, just as his team had discovered that they were one runner short for a relay race. The visualization ended with him running the anchor leg and winning for his team. As it concluded, Ray was visibly relaxed and had a wide smile on his face. It was felt that he would do best combining relaxation and comfort images with ones that were exciting and had an action-oriented focus, because of his particular coping strategies.

Interestingly, feedback was received about Ray's perception of this intervention eight years later, after Ray had been cared for in other settings, and then was seen by a psychologist on an adult service. During his interview with Ray, in the course of asking him what had helped him with his pain in the past, Ray spontaneously mentioned the guided imagery intervention that he recalled from when he was 11, and recalled how good it had felt. It was instructive to learn how meaningful this intervention was for this young man, even though his life in middle and late adolescence had been quite stressful in many ways beyond the reach of the pediatric caregivers who had worked with him when he was younger.

The Treatment of a Child in the Emergency Department after Vehicular Collision

Two busloads of fourth-grade children were on their way to a larger city for a field trip to see a play, when one of the buses was rear-ended by a construction truck and pushed into the back of the second bus. Many of the children sustained minor injuries, although all of them were conscious and walking. They were taken off the buses, and the 18 children with identifiable injuries were transported to a hospital in the larger city by ambulance. Although one car of parent chaperones was following the buses, the vast majority of the 18 children did not have their parents present when they arrived at the emergency department. One of the teachers on the bus was visibly injured and had bleeding from her scalp, adding to the children's anxiety. However, as the children were individually evaluated, it became apparent that their injuries were not serious and that none of the children would require admission to the hospital. The psychologist was called to the emergency department to see two children whose reactions had become worrisome to the staff. When she spoke with the staff, they explained that they had called for help for those two children because they were the children who appeared most anxious and stated that they absolutely, positively would NOT get on a bus again that day. Since two new buses were being summoned to return the children to their home two hours away, the staff was concerned about a difficult scene of anxious children afraid to get on the bus, and possibly infecting the other children with this idea.

Not surprisingly, these two children had injuries that had required more attention than some of the others, including CAT scans and intravenous lines. The psychologist approached one of them, Taylor, just after he was cleared medically. He emphatically confirmed what the nurses had noted—that no way was he getting back on the bus! The question was presented to him hypothetically as to what he would want to do if there was no alternative. He was able to describe several things he would like to do, such as asking the driver not to follow too closely, and making sure the bus had its brakes checked. The therapist suggested that sometimes pretending you were doing something fun was helpful. She asked Taylor what his favorite activity in the world was, and he answered "soccer." They discussed the new professional soccer team that had recently come to a nearby city, and Taylor talked about his desire to attend one of their games. When asked if he could pretend that he was going to a game, he easily entered into a series of increasingly elaborate images about going to a professional game on the bus, getting a player to autograph his ball, having his favorite team win, and playing loud rock music on the bus all the way there and back. When the therapist asked him if he thought he could do this pretending on his own if he did need to get on a bus to go home, he looked surprised as he answered "sure . . . that would be sort of fun." Together, Taylor and the therapist wrote down the key elements of his coping strategies on a card, which the therapist suggested he share with his parents when he got home. As they left the treatment room, Taylor saw the other child who had also expressed anxiety. He ran up to him excitedly sharing his idea of pretending he was going to a soccer game, and started asking his friend where he would like to pretend to go. As the two boys went to join their friends in the waiting room, Taylor coached his friend to think about going to a BMX bicycle race, and was doing a fine job getting his friend to come up with the details that would make his images seem more real. Later that afternoon, the junior therapist and his friend boarded the replacement bus without incident and headed home.

SUMMARY

Guided imagery provides therapists from many theoretical orientations with practical tools with which to assist children. Relaxation, increased mastery of past, present, and future stresses, and increased psychodynamic insight are all appropriate goals for this technique. Children from the preschool years through adolescence can benefit, as can both highly verbal and less verbally oriented children. Psychiatric and medical settings are both appropriate sites for its use, as is normal child-rearing. For many children, the use of guided imagery will feel natural and comfortable. For other children, learning to harness their imaginations on behalf of better coping will in itself have long-term benefits. Psychotherapists may chose to use the technique themselves, to share it with families and others working with the child, or to use audiotape or bibliotherapy to enhance their efforts. While both psychodynamic, behavioral, and cognitively oriented researchers and clinicians have contributed to the literature on guided imagery, much more work needs to be done to continue to refine and expand this technique and to further our understanding of when, with whom, and how it works best.

REFERENCES

Armstrong, F.D., Collins, F.L., Greene, P., & Panzironi, H. (1988). Effects of brief relaxation training on children's motor functioning. *Journal of Clinical Child Psychology, 17*, 310–315.

Brett, D. (1988). *Annie stories.* New York: Workman.

Brigham, D. (1994). *Imagery for getting well: Clinical applications of behavioral medicine.* New York: Norton.

Brown, J.L. (1995). *No more monsters in the closet: Teaching your children to overcome everyday fears and phobias.* New York: Crown.

Dean, A.L. (1990). The development of mental imagery: A comparison of Piagetian and cognitive psychological perspectives. *Annals of Child Development, 7*, 105–144.

DeMille, R. (1981). *Put your mother on the ceiling: Children's imagination games.* Santa Barbara, CA: Ross-Erikson. (Original work published 1967)

Garth, M. (1991). *Starbright: Meditations for children.* New York: Harper-Collins.

Garth, M. (1992). *Moonbeam: A book of meditations for children.* Blackburn, Australia: HarperCollins.

Garth, M. (1994). *Sunshine: More meditations for children.* North Blackburn, Australia: HarperCollins.

Graziano, A.M., & Mooney, K.C. (1980). Family self-control instruction for children's night time fear reduction. *Journal of Consulting and Clinical Psychology, 48*, 206–213.

Hilgard, E.R. (1965). *Hypnotic susceptibility.* New York: Harcourt, Brace and World.

James, B. (1989). *Treating traumatized children: New insights and creative interventions.* Lexington, MA: Lexington Books.

Johnson, M.R., Whitt, J.K., & Martin, B. (1987). The effect of fantasy facilitation on anxiety in chronically ill and healthy children. *Journal of Pediatric Psychology, 12*, 273–283.

Joyner, C.D. (1991). Individual, group and family crisis counseling following a hurricane. In N.B. Webb (Ed.), *Play therapy with children in crisis: A casebook for practitioners* (pp. 396–415). New York: Guilford Press.

Jung, C.G. (1953). *Two essays on analytical psychology.* New York: World.

King, N., Cranstoun, F., & Josephs, A. (1989). Emotive imagery and children's night-time fears: A multiple baseline design evaluation. *Journal of Behavior Therapy and Experimental Psychiatry, 20,* 125–135.

Kohen, D.P. (1986). Applications of relaxation/mental imagery (self-hypnosis) in pediatric emergencies. *International Journal of Clinical and Experimental Hypnosis, 34,* 283–294.

Kohen, D.P. (1997). Teaching children with asthma to help themselves with relaxation/mental imagery. In W.J. Matthews & J.H. Edgette (Eds.), *Current thinking and research in brief therapy: Solutions, strategies, narratives* (Vol. 1, pp. 169–191). New York: Brunner/Mazel.

Kohen, D.P., & Botts, P. (1987). Relaxation-imagery (self-hypnosis) in Tourette syndrome: Experience with four children. *American Journal of Clinical Hypnosis, 29,* 227–237.

Kohen, D.P., & Wynne, E. (1997). Applying hypnosis in a preschool family asthma education program: Uses of storytelling, imagery, and relaxation. *American Journal of Clinical Hypnosis, 39,* 169–181.

Korn, E.R., & Johnson, K. (1983). *Visualization: The uses of imagery in the health professions.* Homewood, IL: Dow Jones-Irwin.

Kosslyn, S.M., Margolis, J.A., Barrett, A.M., Goldknopf, E.J., & Daly, P.F. (1990). Age differences in imagery abilities. *Child Development, 61,* 995–1010.

Krueger, L.D. (1987). Pediatric pain and imagery. *Journal of Child and Adolescent Psychotherapy, 4,* 32–41.

LeBaron, S., & Zeltzer, L.K. (1985). The role of imagery in the treatment of dying children and adolescents. *Development and Behavioral Pediatrics, 6,* 252–258.

Lee, L.H., & Olness, K.N. (1966). Effects of self-induced mental imagery on autonomic reactivity in children. *Developmental and Behavioral Pediatrics, 17,* 323–327.

Leuner, H. (1969). Guided affective imagery (GAI). A method of intensive psychotherapy. *American Journal of Psychotherapy, 23,* 4–21.

Leuner, H., Horn, G., & Klessman, E. (1983). *Guided affective imagery with children and adolescents.* New York: Plenum Press.

Lipovsky, J.A. (1992). Assessment and treatment of post-traumatic stress disorder in child survivors of sexual assault. In D.W. Foy (Ed.), *Treating PTSD: Cognitive-behavioral strategies* (pp. 127–164). New York: Guilford Press.

Martin, M., & Williams, R. (1990). Imagery and emotion. In P.J. Hampson, D.F. Marks, & J.T.E. Richardson (Eds.), *Imagery: Current developments* (pp. 268–306). New York: Routledge & Kegan Paul.

McGrath, P.A. (1990). *Pain in children: Nature, assessment, and treatment.* New York: Guilford Press.

Meichenbaum, D. (1978). Why does using imagery in psychotherapy lead to change? In J.L. Singer & K.S. Pope (Eds.), *The power of human imagination: New methods in psychotherapy* (pp. 381–394). New York: Plenum Press.

Pearce, J.W., & Pezzot-Pearce, T.D. (1997). *Psychotherapy of abused and neglected children.* New York: Guilford Press.

Pederson, C. (1994). Ways to feel comfortable: Teaching aids to promote children's comfort. *Issues in Comprehensive Pediatric Nursing, 17,* 37–46.

Pederson, C., & Harbaugh, B.L. (1995). Nurses' use of nonpharmacologic techniques with hospitalized children. *Issues in Comprehensive Pediatric Nursing, 18,* 91–109.

Piaget, J. (1968). *Six psychological studies* (A. Tenzer, Trans.). New York: Vintage Books. (Original work published 1964)

Piaget, J., & Inhelder, B. (1971). *Mental imagery in the child.* New York: Basic Books.

Rosenstiel, A.K., & Scott, D.S. (1977). *Journal of Behavior Therapy and Experimental Psychiatry, 8,* 287–290.

Ross, D.M., & Ross, S.A. (1988). *Childhood pain: Current issues, research, and management.* Baltimore: Urban & Schwarzenberg.

Schaefer, C.E., & Millman, H.L. (1978). *Therapies for children: A handbook of effective treatments for problem behaviors.* Washington, DC: Jossey-Bass.

Sheikh, A.A., & Jordan, C.S. (1981). Eidetic psychotherapy. In R.J. Corsini (Ed.), *Handbook of innovative psychotherapies* (pp. 271–285). New York: Wiley.

Sherrod, L.R., & Singer, J.L. (1984). The development of make-believe play. In J.H. Goldstein (Ed.), *Sports, games and play* (pp. 1–38). Hillsdale, NJ: Erlbaum.

Singer, D.G. (1993a). Fantasy and visualization. In C.E. Schaefer (Ed.), *The therapeutic powers of play* (pp. 189–221). Northvale, NJ: Aronson.

Singer, D.G. (1993b). *Playing for their lives: Helping troubled children through play therapy.* New York: Free Press.

Singer, D.G. (1994). Imagery techniques in play therapy with children. In J. Hellendoorn, R. van der Kooij, & B. Sutton-Smith (Eds.), *Play and intervention.* Albany: State University of New York Press.

Singer, J.L. (1973). *Boundaries of the soul.* Garden City, NY: Anchor Press.

Singer, J.L. (1973). *The child's world of make-believe: Experimental studies of imaginative play.* New York: Academic Press.

Singer, J.L. (1974). *Imagery and daydreaming methods in psychotherapy and behavior modification.* New York: Academic Press.

Singer, J.L. (1975). *The inner world of daydreaming.* New York: Harper & Row.

Wolpe, J. (1958). *Psychotherapy by reciprocal inhibition.* Stanford, CA: Stanford University Press.

Zeltzer, L.K., & LeBaron, S. (1986). Fantasy in children and adolescents with chronic illness. *Developmental and Behavioral Pediatrics, 7,* 195–198.

CHAPTER 4

Programmed Distance Writing in Therapy with Acting-Out Adolescents

LUCIANO L'ABATE

IN THE last two decades, this author has become aware of the power of writing over the power of talking. Elsewhere, L'Abate (1998, 1999) has argued that in psychological interventions, especially with acting-out adolescents and adults, and in comparison to writing, talk is both cheap and expensive at the same time, an inefficient medium of communication and helping, and difficult if not impossible to control. Distance writing (DW)—writing outside and away from the presence of a mental health professional—and especially programmed distance writing (PDW, i.e., workbooks)—is a much more efficient and controllable medium of communication and helping than talk. A workbook consists of a varying number of written homework assignments, from 3 to 20 or more. Each assignment consists of a variety of questions, exercises, or tasks about a specific topic (see Table 4.1). Acting-out individuals may use talk to con, manipulate, lie, and cheat. It became very difficult to teach such people to think before acting rather than acting before thinking using only talk. Cost-effective workbooks were developed to help people think *before* they act (L'Abate, 1986, 1992, 1997a, 1997b).

Table 4.1
Workbooks and Materials Available from the
Institute for Life Empowerment (ILE)*

I. Workbooks for Individuals

  A. Based on Psychological Test Profiles

    1. *Adult Psychopathy* can be used in conjunction with a short self-report test for incarcerated felons who want rehabilitation (3 assignments +).

    2. *Anxiety, Depression, Fears* are the major emotions that are difficult to control and use positively. This workbook teaches how to control these fears (3 assignments +).

    3. *Beck Depression Inventory-II* is based on the latest revision of this much used inventory (3 assignments +).

    4. *Big Five Markers* consists of L. Goldberg's factor analysis of the Five Factors Model (FFM) of personality (12 assignments +).

    5. *Brief Psychiatric Rating Scale* permits a very quick confrontation of most symptoms of psychiatric disturbance (3 assignments +).

    6. *Butcher Treatment Planning Inventory* written in conjunction with the first instrument to specifically assess treatment resistance (3 assignments +).

    7. *Dependent Personality* deals with items that describe characteristics that put dependent personalities at risk for depression (3 assignments +).

    8. *Five-Factors Model of Personality* (NEO) is one of the most popular, research-based, trait-oriented personality inventories (12 assignments +).

    9. *Hamilton's Anxiety Scale* uses the items from this scale to develop assignments relevant to learning to cope with anxiety (3 assignments +).

    10. *Hamilton's Depression Scale* uses the items from this scale to develop assignments to learn how to cope with depression (3 assignments +).

    11. *Juvenile Psychopathy* can be used either in conjunction with a self-report, paper and pencil test or simply on the basis of persistent acting-out behavior (3 assignments +).

(continued)

Table 4.1   *(Continued)*

12. *Personality Assessment Inventory* (PAI) and Symptom Scale 77 (SS-77) is a combination of two questionnaires that cover most common psychiatric conditions or syndromes, including phobias, anxiety, and traumas, among others (23 assignments).

13. *Personality Disorders* are extremely resistant to talk based interventions. Perhaps through the writing medium and computer-assisted interventions like this workbook these disorders may become ameanable to change (3 assignments +).

14. *Posttraumatic Stress Disorder* is based on the latest factor analytic study of the scale by the same name (3 assignments +).

15. *Posttgraumatic Stress Symptoms* helps people who still suffer from painful experiences from their pasts that are still effecting them in the present (3 assignments +).

16. *Self-Others Profile Chart* are two theory-derived workbooks that allow a quick and focused determination of disturbances in the Self, in intimate Ohers, and in both Self and Others (6 assignments +).

17. *Meyers-Briggs Type Indicator* is based on the theories of Carl Jung concerning personality types. (10 assignments +).

18. *What Kind of Depression?* based on the differentiation between depression derived from overdependency and depression derived from self-criticism (5 assignments +).

B. Based on Referral Question

19. *Addendum to Anger* teaches that there are a variety of angry feelings that can be expressed and controlled in more constructive ways than in the past (7 assignments).

20. *Addendum to Phobias* teaches people to learn to express and control their fears (5 assignments).

21. *Addendum to Social Training* is written from the viewpoint of how many acting out individuals think (10 assignments).

22. *Anger, Hostility and Aggression* derived from the work of Eckhardt, Deffenbacher, Spielberger and his associates (the AHA syndrome) (5 assignments +).

23. *Anxiety* follows the DSM-IV definition of this condition (6 lessons).

Table 4.1   *(Continued)*

24. *Co-dependency* helps partners of addicted individuals to set limits on their partners (13 assignments).

25. *Emotional Expression* teaches respondents who are unable to express feelings to express them in a more appropriate and helpful fashion (3 assignments +).

26. *Loneliness* helps individuals to deal with feelings that make them unable to develop meaningful relationships on their own (6 assignments).

27. *Moodiness* is an all purpose workbook that teaches individuals to express a great many memories that effected their moods (12 assignments).

28. *Multiple Abilities* is based on the theories of H. Gardner, R.J. Sternberg, and P. Salovey about multiple intelligences (15 assignments).

29. *Procrastination* helps individuals become more aware and perhaps learn to deal with and control their procrastination (6 assignments).

30. *Sexual Abuse* for victims of sexual abuse who need to complete it in conjunction with support or therapy groups (9 assignments).

II. Appendices
   A. Annotated Bibliography of Selected Self-Help Workbooks.
   B. Example of Informed Consent Form.
   C. Feedback Sentences for Letters to Respondents.
   D. Self-Other Profile Charts (SOPC): Revised Forms for elementary, middle school, high school, college, and adulthood.

*For more information about these workbooks, please access: http://www.mentalhealthhelp.com.

HISTORICAL BACKGROUND

Writing and especially distance writing (DW) for preventive and therapeutic purposes has a distinguished history.[1] In every decade since the 1940s, writing has been suggested as a tool in psychotherapeutic interventions. In 1942, Allport included personal documents, like diaries, for an understanding of the person and of

---

[1] The historical section was written with the help of Oliver McMahan, Ph.D.

personality. A few years later, Progoff (1975) expanded on the use of autobiographical materials, as suggested originally by Allport. In the 1950s, Landsman (1951), Messinger (1952), and Farber (1953) advocated the integration of writing in clinical practice. In the 1960s, Pearson (1965) published the first APA symposium on the use of DW with psychotherapy patients, with Ellis (1965) advocating DW in therapy in the form of assigned homework between sessions. Phillips and Wiener (1965) pioneered the term "writing therapy." They attempted to empirically validate its outcome with a waiting list control group and pre-post intervention evaluation. In the 1970s, Watzlawick, Weakland, and Fisch (1974) formulated postulates of second-order change, advocating conversion from verbal to written media as a significant component in cognitive patterns of second-order change. Shelton and Ackerman (1974) continued the use of writing with regular homework assignments as part of therapy. Creativity in written therapy in the form of poetry writing was part of the repertoire of Harrower (1972).

In the 1980s, the use of writing expanded even further in psychotherapy. Brand (1989), Kelley (1990), and Scinto (1986) discussed writing as a way to increase cognitive and personality functioning. The use of poetry as a therapeutic intervention grew in that decade (Fuchel, 1985; Mazza, 1981; Rothenberg, 1987). Interactive writing between clients and significant others was proposed by Farley and Farley (1987). Short story writing (Graves, 1984), letter writing (Diets, 1988; Lindahl, 1988), and journal writing (Faria & Belohlavek, 1984) were being used at new levels of formalization and sophistication not heretofore used as therapy.

In the 1990s, the use of DW continued. Nau (1997) advocated the writing of letters by therapists as well as clients as part of therapy. He further advocated DW in the use of problem solving, family systems, grief, and loss counseling. He even instructed a client to write to an amputated leg. Leucht and Tan (1996) affirmed several reasons for the use of written homework between sessions, citing increased number of times clients directly address problems, and "... increasing a client's sense that he or she is not completely dependent on the therapist to produce change" (p. 258) with the application of skills learned in therapy to other life tasks. Riordan (1996) in an approach called, "scriptotherapy," reviewed a variety of formats for DW including, "structured writing," "counseling by correspondence" (p. 266), and written therapy in group work. Lemberg (1994) expanded writing to a journaling technique used by couples, noting that couples felt a "greater sense of active participation in therapy" (p. 65) as a result of writing. Most of the references just cited are based strictly on case reports. More recently, there has been an increase of empirical evidence in support of DW for interventional purposes. Before this evidence is reviewed, however, we will classify various types of DW to better understand its nature.

A CLASSIFICATION OF DISTANCE WRITING INTERVENTIONS

As DW evolved as a part of therapeutic practice, the need for a classification scheme became evident (L'Abate, 1992, 1997a, 1997b). There are at least four overlapping dimensions that can be used to classify DW for interventional purposes:

1. *Structure,* which has four levels ranging from (a) *open-ended* (ODW) as in journals and diaries, to (b) *focused* (FDW), requiring concentration on a specific activity or topic like an autobiography, to (c) *guided* (GDW) consisting of a series of questions based on either ODW or FDW, and (d) *programmed* (PDW), where respondents (clients, counselees, patients, subjects) complete homework assignments consisting of a systematic series of assignments devoted to a particular topic, like depression, anxiety, and others (cf. Table 4.1).
2. *Content* can range from (a) traumatic to trivial, (b) general to specific, and (c) explicit to implicit.
3. *Goals* range from (a) *cathartic,* dealing with painful feelings or memories, to (b) *prescriptive,* dealing with behavioral exercises and tasks.
4. *Level of Abstraction,* ranging from abstract to concrete.

An example of cathartic FDW is "expressive writing" (Pennebaker, 1997). For example, participants wrote about the emotional trauma of job loss. During a five-day period they were instructed to write about "their deepest thoughts and feelings surrounding the layoff and how their lives, both personal and professional, had been affected" (p. 725). Those who participated in expressive writing "were re-employed more quickly than those who wrote about nontraumatic topics or who did not write at all." Further, "expressive writing appeared to influence individuals' attitudes about their old jobs and about finding new employment" (p. 722).

There are additional references about PDW in prevention and psychotherapy (L'Abate, 1986, 1990, 1991, 1992, 1997a, 1997b, 1999). This movement has culminated in the recent publication of workbooks by the Institute for Life Empowerment (Table 4.1), the Psychological Corporation, and one brief therapy planner by Schultheis (1998) devoted exclusively to written homework assignments. Workbooks represent the software for Computer-Assisted Interventions (CAI), which seem the favorite medium of communication for acting-out and impulsive adolescents and adults. (Clements, 1986; Clements & Gullo, 1984; L'Abate, 1992, 1993, 1997a; L'Abate & Torem, in press; Scandura, 1984).

Workbooks could well become the first sieve in a sequence of interventions that follow a cost-effective service delivery model. This model suggests going from the least expensive (PDW and medication) and group-therapy to the most expensive interventions, face-to-face, individual talk psychotherapy, and, in the extreme, jails or hospitals. From ODW, for instance, one can progress to prescribe either FDW or PDW, with GDW being used as feedback for completed assignments.

EMPIRICAL SUPPORT FOR
DISTANCE WRITING (DW)

Distance Writing (DW) as an intervention has been found to be effective in a number of outcome studies (Esterling, L'Abate, Murray, & Pennebaker, 1999; L'Abate, 1997a, 1997b; Smyth, 1998). Consequently, the evidence reported here to support its preventive and therapeutic powers will be selective rather than exhaustive. For example, positive psychological effects were documented by Phillips, Gershenson, and Lyons (1977) who followed-up the first controlled study of DW by Phillips and Wiener (1965). Respondents were given weekly writing assignments that were kept in a notebook. Psychometric measures like the Minnesota Multiphasic Personality Inventory (MMPI) and the Edwards Personal Preference Schedule (Edwards) were used to measure outcome. On the MMPI, the greatest changes were in Psychasthenia, Hypomania, and Social Introversion, with the latter scale showing the greatest change. On the Edwards, reliable changes were in the direction of more assertiveness, more outgoing behavior, and less dependency.

PSYCHOLOGICAL EFFECTS

Psychological effects from PDW have been measured by L'Abate, Boyce, Fraizer, and Russ (1992). They compared the effects of three workbooks for depression, one based on Beck's (1976) cognitive model of depression, another based on L'Abate's (1986) interpersonal model of depression, and the third based on the Minnesota Multiphasic Personality Inventory-2 (MMPI-2) Content Scale of Depression (L'Abate, 1992). Respondents were classified as either high or low in depression based upon the Beck Depression Inventory (BDI) and the Center for Epidemiological Studies Depression (CES-D) Scale. Respondents were randomly assigned to either control or to one of the three different homework groups. Results of post-tests indicated that mean BDI scores of the homework groups decreased significantly in comparison to the control group. While these results indicated that workbooks may lower depression, regardless of whether the initial level of depression varies, a six-month follow-up study yielded no differences between the three experimental groups and the control group (L'Abate, 1997b).

Russ (L'Abate, 1997b) used the Anxiety Content Scale of the MMPI-2 and the Spielberger's State Trait Anxiety Inventory (STAI) to measure the effectiveness of an anxiety workbook that contained six assignments administered through the mail with neither face-to-face interaction with a professional nor feedback. Mean anxiety scores of the intervention group on the STAI were significantly lower ($p < .05$) than control group scores on post-test. There were significant decreases for the State Anxiety scores in a six-month follow-up ($p < .0001$) as well as a significant group x time interaction ($p < .03$). Trait Anxiety scores, however, did not decrease.

Both cognitive and emotional positive changes were reported as a result of FDW about feelings related to interpersonal traumatic events (Murray & Segal, 1994). Emotional effects were the target of Pennebaker's (1997) research on an expressive writing intervention. Respondents used expressive writing as an opportunity to divulge the emotional nature of traumatic experiences, particularly job loss. The emotions expressed included anger and bitterness. The written interventions were important not only to directly connect the emotions with sources of trauma (job loss) but also in coping with effects that emotions had upon relationships and respondents' general demeanor.

COMPARISONS WITH TALK PSYCHOTHERAPY

The effects of DW can be analyzed by comparing it with psychotherapy analogues (Donnelly & Murray, 1991; Murray, Lamnin, & Carver, 1989). Participants were divided into three groups: writing about a very traumatic event, writing about trivial events, and talking to a therapist about a traumatic event. All respondents either wrote or talked for 20 minutes for four days. Psychotherapy respondents reported more changes in feelings and adaptation. However, in content analyses of both written and spoken productions, both DW and psychotherapy produced positive changes in cognitions, self-esteem, and adaptive behavior. A follow-up (Donnelly & Murray, 1991) with more respondents and four sessions of psychotherapy found that talking and DW reduced negative emotions, increased self-esteem, and produced adaptive changes in cognition and behavior. However, significant differences were discovered in positive and negative moods between DW and psychotherapy sessions. In DW, negative mood increased and positive mood declined after each writing session. An opposite effect was found after each psychotherapy session. Yet, the DW group felt more positive overall by the end of the study.

Murray and Segal (1994) further analyzed DW versus talking by isolating vocal expression, a significant component of traditional psychotherapy, and comparing it to distance speaking (DS) with DW as therapeutic treatment. One group of respondents spoke into a tape recorder with no one present. Another group wrote during the same period. Each group was split by content. Half wrote about trivial topics. The other half wrote about the emotional sequelae of a traumatic event. Both DW and DS groups showed positive therapeutic effects and positive changes in the content analysis of their productions. In both groups, there was also an increase in negative moods and decrease in positive moods. These results suggested that differences between DW and DS were due to interpersonal factors. Given that DW seems just as or nearly as effective as DS, one may want to chose the medium that is less expensive than the other. Given statistically insignificant differences between DW and DS, the latter is more expensive because of the costs of transcription from the spoken to the written medium for content and outcome analysis.

To compare effects of emotion versus cognition displayed in DW as an intervention, Pennebaker and Beall (1986) divided respondents into three groups: those who focused just on cognitive process by discussing "only facts" related to a traumatic event they had experienced, those who were to discuss only the emotional aspects of their traumatic event, and those who were to discuss both facts and emotions of their trauma. A control group wrote only about trivial topics. Dependent measures included physician visits to determine the impact of emotions versus cognitions on physical health. There was no significant difference between the trivial and "only facts" groups. The "emotions only" group reported improvement, but there was no measurable impact on physical health. However, the "cognitions and emotions" writing group showed significant long-term mental and physical health benefits.

PHYSIOLOGICAL AND COGNITIVE EVIDENCE

Several studies suggest that FDW facilitates the expression of past hurts, a model pioneered by Pennebaker (1997) and supported by evidence cited above and elsewhere (Esterling et al., 1999), produces positive physical health outcomes. In one of the earliest studies, respondents who were asked to write about traumatic experiences had significant reductions in physician visits in the six months following the study as compared to a control group (Pennebaker & Beall, 1986). Among many replications of this model, Greenberg and Stone (1992) had students write about deeply traumatic events comparing them with students who wrote about mild traumatic events or about superficial topics. The experimental group showed a significant drop in physician visits in comparison to the two control groups. University employees who wrote about traumas once a week for four consecutive weeks had fewer absentee days and improved liver enzyme function two months after writing compared to controls (Francis & Pennebaker, 1992).

Pennebaker (1993) has been successful in finding significant correlations between types of words used in FDW and improvement in physical health, content analysing essays about traumatic events. A computer program called Linguistic Inquiry and Word Count (LICW) measured the use of negative words (sad, angry), positive emotion words (happy, laugh), causal words (because, reason) and insight words (understand, realize). Three linguistic factors were found to be reliably related to physical health. Two factors related to emotions, an increase in positive emotion words and moderate versus very low or very high numbers of negative emotion words. The third factor relating to cognition was the most significant. Increases in causal and insight words were strongly associated with increases in physical health as measured by lower numbers of doctor visits, lower numbers of absences from school, and positive immune system measurements. Furthermore, increases in cognitive words covaried with judges' evaluations regarding increases in cognitive structure. Those who experienced increases in health as a result of FDW gradually increased the organization of their narratives as they wrote at greater lengths.

IMMUNOLOGICAL EFFECTS

Pennebaker, Kiecolt-Glaser, and Glaser (1988) reported that FDW affects the immune system positively. Treatment respondents wrote 15 to 20 minutes each day for four consecutive days. A control group wrote for the same amount of time about superficial topics. At a three-month follow-up, the trauma writing treatment group showed a significant improvement in immune function, had fewer physician visits than controls, and self-reported being significantly happier. The highest positive immune response occurred when respondents were higher self-disclosers. Petrie, Booth, Pennebaker, Davison, and Thomas (1995) used the same model using a hepatitis B vaccination program. Trauma DW had significantly higher antibody levels against hepatitis B than the control group. This study was significant because it measured the effect of writing while the immune system was in operation against a specific viral challenge.

Esterling, Antoni, Kumar, and Schneiderman (1990) validated the findings of Pennebaker and his associates by relating specific immunological benefits with DW interventions. They used Epstein-Barr virus (EBV) response as a dependent measure of immune system variances as a result of FDW using Pennebaker's model. They administered undergraduates a personality inventory and had them write for 30-minutes about a stressful event that they had not yet disclosed fully to anyone. Correlations between personality styles and immunity outcomes indicated that:

> if individuals were aware of but chose not to disclose the emotional intensity of the stressful events through writing because of embarrassment, fear of punishment, or other reasons, the consequence may have been to hold back or inhibit their thoughts, feelings, and behaviors from others. (Esterling et al., 1999)

The result of inhibiting emotional expression was impaired control of latent EBV. Individuals experiencing major stressors who chose to inhibit rather than express in writing were at risk of destabilization in immunological control over herpes viruses such as EBV. In another study (Esterling, Antoni, Fletcher, Margulies, & Schneiderman, 1994), respondents were divided into FDW and FDS groups. They were to write or talk about a stressful event once a week for three weeks. The Control group wrote about trivial topics. As in the earlier study (Esterling et al., 1990), respondents were divided by personality and percentage of emotional words as an index of emotional expressiveness. Both written and verbal modalities resulted in a significant decrease in EBV antibodies over the four-week observation period. However, talking lowered EBV antibodies better than writing. Writing expression produced more total and negative emotional terms. Talking was rated higher in "cognitive change, self-esteem improvements, and adaptive coping strategies" (Esterling et al., 1994, p. 135). This study suggested that the expression of emotions may be the important function of writing. Cognitive change, enhanced self-esteem, and development of coping strategies may be the important function of the verbal medium.

Working at a Distance from Respondents

When working with people at a distance, treatment adherence is a major issue that is concerned with the consistency and integration of the various parts of the treatment process. Houge, Liddle, and Rowe (1996) reviewed several studies regarding treatment adherence, and advocated that researchers find ways to link "treatment specification and manualization, comparative clinical efficacy, and therapeutic accountability . . ." (p. 341). A number of studies (Burns & Nolen-Hoeksema, 1992; Conoley, Padula, Payton, & Daniels, 1994; Neimeyer & Feixas, 1990) focused on the specific area of homework adherence, affirming that homework adherence is vital for positive treatment outcome. Hence, DW is a way to document, measure, and monitor treatment adherence and homework adherence.

Prescriptiveness

PDW is a vital part of treatment planning, relating to all components of the of intervention process, such as assessment, treatment, homework assignments, and post-treatment assessment. PDW guarantees the necessary links between assessment, treatment, and treatment adherence. Consistency of linkages between assessment instruments, therapeutic interventions, post-therapy assessments, and post-therapy follow-ups all are maximized and coordinated through the use of PDW in a way that is difficult or expensive to obtain when interventions are based on talk. Traditionally, most psychological tests were constructed to understand and predict behavior, not to prescribe treatment. They were intended to be descriptive, or at best predictive, but never prescriptive. To match problem with solution, it is necessary to have a catalogue of solutions, such as the list of workbooks in Table 4.1.

These workbooks can be matched with either a test profile or a referral question regarding individuals, couples, and families. The larger the list of possible solutions, the greater is the possibility of matching a specific problem with a specific solution. For instance, there are now at least five workbooks for impulsive and psychopathic character disorders. As shown in Table 4.1, there are at least six different depression workbooks: one derived from Beck Depression Inventory-II, one derived from Hamilton's Revised Depression Scale, one derived from Morley's Personality Assessment Inventory (Morey & Henry, 1994), two derived from a model of depression consisting of two factors, self-criticism and overdependency, and another about the depressive personality. In addition to these workbooks, there is one derived from depression in couples (L'Abate, 1986) and one derived from the MMPI-2 (L'Abate, 1992). Given all these workbooks representing various theoretical viewpoints, the question remains as to which workbook will produce the best results with a particular disorder. Future research will be oriented toward comparative evaluation of effectiveness for workbooks derived from different theoretical viewpoints.

PSYCHOTHERAPY AND PDW

PDW has become a standard operating procedure in this author's private practice for at least three reasons, to: (1) help adolescents to assume more responsibility for changes in their impulsivity and acting out, (2) save the therapist's time and energy, and (3) make psychotherapy more cost-effective. Many juveniles are either in detention, do not want face-to-face contacts with a therapist, or make nuisances of themselves in the therapy office. The energy expended in trying to help these youngsters through talk is draining and often unproductive. Programmed writing assignments, or workbooks, on the other hand, can often succeed where all else fails. In this author's practice, juveniles and patients with character disorders, whether individuals, couples, or families, have to agree (in writing) to complete written homework assignments that match one hour of homework with one hour of therapy (L'Abate, 1986). Additionally, workbooks, as specific applications of PDW, can be administered nomothetically as a general approach for everybody. They can be administered idiographically to fit the individual needs of each respondent. Given the same number of assignments, as necessary for research purposes, it is still possible to vary the nature of each assignment to fit individual needs at the same time that a standard administration format is followed.

Some teenagers are difficult to control in family therapy sessions. Some acting-out teenagers tend to distract the session with irrelevant issues, to disobey instructions, and to continue to act out in therapy sessions. Using workbooks, these individuals do not have to attend therapy sessions if they resist face-to-face contacts. However, they might be told that they have to complete written assignments if they: (1) want to stay in the family, (2) do not want to be referred to a court for status considerations, (3) have to live with the disliked, noncustodial parent, or (4) go to detention. Talk therapy with the family may be continued, but, when a juvenile consistently disrupts and distracts during therapy sessions, it is much more practical to contract with him or her for the completion of written homework assignments outside therapy sessions. An added incentive is to have adolescents pay the whole fee for the entire program beforehand (with written feedback from the therapist through the mail or through e-mail). This fee may be taken partially from their weekly allowance or paycheck for part-time work. If and when they complete the whole workbook and a post-test, they receive one-third of the fee back.

Originally, the basis for using PDW was strictly pragmatic. To use time more effectively, the author found it helpful to prescribe one hour of written homework for each hour of family therapy from the very outset. Relying on talk was given up for greater reliance on PDW. This position has been supported by the research previously summarized and by a review by Simon (1998). She questioned whether talk-based treatments for criminal offenders work. In reviewing the meta-analyses literature on the effectiveness of psychological treatments based on talk, she concluded that: ". . . offender treatment [including juveniles] yields consistently small effect size, the effect of offender treatment is less than half that of the overall effects in meta-analyses of psychological interventions in general" (p. 139). Simon focused her discussion on policy rather than on treatment implications of her rather disheartening conclusion.

Since writing the first workbook for impulsive individuals (L'Abate, 1992), the author expanded this approach by designing additional workbooks that can be administered to juveniles through the mail, by fax, or on personal computers. Computers are increasingly found in public libraries, clinics, jails, and hospitals. Hence, not owning a computer is no longer an excuse for not using one. Most juveniles hate to write using a pen or pencil because they believe it is "sissy" or too feminine. Using a computer seems to be more masculine and more likely to project a "macho" exterior. Most juveniles have no objection, in fact, are quite enthusiastic, about communicating through a computer. The PDW approach was first used with jailed felons because they could not be seen face-to-face in jail. Feedback about each assignment took place through the mail (L'Abate, 1992). However, there is no reason why such feedback could not be given through a computer.

In PDW, family members often need to model the same behavior at home by answering, in writing, homework assignments given by the therapist. Each family member is given either a specific workbook for an individual condition, like depression, or couples and families may be given the same assignments, provided that they answer the assignments independently of others. Then, an appointment is made for family members to get together at home to compare and contrast their answers. They keep running notes of what happened at this meeting. These notes, together with the completed assignments, are shared with the therapist in face-to-face sessions and become part of the therapist's file folder. If respondents want to keep their records, they may make copies of their assignments.

WORKBOOKS FOR ACTING-OUT JUVENILES[2]

This section describes in more detail the workbooks listed in Table 4.1 that are written specifically for juveniles. Workbooks are classified according to whether they were written on the basis of an existing test or test profile or whether they were written on the basis of a referral question for individuals, couples, and families. Each assignment or series of assignments matches the same isomorphic dimension on a test-profile. If a test profile shows a high score on anxiety, for instance, then the anxiety workbook would be assigned. These homework assignments can be administered to bolster the effects of any preventive or psychotherapeutic (i.e., face-to-face, talk-based) approach. As explained at greater length in a manual (L'Abate, 1997b), the use of workbooks can take place alongside, in preparation for, or termination from any face-to-face talk intervention. A workbook may be assigned in addition to an ongoing preventive program, like psychoeducational social skills training, as an alternative to such a program, or therapeutically, in addition or as an alternative to psychotherapy and rehabilitation.

Social Training Workbook

The original text for the *Social Training Workbook* can be found in L'Abate (1992). It was written from the viewpoint of "shoulds," that is, what acting-out teenagers need to learn to improve thinking and planning before acting. This workbook was designed to teach externalizing, impulsive, and acting-out individuals how to think before acting. It consists of 18 to 22 assignments asking respondents to rehearse and repeat new and more constructive behaviors. These assignments will be reviewed in the case illustration that follows. The MMPI results before, immediately after, and six months after completion of this workbook with two incarcerated felons (ages 18 and 20) are reported in L'Abate. A complete transcript of the evaluation and correspondence (assignments and feedback) with one of them, illustrating the whole process of PDW,

---

[2] Please note that the sample assignments contained in this chapter are protected by copyright laws. They cannot be used clinically or otherwise without the expressed permission of the Institute for Life Empowerment.

is included with pre-post and follow-up MMPI profiles (L'Abate, 1992). The reader should keep in mind that these interventions took place ten years ago and since then additional workbooks have been created.

Addendum to Social Training Workbook

Assignments from the original *Social Training Workbook* were drawn from clinical practice. They were meant to be pragmatic in teaching respondents semantic retraining for topics that needed to be learned by an acting-out adolescent ("shoulds"). An Addendum adds a greater number of supplementary and complementary assignments. This Addendum was written from the viewpoint of how acting-out youngsters think rather than what and how they "should" think.

Furthermore, assignments in this Addendum are drawn from a relational selfhood model of externalizing behavior derived from a developmental, relational, and contextual theory of personality socialization (L'Abate, 1993, 1994, 1997b). Impulsive and acting-out individuals, mostly males, show a prepensity toward Selfishness, while co-dependent individuals, mostly females, married or living with selfish men, show a propensity toward Selflessness. A workbook for the latter (L'Abate & Harrison, 1992) is also available (see Table 4.1).[3]

Assignments from the previously published *Social Training Workbook* (L'Abate, 1992) were theory-independent. Those included in this workbook are more theory-derived and theory-dependent. In spite of this distinction, assignments from both workbooks, and the additional workbook for juvenile psychopathy described next, can be administered complementarily. These workbooks overlap with each other, as do two additional workbooks. One Addendum on Anger, and a second on Anger, Hostility, and Aggression, which are distinctive characteristics of many acting-out impulsive individuals. A sample of the introductory assignment of the former *workbook* is found in Table 4.2.

---

[3] An annotated bibliography of over 50 mental health workbooks published commercially is available from the Institute for Life Empowerment (http://www.mentalhealthhelp.com).

Table 4.2
First Assignment for Addendum to Social Training
Workbook: Life as a Power Struggle

The purpose of this workbook is to help you understand behavior that may have gotten you in trouble (with the law) in the past and that may get you in trouble in the future.

The purpose of the first assignment is to help you understand whether life is a power struggle or whether life is what you make it. It can be a power struggle if you want to make it that way, or, it can be a more peaceful process if that is what you want to make it. *It is up to you.* Do you want to make life a power struggle or a more peaceful process? If you want to go on making life a power struggle you do not need to work on this workbook or this lesson. If you want to make life a more peaceful process for you, go on and answer the questions asked in this lesson.

1. By a power struggle is meant that in any human relationship there are winners and losers. As a result, life becomes a struggle to win or loose, where defeating others seems to be necessary to survive. How much is life a power struggle for you?

    a. A great deal   _____
    b. Often times   _____
    c. Not at all   _____

2. If you have checked *a* and *b* go ahead with this lesson. If you checked *c* you may not be ready or willing to undertake this workbook and a different workbook or approach may be necessary for you.

3. How did life begin as a power struggle for you?

    a. Write as far as you can remember how victories and losses became part of your life.

    b. Who won at whose expense?

    c. Who lost and lost again?

    d. How did you learn to defeat others before they defeated you?

    e. Do not limit yourself to answering the questions asked above. Write as much as you can to answer these questions.

Table 4.2 *(Continued)*

4. Would you say that you learned to lose by defeating others?

   a. How did learn to do that?

   b. Write as many situations where you lost by defeating others.

5. Did you ever win by defeating others?

   a. Write as many situations where you felt you won by defeating others.

   b. Who were they and how did you do it?

6. Do you want to go on with this power struggle or do you want to give it up? If you want to go on with it, you do not need to complete this lesson and you can quit right now. If you want to give up this power struggle, what kind of life do you want to lead for yourself? Rank order all the statements below according to what you want the most (No. 1) to the statement that you want the least.

Life Goals	Rank
a. I want a peaceful life.	_____
b. I want a self-enhancing life.	_____
c. I want to learn to give up the power struggle.	_____
d. I do not know what I want.	_____
e. I want to learn to win rather than to defeat myself and other.	_____
f. I want to learn to win at no one else's expense.	_____
g. (Write here what you want that is not stated above.)	_____

Homework: During the next week, write down how you would like to achieve the Life Goals you have just ranked. Write first about Life Goal ranked No. 1. When you are finished, then write about Life Goal ranked No. 2, and so on, until you have written about all the Life Goals you want to achieve. Make sure you receive feedback from a professional about what you have written.

Juvenile Psychopathy

This workbook consists of written homework assignments that are isomorphic with dimensions evaluated by the *Child Psychopathy Scale* (CPS; Lynam, 1997). It can be administered on the basis of either the presenting referral symptom or on the basis of an objective measure of juvenile acting out. Preferably, these measures should be administered before and after completion of each workbook, as well as months after termination. This workbook was designed to lower the chances of respondents behaving in destructive fashions toward others, and ultimately to the self. Since there is always the danger that the workbook may "train" juveniles to answer the test without any real change in behavior, it is recommended that a different measure of impulsivity or juvenile psychopathy be used, including ratings from external observers (Webster & Jackson, 1997).

The order of administration of these assignments can follow the subjective ranking of each respondent, or it can follow the objective ranking derived from test scores, either from the most severe to the least severe dimension, or vice versa. Ordering of assignments in the absence of evidence to support it, at this point, needs to be left to the clinical judgment of the professional. A sample of the first introductory assignment is found in Table 4.3.

Addendum to Anger Program

This workbook is written to complement and possibly improve on assignments published previously about the same topic (L'Abate, 1992) and on the workbooks described previously. Anger is an important determinant of acting-out and impulsivity (L'Abate, 1993, 1994, 1997d) and needs to be considered in any rehabilitation plan with juveniles. In contrast to assignments already published (L'Abate, 1992), this workbook recognizes the multidimentional nature of anger and its multiple determinants. It consists of seven assignments: (1) Introduction: There Are Different Kinds of Anger (see Table 4.4), (2) Direct and Indirect Negative Expressions of Anger, (3) Practicing Your Anger Directly, (4) Practicing Your Anger Indirectly, (5) Feeling Angry versus Expressing Anger, (6) Distinguishing Anger from Other Feelings, and (7) Positive (Joining)

Table 4.3

First Assignment for Juvenile Psychopathy Workbook:
Behaviors That Got You or Might Get You into
Trouble with the Law

The purpose of this workbook is to help you learn more about behaviors that have gotten you in trouble in the past. These behaviors might get you into trouble or even in jail again in the future. If you do not want to learn about these behaviors, of course, you do not have to go on with this assignment.

If you do want to: (1) learn more about behaviors that have gotten you into trouble (and possibly in jail), and (2) avoid getting into trouble in the future, please complete this assignment. The purpose of this assignment is to learn more about which behaviors might get you into trouble with the law.

1. Below there is a list of behaviors that get many young people in trouble with the law. You need to define each behavior as you understand it. You may want to check in a dictionary, ask your buddies, adults, parents, brothers and sisters, or relatives. It may take you a week or longer to complete these definitions. Feel free to use any examples from your experience to define these behaviors. Take your time. It is important that you understand what these behaviors are and how they might get you in trouble with the law.

What Do You Understand by the Following?	Examples
a. Glibness/superficial charm:	
b. Pathological lying:	
c. Conning/manipulative:	
d. Lack of remorse or guilt:	
e. Shallow affect:	
f. Callousness/lack of empathy:	
g. Failure to accept responsibility for own actions:	
h. Parasitic lifestyle:	

(continued)

Table 4.3 *(Continued)*

---

   i. Poor behavioral controls:

   j. Lack of plans:

   k. Impulsivity:

   l. Irresponsibility:

  m. Criminal versatility:

2. Now that you have completed the first part of this assignment comes the hard part: Below are listed the 13 behaviors that you have defined during the past week or so. Rank each of them according to how each (mis)behavior applies to you. Rank as No. 1 the (mis)behavior that applies to you the best (or most!). Rank as No. 2 the (mis)behavior that applies to you next best. Rank as No. 3 the behavior that applies to you next. Go on until you find (mis)behaviors that do not apply to you at all. Just write N/A (non applicable) instead of a rank number next to these behaviors.

Behaviors	Rank
a. Glibness/superficial charm	_____
b. Pathological lying	_____
c. Conning/manipulative	_____
d. Lack of remorse or guilt	_____
e. Shallow affect	_____
f. Callousness/lack of empathy	_____
g. Failure to accept responsibility for own actions	_____
h. Parasitic lifestyle	_____
i. Poor behavioral controls	_____
j. Lack of plans	_____
k. Impulsivity	_____
l. Irresponsibility	_____
m. Criminal versatility	_____

3. Write down why you rank-ordered yourself the way you just did:

Table 4.3 *(Continued)*

4. Now that you have completed this assignment, write how you feel about it. Check which of these answers tells how you felt about it. There is also space for you to explain further, if you want to:

   a. I did not like it at all, a waste of time. I want to quit this stupid workbook. _____

   b. I did not like it very much, but I want to go on with this workbook. _____

   c. I liked it and I want to go on with this workbook. _____

   d. I liked it a lot and I wish I had something like this workbook earlier. _____

   e. I liked it so much that I wish all juveniles could get something like this workbook to work on. _____

5. Give, mail, or e-mail your answers to whoever has given you this lesson.

Homework: During the coming week think more about the behaviors that got you into trouble and whether you want to change the rank order of these behaviors as listed above, or start working on the next assignment.

Expressions of Anger. A sample of the first introductory assignment is found in Table 4.4.

SELF-OTHER PROFILE CHART WORKBOOKS

According to the selfhood model mentioned earlier, selfishness is defined as a personality propensity where self-importance is asserted at the expense of somebody else, usually an intimate but often non-intimates (L'Abate, 1997b). This propensity leads to extremes in acting-out and criminal behavior. By the same token, selflessness is defined as a personality propensity where self-importance is denied and importance of others is asserted. This propensity leads to extremes in affective and dependent disorders like co-dependencies, depressions, and suicides. Many acting-out juveniles are children of either depressed mothers and selfish fathers, or both. This model has been evaluated with a

Table 4.4
First Assignment of Anger Workbook:
There Are Different Kinds of Anger

The purpose of this workbook is to help you learn more about your anger. Possibly if you learn more about your anger, you may learn to express it in more helpful ways that you may have done in the past.

1. The purpose of this introduction is to help you find out which kind of anger controls you. There are at least two ways of looking at anger:
   a. As an immediate, internal response to a situation without external behavior.
   b. As an explosion from keeping inside many unexpressed feelings. Which of these two ways is characteristic of your anger? Circle one or both.

2. What do you do when you get angry? Please explain in detail:

3. How often do you get angry?
   a. At least once a day or more.   _____
   b. Two or three times a week.   _____
   c. A couple of times a month.   _____
   d. Once or twice a year.   _____

4. How angry do you get?
   a. Extremely angry, rageful.   _____
   b. Angry enough but without rage.   _____
   c. Irritated rather than angry.   _____
   d. Annoyed rather than angry.   _____

5. How destructive is your anger?
   a. Extremely.   _____
   b. Somewhat.   _____
   c. Not at all.   _____

6. Anger may come out from a variety of sources or causes. Which of these sources seems to be more related to your anger?

Note that all these types of anger are not mutually exclusive and they may overlap.

Table 4.4 *(Continued)*

a. *As a reaction to frustrations.* What would these frustrations be for you? Please expand on your answer as much as you like (use another piece of paper if necessary):

b. *As a reaction to hurt(s):* What would these hurts consist of for you? Please list all the hurts that seem related to your anger:

c. *As a form of manipulation for situations you feel unable to control.* What would these situations be? Please expand on these situations as much as you like:

d. *As habitual imitation of past models.* What would these models be? Please expand on the influence of these models as much as necessary:

e. *As a form of learned abuse.* How did you learn to use anger as abuse? Expand at will:

f. *As self-indulgence.* How did this form of self-indulgence develop in you? Please expand at will:

g. *As fear of failure.* Expand on how anger developed from this fear:

h. As part of *a quest for perfection* and perfectionism. Expand at will:

i. As a result of *feeling helpless* and inadequate to deal with a situation. Expand at will:

j. As a result of *guilt and shame* about certain behavior you are not proud of. Expand at will:

k. As a way of asserting and expressing your importance when you feel put-down:

l. There may be another source or cause that is not included in the list above. Feel free to list another source of anger and expand on how it developed within you.

(continued)

Table 4.4   *(Continued)*

7. Now rank these types of anger in how they apply to you, ranking No. 1 the type of anger that applies to you the most, rank as No. 2 the anger that applies to you second best, and so on, until you reach the types of anger that applies to you the least or not at all (N/A):

Types/Sources of Anger	Rank
a. Frustrations	_____
b. Hurts	_____
c. Manipulation	_____
d. Habit	_____
e. Abuse	_____
f. Self-indulgence	_____
g. Failure	_____
h. Perfectionism	_____
i. Helplessness	_____
j. Guilt & Shame	_____
k. Importance	_____
l. Other source ( )	_____

8. Write down at least three instances when anger was used helpfully:
   a.

   b.

   c.

9. Write down at least three instances when anger was used hurtfully:
   a.

   b.

   c.

10. Write down any reactions, thoughts or feelings (including anger!) that have come out as a result of completing this lesson:

Homework: During the next week, log (write down) how often you got mad as well as the situation that brought about your anger. It is very important that you complete this homework because the information you write down will be useful in future assignments.

Self-Others Profile Chart whose psychometric properties (validity and reliability) have been evaluated (L'Abate, 1997d). There are five versions of this chart depending on age, from elementary, middle school, high school, college, to adulthood (L'Abate, 1992).

These workbooks (see Table 4.1) are isomorphic with the two major dimensions, self/others of this test and could be administered to juveniles who score high on self and low on others. These workbooks can be administered to children because of the simplicity of their wording, instructions and concepts underlying their use. Children who are low on Self-Importance could receive the Self workbook. Children low on importance of Others, who might be already acting out, would need to work on the Others workbook.

Anger in Children and Teenagers Workbook

This workbook is based on the factor-analysis of Lahey et al. (1990) and the work of Feindler (1995). Before the administration of this workbook, it would be very helpful if there were external observations (ratings, checklists, and the like) of angry behaviors from observers for two purposes: (1) to verify whether these observations match with the self-report of angry behaviors from the child or teenager and (2) to verify whether the administration of this workbook resulted in positive changes, regardless of self-reports from respondents.

After the administration of the first assignment, all the following assignments are based on the rank-orders given by respondents in this first assignment. The behavior ranked as No. 1 is listed in the title of the second assignment, using the same standard form for all the following assignments. The behavior ranked as No. 2 becomes the third assignment, and so until all the assignments rank-ordered as needing change have been administered. For research purposes, the number of assignments may be constant for all respondents. However, the titles of the assignments may change from one respondent to another, allowing this approach to be idiographic as well as nomothetic. It is highly recommended that self-report, paper-and-pencil tests to measure degree, duration, frequency, and intensity of anger, hostility, and aggression, be administered before, during, and after completion of this workbook.

Even better, it would be very useful to have external measures of anger, such as observations or reports from family members, relatives, coworkers, or friends, as well as therapists, or others who have experienced first-hand the anger, hostility, or aggression reported by respondents. This workbook consists of a two-step procedure. The first step consists of dealing with each reaction ranked by respondents as needing change. The second step consists of specific suggestions on how to deal with anger, hostility, or aggression in constructive ways.

The purpose of the first assignment in this workbook is strictly prescriptive, to find out what angry, hostile, or aggressive reactions respondents want to change. Consequently, all the subsequent "standard" assignments are based on the rank-order given by each respondent in this assignment. The "reaction" ranked as No. 1 is administered as the second assignment. The reaction ranked as No. 2 is administered as the third assignment and so on, for as many reactions as have been ranked by respondents.

For research purposes, of course, the number of assignments would be the same for all respondents, even though their sequence may vary from one respondent to another, hence combining both nomothetic and idiographic approaches without sacrificing standard operating procedures. The first assignment of this workbook is shown in Table 4.5.

DIVORCE ADJUSTMENT FOR CHILDREN WORKBOOK

Karin Jordan (1999) has developed a *Divorce Adjustment for Children Workbook* of elementary school age consisting of seven assignments to be used in addition to face-to-face therapy: (1) discussion of the impact of the divorce on the child and the family, (2) what it means to have two families instead of one, (3) feelings about the breakup, (4) custody and where do I live? (5) about my mom and dad, (6) I am a child, not a grown-up, and (7) changing families. This workbook is relevant to the extent that many juveniles come from broken homes. It remains an open question whether dealing with the divorce at a younger age, expressing feelings that would not be expressed otherwise, would have had some preventive effect on curbing acting-out years later.

Table 4.5
First Assignment of Anger, Hostility, and Aggression Workbook

---

Assignment 1. How I Deal with My Anger

Name_____   Date_____

The purpose of this workbook is to help you with your anger and the hurtful behaviors that go with it. The purpose of this assignment is to learn more about how you express your anger to help you deal with it in better ways for you than in the past.

1. Which of these behaviors apply to you? Most of the Time, Sometimes, and Never? Please check which behavior applies to you.

	Applies to Me			
Angry Behaviors	Most of the Time	Sometimes	Never	Rank-Order
Hurting animals	_____	_____	_____	_____
Attacking others	_____	_____	_____	_____
Bothering others	_____	_____	_____	_____
Swearing	_____	_____	_____	_____
Firesetting	_____	_____	_____	_____
Spiteful	_____	_____	_____	_____
Touchy	_____	_____	_____	_____
Running away	_____	_____	_____	_____
Stealing	_____	_____	_____	_____
Blaming others	_____	_____	_____	_____
Temper tantrums	_____	_____	_____	_____
Cruel with others	_____	_____	_____	_____
Destroying property	_____	_____	_____	_____
Fighting	_____	_____	_____	_____
Arguing	_____	_____	_____	_____
Truant from the law	_____	_____	_____	_____
Lying	_____	_____	_____	_____

(continued)

Table 4.5   *(Continued)*

| Angry Behaviors | Applies to Me | | | Rank-Order |
	Most of the Time	Sometimes	Never	
Hitting others	_____	_____	_____	_____
Defying others	_____	_____	_____	_____
Stubborn	_____	_____	_____	_____
Breaking rules	_____	_____	_____	_____
Bullying, threatening	_____	_____	_____	_____
Doing the opposite of what you are told	_____	_____	_____	_____
Drinking, smoking, using drugs	_____	_____	_____	_____
Angry	_____	_____	_____	_____
Breaking things	_____	_____	_____	_____
Uncooperative	_____	_____	_____	_____
Talking back	_____	_____	_____	_____
Irritable, hot tempered, easily angered	_____	_____	_____	_____
Arguing & quarreling	_____	_____	_____	_____
Sulking & pouting	_____	_____	_____	_____
Denying mistakes	_____	_____	_____	_____
Pushing limits, persisting	_____	_____	_____	_____
Nagging, and not taking "No" for an answer	_____	_____	_____	_____
Picking on others to get attention	_____	_____	_____	_____
Bragging & boasting	_____	_____	_____	_____

Table 4.5 *(Continued)*

	Applies to Me			
Angry Behaviors	Most of the Time	Sometimes	Never	Rank-Order
Teasing others	_____	_____	_____	_____
Not sharing with others	_____	_____	_____	_____
Other (write what it is)	_____	_____	_____	_____

2. Now that you have checked how these behaviors apply to you, it is important for you to rank-order angry behaviors that apply to you most of the time or sometimes. This rank-order, of course, depends on whether you want to change those angry behaviors or not. If you do not want to change any angry behavior then you are wasting your time going on with assignment. You may as well quit now. However, if you do want to change angry behaviors that apply to you most of the time or sometimes, rank-order as No. 1 as the angry behavior you want to change the most. Then rank-order as No. 2 the angry behavior you want to change next. Rank-order as No. 3 the angry behavior you want to change next and so on until all the angry behaviors that apply to you are in rank-order according to how much you want to change them.

3. Now that you have finished this rank-order, explain why you rank-ordered those angry behaviors the way you did:

Homework: During the coming week think more about your angry behaviors and what they get you. Think also whether you want to change the rank-order of angry behaviors you want to change.

DEALING WITH RESISTANT JUVENILES: BUTCHER TREATMENT PLANNING INVENTORY (BTPI)

To deal with resistance to psychological interventions, a workbook that relates to the Treament Resistance Content Scale of the MMPI-2 was developed (L'Abate, 1992). More recently, with the advent of the Butcher's Treatment Planning Inventory (in press), a workbook isomorphic with the dimensions (i.e., areas), measured by this inventory was developed (see Table 4.6). The purpose of this workbook is to help juveniles as well as adults become more aware of areas in their lives that are relevant to the development of a specific treatment plan tailor-made for them. The purpose of the first assignment is strictly diagnostic and prescriptive. It requires respondents to list some of the most common areas of their personality that are relevant to treatment planning. The remainder of this workbook consists of assignments that are drawn from this list. An example of the areas covered by this workbook and initial instructions for its administration is given in Table 4.6. By asking respondents to define all these terms, it is possible to: (1) enlarge the cognitive realm of respondents, (2) develop a common language between respondents and professionals, and (3) confront issues of evaluation and treatment that are difficult if not impossible to confront directly through talk therapy.

The order of homework assignments can be performed in two ways: follow the rank order given by the respondent in the first assignment, or follow the test profile, either from the most elevated score to the least elevated one or vice-versa, from the least to the most elevated score. A third alternative, especially if there is a large discrepancy between the subjective order of the respondent and the objective profile, would be to discuss this discrepancy with the respondent and arrive at a compromised, negotiated order of assignment administration.

CASE ILLUSTRATION

The case reported here concerns a 15-year-old boy, Kent[4] (not his real name) who was referred for treatment after he was expelled from his fourth school placement. In therapy, his acting-out was related to the mother's depression. ("You should be congratulated for helping mother become angry rather than depressed.") After initial protests from the mother about her depression, on a third evaluation visit, she finally reported that over the years she had

---

[4] Kent's mother gave a written consent to publish this case provided anonymity was guaranteed.

Table 4.6
Areas of Personality to Define in Butcher
Treatment Planning Inventory (BTPI) Workbook

Please define in writing what the areas of personality listed below mean to you. If necessary use a dictionary, ask a friend, or ask the professional your are working with at the present time. Also use examples that come to mind to complete each definition.

a. Consistency of self-definition.

b. Presentation of self.

c. Reason for seeking treatment.

d. Closed mindedness.

e. Problems in forming relationships.

f. Somatization of conflicts.

g. Low expectations of therapeutic benefit.

h. Self-oriented centeredness.

i. Lack of support.

j. Sadness/depression/self-defeating behavior.

k. Disabling anxiety.

l. Intense anger expression.

m. Anger turned against the self.

n. Unusual thinking or bizarre beliefs.

gotten up at night (whenever her husband was out of town, which was frequently) to write "about her demons." She refused to report about the nature of these "demons" except to imply that they were related to loneliness and frustration about her husband's frequent work-related trips and his inability to help out with the son's acting-out in school.

Kent's reactions were predictably negative and limited. He did not view therapy as necessary or relevant. There was nothing wrong with his being expelled from four schools because he was bright enough to pass. The fact that he would fail a grade because of not finishing the school year did not seem to concern him at all. During a session with his mother and once with his father, Kent continued to behave oppositionally, negativistically, and in a distracting manner. The only way to get his attention was to bet him money ($5) that he would get into trouble during the forthcoming week because of his loyalty to his mother and his need to keep her in an angry mood rather than to see her cry when she felt depressed (Weeks & L'Abate, 1982). He won two bets for two consecutive weeks, by not acting out, staying in his fifth school placement, and perhaps, passing to the next grade if he completed the school year in good standing. The fifth high school accepted him because of his unusual ability in an individual sport. His MMPI-A predictably scored at the 90% on the Pd scale, with all the other validity and clinical scales within "normal" limits, that is, below the 70th percentile.

In spite of these positive gains, it was clear that he was always pushing limits with his teachers. Even though his grades were above average, his oppositional and negativistic attitude toward authorities and his need to receive negative attention kept him in the principal's office. Consequently, it was agreed that to prevent being thrown out of school and failing the year, he would need to complete weekly homework assignments related to his impulsivity and self-defeating attitudes. These attitudes kept him "winning" phyrric victories even though he was losing the war. He agreed (through a signed informed consent form) to continue working on the *Social Training Workbook* even though his family was moving out of state, when his father was promoted. Kent completed the 18 assignments of the *Social Training Workbooks* through correspondence as well as the post-MMPI-A. Selected summaries of his answers to each assignment follow.

Assignment No. 1. Goals and Wants

Here Kent expressed his awareness of how his behavior was "tearing my family apart" and "separating my parents." He wanted to lead "a normal life," and "lower the stress" level of the family by trying "to turn my life around." These answers, among others, were surprising because not once during the five talk-therapy sessions with either his mother or his father present, did Kent express these sentiments verbally. It makes one think about PDW reaching aspects that are difficult to express verbally and in face-to-face sessions with juveniles.

Assignment No. 2. Mistakes

Kent acknowledged "breaking into the school Snack Bar," an admission he had not made verbally, and "I sure do not have respect for authority." He was aware of the consequences that would follow his "mistakes," relating to taking drugs and driving his car without permission.

Assignment No. 3. Control

To Kent control meant using "common sense to produce positive results." He listed incidents in which he failed to exercise control over himself, relating "mistakes" to failures to control himself and making positive decisions about the ability to control.

Assignment No. 4a. Law

Kent defined this term as "a rule set up by the government that everyone must follow." He was able to separate laws from authority and connecting failures to obey laws with contingent punishments. At the end of this assignment respondents are asked how they feel when someone cheats, lies to, or robs them. This theme is the topic of the next assignment.

Assignment No. 4b. Law

The theme of this assignment is following the Golden Rule. Kent was aware of the fact that he would be treated the way he treats others, relating the outcome of using derogatory remarks with two girls and staying too long on the phone. He did apologize to one girl for his name-calling and she forgave him.

Assignment No. 5. Responsibility

Kent recognized that he was responsible for his behavior and positive and negative consequences of his behavior. He was asked to list four instances of responsible and four instances of irresponsible behaviors with their consequences. As an assignment for the following week, he was asked to write three instances when his behavior went *against* himself and three instances when his behavior was *for* himself.

Assignment No. 6. Self

Kent described himself as "witty" and "sometimes smart," wanting to become "charming" and "intelligent." He admitted not having confidence in himself and being fearful of enbarassing himself. One cannot help wondering whether he, or any other acting-out juvenile for that matter, would have been able to admit to weaknesses of this kind verbally.

Assignment No. 7. Love

For Kent, love meant "to care and show feelings toward another. He related love to "something good" and failure to love to "hurt feelings." Giving love is better than not giving it "because if you give love it will be much more appreciated and you will probably receive it." During the coming week, he was asked to list four instances where he failed to show love and four instances where he was successful in showing love to others.

Assignment No. 8. Care

According to Kent, "Caring is when something matters enough to you that you do something about it." He was asked to list: (1) four reasons why anybody should care for him, (2) four examples of how he cared for himself, with results of what happened when he cared for himself, (3) four examples of how he cared for others, with related outcomes, (4) four examples of how others cared for him, (5) four examples of how he failed to care for himself, and (6) four examples of how others failed to care for him. For the coming week, he was asked to record and list four times when he showed care for himself. Among the four instances, Kent stated: "I cared enough to go to school, make up my tests, do these lessons, and go to see you.

Assignment No. 9. Seeing the Good

Having a positive attitude about things. When one fails to have this positive attitude, "You do bad things," "You don't care about yourself," "You don't look at things in a positive way," and "You tend to be pessimistic." When others fail to see the good in him, Kent listed four results: "I become upset," "I try to make others see the good in me," "I become discouraged," and " I try to prove them wrong." By the same token, he was asked to list what happens when he fails to see the good in himself and others, giving four reasons why "seeing the good is better than seeing the bad." For the coming week, Kent was asked to list four instances when he saw the good in himself and how he felt about each instance. He also had to list four instances when he saw bad in himself and how he felt about each instance. Among the benefits of this assignment Kent listed "I learned that I could easily be good."

Assignment No. 10. Forgiveness

Kent defined forgiveness as "To forget about something bad someone has done," relating this process to positive consequences to himself and others. Among past mistakes that he had to forgive, Kent listed: (1) smoking pot twice, (2) wrecking his motorcycle twice, (3) failing two tests, and (4) failing to qualify in his chosen sport. He was asked why others should forgive him if he could not forgive himself. His answers pertained to not making the same mistake twice and feeling "truly sorry." During the coming week, Kent was asked to list four instances of how he forgave himself and others and how he felt after he forgave. He was able to list four instances but failed to relate any feelings to them.

Assignment No. X. Respect for Parents

Kent expressed his positive feelings toward his mother in terms of "things" rather than feelings, and "restrictions" rather than affection and warmth. Kent did not feel as close to his father as he felt about his mother because he saw his father as "not understanding," but caring for Kent by buying things he wanted in spite of Kent's "rebelliousness." His behavior was related to forgiveness, but Kent admitted to not "wanting to forgive himself" lest he repeat the same destructive behavior. Here Kent admitted to "destroying a church" building but he did not elaborate. He was aware of the consequences of not respecting his parents and authorities. For the coming week, he had to list four examples of respect for authority: (1) "I went to school," (2) "I cleaned my room," (3) "I didn't smoke in school," and (4) "I did what my teachers said." For Kent, this assignment meant that "there are consequences" to defing authority, not only from my parents, but others also.

Assignment No. 11. Situations

The purpose of this assignment is to relate behavior to specific situations where the respondent was responsible for what happened (in those situations). Many acting-out juveniles externalize their behavior on external "situations," as if these situations happened without taking responsibility for their behavior in those situations. Kent was asked to distinguish between "helpful" and "hurtful" situations, listing four outcomes of behaving helpfully and four outcomes of behaving hurtfully. For the coming week, he was asked to list four helpful and four hurtful situations and their outcomes on him. Given the opportunity to choose between helpful and hurtful situations, he had to choose which situation he wanted (helpful).

Assignment No. 12. Actions and Decisions

Kent rehashed actions that got him into trouble in the past, adding a new one ("I got really drunk on New Year's Eve"). Among the actions that did him some good, he listed making straight As, practicing his chosen sport, staying out of trouble in school, and deciding not to smoke at school with a friend. Letting his peers control and influence his actions was an issue that he dealt with by not associating with his old friends and making new, more positive friendships. He also listed helpful and hurtful actions and what they got him in return. He conceded that he enjoyed being helpful.

Assignment No. 13. Emotions and Feelings

Kent was asked to write as many feelings as he was aware of. He listed 21 feelings and was asked to give four reasons why feelings and emotions are important: (1) they let you express yourself, (2) they let everything that's building up in you out, (3) they show others how you feel about things, and (4) they help you make important decisions. Going into action rather than staying with his feelings lead him to "make bad decisions." Other questions in this assignment focused on separating feelings and emotions from actions. He answered these questions appropriately, concluding that feelings and emotions discriminate "right from wrong."

Assignment No. 14. Thinking

"Thinking helps you decide whether something is right or wrong." *What happens to you when you do not think? Give four results that come from your failure to think:* He answered in terms of doing something "stupid," "hurtful,""saying or doing the wrong thing," "making a bad decision," and "doing something impulsive." He had to list four outcomes of acting before or without thinking and poor versus good thinking. He had to list when poor thinking got him into trouble and when good thinking got him out of trouble. During the coming week, his task was to list four times when he used good thinking.

Ad Hoc Assignment No. 16. Rejection

After mailing these assignments to the author, Kent received a lengthy feedback letter where three issues were presented to him in three different assignments. In the first assignment, he was confronted with his need to be rejected and to reject. Apparently, questions in this assignment, written specifically for him, hit a receptive cord because he admitted to being involved in this process: "When I feel rejected, I do something stupid to forget about it."

Ad Hoc Assignment No. 17. Repetition

This issue confronted how he made the same mistake so often. The reasons for this repetions were: (1) I don't respect authority, (2) I am impulsive, (3) I always want to see if I can get away with something. He admitted that he "must take more time in making decisions and recognize when I do something wrong." Opposing authories was confronted as part of repetitive behavior that is harmful to him. Another repetitive pattern was treating others in ways that are designed to achieve rejection by not following the norm of reciprocity. Acting before thinking was another repetitive pattern that he had to confront. He answered that he was using thinking before acting much more now than he did in the past.

Ad Hoc Assignment No. 18. Sad Feelings

Issues of conditonal versus unconditional love were brought out in relation to his parents, including the responsibility of making himself "lovable" rather than "unlovable." Last, his continuous avoidance of sad feelings was brought out and he admitted to it readily: "I do something to avoid the sadness." *When your mother cries, you:* "usually do something that keeps her preoccupied so that she will avoid the sadness." *I don't cry because:* "I feel that it is a sign of weakness. . . . I don't want people to think I'm weak." Eventually, he came around to admit that "Sometimes crying is a sign of strength."

Assignment No. 19. Putting It All Together

Asked what he learned from working on this workbook, Kent wrote: "I have become more aware of my problems and now I try to control them," admitting, however, that he still "did impulsive things." He had to change because he did not like himself as a person, was tired of hurting his parents, his life was going down hill, to become "more aware and responsible because my parents won't always be able to protect me." He learned from all assignments, but the one that was more difficult for him was the one on "Thinking." His goals were to go to college, get a job, get married, and achieve a high place in society."

From March (date of pre-test) to July of the same year (date of post-test), his profile showed a decrease in the Pd scale to the 75th percentile with a parallel increase to the same percentile on the Mf scale, and increased to the 65% on the Pt and Sc scales. The rest of the profile remained essentially unchanged. According to a letter from his parents, he had completed the school year successfully and was promoted to the next grade.

INDICATIONS/CONTRAINDICATIONS

Working at a distance from juveniles using DW and PDW involves certain dangers. An informed consent form (available from the Institute for Life Empowerment) and a pretest battery are minimum requirements for the application of PDW with juveniles.

The first danger relates to being conned. This manipulation can be seen through extreme obsiquousness and blind, uncritical compliance without relevant and open feedback. One way to break through this facade is to administer anger-related assignments as well as regular, pre-, during, and post-evaluations. The null hypothesis, that no change is taking place, inspite of their efforts, is extremely threatening to juveniles, and can be used from time to time whenever such a hypothesis is relevant and timely. Also, precautions must be taken to assure that assignments are completed by the respondent. Parents, teachers, counselors, or detention officers must make sure that the respondent and no one else is completing the assignments. If certain behavioral tasks are assigned, as many assignments do, an external observer needs to be enlisted to assure that the behavior reported in writing was paralled by actual behavior *in situ*.

RANGE OF APPLICATIONS

We do not yet know the limits and shortcomings of the PDW approach with juveniles. Certainly, to complete workbooks and their assignments, it would be helpful if juveniles were under controlled, structured conditions, with specific rules and outcomes for their behavior, either in detention, jail, or firm parental supervision. The latter is usually hard to come by, because if there had been firm and consistent limits to begin with, the acting-out would have not developed.

PDW and CAI offer two challenges for those who want to use this approach. The first challenge relates to applications of this approach with children. How young should a child be to profit by this approach? Most youngsters grow up with computers. However, the software (i.e., programmed workbooks), will need to be re-written to their level. How young a level? Thus far, he youngest patient who was administered the *Social Training Workbook* (L'Abate, 1992) was a bright 14-year-old girl who wrote massive assignments with great enthusiasm. She eventually graduated from college and has become a successful career woman on a 10-year follow-up.

CRITICAL ISSUES

The major issue in the use of PDW with juveniles is one of research. None of the workbooks described has as yet been subjected to rigorous evaluation. Only through rigorous research will we be able to find whether: (1) workbooks do produce the changes we expect of them; (2) certain types of juveniles will be more receptive to work in this fashion than other juveniles; or (3) any immediate outcome will last for at least two to three years after termination of treatment.

Evidence reviewed elsewhere suggest that writing and especially PDW could be considered as a cost-effective way to reach a large number of people on a preventive basis. A major issue in this regard is feedback. Is it necessary? It may not be necessary with fairly functioning undergraduates, but it might become necessary if not vital with extreme cases where acting out may reach murderous proportions. With recent advances in computerized essay analysis, this problem, however, can be solved. There is no technological barrier to the creation of such feedback. There is a need for more evaluation of which workbooks are most useful for which kinds of problems.

Recently, Ben-Porath (1997) reviewed the use of personality assessment instruments in empirically guided treatment planning, summarizing a variety of reasons for the need to construct a whole new kind of assessment instruments to prescribe treatment. This viewpoint parallels similar arguments made in relation to the use of PDW in psychotherapy and prevention. L'Abate (1990, 1991, 1992, 1997a, 1997b, 1997c, 1999) has argued that as long as psychological treatment is based solely on the spoken medium, it will be very expensive to validate what therapists did or said and what they think they did or said. One would have to tape-record what was said in the therapy session, transcribe it, and eventually code it for classification. This process, although relevant and important, is limited to a handful of researchers who have the tenacity and motivation, including grant money, to verify the validity of the therapeutic process and link it to an assessment instrument. Nonetheless, linking evaluation with the spoken medium is difficult, expensive, and limited to those few who receive grants to research this area.

To support these arguments in favor of using the written word as a much more specific way to intervene and to link evaluation with treatment, a variety of workbooks that are isomorphic with their corresponding assessment instruments were developed. To date, there are workbooks for the 15 Content Scales of MMPI-2 (L'Abate, 1992), including an assignment derived from the scale on treatment resistance that preceded this chapter (Table 4.1).

The matching of homework assignments recognizes the importance of individual characteristics in the overall functioning of juveniles and their families. With individuals, these assignments can be administered in cases of co-morbidity, where one clinical condition is treated through the verbal, face-to-face approach, while the other condition can be treated through PDW or CAI. The latter allow more precise tailor-making of preventive or therapeutic approaches than it is possible verbally.

As with all the workbooks provided by the Institute for Life Empowerment (ILE), qualified (i.e., licensed or certified) professionals using them should make extra copies of them as needed. When converting these workbooks to computer use, or to make extra copies, professionals can draw extra lines after each question to allow space for respondents to answer questions. The number of lines should be based on the length of the expected answer. Otherwise, respondents could be asked to number their written answers on separate sheets of paper to match the corresponding questions given to them.

IMPLICATIONS FOR EVALUATION
AND CONCLUSION

All these workbooks point toward the need to construct a whole new class of assessment instruments that are constructed to encompass not only the old standby criteria of *diagnosis* and *prediction* but that must include also a third criterion of *prescription* (L'Abate, 1990, 1992, 1997b, 1997d, 1999). One example of such instrument is the *Problems in Relationships Scale and Workbook* made up of 240 items to cover 20 dimensions of couple relationships matched with 20 lessons derived from those lessons (L'Abate, 1992). The discrepancy score between partners was correlated significantly with the Dyadic Adjustment Scale, among other significant correlations with the NEO, the Self-Other Profile Chart, and an Adlerian lifestyle test (McMahan, 1998).

One can take any assessment instrument and develop from its profile a matching programmed workbook. The workbooks summarized in this chapter and listed in Table 4.1 demonstrate that given any evaluated and even non-evaluated dimension, it is possible to develop a matching series of assignments for any area or dimension covered by the instrument or by the referral question (L'Abate, 1992, 1998).

REFERENCES

Allport, G.W. (1942). *The use of personal documents in psychological science.* New York: Social Science Research Council.

Beck, A.T. (1976). *Cognitive therapy and the emotional disorders.* New York: Meridian Press.

Ben-Porath, Y.S. (1997). Use of personality assessment instruments in empirically guided treatment planning. *Psychological Assessment, 9,* 361–367.

Brand, A.G. (1989). *The psychology of writing: The affective experience.* New York: Greenwood Press.

Burns, D.A., & Nolen-Hoeksema, S.K. (1992). Therapeutic empathy and recovery from depression in cognitive-behavioral therapy: A structural equation model. *Journal of Consulting and Clinical Psychology, 60,* 441–449.

Butcher, J. (in press). *Psychological treatment planning inventory: Test manual and interpretative guide.* San Antonio, TX: Psychological Corporation.

Clements, D.H. (1986). Effects of Logo and CAI environments on cognition and creativity. *Journal of Educational Psychology, 78,* 309–318.

Clements, D.H., & Gullo, D.F. (1984). Effects of computer programming on young children's cognition. *Journal of Educational Psychology, 76,* 1051–1058.

Conoley, C.W., Padula, M.A., Payton, D.S., & Daniels, J.A. (1994). Predictors of client implementation of counselor recommendations: Match with problems, difficulty level, and building on client strengths. *Journal of Counseling Psychology, 41,* 3–7.

Diets, B. (1988). *Life after loss: A personal guide to dealing with death, divorce, job change, and relocation.* Tucson, AZ: Fisher Books.

Donnelly, D.A., & Murray, E.J. (1991). Cognitive and emotional changes in written essays and therapy interviews. *Journal of Social and Clinical Psychology, 10,* 334–350.

Eckhardt, C.I., & Deffenbacher, J.L. (1995). Diagnosis of anger disorders. In H. Kassinove (Ed.), *Anger disorders: Definition, diagnosis, and treatment* (pp. 27–47). Philadelphia: Taylor & Francis.

Ellis, A. (1965). Some use of printed, written and recorded words in psychotherapy. In L. Pearson (Ed.), *The use of written communication in psychotherapy* (pp. 21–29). Springfield, IL: Thomas.

Esterling, B.A., Antoni, M.H., Fletcher, M.A., Margulies, S., & Schneiderman, N. (1994). Emotional disclosure through writing or speaking modulates latent. Epstein-Burr virus antibody titers. *Journal of Consulting and Clinical Psychology, 62,* 130–140.

Esterling, B.A., Antoni, M.H., Kumar, M., & Schneiderman, N. (1990). Emotional repression, stress disclosure responses, and the Epstein-Barr viral capsid antigen titers. *Psychosomatic Medicine, 52,* 397–410.

Esterling, B.A., L'Abate, L., Murray, E.J., & Pennebaker, J.W. (1999). Empirical foundations for writing in prevention and psychotherapy: Mental and physical health outcomes. *Clinical Psychology Review, 19,* 79–96.

Farber, D.J. (1953). Written communication in psychotherapy. *Psychiatry, 16,* 365–374.

Faria, G., & Belohlavek, N. (1984). Treating female survivors of adolescent incest. *Social Casework: Journal of Contemporary Social Work, 65,* 465–471.

Farley, J.W., & Farley, S.L. (1987). Interactive writing and gifted children: Communication through literacy. *Journal for the Education of the Gifted, 10,* 99–106.

Feindler, E.L. (1995). Ideal treatment package for children and adolescents with anger disorders. In H. Kassinove (Ed.), *Anger disorders: Definition, diagnosis, and treatment* (pp. 173–195). Philadelphia: Taylor & Francis.

Francis, L.J., & Pennebaker, J.W. (1992). Putting stress into words: The impact of writing on physiological, absentee, and self-reported emotional well-being measures. *American Journal of Health Promotion, 6,* 280–287.

Fuchel, J.C. (1985). Writing poetry can enhance the psychotherapeutic process: Observations and examples. *Arts in Psychotherapy, 12,* 89–93.

Graves, P.L. (1984). Life event and art. *International Review of Psychoanalysis, 11,* 355–365.

Greenberg, M.A., & Stone, A.A. (1992). *Psychological aspects of depression: Toward a cognitive-interpersonal integration.* New York: Wiley.

Harrower, M. (1972). *The therapy of poetry.* Springfield, IL: Thomas.

Houge, A., Liddle, H.A., & Rowe, C. (1996). Treatment adherence process research in family therapy: A rationale and some practical guidelines. *Psychotherapy, 33,* 332–345.

Jordan, K. (1999). *Programmed distance writing: Divorce adjustment for children.* Paper submitted for publication. Department of Counselor Education, University of Colorado at Denver.

Kelley, P. (1990). *The uses of writing in psychotherapy.* New York: Haworth.

L'Abate, L. (1986). *Systematic family therapy.* New York: Brunner/Mazel.

L'Abate, L. (1990). *Building family competence: Primary and secondary prevention strategies.* Newbury Park, CA: Sage.

L'Abate, L. (1991). The use of writing in psychotherapy. *American Journal of Psychotherapy, 45,* 87–98.

L'Abate, L. (1992). *Programmed writing: A self-administered approach for interventions with individuals, couples, and families.* Pacific Grove, CA: Brooks/Cole.

L'Abate, L. (1993). A family theory of impulsivity. In W.G. McCown, J.L. Johnson, & M.B. Shure (Eds.), *The impulsive client: Theory, research, and treatment* (pp. 93–118). Washington, DC: American Psychological Association.

L'Abate, L. (1994). *A theory of personality development.* New York: Wiley.

L'Abate, L. (1997a). Distance writing and computer-assisted training. In S.R. Sauber (Ed.), *Managed mental health care: Major diagnostic and treatment approaches* (pp. 133–163). Bristol, PA: Brunner/Mazel.

L'Abate, L. (1997b). *Manual: Distance writing and computer-assisted interventions in mental health.* Atlanta, GA: Institute for Life Empowerment (ILE).

L'Abate, L. (1997c). The paradox of change: Better them than us! In R.S. Sauber (Ed.), *Managed mental health care: Major diagnostic and treatment approaches* (pp. 40–66). Bristol, PA: Brunner/Mazel.

L'Abate, L. (1997d). *The self in the family: A classification of personality, criminality, and psychopathology.* New York: Wiley.

L'Abate, L. (1999). Taking the bull by the horns: Beyond words in psychological interventions *The Family Journal: Counseling and Therapy with Couples and Families, 7.*

L'Abate, L., Boyce, J., Fraizer, L.M., & Russ, D. (1992). Programmed writing: Research in progress. *Comprehensive Mental Health Care, 2,* 45–62.

L'Abate, L., & Harrison, M.G. (1992). Treating codependency. In L. L'Abate, J.E. Farrar, & D.A. Serritella (Eds.), *Handbook of differential treatments for addictions* (pp. 286–306). Boston: Allyn & Bacon.

L'Abate, L., & Torem, M.S. (in press). *Distance writing and computer-assisted interventions in psychiatry and mental health.* Samford, CT: ABLEX.

Lahey, B.B., Frick, P.J., Loeber, R., Tannenbaum, B.A., Van Horn, Y., & Christ, M.A.G. (1990). *Oppositional conduct disorder: I. A meta-analysis review.* Unpublished manuscript. University of Georgia, Athens.

Landsman, T. (1951). The therapeutic use of written materials. *American Psychologist, 5,* 347.

Lemberg, R. (1994). Couples journaling technique: A brief report. *Family Journal: Counseling and Therapy for Couples and Families, 2,* 64–65.

Leucht, C.A., & Tan, S.Y. (1996). "Homework" and psychotherapy: Making between-session assignments more effective. *Journal of Psychology and Christianity, 15,* 258–269.

Lindahl, M.W. (1988). Letters to Tammy: A technique useful in the treatment of a sexually abused child. *Child Abuse & Neglect, 12,* 417–420.

Lynam, D.R. (1997). Pursuing the psychopath: Capturing the fledging psychopath in a nomological net. *Journal of Abnormal Psychology, 106,* 425–438.

Mazza, N. (1981). The use of poetry in treating the troubled adolescent. *Adolescence, 16,* 403–408.

McMahan, O. (1998). *Programmed writing, personality variables, and couples' adjustment.* Unpublished Ph.D. dissertation, Department of Counseling and Psychological Services, Georgia State University, Atlanta.

Messinger, E. (1952). Auto-elaboration: An adjuvant technique in practices of psychotherapy. *Disorders of the Nervous System, 13,* 339–344.

Morey, L.C., & Henry, W. (1994). Personality assessment inventory. In M.E. Maruish (Ed.), *The use of psychological testing for treatment planning and outcome assessment* (pp. 185–216). Hillsdale, NJ: Erlbaum.

Murray, E.J., Lamnin, A., & Carver, C. (1989). Emotional expression in written essays and psychotherapy. *Journal of Social and Clinical Psychology, 8,* 414–429.

Murray, E.J., & Segal, D.L. (1994). Emotional processing in vocal and written expression of feelings about traumatic experiences. *Journal of Traumatic Stress, 7,* 391–401.

Nau, D.S. (1997). Andy writes to his amputated leg: Utilizing letter writing as an interventive technique in brief therapy. *Journal of Family Psychotherapy, 8,* 1–12.

Neimeyer, R.A., & Feixas, G. (1990). The role of homework and skill acquisition in the outcome of group cognitive therapy for depression. *Behavior Therapy, 21,* 281–292.

Pearson, L. (Ed.). (1965). *The use of written communication in psychotherapy.* Springfield, IL: Thomas.

Pennebaker, J.W. (1993). Putting stress into words: Health, linguistic and therapeutic implications. *Behavior Research and Therapy, 31,* 539–548.

Pennebaker, J.W. (1997). *Opening up: The healing power of confiding in others.* New York: Guilford Press.

Pennebaker, J.W., & Beall, S.K. (1986). Confronting a traumatic event: Toward an understanding of inhibition and disease. *Journal of Abnormal Psychology, 95,* 274–281.

Pennebaker, J.W., Kiecolt-Glaser, J., & Glaser, R. (1988). Disclosure of traumas and immune function: Health implications for psychotherapy. *Journal of Consulting and Clinical Psychology, 56,* 239–245.

Petrie, K.J., Booth, R.J., Pennebaker, J.W., Davison, K.P., & Thomas, M.G. (1995). Disclosure of trauma and immune response to a hepatitis B vaccination program. *Journal of Consulting and Clinical Psychology, 67,* 787–792.

Phillips, E.L., Gershenson, J., & Lyons, S. (1977). On time-limited writing therapy. *Psychological Reports, 41,* 707–712.

Phillips, E.L., & Wiener, D.N. (1965). *Short-term psychotherapy and structured behavior change.* New York: McGraw-Hill.

Progoff, I. (1975). *At a journal workshop.* New York: Dialogue House Library.

Riordan, R.J. (1996). Scriptotherapy: Therapeutic writing as a counseling adjunct. *Journal of Counseling & Development, 74,* 263–269.

Rothenberg, A. (1987). Self-destruction, self-creation, and psychotherapy. *American Journal of Social Psychiatry, 7,* 69–77.

Scandura, J.M. (1984). Cognitive instructional psychology: System requirements and research methodology. *Journal of Computer-Based Instruction, 11,* 32–41.

Schultheis, G.M. (1998). *Brief therapy homework planner.* New York: Wiley.

Scinto, L.F.M. (1986). *Written language and psychological development.* Orlando, FL: Academic Press.

Shelton, J.L., & Ackerman, J.M. (1974). *Homework in counseling and psychotherapy: Examples of systematic assignments for therapeutic use by mental health professionals.* Springfield, IL: Thomas.

Simon, L.M.J. (1998). Does criminal offender treatment work? *Applied & Preventive Psychology, 7,* 137–159.

Smyth, J.M. (1998). Written emotional expression: Effect sizes, outcome types, and moderating variables. *Journal of Consulting and Clinical Psychology, 66,* 174–180.

Spielberger, C.D., Reheiser, E.R., & Sydeman, S.J. (1995). Measuring the experience, expression, and control of anger. In H. Kassinove (Ed.), *Anger disorders: Definition, diagnosis, and treatment* (pp. 49–67). Philadelphia: Taylor & Francis.

Watzlawick, P., Weakland, J., & Fisch, R. (1974). *Change: Principles of problem formation and problem solution.* New York: Norton.

Webster, C.D., & Jackson, M.A. (Eds.). (1997). *Impulsivity: Theory, assessment, and treatment.* New York: Guilford Press.

Weeks, G., & L'Abate, L. (1982). *Paradoxical psychotherapy: Theory and practice with individuals, couples, and families.* New York: Brunner/Mazel.

PART TWO

ADVENTURE-BASED TECHNIQUES

CHAPTER 5

Wilderness Therapy for Adolescents

DENE S. BERMAN and JENNIFER DAVIS-BERMAN

INTRODUCTION

IT SEEMS that a fascination with and interest in the wilderness for its curative and restorative powers has been a central and compelling part of the human experience since the early part of the twentieth century. The story of Joe Knowles, the Nature Man, exemplifies this fascination. In 1913, Joe Knowles stripped off all of his clothes and entered the Maine woods, where he was to live, with no clothing, food, or human contact for 60 days. This story so captivated the public that the *Boston Post*'s circulation grew to 400,000, with an equal number of people congregating at a rally in Boston to greet Joe when he emerged in good health. Joe's adventures made the front page of nearly every newspaper in the United States. Joe was to replicate this endeavor in the Siskiyou Mountains of Oregon and the Adirondacks of New York. He even wrote a best-selling book about his adventures, which was called the greatest local story in San Francisco since the great fire (Davis-Berman & Berman, 1994). It was only the outbreak of the First World War that relegated Joe's story to obscurity. Contemporary interest in nature, adventure travel, and the perceived healing qualities of being in the wilderness continues, as reflected in popular culture (e.g., Bryson, 1998; Krakauer, 1997).

This chapter explores and describes a program designed to deal with troubled adolescents that capitalizes on this fascination with the wilderness. First, we place wilderness therapy programs in context by examining their history and the philosophy behind their development. After describing early programs, we will review some of the literature in this field. Finally, we will present and discuss elements of a model program. Although not a duplication of our own wilderness therapy program (Berman & Davis-Berman 1989, 1991), the discussion of a model program is based on our program. An expeditionary type program, our wilderness therapy program and our experiences in this area form the basis for our thoughts and perspectives. This chapter ends with a discussion of some critical issues in the field. Although not meant to be a cookbook approach, we have tried to be detailed and concrete enough to inspire interested clinicians to think about participating in wilderness therapy programs.

HISTORICAL BACKGROUND

During the colonization of the New World by early European explorers, there existed the conception of the wilderness as dangerous, harsh, and threatening (Nash, 1982). Everything was uncertain and danger seemed to lurk around every corner. This perceived threat clearly helped shape these early explorer's views of Native Americans who were seen by early settlers as heathen, deficient, savage creatures who were in need of redemption. Thus, a common theme during this time was the need to conquer and control the wilderness and all that lived therein. Implicit in this framework was the belief that the White man was superior, and had the right to overtake people and environments (Huth, 1990).

Following the initial occupation of the colonies in the New World, perceptions of threat diminished. Out of the conception of the wilderness as dangerous grew notions about the wilderness as romantic. Surely, one of the most influential proponents of this conception was Thoreau, who illuminated the beauty and restorative powers of the wilderness for ordinary readers (Krutch, 1982). Thoreau even went so far as to draw a parallel between walking in the wilderness and the divine when he spoke of *sauntering* as referring to those who trek to the Holy Land (Thoreau, 1906). Further, he drew parallels between confronting physical frontiers and emotional growth when he said: "The frontiers are not east or west, north or south, but wherever a man *fronts* a fact, though that fact be his neighbor, there is a wilderness . . . between him and *it* [emphases in original]" (Krutch, 1982, p. 81).

To be sure, Thoreau was not the only voice in the movement to revere and preserve the wilderness. During this time, the popularity of outdoor writers grew, and general interest in protecting and enjoying natural areas burgeoned. Consider the writings of James Fenimore Cooper, William Cullen Bryant, and Washington Irving or the paintings of Fredrick E. Church, Albert Bierstadt, and Thomas Moran. These and other voices reflected a movement often referred to as *romanticism* (Nash, 1982). Romanticism reflected the idea that there were aesthetic values in the wilderness, rather than the previous focus on the taming or exploitation of what was wild.

The early part of the nineteenth century found increasing controversy as advocates fought for the preservation of the land. Central figures like John Muir emerged at this time, as well as organizations like the Sierra Club and the National Park Service (Wellman, 1987). Thus, conceptions of the wilderness rapidly moved from viewing it as a place to be feared and conquered to a place to be protected and revered. As these beliefs began to change, people began to seek to have experiences in the wilderness environment. These beliefs were reflected in the movement to preserve the wilderness through the establishment of parks, like Yellowstone (2,000,000 acres, established in 1872) and the Adirondacks (715,000 acres, established in 1885).

In the mid-1800s, camping as recreation emerged, through the leadership of Thomas Hiram Holding (A. Mitchell, Robberson, & Obley, 1977). Early camps were privately funded and were based on the notion that the out-of-doors was restorative. The Good Will Farm for Boys and Camp Baldhead were examples of camps that tried to capitalize on the healing aspects of the out-of-doors.

Implicit in these programs were the ideas that self-esteem and positive behavior can improve with exposure to the out-of-doors (Gibson, 1973; A. Mitchell et al., 1977). The notion of wilderness as therapeutic was further developed through the tent therapy programs in the early 1900s.

Developed almost as an accident, these tent therapy programs emerged as a result of overcrowding at the Manhattan State Hospital. Due to lack of space, psychiatric clients were housed on the hospital lawn during a tuberculosis epidemic. After the summer, the program was discontinued. However, the clients showed dramatic improvement after being housed outdoors; some improved enough for discharge (*American Journal of Insanity*, 1906, 1910).

This early tent therapy experience helped form the foundation for the therapeutic camping movement which is still with us today. During the first half of the 1900s, camps were developed that included recreation and socialization as goals. Camp Ahmek focused on socialization, cooperation, and role modeling (Dimock & Hendry, 1939). Other camps during this time were even more therapeutic in their approach, using psychiatrists and social workers as consultants (Scheidlinger & Scheidlinger, 1947).

Subsequent to these early therapeutic programs, but still prior to 1950, camps increased and grew in the sophistication of their therapeutic programming. The University of Michigan Fresh Air Camp utilized diagnosis, treatment plans, and psychotherapy (Morse, 1957). The Salesmanship Club of Dallas, still in existence today, tried to incorporate troubled kids into their program. They focused on behavioral change and emotional growth (Smith, 1958).

Finally, one cannot discuss modern therapeutic camping without mentioning Outward Bound, founded by Kurt Hahn in the early 1940s to bolster the inner resources of merchant marines. The program came to America in 1962 with the opening of the Colorado Outward Bound School. It has since grown to have schools all over the world. Early Outward Bound courses included work with ropes, physical conditioning, climbing, and camping (Miner & Boldt, 1981) to encourage personal growth and interpersonal skills (Katz & Kolb, 1967).

Outward Bound is certainly a renowned outdoor program, with offerings throughout the world. Its early conceptualization was probably less therapeutic in its orientation, and was epitomized by the phrase, the Mountains Speak for Themselves (MST). In other words, the wilderness environment was healing and restorative in and of itself, thus there was little need for reflection or therapy. Later, Outward Bound utilized reflection and debriefing with much more frequency. They have since developed specific courses for at-risk and identified risk populations, thus, moving some aspects of their program into the therapeutic realm (e.g., James, 1993; Katz & Kolb, 1967; Miner & Boldt, 1981).

CURRENT PROGRAMS

Recent years has seen the continued popularity of therapeutic wilderness programs for youth. Outward Bound has grown and expanded, and offers a wide variety of therapeutic programs. To learn more about the variety of existing wilderness therapy programs, we conducted a national survey of 31 wilderness therapy programs (Davis-Berman, Berman, & Capone, 1994).

It is interesting to note that the majority of these therapeutic programs serve adolescents (Davis-Berman et al., 1994). When administrators were asked to describe their programs in this survey, they had difficulty precisely describing the therapeutic methodologies used in the programs. Many mentioned the use of group therapy, and most talked about the use of the wilderness environment as a metaphor for real-life events and relationships. When asked about the credentials of staff working in these wilderness programs, inconsistent findings emerged. Some programs utilized more professional staff, with Master's degrees, while most required Bachelor's degrees or less. The activities utilized in these programs ranged from backpacking expeditions, to canoeing, to ropes courses. Some programs were hours long, while others were residential programs, months in length.

A more recent study (Friese, Hendee, & Kinziger, 1998) started their survey with a database of 700 wilderness experience programs (WEPs), organizations that take customers into the wilderness for personal growth, therapy, leadership, or organizational development purposes. They identified 14 counseling programs, which they summarized as focusing on correcting behavior, utilizing group feedback and the milieu, and where the leadership style involved active engagement of clients. Thus, counseling or therapy programs do not constitute the majority of outdoor programs, but are nevertheless significant and worthy of examination.

Before presenting a model for a wilderness therapy program in this chapter, we need to set the stage and identify the characteristics of wilderness programming that might be considered to be therapeutic. In other words, what is it about the use of the wilderness in these current programs that is therapeutic? Following this discussion, we will briefly examine some of the outcome data generated from current programs.

CONCEPTIONS OF CHANGE

As varied as the therapeutic wilderness programs are the models for how change occurs in these programs. Consistent with the emerging belief in the healing properties of the wilderness, we can identify qualities of this relationship that have been attributed to the therapeutic nature of this environment. Some programs, like the early Outward Bound MST model focused on the wilderness as therapeutic in and of itself. Other programs focus on the milieu, with its qualities to facilitate the process of growth and change among those who spend time there (Davis-Berman & Berman, 1994). Some of the key elements in this regard include the ability of the wilderness to impose natural consequences, the need for cooperation, the need for enhanced communication, the challenge of an unfamiliar environment, physical fatigue, positive interactions and relationships with authority figures, and the healing aspect of a beautiful, pristine environment (Davis-Berman et al., 1994). Others write of the ability of the wilderness environment to facilitate pushing out of the comfort zones (Nadler, 1995) and of the wilderness as a metaphor for many life events and struggles (Gass, 1993). More recently, narrative (Luckner & Nadler, 1997) and solution-focused (Gass & Gillis, 1995) approaches have been discussed in relation to adventure counseling.

Regardless of the theoretical model that one uses, we would make a distinction between those programs that are therapy, per se, and those programs that are therapeutic. This distinction is akin to psychological discussions about therapy as a planned process, designed to meet specific treatment goals, with measurable objectives, and efficacious techniques (Berman & Davis-Berman, 1995).

In examining wilderness therapy programs, some critical questions emerge. First, how does one distinguish between therapy programs and therapeutic programs? Related to this distinction, what are the qualifications of the staff in each of these types of programs? What are the therapeutic modalities utilized in these programs? Finally, do these programs make a difference, and if so, in what ways do they facilitate change in participants? It is to this latter question that we now turn.

Outcome Data

Early attempts to document the ability of wilderness therapy to change lives were largely anecdotal (e.g., Barley, 1972). However, some reasonably well-designed research studies began to appear in the literature at the same time (Davis-Berman & Berman, 1994).

Generally, studies have indicated that negative behaviors tend to decrease following participation in wilderness therapy programs, as compared to adolescents who were not in these programs (e.g., Berman & Davis-Berman, 1989; Chenery, 1981; Krieger, 1973; Shniderman, 1974). Probably the most consistent change has been found in self-esteem or self-concept, with these measures increasing following participation in a wilderness therapy program (e.g., Berman & Davis-Berman, 1989; Kaplan, 1974).

More recent evaluation has supported these results in both adolescent and adult populations. The impact on participants on a transatlantic sailing voyage was assessed. The results suggested that participants reported an increase in self-esteem and coping ability as compared to a comparison group (Norris & Weinman, 1996). Very positive results were also found in an outdoor program affiliated with an outpatient mental health facility. Participants were clients receiving outpatient services, many of whom had serious, chronic psychiatric diagnoses. Following a nine-week adventure program consisting of daily adventure activities, the treatment group demonstrated significant changes. Significant increases in self-efficacy, physical self-efficacy and self-esteem were found, as compared to no change in the comparison group (Kelley, Coursey, & Selby, 1997). Self-efficacy was used as a framework in yet another recent evaluation. Following participation in a wilderness program, behaviorally disordered adolescents displayed a significant increase in cooperation, especially in their school settings (Sachs & Miller, 1992).

Applying the use of the wilderness to working with families and troubled teens, Bandoroff (1993) found that family functioning, adolescent behavior, and self-esteem improved among those participating in the wilderness program as compared to 39 comparison families. Increases in self esteem and self concept were again seen in a study of twelfth grade students. Attitudes toward the environment did not change in the sample (Gillett, Thomas, Skok, & McLaughlin, 1991).

As has always been the case, much work has been done on the evaluation of the impact of wilderness programs on delinquent populations. The recent research continues this trend, and presents mixed results. Castellano and Soderstrom (1992) examined the impact of a wilderness program on recidivism. Interestingly, they found a decrease in the wilderness group as compared to a control group at one year post-test. However, this difference was not apparent at two years. Another study compared standard probation with an outdoor adventure program for delinquents. The results suggested that there were no differences in recidivism between the two groups (Elrod & Minor, 1992).

Despite the fact that the number of studies has sharply increased, the evaluation of these programs has still been criticized as inadequate (Davis-Berman & Berman, 1994; Gillis, 1995), however, recent meta-analyses (Cason & Gillis, 1994; Priest, 1992) are moving evaluation to a more global level. In their analysis, Cason and Gillis examined 43 adventure oriented studies of programs serving adolescents. Following treatment, the participants were found to be more internal in their locus of control. Adventure programs were also associated with better grades, more positive attitudes and increased self-concept.

Other examples of this type of analysis include Priests' (1992) attempt to examine the actual dimensions of an adventure experience, in order to move toward model construction. Additionally, a recent meta-analysis has been done that attempts to examine the impact of adventure-based programs across studies on the dimensions of: self-concept, leadership, academic, personality, interpersonal, and adventure orientation. Participants of adventure programs were found to change in a positive direction on these dimensions, with change remaining stable at follow-up (Hattie, Marsh, Neill, & Richards, 1997).

These types of studies bring us closer to addressing some of the earlier identified problems in the literature like defining and understanding the process of wilderness programs (Davis-Berman & Berman, 1994). Increased specificity and further depth in research is essential if the field of adventure therapy is to grow and is to receive mainstream acceptance. However, numerous dissertations, and work from established scholars lead us quickly toward the goal of presenting wilderness or adventure therapy as an effective methodology. In fact, a recent review of meta-analyses on outdoor education has concluded (Neill & Richards, 1998):

> Overall, these studies, representing 12,000 participants, show that outdoor education has a small to medium impact on typically measured outcomes such as changes in self-concept, self-confidence and locus of control. These effects seem not only to be retained over time but to increase still further, which is impressive. The most effective programs are longer, involve adult-age participants and to be [sic] conducted by some particular organisations. (p. 2)

There are other aspects of this treatment approach that lend themselves for adoption besides outcome data. These include the fact that wilderness therapy may represent a less restrictive environment than other residential programs (Davis-Berman & Berman, 1994). Additionally, adolescents are often difficult to work with in traditional settings—either outpatient or inpatient. In order to succeed in traditional therapy, adolescents must be attentive, verbal, and cooperative in an office setting. They are usually asked to be open and disclose without any prior experience with the therapist geared toward gaining and building trust (Saffer & Naylor, 1987). Often adolescents with problems like attention deficit disorder (American Psychiatric Association [APA], 1994) have difficulty focusing on verbal stimuli and may struggle with traditional talk therapy. With adventure or wilderness therapy, adolescents can be exposed to active, action-oriented methods. Some can use these experiences as a catalyst, while others may become sophisticated with the use of metaphors based in their experiences (Gass, 1993).

With the obstacles to change inherent in traditional therapy, and the appeal of action-oriented approaches, we believe that it is important to pursue alternatives. Therefore, it is as a result of our belief in the power of wilderness programs that we next turn to a description of a model program.

DESIGNING A MODEL PROGRAM

PROGRAM CONSIDERATIONS

Many types of programs can be designed, from a partial day ropes course designed as an adjunct to a school-based program to a month-long component of a residential program. While we have conducted a number of different types of programs, the ones we are most comfortable with are backpacking expeditions at least one week in length. The model program we will be discussing will lean toward the elements of programs with which we are most experienced and comfortable.

Our own program, the Wilderness Therapy Program, is a component of our counseling practice. Through the Wilderness Therapy Program, we conduct counseling programs primarily for youth, in settings that include wilderness areas and rivers. The Wilderness Therapy Program also conducts training for counselors and outdoor leaders, as well as consultations to, and contract programs for educational, social service, and juvenile justice organizations.

Consideration of a wilderness therapy program is similar to designing any type of therapy program in that planning needs to take into account variables such as the client characteristics and needs, the goals and objectives of the program, the modality of treatment, treatment planning, as well as specifics about how the therapy will be conducted. Each of these topics will be covered in this section. Two other topics that will be discussed are crisis intervention and termination of the program.

CLIENT CHARACTERISTICS AND SELECTION CRITERIA

Although we are often tempted to design our programs to be all inclusive, excluding no one, we must resist this temptation in a wilderness therapy program. Through our experience, we have discovered that the needs and characteristics of adolescents in outpatient and inpatient settings vary widely. Further, the qualities and needs of those in the juvenile justice system are also different. As such, we recommend that programs make a decision to offer wilderness and adventure therapy programs for homogeneous groups. For example, one program or trip could be designed and offered for adolescents in outpatient counseling, while another trip or program could be planned for adolescents in residential treatment settings.

We have found that wilderness therapy experiences seem to be most helpful to adolescents who are depressed, withdrawn, and have difficulty relating to others (Berman & Anton, 1988; Davis-Berman & Berman, 1989). We have also had a great deal of success in working with adolescents who have trouble controlling their acting-out behavior. With both of these populations, in particular, and all potential participants, it is critical to screen clients for their potential to harm self or others. Nevertheless, we advocate that programs carefully consider who attends their programs, and that each program develop exclusionary criteria. In our own program, we have excluded adolescents who were actively psychotic, those with severe attention deficit disorder, and those with retardation. We have also attempted to exclude those who might be a serious threat to harm themselves or someone else. The notion of excluding some potential participants does not imply passing judgment. Rather, it suggests that programs must recognize the power of the group, the impact that each participant has on the functioning of the group, and the expertise of the therapists. As such, decisions must be made with the whole group in mind.

Although there are some programs that take participants against their will, we advocate for voluntary participation with informed consent. Excessive hostility and resentment about being forced to participate will be counter-productive. Extreme examples of programs that force adolescents into participation set the stage for potentially tragic results, such as the deaths that have occurred in wilderness therapy programs or programs that utilize more of a boot camp philosophy (e.g., Carpenter, 1995; Griffin, 1995; Matthews, 1991).

GOALS

Prior to the decision to implement a wilderness therapy program, the issue of goals must be carefully considered. If the setting is an agency, how do the goals of the agency mesh with the goals one might have in implementing a wilderness program? If the wilderness program will be free-standing, what are the specific goals to be met through this program? Why not stay with a traditional program? What does the use of the wilderness have to offer the clients that a traditional program does not have?

   In broadly construing goals for wilderness therapy, we have suggested that wilderness therapy programs are a good fit in programs whose philosophies include the following (Berman & Davis-Berman, 1991, p. 375):

1. Service delivery systems for adolescents should encompass a range of settings.
2. Services should be provided in the least restrictive environment.
3. Counseling services for adolescents should be flexible and not necessarily constrained by office walls.
4. Some adolescents are in need of situations in which consequences for behavior are immediate, naturally occurring, or contingent on one's behavior.

   Another critical issue to be dealt with in developing program goals is the extent to which the wilderness program is a therapy program or a therapeutic program. Therapy and therapeutic programs are different, and as such require different structures and staffing patterns (Davis-Berman & Berman, 1993, 1994). Therapy programs require diagnoses, treatment plans, and certified therapists, while therapeutic programs may not necessarily require this level of credentialing (Berman & Davis-Berman, 1995; Berman, Davis-Berman, Chamberlain, & Dandaneau, 1997). Obviously, the decision whether or not to provide structured psychotherapy within the framework of the wilderness program is critical and sets the stage for all further program planning.

Finally, setting carefully thought-out goals is essential to program evaluation. Although it may seem premature to think about evaluation prior to even starting a program, it is precisely at this time that evaluation must be kept in mind (Davis-Berman & Berman, 1994). Goals should be carefully constructed. They must be concrete, easily understood, and operationalized. Finally, the criteria for successfully meeting the program goals must be explicitly stated.

ASSESSMENT AND TREATMENT PLANNING

Just as in therapy, an assessment of each participant is critical prior to the actual wilderness therapy experience. A clinical interview is essential for good treatment planning, and it is always helpful if other family members are involved. An attempt should be made to identify the client's strengths and weaknesses, treatment goals, and diagnosis, from the *DSM-IV* (APA, 1994). In those instances when our own staff is not able to conduct a screening interview, a release of information is obtained, and the client's therapist is contacted.

This assessment information forms the basis of the individual treatment plans that are essential to wilderness therapy. Ideally, the results and impressions gleaned from the clinical interviews are shared with the adolescent and his or her parents. In our program, we generally like to develop the treatment plans in a group setting. All of the program participants meet prior to the trip with their parents. At this meeting, each adolescent is asked to identify three or four goals that he or she would like to work on during the trip. They are then asked to rate how well they are currently functioning on this dimension. For instance, if an adolescent identified anger management as a goal, he or she would then be asked to rate the extent to which he or she was currently dealing with anger.

Following this disclosure, the parents have an opportunity to comment on the goals selected by their child and to suggest others. In setting measurable outcomes, one consideration is a goal attainment scale, thus the parents rate the extent to which they believe their child is currently meeting their goal. With a little negotiation, we have developed a treatment plan. Importantly, this plan has been developed in concert with parents. We also feel that by talking about these issues with all participants present, we begin to work on group formation. Participants begin to get to know each other, and an immediate atmosphere of openness and communication is established.

RANGES OF ACTIVITIES

Adventure and wilderness therapy programs utilize a very wide range of experiential modalities in their programs. Our national survey demonstrated that the variety of outdoor experiences was rich. A large number of programs utilized ropes courses. Others included backpacking, canoeing, climbing, horseback riding, biking, and experiential games (Davis-Berman et al., 1994). For a broader view of the range of outdoor activities used, and specifically the use of experiential games and initiatives, the reader is referred to Gass (1993) and Rohnke (1989, 1991).

The selection of the activities that will be used, and their sequence and position in your program are critical. In making these decisions, consider that the more intense, expeditionary programs are the ones that have been evaluated more frequently and show the most promise (Davis-Berman et al., 1994). These types of programs are able to capitalize on the richness and remoteness of the wilderness environment that ropes course programs do not. The power and intensity of the group is also more of a factor in expeditionary programs.

A further consideration regarding the type of activity involves a risk assessment (Berman & Davis-Berman, 1996). One approach to risk assessment is to look at the risks inherent in the population, assuming that some populations are more at risk for emotional crisis than others. Further, one needs to consider the counseling goals of the program, bearing in mind that programs that focus on the soul-searching, angst-producing components of therapy are more likely to contribute to the risk of crisis than are counseling programs aimed at growth-enhancement. Finally, one also needs to take into account the skills of the program leaders/therapists. While some therapists are skilled with more difficult clients, others may not have the experience or training to deal with at-risk or chronic clients. The same rationale can be used when considering the outdoor skills of leaders. Some leaders are trained and certified to teach activities as risky as white water kayaking, while hiking on a well-marked trail may challenge other leaders.

When we put all of these factors contributing to risk together—client characteristics, the intensity of therapy, the skills of the leaders—we have a better way of considering activities. For example, with less skilled leaders and clients at risk, the activities should involve less risk, in order to help clients maintain stability and avoid crisis. Or, with highly skilled staff, including therapists and outdoor leaders, with a backup staff that can be mobilized, if needed, the activities can be more challenging while still having reasonable assurance that crises can be averted.

Group Therapy

As suggested, the act of developing treatment plan goals as a group serves as an initial phase in group formation and therapy. When the actual trip begins, group therapy becomes a central part of the experience. Generally, we like to convene therapy sessions after lunch, before participants get too tired from hiking. Usually, the first group revolves around feelings about adjusting to the trip. The leader is also concerned with facilitating group formation and cohesion. During these initial sessions, the group leaders are quite active as therapists. As the trip progresses, problems, issues, or concerns become group tasks. Thus, the group becomes a vehicle for therapy, problem solving, and a model for living.

While on the trail, the group therapy seems to operate at two levels. First, the group becomes the metaphor for life and for relating to others. Participants work all things out within the group. They are also given immediate feedback as to how they relate and are perceived by the group. Additionally, traditional therapy issues are worked on in group therapy. For example, we might decide to focus on anger management for a group session. Thus, the group itself might be topical in nature. However, we are always integrating the behaviors, attitudes, and verbalizations of the participants as they complete the program. The wilderness does provide a therapeutic backdrop, and we are always observing and tracking participant progress.

Despite the fact that our program emphasizes the use of group therapy, participants are provided individual therapy as needed and desired. This can and does occur in the most unlikely of places—on a rock ledge, while walking down the trail, around a campfire at night. The good thing about being in the wilderness environment is that there is no place to hide. We are able to observe continually and approach an adolescent for an individual session immediately. We feel that this kind of intensity and timeliness of therapy greatly facilitates insight and change.

Another therapeutic tool that we use is journaling. In order to facilitate this process, we even suggest certain themes to be covered in the daily journals. Examples of themes might include trip goals, feelings about leaving home, feelings about interacting with others on the trip, maintaining change at home. The leaders model good writing habits by taking and recording progress notes on the group and individual therapy of each participant on a daily basis.

Good documentation is as important in a wilderness therapy program as it is in the clinic or office. We have tried bringing charts into the field with us, taking notes on a daily basis, and have also dictated notes into a small tape recorder. We have no specific preferences for the method for documentation, as long as the results are thorough.

HANDLING EMERGENCIES

In spite of the best made plans, problems can occur. All programs should have staff with the appropriate emergency first aid and other emergency training credentials. This is essential, and there is no room for compromise. Programs should also have an agreed upon evacuation plan to be used if necessary. All staff should be able to implement this plan if needed. It is also important to have staff that possess appropriate outdoor leadership credentials, gained ideally through organizations like the Wilderness Education Association. In short, staff need sufficient outdoor and counseling expertise that they are prepared to take over the wilderness therapy trip if another staff should become incapacitated.

In addition to preparing and dealing with physical emergencies, wilderness therapy programs must anticipate and be able to deal with psychiatric or emotional crises in the field. It is our contention that staff must be as well trained in dealing with emotional safety as they are in physical safety. This is a relatively new area of discussion in the field of adventure and wilderness therapy. We have advocated in many places (e.g., Davis-Berman & Berman, 1993, 1994) that wilderness therapy programs employ trained and credentialed therapists. We have suggested that program participants are entitled to services from staff with the same credentials that one would encounter in an office setting.

It can be suggested that wilderness therapy programs, by definition, might set the stage for the development of emotional crises. Some adventure or wilderness therapy programs focus on pushing the client out of the comfort zone in order to facilitate growth and change (Luckner & Nadler, 1997). Even if this element of stretching zones of comfort is not present, the simple act of leaving home and entering the wilderness environment may set the stage for crisis for some (Berman, Davis-Berman, & Gillen, 1998).

In addition to skills and knowledge about crisis intervention, it can be argued that staff of wilderness therapy programs need to know how to diffuse emotional situations in an effort to prevent escalation. This training involves teaching staff to deal with anxiety, disruptive and harmful behavior. Finally, we have suggested that staff of wilderness therapy programs be trained in techniques to deal with emotional crises once they have occurred (Berman et al., 1998). One such approach is Critical Incident Stress Debriefing (CISD). This model involves seven formal steps that can be taken in order to prevent the development of a more traumatic, serious response to the crisis (J. Mitchell & Everly, 1995).

A final suggestion about the prevention and management of crisis is the adoption of a risk management plan for emotional crises.

An example of such a plan can be found in *The Wilderness Education Association's Affiliate Handbook* (Wilderness Education Association, 1996). This plan contains 21 points to consider, ranging from evacuation planning to the initial screening of participants.

ENDING THE TRIP

As the trip winds down, participants are encouraged to write a letter to their parents discussing the gains that they feel they have made on the trip, and suggesting things that the adolescent would like to see change in the family upon their return. These letters are often difficult to write, and even more challenging to put into action upon returning home. These letters, however, can serve as a beginning for family therapy. We encourage wilderness therapy programs to offer follow-up groups to adolescents and families to work on the issues and changes experienced while in the program. A major criticism of wilderness therapy programs is that many of the changes experienced seem to be temporary. That is, adolescents grow, change, and stretch themselves while on the trip. When back in the routine environment, however, these changes go by the wayside. Intensive follow-up groups can facilitate the permanence of change, and can help participants generalize their changes to different life situations and events.

The focus on this aspect of the program is on the maintenance and generalization of gains. This can be accomplished through the use of metaphors (Bacon, 1983; Gass, 1993; Hovelynck, 1998) and, in fact, the successes that a participant has on a trip can be a metaphor for creating successes when home. Another strategy for generalization is to help participants change their narrations about their lives (e.g., Luckner & Nadler, 1997). Some programs help participants create mandalas (Davis-Berman & Berman, 1994), in a fashion similar to that discussed by Jung as a symbol of transformation (Hall & Nordby, 1973). A final suggestion is one used by many programs, in which participants are urged to write a letter to themselves at some point of success or contemplation during the program. These letters are mailed back to the participant at some later point, for example, six months after the program ends.

EVALUATION

As we stated earlier in this chapter, evaluation begins with the earliest planning of wilderness therapy programs. We also assert that it is essential to evaluate programs in order to compile efficacy data. In our program, we advocate the use of a systems-oriented assessment procedure. First, the impressions of the clinicians in the program provide valuable evaluative information. Additionally, every day, the therapists write detailed progress notes for each participant on the trip. These records provide important information about change.

Objective measures of change can also be used to evaluate participant change. These instruments are usually administered pre-trip and post-trip, with follow-up data collection efforts adding to the data collection process. As was seen in the literature review in this chapter, self-esteem, self-concept, self-efficacy, and behavior checklists are often used as assessment tools (e.g., Achenbach & Edelbrock, 1983; Piers & Harris, 1969). We have also developed a behavioral checklist, the Wilderness Therapy Checklist (Berman & Anton, 1988). This instrument asks the therapist to rate participants both before and after the trip on a number of behaviors related to: interactions with peers, affect, self-esteem, conflict, response initiation, and cooperation.

Research needs to be done not only on the quantitative evaluation of wilderness therapy programs, but also on the qualitative nature of these programs (Davis-Berman & Berman, 1994). What is the therapeutic process like in these programs? How does the wilderness environment actually facilitate change? What is the power behind this approach to therapy? Participants are encouraged to help answer these questions through open-ended discussions, and journal, poetry, and song writing.

OTHER ISSUES TO CONSIDER

An important issue to consider concerns networking and collaboration. Very few individuals possess all skills and credentials needed to be both a therapist and an outdoor leader. This calls for the need to identify staffing resources. Once this is accomplished, it is recommended that these staff train together, so that they make an effective team. Successful programs have a team of consultants to address medical concerns, nutritional, and technical outdoor concerns. Backup resources must also be identified to teach and conduct technical components of programs (e.g., white water rafting). At a minimum, we believe that each staff person must be able to fill in for the other in the event of an emergency. Thus, therapists on a backpacking trip must be able to handle physical emergencies and evacuations, should they be needed.

Marketing of programs is a topic that is beyond the scope of this chapter except to suggest that getting the word out, and referrals in, is as important for a wilderness therapy program as it is for any other therapy program.

Programs of the sort discussed in this chapter involve large commitments of staff time and energy, and include relatively small staff to client ratios. This makes wilderness programs expensive to run. Certainly financial and budgetary considerations must be addressed, if one is to run a successful program.

CRITICAL ISSUES

As the popularity of wilderness therapy programs continues to grow, it is important to mention some critical issues in the field, both to foreshadow emerging topics of concern and in an attempt to suggest directions for a burgeoning field. Programs must continue to work on evaluation of both outcome and method if they are to grow in size and credibility. It is critical that this data establish wilderness therapy as a legitimate and efficacious methodology. A suggested direction for this endeavor is to establish wilderness therapy as an empirically validated therapy (Chambless et al., 1996, 1998). This would require well-conducted experiments demonstrating efficacy, with clearly specified clients, treatment manuals, and more than one investigative team.

Mental health practice must be responsive to third-party payments. Wilderness therapy is not, nor is it likely to be, recognized as a practice setting, as are inpatient, outpatient, and residential settings. To qualify for payment, wilderness therapy programs will have to learn the "language" of insurance companies. One way for this to happen is to educate insurance and managed care companies to the literature on the effectiveness of wilderness therapy, and then to present financial information to these companies demonstrating some cost savings over traditional methods of treatment.

Directly related to legitimacy in the eyes of insurance companies is the issue of staff training and qualifications. Earlier in this chapter, we have made the case for stringent requirements for first aid training and certification for outdoor leaders for the trip. We also advocate for professional credentialing for those involved in working with troubled or at-risk participants of a wilderness therapy trip. Recognizing that it is a rare person who is qualified both as an outdoor leader and a therapist, we have recommended cross training of professionals (Davis-Berman & Berman, 1994). Although controversial, we suggest these stringent requirements in light of recent deaths in wilderness therapy programs (Griffin, 1995). We take this position for a few reasons. First, we believe that participants in wilderness programs have as much right to qualified staff as do those seen in office settings. Second, staff must have the professional education and clinical experience with which to deal with emotional and psychiatric issues that arise in wilderness settings. Finally, managed care companies are adopting very strict credentialing requirements for the provision of services.

A final issue for discussion, certainly related to the professionalization issue is program accreditation. Currently, the Association for Experiential Education is among a small group of organizations reviewing and accrediting programs (Association for Experiential Education, 1995). While not a guarantee for asserting legitimacy, accreditation of wilderness therapy programs is one way of ensuring the integrity of programs.

SUMMARY AND CONCLUSIONS

With its humble beginning in the camp movement of the mid-1800s and tent therapy in state hospitals in the 1910s, wilderness therapy began to grow as mental health professionals subsequently became involved with summer camps. When Outward Bound came to the United States, a new interest in growth in the out-of-doors blossomed. Both Outward Bound and other programs began taking psychiatric clients into the wilderness and documenting the changes occurring therein.

Surveys of wilderness programs in the last five years have started with data bases of hundreds of programs (Davis-Berman et al., 1994; Friese et al., 1998). These surveys have included wilderness therapy programs. Most wilderness therapy programs serve adolescents. One of the central findings of these surveys is the diversity of programs. In terms of the range of activities, programs may focus on backpacking expeditions to horseback riding. While some programs are day programs, others are residential in nature. And while some programs hire trained therapists, others rely on those without graduate mental health degrees to function as therapists.

Despite the diversity of programs, there is empirical support for wilderness therapy, although there have been critical methodological reviews of these studies (Davis-Berman & Berman, 1994; Gillis, 1995). The results of studies suggest that enrollment in wilderness therapy programs can reduce the number of negative behaviors, increase self-concept, increase internal locus of control, and even lead to improvements in academics and interpersonal relationships. Meta-analyses (Cason & Gillis, 1994; Hattie et al., 1997) indicate that wilderness therapy programs result in small to moderate change that is stable at follow-up. It was suggested that a future direction for research is to conduct multisite evaluations with a well-specified population, using treatment manuals. Results that can show this approach to be superior to control groups or more traditional treatments would help establish wilderness therapy as an empirically validated therapy.

It is our hope that readers will appreciate the presentation of many of the details of our own Wilderness Therapy Program to use as a model for discussion and implementation of other programs. Toward that end, we began our model with a number of pre-trip considerations, including the goals of the program, and criteria for client selection. It is important for programs to have both inclusionary and exclusionary criteria for clients, along with the expertise of the staff. A component of client selection is assessment of client needs, problems, and strengths. This should result in an individual treatment plan, just as one would expect in a community-based program.

Wilderness programs can involve a range of activities. While our program most often uses backpacking as the mode of travel, other programs may choose activities as diverse as sea kayaking or snow shoeing. A model was outlined to help determine the type of activities that may be appropriate, based on the amount of challenge or risk inherent in that activity.

Wilderness therapy programs utilize the group as the primary agent of change, making group therapy paramount. While there are times when individual intervention is needed and desirable, wilderness therapy occurs within the milieu of the group. Our own groups meet during the day, while participants are still fresh, and focus on the functioning of members within the group. Once the group is functioning well, attention can be given to the specific needs of individuals within the group. An important focus of the group is on maintenance and transfer of gains made in the program back to the home setting.

A risk management plan is an essential component of a wilderness therapy program, for it minimizes and prevents problems that may arise. It would be unrealistic to expect, however, that individuals will not need crisis intervention, for even in the best planned programs physical and/or emotional crises can arise. The best approach to dealing with crises is by preparation. This can occur by way of staff training in first aid (e.g., wilderness first responder certification) and crisis intervention that may include training in dealing with physical acting out and aggression and even critical incident stress debriefing.

Other topics of concern include program evaluation, marketing, financial considerations, staff recruitment, and training. Future directions for wilderness therapy include empirical validation of this approach, with inroads into the managed care market. Accomplishment of these goals will necessitate consideration of increases in staff training and program certification.

REFERENCES

Achenbach, T.M., & Edelbrock, C. (1983). *Manual for the child behavior checklist and revised child behavior profile.* Burlington: University of Vermont.

American Journal of Insanity. (1906). 63.

American Journal of Insanity. (1910). 67.

American Psychiatric Association. (1994). *Diagnostic and statistical manual* (4th ed.). New York: American Psychiatric Association.

Association for Experiential Education. (1995). *Journal of Experiential Education, 18*(2), 1, 7.

Bacon, S. (1983). *The conscious use of metaphor in Outward Bound.* Unpublished manuscript, Colorado Outward Bound School.

Bandoroff, S. (1993). Wilderness family therapy: An innovative treatment approach for problem youth. *Dissertation Abstracts International, 53*(11-B), 59–66.

Barley, F. (1972). Camp can change campus attitudes. *Camping Magazine, 44*(7), 18.

Berman, D.S., & Anton, M. (1988). A wilderness therapy program as an alternative to adolescent hospitalization. *Residential Treatment for Children and Youth, 5,* 39–52.

Berman, D.S., & Davis-Berman, J.L. (1989). Wilderness therapy: A therapeutic adventure for adolescents. *Journal of Independent Social Work, 3*(3), 65–77.

Berman, D.S., & Davis-Berman, J.L. (1991). Wilderness therapy and adolescent mental health: Administrative and clinical issues. *Administration and Policy in Mental Health, 18,* 373–379.

Berman, D.S., & Davis-Berman, J.L. (1995). Adventure as psychotherapy: A mental health perspective. *Journal of Leisurability, 22*(2), 21–28.

Berman, D.S., & Davis-Berman, J.L. (1996). Training adventure therapists: A mental health perspective. *The Bradford Papers, 7,* 41–48.

Berman, D.S., Davis-Berman, J.L., Chamberlain, R., & Dandaneau, C. (1997). *Adventure therapy: What it takes to do the job.* Paper presented at the International conference of the Association for Experiential Education, Asheville, NC.

Berman, D.S., Davis-Berman, J.L., & Gillen, M. (1998). Behavioral and emotional crisis management in adventure education. *Journal of Experiential Education, 21,* 96–101.

Bryson, B. (1998). *A walk in the woods: Rediscovering America on the Appalachian Trail.* New York: Broadway.

Carpenter, B. (1995). Taking nature's cure: Do expensive wilderness therapy camps help or hurt troubled teens? *U.S. News and World Report, 118*(25), 54–58.

Cason, D., & Gillis, H.L. (1994). A meta-analysis of outdoor adventure programming with adolescents. *Journal of Experiential Education, 17*(1), 40–47.

Castellano, T., & Soderstrom, I. (1992). Therapeutic wilderness programs and juvenile recidivism: A program evaluation. *Journal of Offender Rehabilitation, 17*(3/4), 19–46.

Chambless, D.L., Baker, M., Baucom, D.H., Beutler, L., Calhoun, K.S., Crits-Christoph, P., Daiuto, A., DeRubeis, R., Detweiler, J., Haaga, D.A., Johnson, S.B., McCurry, S., Mueser, K.T., Pope, K.S., Sanderson, W.C., Shoham, V., Stickle, T., Williams, D.A., & Woody, S. (1998). Update on empirically validated therapies: II. *Clinical Psychologist, 51,* 3–16.

Chambless, D.L., Sanderson, W.C., Shoham, V., Johnson, S.B., Pope, K.S., Crits-Christoph, P., Baker, M., Johnson, B., Woody, S., Sue, S., Beutler, L., Williams, D.A., & McCurry, S. (1996). An update on empirically validated therapies. *Clinical Psychologist, 49,* 5–15.

Chenery, M. (1981). Effects of summer camp on child development and contributions of counselors to those effects. *Journal of Leisure Research,* 3rd quarter, 195–207.

Davis-Berman, J.L., & Berman, D.S. (1989). The wilderness therapy program: An emperical study of its effects with adolescents in an outpatient setting. *Journal of Contemporary Psychotherapy, 19,* 271–281.

Davis-Berman, J.L., & Berman, D.S. (1993). Therapeutic wilderness programs: Issues of professionalization in an emerging field. *Journal of Contemporary Psychotherapy, 23,* 129–136.

Davis-Berman, J.L., & Berman, D.S. (1994). *Wilderness therapy: Foundations, theory and research.* Dubuque, IA: Kendall/Hunt.

Davis-Berman, J.L., Berman, D.S., & Capone, L. (1994). Therapeutic wilderness programs: A national survey. *Journal of Experiential Education, 17*(2), 49–53.

Dimock, H., & Hendry, C. (1939). *Camping and character: A camp experiment in character education.* New York: Association Press.

Elrod, H., & Minor, K. (1992). Second wave evaluation of a multifaceted intervention for juvenile court probationers. *International Journal of Offender Therapy & Comparative Criminology, 36*(3), 247–262.

Friese, G., Hendee, J.C., & Kinziger, M. (1998). The wilderness experience program industry in the United States: Characteristics and dynamics. *Journal of Experiential Education, 21,* 41–45.

Gass, M. (1993). *Adventure therapy: Therapeutic applications of adventure programming.* Dubuque, IA: Kendall/Hunt.

Gass, M., & Gillis, H.L. (1995). Focusing on the "solution" rather than the "problems": Empowering client change in adventure experiences. *Journal of Experiential Education, 18,* 63–69.

Gibson, H. (1973). The history of organized camping: Establishment of institutional camps. In D. Hammerman & W. Hammerman (Eds.), *Outdoor education: A book of readings* (pp. 69–76). Minneapolis: Burgess.

Gillett, D.P., Thomas, G.P., Skok, R.L., & McLaughlin, T.F. (1991). The effects of wilderness camping and hiking on the self-concept and the environmental attitudes and knowledge of twelfth graders. *Journal of Environmental Education, 22*(3), 33–44.

Gillis, H.L. (1995). If I conduct outdoor pursuits with clinical populations, am I an adventure therapist? *Journal of Leisurability, 22*(2), 5–15.

Griffin, K. (1995). Dangerous discipline. *Health, 9*(3), 94–99.

Hall, C.S., & Nordby, V.J. (1973). *A primer of Jungian psychology.* New York: Mentor.

Hattie, J., Marsh, H., Neill, J., & Richards, G. (1997). Adventure education and Outward Bound: Out-of-class experiences that make a lasting difference. *Review of Educational Research, 67*(1), 43–87.

Hovelynck, J. (1998). Facilitating experiential learning as a process of metaphor development. *Journal of Experiential Education, 21,* 6–13.

Huth, H. (1990). *Nature and the American: Three centuries of changing attitudes.* Lincoln: University of Nebraska.

James, T. (1993). *The only mountain worth climbing: The search for roots.* Unpublished manuscript.

Kaplan, R. (1974). Some psychological benefits of an outdoor challenge program. *Environment and Behavior, 6,* 101–115.

Katz, R. & Kolb, D. (1967). *Outward Bound and education for personal growth.* Reston, VA: Outward Bound.

Kelley, M., Coursey, R., & Selby, P. (1997). Therapeutic adventures outdoors: A demonstration of benefits for people with mental illness. *Psychiatric Rehabilitation Journal, 20*(4), 61–73.

Krakauer, J. (1997). *Into thin air: A personal account of the Mount Everest disaster.* New York: Villard.

Krieger, W. (1973). Study on self-concept change in campers. *Camping Magazine, 45*(4), 16–17.

Krutch, J. (Ed). (1982). *Walden and other writings by Henry David Thoreau.* New York: Bantam.

Luckner, J.L., & Nadler, R.S. (1997). *Processing the experience: Strategies to enhance and generalize learning* (2nd ed.). Dubuque, IA: Kendall/Hunt.

Matthews, M. (1991). Wilderness programs offer promising alternative for some youth: More regulation likely. *Youth Law News, 12*(6), 12–15.

Miner, J., & Boldt, J. (1981). *Outward Bound U.S.A.: Learning through experience in adventure-based education.* New York: Morrow.

Mitchell, A., Robberson, J., & Obley, R. (1977). *Camp counseling* (5th ed.). Philadelphia: Saunders.

Mitchell, J., & Everly, G. (1995). Critical incident stress debriefing (CISD) and the prevention of work-related traumatic stress among high risk occupational groups. In G. Everly & J. Lating (Eds.), *Psychotraumatology: Key papers and core concepts in post-traumatic stress.* New York: Plenum Press.

Morse, W. (1957). An interdisciplinary therapeutic camp. *Journal of Social Issues, 13*(1), 15–22.

Nadler, R.S. (1995). Edgework: Stretching boundaries and generalizing experiences. *Journal of Experiential Education, 18,* 52–55.

Nash, R. (1982). *Wilderness and the American mind* (3rd ed.). New Haven, CT: Yale University Press.

Neill, J.T., & Richards, G.E. (1998). Does outdoor education really work? A summary of recent meta-analyses. *Australian Journal of Outdoor Education, 3,* 2–9.

Norris, R., & Weinman, J. (1996). Psychological change following a long sail training voyage. *Personality and Individual Differences, 21*(2), 189–194.

Piers, E., & Harris, D. (1969). *Manual for the Piers-Harris children's self-concept scale.* Nashville: Counselor Recordings and Texts.

Priest, S. (1992). Factor exploration and confirmation for the dimensions of an adventure experience. *Journal of Leisure Research, 24*(2), 127–139.

Rohnke, K. (1989). *Cobras and cowtails II.* Dubuque, IA: Kendall/Hunt.

Rohnke, K. (1991). *Bottmomless baggie.* Dubuque, IA: Kendall/Hunt.

Sachs, J., & Miller, S. (1992). The impact of a wilderness experience on the social interactions and social expectations of behaviorally disordered adolescents. *Behavioral Disorders, 17*(2), 89–98.

Saffer, J., & Naylor, K. (1987). Difficulties encountered in the treatment of outpatient adolescents. *Adolescence, 22,* 143–147.

Scheidlinger, S., & Scheidlinger, L. (1947). From a camp of a child guidance clinic: The treatment potentialities of the summer camp for children with personality disturbances. *The Nervous Child, 6,* 232–242.

Shniderman, C. (1974). Impact of therapeutic camping. *Social Work, 19,* 354–357.

Smith, B. (1958). *The worth of a boy.* Austin, TX: The Hogg Foundation.

Thoreau, H. (1906). *The writings of Henry David Thoreau.* Boston: Houghton Mifflin.

Wellman, J. (1987). *Wildland recreation policy: An introduction.* New York: Wiley.

Wilderness Education Association. (1996). *The Wilderness Education Association's Affiliate Handbook* (4th ed.). Fort Collins: Colorado State University.

CHAPTER 6

Rational-Emotive Adventure Challenge Therapy

STUART LEEDS

THERE HAS been a recent trend in the professional literature proposing the beneficial treatment results gleaned from wilderness adventure–based therapy programs. As these less traditional treatment modalities become more accepted as viable tools for innovative change within a variety of populations and disorders, research has yet to substantiate the generalizability and lasting effects of these particular experiential interventions. It is hypothesized that combining a structured and well-established form of clinical therapy, specifically rational-emotive behavior therapy (REBT), with a wilderness adventure–based program, will create a more pervasive, meaningful, and deeper impetus for change.

In other words, it is proposed that the benefits of positive therapeutic change would be significantly enhanced when the wilderness adventure–based therapy experience is capsulized within the principles and philosophy of the REBT format. This would bring together clinical expertise and a structured treatment modality into the experiential learning and environment of the therapeutic wilderness. The challenges, obstacles, and problems encountered in the wilderness program would be processed utilizing REBT for a more effective and readily generalizable treatment experience.

In summary, it is suggested that wilderness adventure–based therapy can be significantly enhanced in its overall therapeutic effectiveness, generalizability, transfer of learning, and clinical duration when incorporating the rational-emotive behavioral modality. As both wilderness adventure therapy and REBT are quite similar in philosophy, that is, both take on an active-directive, experiential, and humanistic approach to treatment, neither theory would be compromised.

WHY ADVENTURE-BASED THERAPY?

Overall, professional literature has proclaimed the benefits of wilderness adventure-based therapy to a wide variety of populations. In the beginning, it was seen as being a useful tool, or at least a last-ditch effort, to reform America's growing youth problems with a stringent Outward Bound or survival school experience. However, as research progressed and different populations benefited from wilderness programs, more interest focused on the specific components and intervention strategies that were employed to change what were thought of as unchangeable persons (Gass, 1993).

Adventure-based therapy has the unique distinction of taking therapy out of the office, thereby reducing resistance and increasing group conformity due to the uncommon unfamiliarity of the natural surroundings. As a group experience, it plunges clients into working through the early stages of group dynamics (which may take several sessions normally) and into immediate work stages (Mitten, 1995). Additionally, with the proper circumstances in adventure therapy, stronger, more immediate bonds are made between leaders and the client peer group, including trust fostered through several group exercises.

The benefits to adventure-based training are plentiful in the literature, especially in regard to building confidence, goal-directed behaviors, social skills, and problem-solving skills. However, it is the therapeutic interventions and processing of what the client is actually going through at the time that makes the experience therapeutic, generalizable, and long lasting. The problem with most adventure-based therapy programs is the variety of treatment modalities present when processing these experiences, including no treatment interventions whatsoever. Some programs make a valiant attempt at incorporating their own style of therapy based strictly on wilderness experience (Gass & Gillis, 1995a; Marx, 1988; Mitten, 1995; Nadler, 1995; Ringer & Gillis, 1995) and in several innovative therapeutic styles. Although these are reported to have beneficial effects, the lack of consistency and research does little for future replication of those techniques. Many of the existing group-processing experiences are based on deepening the psychological level of meaning in the process. These group-processing experiences have a focus in the past rather than the here-and-now focus more in tune with current brief psychotherapies (Ringer & Gillis, 1995).

The overall problem when describing the therapeutic modalities utilized in wilderness adventure–therapy programs is the general lack of description or operationalized definitions of technique, processing, or therapeutic methods (Davis-Berman, Berman, & Capone, 1994). The nonspecific mechanisms of treatment coupled with a dearth of skilled psychological staff members lead to additional confounds and a "watering down" of therapeutic effect. Virtually all of the existing programs consist of brief processing of specific goal-directed events. A structured approach to a group psychotherapy experience, conducted by trained professionals, would maximize the benefit of the therapeutic experience.

WHY RATIONAL-EMOTIVE BEHAVIOR THERAPY?

After reviewing the current literature on therapeutic interventions in a nonclinical environment, it appears that a cognitive-behavioral approach, specifically REBT, is most consistent in structuring the goal-oriented achievements within wilderness adventure–based therapy. Because REBT is strongly cognitive, emotive, and behavioral, it assesses not only people's irrational beliefs but also their inappropriate feelings and self-defeating behaviors. These components strongly parallel adventure-based therapy and are in fact reframed within metaphors, analogies, and examples of everyday problems. The philosophy of REBT also takes into consideration a new way of thinking emphasized by *doing* and therefore connects with the very active nature of the wilderness experience. The use of humor and sometimes profanity is also expressed as a usual hallmark within the wilderness environment. REBT programs have been shown to be effective with both delinquent adolescent populations (Larson, 1990) and adult inpatient and outpatient groups (Nottingham & Neimeyer, 1992). Additionally, REBT group-oriented programs have been effective with long-lasting change (Kushnir & Malkinson, 1993; Leaf, Krauss, Dantzig, & Arlington, 1992).

Teaching and understanding the basic ABCs of REBT and how they relate to wilderness challenge experiences and real-world problems would not be complicated. Group settings for REBT have already been established (Walen, DiGiuseppe, & Dryden, 1992) and work well with a variety of populations, such as juvenile sex offenders (Jenkins-Hall, 1994; Larson, 1990; Laws, 1989) and those from inpatient and outpatient programs (Friedberg, Fidaleo, & Mikules, 1992). Also, many of the main hypotheses of REBT fit well with mainstream wilderness treatment and process situations (Ellis & Grieger, 1977), such as active-directive homework, role play, modeling, and redirecting negative self-statements and tendencies to self-rate and to display low frustration tolerance.

The research literature presents strong evidence that therapeutic adventure programs are effective (Ewert, 1989; Kimball, 1979; Walsh & Gollins, 1976). However, many are unsure as to why it works. Several early programs such as Outward Bound give enormous weight to "just being in the great outdoors" as the primary therapeutic element (Stich & Gaylor, 1983). Most other programs, when surveyed (Davis-Berman & Berman, 1993; Long, 1987), were unable to define what theoretical orientation or framework their programs could be ascribed to. Most stated that the experiential components and group processes enhanced treatment effectiveness (Miles, 1987). It is important to note that the group development model is indeed essential to the success of wilderness adventure–based therapy (McPhee & Gass, 1993). Awareness of group stage development within the adventure-based therapy model assists with assessment and transition for change and provides a framework for counselors to judge the group's progress. Many wilderness programs espouse that warmth, empathy, and feelings of being "liked" by the therapist will facilitate group change (Mitten, 1995; Rogers, 1973), but that is yet to be substantiated within current adventure-based programming. Perhaps more apparent, and similar to group therapy in a clinical setting, for an outdoor therapeutic experience to be positive there have to be positive relationships between leaders and participants. Research has shown that successful therapists establish relationships with clients that offer them "high levels of accurate empathy, nonpossessive warmth and genuineness" (Mitten, 1995, p. 85).

CURRENT ADVENTURE-BASED THEORY

Although there is more than one accepted method of conducting adventure-based therapy (Davis-Berman & Berman, 1993; McPhee & Gass, 1993; Miles, 1987; Nadler, 1995), there are several critical components that serve as a foundation for most well-established adventure-based therapy programs. This principle provides a rationale as well as a theoretical framework for conducting adventure experiences for therapy. It is important to note that in most cases, adventure-based therapy is not used to replace other therapeutic interventions and practices. Instead, adventure-based therapy is used to enhance established treatment objectives and to provide a richer therapeutic environment for change so that therapy is more successful (Berman, 1995; Davis-Berman & Berman, 1993; Herbert, 1996; Maguire & Priest, 1994). Currently, there is a wealth of literature and research that substantiates the positive effect of using adventure-based programs with many diverse age groups and populations (Clagett, 1992; Ewert, 1989; Marx, 1988; Mason, 1987). Most wilderness challenge programs are designed to encourage participants to reach beyond their present behavior and accomplish a task that they may have thought themselves incapable of handling. Adventure activities such as those offered by Outward Bound or therapeutic programs like Project Adventure are examples of this type of experience. The intent of these programs is to bring the individual to a better understanding of self in relation to the environment and to provide the opportunity for growth in knowledge, ability, and self-concept (Bacon, 1988; Finkenberg, Shows, & DiNucci, 1994; Gillett, Thomas, Skok, & McLaughlin, 1991; Hazelworth & Wilson, 1990).

The rationale and credibility for using therapeutic adventure-based therapy programs are well documented (Ewert, 1989; Gass, 1993; Nadler & Luckner, 1992). Adventure-based learning is a type of experiential education and therapeutic program in which adventure pursuits that are physically and psychologically demanding are used within a framework of safety and skills development to promote interpersonal growth (Davis-Berman & Berman, 1989; Gass & Gillis, 1995b). Although adventure-based therapy has developed as a discrete addition to the mental health field, its origins and many of its principles and philosophies are founded in the field of experiential education.

CHARACTERISTICS OF ADVENTURE-BASED THERAPY

Adventure-based challenges are, by design, a frontal assault on learned helplessness, dependency, and feelings of low self-worth (Gass, 1993). Through performance-based success and mastery, participants are able to discover previously untapped inner resources. Adventure-based therapy fosters perceptions of capability, group cohesiveness, self-empowerment, and significance. These perceptual changes are the key to behavioral, motivational, and emotional changes, especially in troubled youth (Davis-Berman et al., 1994).

Adventure-based therapy seeks to snap participants out of self-defeating attitudes and perceptions and to replace anomie, cynicism, and alienation with feelings of empowerment, perseverance, and self-confidence. Programs are designed to be incremental in increasing problem-solving skills, learned skills, and group skills to further develop autonomous experiential learning. Problems offer real consequences, and success or failure is readily apparent. Feedback to the learner is immediate. Because the outcomes are consequential, the individual and the group learn to assume responsibility for their actions and choices (Castellano & Soderstrom, 1992). Problem resolution requires participants to draw on the full complement of their physical, emotional, and cognitive resources.

THERAPIES UTILIZING THEORY

Some of the difficulties of adventure-based therapy programs arise when the exact modality of change cannot be identified. Although all programs state that they use a particular or eclectic method regarding theory, some regard the wilderness itself as a learning environment that is significant enough alone to exact change in a positive direction (Bacon, 1988; Miles, 1987). However, most recent programs agree that the wilderness is not enough, and theory, therapy, and integration of treatment modalities are what make adventure-based therapy successful (Davis-Berman & Berman, 1993). A recent study by Parker and Stoltenberg (1995), in which a study was completed between three groups—therapy only, adventure-based therapy, and a control group—found that the only long-term effectiveness was with adventure interventions integrated with ongoing counseling.

In terms of therapy, the approaches reported are as diverse as the clients served and the program designs. It appears that substance abuse adventure programs seem to rely on the 12 step approach or some variation of this model. Many rely on "metaphor therapy" akin to the Outward Bound model (Gass, 1993), and some programs use group, family, and individual approaches without providing specific information as to the implementation of this therapy (Davis-Berman & Berman, 1993).

A minority of programs did appear to have a specific theory used for clinical populations. These programs emphasized the need for a specific model or map based on clinical theory to implement, describe, utilize, and structure therapeutic gains (Gass & Gillis, 1995; Hughs & Dudley, 1973; Kimball, 1979; Marx, 1988; Mason, 1987; Nadler, 1995; Sachs & Miller, 1992). These programs claimed a variety of theoretical backgrounds, including psychoanalytic theory (Hughs & Dudley, 1973), Bandura's (1977) self-efficacy theory (Stich & Gaylor, 1993), systems theory (Clapp & Rudolph, 1990; Gass, 1993), reality therapy (Clagett, 1992), and various new and customized forms of group therapy.

Groups allow time for bonding, trust, support, laughter, and modeling behaviors to occur. Similar to group therapy in a clinical setting, relationships are important in fostering positive feedback from peers, empathy, and genuineness for optimum therapeutic gain (Mitten, 1995). The group is the central place where problems are directed (Neely & Kling, 1987).

Group therapy is an emotional and corrective experience. Participants must experience something strongly (as in an adventure-based activity), but they must also understand the implications of that emotional experience. A corrective emotional experience can occur in a group when basic tensions and modes of relating are allowed to emerge in a safe and honest environment, followed by examination of and learning from the ensuing interpersonal interactions. What makes group psychotherapy an ideal arena, especially within the adventure-based experience, is that group members create characteristic interactional tensions and engage in modes of relating to others right there in the group setting. The group then becomes a social microcosm for each of its members, which then can serve as a learning point to undergo a corrective emotional experience (Yalom, 1985).

MAKING THE TRANSFER TO THE "REAL WORLD"

One of the major criticisms of adventure-based counseling research is that there are insufficient follow-up data to ascertain whether reported therapeutic benefits are sustained and if they generalize to other life areas (Davis-Berman & Berman, 1994; Ewert, 1989). However, even the data of participants not transferring learning can be diagnostic and used later in individual or group psychotherapy follow-ups (Davis-Berman & Berman, 1994; Ewert, 1989). It then becomes even more important to utilize strategies and opportunities to practice transfer learning while still in the adventure activities for the strongest impact to occur (Herbert, 1996). This hands-on learning will then be translated into positive attitudinal and behavioral changes that persist beyond the wilderness setting (Castellano & Soderstrom, 1992).

It is the transference back to everyday life that distinguishes sound adventure-based therapy from just another romp in the woods. The primary objective of this type of training is not to take people into an outdoor setting and draw direct parallels between that experience and experiences at home. But if you can get people to take risks trying something they are sure they cannot do, and they discover they can do it, that realization translates into their whole approach to life, work, school, and relationships (Gall, 1987).

Transfer of learning becomes more apparent and somewhat easier when taken in the context of the integrated program. REBT becomes a built-in mechanism whereby learning is a process of continued practice, behavioral assignments, and groups within a series of pre-, during, and posttrip activity follow-up. REBT provides an already established set of ideas, a treatment regimen, techniques, and various methods to assist with a more enduring philosophic change toward real-world gains and goals.

DEFINITIONS OF
ADVENTURE-BASED THERAPY

Adventure-based programs are usually conducted in remote outdoor settings, although they can exist in urban settings as well (Levine, 1978). Activities such as backpacking, hiking, camping, rock climbing, rafting, high and low ropes course initiatives, rappelling off vertical cliffs, community service projects, and individual and group problem-solving projects are the kinds of activities often found in adventure-based programs. Many of these activities have been used for recreational purposes with a variety of clientele, including people with long-term mental illness (Banaka & Young, 1985; Berman & Anton, 1988), mental retardation (Dillenschneider, 1983), substance abuse problems (Gass & McPhee, 1990; Stich & Gaylor, 1983), and physical disabilities (Ewert, 1989), and bulimia nervosa patients (Maguire & Priest, 1994), rape victims and survivors of violence (Cole, Erdman, & Rothblum, 1994; Webb, 1993), juvenile sex offenders and juvenile delinquents (Clagett,

1989; Harris, Mealy, Matthews, Lucas, & Moczygemba, 1993; Kjol & Weber, 1993), families (Clapp & Rudolph, 1990; Gass, 1993), geriatric terminally ill, and cancer and AIDS patients (Ewert, 1989). Participation in these activities alone does not constitute adventure-based therapy. Any of these adventure activities can be used for a variety of educational, physical fitness, recreation, and counseling purposes (Schoel, Prouty, & Radcliffe, 1988). A critical difference between simply participating in adventure activities as a recreational endeavor and doing so within an adventure-based therapy context is that, in the latter case, activities are conducted for the purpose of creating individual therapeutic change (Stich, 1983). In addition, adventure activities are designed for the purpose of focusing on behavior and, if necessary, changing it.

PROGRAM DESIGN AND DEVELOPMENT

Currently, there are a variety of adventure-based programs that abide by a highly structured program regimen that emphasizes gains within a therapeutic model. The proposed Rational-Emotive Adventure Challenge Therapy (REACT) model would incorporate the advantages of these programs into a multimodal approach for the optimum experience and peak design. Properties are exemplified from the CHANGES (Context, Hypothesizing, Action that is Novel, Generating information, Evaluation, Solutions) model (Gass & Gillis, 1995a), which emphasizes assessments, information gathering, goal orientation, and psychotherapeutic processing, and requires therapists to be well trained and competent in both psychology and adventure-based activities.

Reldon Nadler's (1995) Edgework program stresses the importance of group processing and dynamics coupled with the use of *eustress* in pushing people through their comfort levels for a positive experience and optimum change. Eustress is the term used to describe a constructive level of anxiety, or the healthy use of stress, whereby the individual converts the uncomfortable feeling into a manageable yet challenging manner. The levels of processing are readily defined and structured and are easily replicated for maximizing transfer of learning.

Mason (1987) integrates Carl Whitaker's systems theory into a model of wilderness family therapy exemplifying group work within the systemic model. She emphasizes the cognitive-affective domain in treatment and focuses on issues of trust, immediate feedback, real versus perceived fear, eustress, empathy, gender equality, and "edgework." Nadler (1995) describes Edgework as the process in experiential therapy by which participants reach the threshold of their comfort level during a specific event or activity and are faced with a choice. When participants arrive at that uncomfortable, unexplored boundary or edge, they make a choice between retreating into the comfort of known and predictable yet destructive patterns, or breaking the pattern and forging ahead in the exploration of areas yet untouched. This edgework relies on motivation, trust, and a willingness to push oneself beyond conventional barriers for a breakthrough to occur.

Arthur Clagett (1989, 1992) presents the closest model of integrated adventure-based therapy within a structured cognitive-behavioral framework, particularly within the reality therapy approach. Main issues include the use of empirical measures and personality test, pre- and posttest developments, individual responsibility for one's actions, increased client commitment and use of behavioral contracts, a "no excuses policy," praise over punishment, and control over extraneous variables. Clagett also uses aftercare follow-up and group processing after the wilderness experience has occurred. Psychoeducation, treatment planning, involvement with family and significant others, and continuance of a service plan all contribute to the success of this program.

SAFETY AND ETHICAL CONCERNS

With the physical dangers and strenuous activities that accompany adventure-based activities come unique safety and ethical issues to be addressed. Examined are issues involving physical safety, that is, individual capabilities due to physical condition, weight, and age as well as instruction on and the use of the equipment, and the physical environment where the activity is taking place. The emotional and psychological safety of participants is reviewed, in addition to more common ethical standards of training requirements and supervision of group leaders. The actual versus perceived risks of the activities involved are also explored (Gass, 1993).

Adventure activities may focus on physical challenges in the natural or adventure-designed environment. True physical risk taking is not the goal here: emotional and intellectual risk taking is. Experts proclaim that perceived physical risk is what makes the program exciting and challenges participants to do their personal best (Gall, 1987). The perceived risk may seem to be high, but in fact there is a low probability of actual physical harm. This view is consistent with the adventure program model designed by Priest (1995) in which he defines adventure as having a higher level of competence than risk. However, ethical considerations require that practitioners be adequately trained and participants informed of potential health risks (Bunting, 1995).

It is important that counselor skills be comprehensive enough to manage outdoor challenges while supporting client efforts, including use of reassurance, empathy, reframing, and problem solving (Marx, 1988). Within adventure-based therapy programs, there may be an increased abuse potential and more intense overdependency on counselors than in traditional therapies. Staff need to be well aware of their own personal issues and inadequacies, for clients may be at their most vulnerable both psychologically and literally, for example, hanging from a rope off a cliff. Therefore, skilled leaders must recognize symptoms of psychological stress, noting signs of signal symptoms and reading behavioral cues for early and immediate intervention. A standard professional responsibility is thorough documentation by credible therapists of such critical incidents and interventions (Gray & Yerkes, 1995).

Managing psychological depth is a small part of the complexity of leading groups. Noting if a participant is divulging too much too soon and gauging the responses of others are skills necessary for safe and effective therapy. Using group therapy skills and maintaining proper psychological depth require sound psychological health, well-developed intuition, and creativity (Yalom, 1985). If leaders are to maintain emotional safety within a group and therefore attempt to avoid psychological harm, are therapists solely responsible for creating emotional safety? Defining emotional safety as a perceived freedom from psychological harm puts more emphasis on individual reactions to situations. Vincent (1995) argues that emotions are dependent on individual perceptions.

Focusing emotional safety on individual perceptions can help therapists identify how emotionally safe someone is by examining the individual as well as the situation. Techniques used in REBT that focus on altering a participant's irrational perceptions may then assist in fostering individual and group emotional safety and enhance participation. The ethics of adventure-based counseling require that practitioners be competent to carry out the work they undertake in a way that respects the needs and rights of participants.

LIMITATIONS WITH ADVENTURE-BASED THERAPY PROGRAMS

In the rapidly evolving field of adventure-based therapy, many questions have arisen about the treatment effectiveness of these programs. Questions inherent in the design of a new program include who is qualified to conduct therapeutic adventure experiences, what are proper evaluation procedures, which empirical measures should be used, what are the ethical and safety concerns, what are the recidivism rates, what is the potential for transfer of learning, what is the abuse potential, and many more factors.

"When reviewing the literature on program evaluation, one is immediately struck by the lack of consensus on just what program evaluation is and how it is done" (Davis-Berman & Berman, 1994, pp. 14–15). There is no clear agreement as to the definition of program evaluation, especially because adventure-based programs are inconsistent in design and treatment populations. There is also controversy over using quantitative versus qualitative research methods. Issues related to standardization of instruments, outcome studies, subjective measures, clinical impression, and objective rating scales further cloud evaluative procedures (Cason & Gillis, 1994; Ewert, 1989; Marx, 1988). Not only has there been very little research done, but many of the evaluation methods were not standardized, empirically based, or objective in nature. Further confounding variables consisted of the lack of theory behind the "therapeutic" adventure-based programs.

The topic of evaluation research is made even more confusing by the fact that not only are there no real definitions of what evaluation is, but the definitions of adventure-based therapy programs are also obscured. Because each program either defines itself as using eclectic methods, group dynamic focus, systemic, newly evolved theoretical viewpoints, or no focus whatsoever, attempts to accurately define and assess the efficacy of these programs are further disrupted.

RATIONAL-EMOTIVE BEHAVIOR THERAPY

Based on the work of Albert Ellis, REBT is a counseling theory and intervention generally based on the assumption that emotional problems result from faulty thinking about (perception of) events rather than from events themselves. As such, it involves a cognitive-emotional-behavioral system. This idea is explained by the ABC theory of emotional disturbance, where A is an activating event, B are beliefs about the event, and C is the emotional and behavioral consequence (Ellis, 1994).

Many people believe that activating events of situations cause emotional and behavioral consequences. However, REBT thinking holds that beliefs about the event intervene and are critical in determining these consequences. If beliefs are rational, the result is moderate, healthy emotions (positive or negative) that enable people to act constructively and achieve their goals. In contrast, irrational beliefs lead to disturbed, unhealthy emotions such as anger, anxiety, or depression, thus making goal attainment difficult (Bernard, 1991).

The core construct of REBT is that emotional upset stems from three major irrational beliefs, or "musts." These demands and rigid patterns of thinking result in creating habits of nonproductive feelings and attitudes. Once such irrational beliefs are identified, the D and E of the ABC paradigm become operative. Disputing (D) means challenging irrational beliefs by vigorously questioning assumptions about the event. As disputing occurs and rational beliefs replace irrational ones, more moderate emotions will lead to the effective (E) new philosophy result (Ellis, 1996; Ellis & Dryden, 1997).

In summary, one of the basic principles of REBT is that cognition is the most important, though hardly the only, determinant of emotion. Irrational thinking often produces dysfunctional emotional states, and the most effective way to reduce emotional distress is to change our thinking. We have a natural or biological tendency to think irrationally and upset ourselves, which gets reinforced by the environment. We perpetuate our emotional distress by repropagandizing ourselves with our irrational beliefs. Therefore, changing those long-standing irrational beliefs will not necessarily be easy work, but will require persistence and practice of REBT on the part of students and clients (Grieger, 1985; Walen et al., 1992).

THE RATIONAL-EMOTIVE ADVENTURE CHALLENGE THERAPY PROGRAM

GOALS FOR TREATMENT

As with most treatment modalities, defining specific goals for treatment to facilitate a more focused, directional path for both client and professional staff will be necessary. Individuals and groups will arrive with a multitude of problems and difficulties, but most share the same basic problems and goals that can be addressed within REACT. Several of these basic premises will be detailed.

Planning and identifying goals *with* the client, not *for* the client, places the responsibility on both the individual and the group. As adventure-based therapy is group-oriented, it is important to begin setting group norms and goals to maintain adherence to group goals. Agreeing on the commitment, confidentiality, and compromise of goals, as per other group therapies, is a standard procedure. However, adventure-based therapy is not only brief in duration, but contains an element of perceived physical as well as emotional danger that is not present in sit-down group therapy. Implementing a Full Value Contract (Schoel et al., 1988) between facilitators and members is an important part of treatment. Briefly, full value behavior consists of agreements to work together as a group toward individual group goals to adhere to certain safety and group behavior guidelines, and to give and receive positive and negative feedback. Members also agreed to work toward changing behavior when appropriate (Schoel et al., 1988).

Specific types of goals can be identified and monitored within REACT. Behavior-oriented, psychosocial, and cognitive development goals may all be addressed. Based on the specific population and treatment directives, goals can be targeted within a wide range of problems. For example, behavior-oriented goals may consist of improving communication skills, increasing an individual's abilities to change his or her life in a positive manner, providing motivation to change existing lifestyles to discover new positive recreational experiences, and reducing the incidence of problem drinking and addictive behaviors.

Psychosocial and emotional goals may include understanding of unconditional self-acceptance, increasing levels of trust in self and others when appropriate, creating the ability to accept self-responsibility, confronting one's own fears and feelings, reassessing one's own potential and personal values, and increasing levels of independence and maturity. One other distinctive goal is to have clients let go of the past or accept it, and to gain insight as to how beliefs in the past may be irrationally influencing the present.

Cognitive goals such as goal-setting strategies, insight into understanding of current dysfunctional patterns of behavior, and how we as humans contribute to our own emotional difficulties are explored. Participants learn that they can regain control to live in a more healthy frame of mind through the understanding and practice of the ABCs of REBT. This also includes increasing cognitive awareness and accurate perceptions, including identifying positive and negative self-talk.

One particular goal for treatment, which has been shown to be quite important and effective in the motivation of learning and outcome for therapy, is that the learning environment be fun. Adventure-based therapy has built-in elements of fun and play where clients can and often will be in playful and silly situations. These can be equated with the well-known "shame attacking" exercises of REBT and assist with normalizing the fallibilities and commonalities of human interaction. Laughter and fun create stress reduction and a relaxed alertness that is not only a positive by-product of an intense therapeutic interaction, but increases the likelihood that clients will seek help if they remember that doing so can be a fun experience (Bisson & Luckner, 1996).

Many of the group adventure activities and initiatives are designed to test and challenge clients' abilities in frustrating situations. One of the main principles of REBT regarding emotional disturbance is the teaching and understanding of low frustration tolerance. Group activities on the challenge course quickly and continuously assess frustration tolerance. Increasing frustration tolerance, in all likelihood, will become a goal for those participants who perceive the event or problem as more than frustrating. This type of therapy lends itself to creating situations that can be utilized in the present to gain insight into and practice tolerating frustrations in one's life, and not just successfully problem solving through them (Nadler & Luckner, 1992).

Additional goals are to practice active disputing of irrational beliefs that interfere with healthy functioning and replacing those with more realistic beliefs, which can then be readily observed, challenged, and implemented by peers and facilitators. This will lead to goals of *preferential* thinking versus demanding that things *should* or *ought* to be different, and issues of demandingness can then be processed within the debriefing sessions.

Finally, goals can be modified through the process of ongoing assessment and reevaluation during group activities and processing. Therefore, goals to *change goals* as the individual or group progresses or digresses can be built in to cater more specifically to the needs of the group. As with all group psychotherapies, reassessment is an ongoing practice, and group input will therefore enhance personal responsibility and empowerment to change.

Setting goals and parameters becomes a strong mechanism for change and may motivate clients to achieve those goals. Additionally, clients can literally see the changes they make when taking risks that they once thought they were unable to take. Using both concrete (challenge activities) and cognitive-emotive (disputing irrational beliefs and exchanging those beliefs with the more effective philosophy) methods to enhance behavior change and reach desired goals becomes a very effective, enduring strategy for full lifestyle improvement:

Patients are not only able to develop specific behavioral skills but also identify "in vivo" underlying irrational beliefs that may interfere with performance and create feelings of depression, anxiety, anger, and frustration. Adventure activities provide patients an opportunity to assess these irrational beliefs in a more vivid fashion, e.g., while standing on a platform 100 feet off the ground, anticipating zipping down a cable, and feeling profoundly anxious. (Nottingham & Neimeyer, 1992, p. 66)

The interaction of REBT principles and adventure-based therapy encourages goal clarification and problem definition. Therapists can be directive in assisting clients to set attainable goals. These goals should be within the person's control, stated positively, observable, achievable, health promoting, and in the client's best interest. Also, acceptable goals must be consistent with the person's ethical code, must not harm others, and must be legal (Dryden, 1995).

POPULATIONS AND CLINICAL PROBLEMS

It would be easier to discuss the populations and disorders that would be unlikely to benefit from REACT than those that would. People in poor physical health for whom it is a danger to be outdoors or to physically exert themselves should be excluded. Clients that are actively psychotic, delusional, aggressively dangerous, or suicidal are also poor candidates. Although mentally retarded clients are commonly utilized as a treatment group in adventure-based therapy, this population has not been shown to benefit from REBT (Ellis, 1994). Barriers for the physically handicapped can be adjusted for, as there are a growing number of wilderness parks and ropes courses now catering to these populations. It has been suggested that the more difficult treatment populations, such as clients with a poor prognosis for the more traditional psychotherapeutic approaches, seem to do very well with adventure-based programs and respond to cognitive-behaviorally based treatment as well. These include adjudicated youth, sex offenders, and those with conduct disorders, drug and alcohol addictions, and severe personality disorders (Castellano & Soderstrom, 1992; Ellis, 1991; Laws, 1989; Whitford & Parr, 1995).

Finally, there has been tremendous success in the nonpsychiatric or deviant populations in both REBT and adventure-based programs. Leadership skills training and corporate development courses have documented numerous positive outcome studies (Davis-Berman & Berman, 1994; Ellis, 1972); these populations may benefit even more from this combined program.

TREATMENT MODALITIES AND TECHNIQUES

Many of the treatment modalities and techniques utilized in adventure-based therapy can be applied with groups in other types of therapeutic activities. Peer pressure, silences, and conflict resolution are used in group formation, development, and growth. Experiential therapy has much in common with the techniques used in REBT; the main differences reside in the emphasis and focus of particular domains. Experiential therapy tends to emphasize activity in that the therapist is involved in the proceedings and may participate in the therapeutic experiences. "But it does not stress directiveness or authoritativeness, especially in individual therapy" (Ellis, 1974, p. 7). Methods of didactic teaching by the therapist or group leader are more akin to REBT than the adventure-based therapies.

It is important to understand that the REACT program includes a more philosophic goal that transcends the process of adventure-based therapy. Whereas adventure-based therapy utilizes a process of experiences leading to specific goal oriented procedures, the REACT program uses these experiences within the context of Rational-Emotive Behavior Therapy. This form of therapy trains the client to actually develop a new philosophy and lifestyle change through the development of new patterns of healthier thinking to minimize unhealthy and over exaggerated forms of distress. There are several main contexts in which therapeutic techniques are facilitated to foster change: cognitive, emotive, behavioral, and experiential methods. The various techniques of adventure-based counseling fall within these methods; therefore, making use of these methods becomes an integral part and strategy of the REACT program. Table 6.1 lists the techniques used within these categories. There is considerable overlap as methods

Table 6.1

Therapeutic Categories Addressed by REACT Program

Cognitive Techniques

Disputation of irrational beliefs and thoughts.

Use of scientific reasoning and logicoempirical methods.

Psychoeducation.

Bibliotherapy.

Identification of rational and irrational self-talk.

Inference chaining (a method similar to the downward arrow technique).

Problem solving and conflict resolution.

Semantic methods such as language style, hypnotic language, and persuasion.

Verbal and physical instruction.

Rational-emotive imagery and time projection methods.

Role play.

Therapeutic metaphor.

Audio- and videotapes of sessions or activities for replay.

Evaluating group goals.

Paradoxical intention.

Reframing the problem or belief.

Emotive Techniques

Primarily focus on change through feelings.

Modeling.

Use of humor, fun, and laughter.

Unconditional acceptance.

Stories and narratives specific to the group or individual situation.

Myths and use of fantasy (e.g., We are all on a deserted isle).

Eustress, a form of therapeutic stress that motivates change by increasing discomfort levels.

Initiative games, usually a goal-oriented or problem-solving cooperative activity.

Shame attacking exercises.

In vivo desensitization.

Table 6.1 *(Continued)*

Behavioral Techniques

Rely on the physical initiative of the individual or group.

Practice and repetition.

Risk taking or behavioral and physical challenge.

Written homework assignments.

Flooding techniques.

Journal writing.

Behavioral experiments.

Reward and punishment.

Basic outdoor skills training.

Behavioral disputes (clients act against their irrational beliefs).

Rational role reversal.

Experiential Techniques

Learning is primarily accomplished by doing, experiencing, and participating in activities that combine cognitive, behavioral, and emotive concepts with physical action.

Peak achievements, such as completing an obstacle course or rappelling off a cliff.

Use of healthy competition, both versus self and others.

Handicapping, to emphasize a new disability and coping strategy by blindfolding, making a limb ineligible, tying people together at the feet, etc.

Trust activities (e.g., trust fall).

Touching and hugging (this can happen as part of peer bonding and after accomplishments when appropriate; physical touch under supervision may be quite therapeutic where previously touch may have been fear-provoking, dangerous, or overstimulating).

Low and high ropes course.

High adventure activities (e.g., rafting, canoeing, rappelling).

Overnight expeditions (long-term, minimum three-day excursion into the wilderness).

are often combined in multiple domains to increase effectiveness. Although the categories of cognitive, emotive, behavioral, and experiential methods have been selected, the theory behind REBT insists that all are interrelated and that the purpose is to emphasize the major modality of each technique. "Pure" techniques probably do not exist.

When participants experience various problems and sensations that the adventure activities were designed to elicit, a combination of techniques is often used to enhance the process of therapy. Trained counselors are able to formulate these incidents within the REBT paradigm for optimal transfer of learning to the everyday world. Certain adventure activities may be best suited to specific populations and situations, and should be carefully planned within each treatment group. Adventure-based activities create numerous opportunities for the therapist to utilize the many techniques available for relating the immediate exchange among the client's thoughts, feelings, and behaviors.

For example, the cat walk is a high-element ropes course activity that requires a belay hookup to the participant who is attempting to walk across a horizontal telephone pole suspended 30 to 40 feet above the ground. Belay is a technique of protecting the climber in the event of a fall: a rope from the climber's harness is anchored to a belay device which controls the rate at which the rope passes through that system or around the body. The belayer is someone who holds the rope and stops the fall of the climber using the friction created by the belay device (Priest, 1995). The walk is usually a distance of 10 to 20 feet. The perceived risk of falling heightens the participant's stress in challenged situations, encourages trust in self and others, and helps overcome natural fears and perceptions of insecurity. The actual risk is minimal due to the belay system and ropes. Participants may choose their level of intensity, from crawling along the pole to walking across blindfolded.

The premise behind adventure activities is similar to that of the rational-emotive imagery technique, where clients elicit emotion and assess thinking or self-talk at that particular moment of the imagery exercise. The distinct advantage in utilizing adventure activities is that counselors and peers can now directly observe, assess, and intervene during critical moments. A participant may experience and display a variety of emotions while attempting the cat walk. Participants may be afraid to step onto the log, may freeze, get angry, make excuses, cry, or utilize any deficient coping strategies within their personal repertoire. When such reactions occur, counselors are advised to respond with the interventions appropriate to the situation, such as identifying the negative self-talk "They will think I'm scared": inference chaining; uncovering core irrational beliefs, such as "I'm a failure" or "I must do this perfectly"; and using the peer group to assist in actively disputing these beliefs. Other methods can then be used in the postprocessing group or during the review of the videotape.

Emotive techniques such as watching a peer face challenges and succeed or fail without ridicule from the group can help create an empowering experience for all participants and enhance the unconditional acceptance of self and others. Framing the passage along the pole as the choice to free oneself of substance abuse assists in metaphoric learning. Even a fall (like relapse) may not be a catastrophe when there is the support of the rope or belayer (family, peer group, or other support). Actually experiencing the eustress as being uncomfortable but positive can help decrease low frustration tolerance. The risky walk often leads to self-empowerment and success. Shame attacking during a cat walk can take the form of a participant's singing "Yankee Doodle" or something equally uncomfortable or embarrassing and finding out that it was not "so terrible." The flooding technique may be effective for participants who are afraid of heights or claim they have an inability to trust others. Peer support becomes essential for emotional safety and participation in these activities. Participants can reward themselves for their accomplishments or use self-derived punishment for failing to attempt the activity.

These methods and techniques need to be well thought out and sequenced in the proper order dependent on clientele and problem areas. Often, they are used in combination for optimum experience and effect. Skilled therapists are flexible enough to modify the task or sequence based on progress and outcomes during the event. It should be clear that a program such as this is a multimodal form of therapy that employs the techniques of many different theories and domains. However, it is the long-term gain that is focused on and not just what may "feel good" at the moment. Therefore, various therapeutic techniques are avoided.

212 ADVENTURE-BASED TECHNIQUES

RATIONALE FOR COMBINING TREATMENTS

There is a common theme in all adventure-based therapy programs that reflects many of the basic tenets of classic REBT. Its critical components not only provide the rationale for integrating the theoretical treatment modalities but also include ways to enhance treatment effectiveness within a new theoretical framework. "Experiential adventure therapy focuses on placing clients in activities that challenge dysfunctional behaviors and reward functional change" (Gass, 1993, p. 5).

The critical components of adventure-based therapy include experiences that are action-centered, turning the more passive talk therapy into a physically concrete experience directly interacting with the individual. This immediately transforms the behavioral aspect of REBT into a simultaneous cognitive, emotive, behavioral experience, much like the homework assigned between REBT sessions. As M. A. Gass points out (1993):

> Action-centered therapies also heighten the amount of non-verbal interaction between clients (Gillis & Bonney, 1986), allowing a greater examination of how clients truly interact. Mason (1987) has also pointed out that in a therapeutic context, non-verbal communication is five times more believable than verbal communication. This adds to the increased validity of client interaction and the resulting beneficial change. This enriched perspective provides therapists with a multidimensional perspective of client interaction for generating positive change based on observed behavior. (p. 6)

Similar to the working premise of REBT, when using such techniques as shame attacking (Ellis, 1994) and paradoxical strategies where the introduction of novel stimuli and situations can reduce client resistance, the unfamiliar wilderness adventure environment sets up a break in the homeostasis of treatment. An inherent goal in many adventure experiences is to take participants out of familiar settings and immerse them in situations that are new and unique. This is also similar to the REBT use of flooding or direct exposure techniques rather than more gradual techniques of systematic desensitization, and provides clients with few expectations or preconceived notions about their success.

In the REACT program, the wilderness and adventure activities provide a nonrisk atmosphere for clients to explore problems rather than be overwhelmed or incapacitated by them. This new environment can also assist both client and therapist in accurately assessing activating events (A) and irrational beliefs (B) leading to irrational consequences (C), as observed by all involved. This helps clarify initial problems and leads to generalization to similar difficulties both past and present.

Another striking similarity between traditional REBT methods and adventure-based therapy is their focus on successful rather than dysfunctional behaviors. In this new adventure environment, participants begin on an equal footing with each other and are thereby given opportunities to focus on their strengths and abilities rather than on previous dysfunctions. With the proper sequencing of the therapeutic program, clients' initial defenses will lead to healthy change upon completion of progressively more difficult and rewarding tasks. More important, it is not task completion that is most important, but, as in group psychotherapy, the process that challenges, motivates, and fosters growth so that lasting and profound change can occur. Clients are challenged to stretch perceived limitations and irrational beliefs while discovering untapped resources and a variety of positive gains.

Group development and process is an integral part of integrating REBT and adventure-based therapy. REBT practitioners teach that group psychotherapy is an educational process that improves mental health; because experiential methods confer mental health benefits, it is believed that such adventure activities should generally be used to exemplify the principle of the rational-emotive behavior philosophy (Leaf et al., 1992). It is within the group that processing of the here and now of the day's events occurs. These cooperative events, combined with the preinstructed underpinnings of the basic ABCs of REBT, lead to the brief yet profound insight necessary for lasting change.

Currently, there are many methods utilized within the group therapy context for adventure-based therapy. A true systemic perspective is taken as group members struggle with individual and group needs. The successful use of family REBT within a structural family systems perspective is well documented (Huber & Baruth, 1989). Therapists do more than offer a variety of activities for enjoyment; they use these activities to foster change. Designing adventure activities for therapeutic gain has an obvious correlation to group therapy. As recommended by Gillis and Bonney (1989), adventure-based therapy should frame the physical involvement of such activities around specific psychological and behavioral issues. These issues should focus on changing dysfunctional behavior patterns, including dysfunctional cognitions and beliefs, by using an active, directive, and problem-solving method.

Adventure-based therapies have the potential for outstanding results within the psychotherapeutic community as well as just about all other populations. By combining an already established, well-documented, and tested form of therapy such as brief REBT with adventure-based therapy, the relevant hypothesis would be an increased step in efficiency for long-term change. Adventure-based therapy currently stands as a more inelegant adjunct to therapy, but with minor modifications and adaptations it can be utilized as a powerful, elegant method of short-term psychotherapy. REACT treatment would further benefit other populations and groups, such as corporate professionals, participants in leadership and assertiveness training programs, and those dealing with handicaps, addictions, or terminal illnesses, those suffering from dysfunctional thinking or irrational beliefs, and persons who create their own misery.

As with other experiential therapies, individuals are responsible for their own behavior and experiences. It is experiential in that the clients come to grips with what they are thinking, feeling, and doing as they interact with the therapist (e.g., Gestalt therapies). One assumption is that growth occurs through personal contact rather than through the therapist's techniques or interpretations. Another basic assumption is that clients have the capacity to do their own seeing, feeling, sensing, and interpreting; thus, client autonomy is fostered, and participants are expected to be active in therapy. The goal is challenging the client to move from environmental support toward self-support and to gain increased and enriched awareness of moment-to-moment experiencing, which by itself is curative (Gass, 1993).

The experience is intensified so that optimum learning can be achieved by pointing out the process in a more active-directed, didactic, and educational manner. This is sufficient to enhance the certainty of the experience. The goal of the REACT program is to eliminate a self-defeating outlook on life and acquire a more rational and tolerant philosophy. Clients are taught that life events themselves do not disturb us; rather, our interpretation of events is critical to our emotional and behavioral responses to those events.

Several powerful and therapeutic mechanisms that the adventure-based therapy approach utilizes are unique in facilitating change. Where the goals may be the same, the wilderness and adventure activities combined with skilled therapeutic processing have the advantage of quickly and readily producing feelings and challenging cognitions that in more traditional therapies may take much more time, energy, and persuasiveness and create greater resistance to change. In Mason's words (1987):

> Feedback from one's actions and deliberate inaction is very clearcut. . . . on the rock, for example, we know clearly when we are on top, when we are stuck, and when we are frozen at the bottom, looking up. The metaphor of rock climbing can thus allow us to become more honest with ourselves. Another example of a mechanistic component might be a "trust fall" where a participant might be asked to stand in a tree six or seven feet off the ground and fall backwards into a group's waiting arms. Depending on the participant's stage of recovery or particular issues being addressed, the goal of this exercise might be to break through denial and bring to the surface powerful feelings related to the shattering of trust that results from abuse or other type of victimization. These feelings can then be worked on in the group and ongoing therapy (Cole et al., 1994). As with rock climbing, belayer trust, and self-reliance in the wilderness, many issues spring to the surface that are not usually tested so fully in our everyday environment. Trust issues can be worked on more directly within the REACT program, lending more power and validity to what usually is a more verbally and cognitive-based treatment. (p. 93)

The strong rationale for integrating the experiential adventure-based therapy into the overall framework of REBT seems quite sound. Ellis (1996) relates how REBT has always used forms of experiential therapy in that it has encouraged participants to take risks of failure and rejection in vivo, to face their physical and emotional fears and thereby help themselves overcome their irrational phobias. The experiential aspect of REBT has an emotive-evocative quality that often works very well: "It introduces a novel, forceful, vigorous element into therapy; and the exercises used are also behavioral and encourage a pronounced active-directive change" (Ellis, 1996, p. 17).

As expressed by Ellis (1994), when used by itself without adequate cognitive disputing and other techniques, experiential therapy has its distinct limitations and disadvantages. One limitation is that despite initial and often dramatic improvement within a profound and successful experience, these effects are mostly temporary. Almost all participants revert to old dysfunctional thoughts and habits; others may make lasting changes but may do so in "unhealthy" ways. Without proper insight, new dysfunctional beliefs may replace previous, even less functional ones, but at the expense of a quality lifestyle. Other disadvantages may include inadequately trained mental health professionals who encourage "feel-good" therapy or are unable to recognize when psychotropic medication is required.

Therefore, by implementing the adventure-based therapy program into the framework of REBT, short-term and often profound gains can be structured into long-term philosophic change. By utilizing the standard methods of REBT, such as practice, psychoeducation, cognitive disputing, and ongoing treatment beyond the adventure experience, the full treatment modality can be used to take advantage of both treatments for additional and more enduring, effective change.

REACT PROGRAM REQUIREMENTS

Specific elements taken from various REBT group inpatient and outpatient programs include staff qualifications, training and supervision of REBT methods, bibliotherapy, group therapy, individual psychotherapy, and psychological assessments. Others include medication referrals, use of a sense of humor, shame-attacking exercises, and group irrational belief disputational exercises. REBT programs that have used a ropes and initiative course have yielded positive results (Nottingham & Neimeyer, 1992). Current REBT group programs emphasize the importance of the therapeutic environment and need for creativity (Friedberg et al., 1992); the use of continual progress reports and empirical measures (Leaf et al., 1992); consistent and highly structured methods of instruction (Lange, 1986); and the need to quickly break through stages of denial and resistance and overcome fears from cognitive distortions and irrational beliefs (Laws, 1989).

Given this information, the proposed REACT program rests on the basic foundation of existing models to be successful. This new program consists of a highly structured and organized method of therapy and adventure activities individualized to the needs of each group of participants. Duration varies from a 1-day intensive, a weekend trip, a 3- to 5-day excursion, to the 7- to 10-day marathon therapeutic adventure; this is also dependent on the needs of the group and specific problems to be addressed. However, utilizing all of the above advantages and integrating them within the rational-emotive behavioral approach is not that complicated.

The first step is to hire and train staff who are or will become competent in REBT and adventure-based activities. It is the lack of consistency of theoretical orientation that appears to water down the therapeutic effectiveness within other programs. Once the counselors and adventure therapists have been sufficiently trained in the principles of REBT and cross-trained with the adventure activities, a selection process of particular participants is made. This can be based on previous diagnosis, homogeneity of a specific problem type, physical ability, and age group. Gender separation is reserved for select populations such as sexual abuse victims or for another pertinent reason where emotional safety may be a factor.

The assessment procedure also comprises exclusionary criteria for clients not ready or able to participate and benefit based on program design, staff qualifications, or activity or locations planned. Individuals who would likely be excluded are those whose cognitive ability is limited by psychosis, severe attention deficit disorder or retardation, or psychiatric disturbances so severe that they may not gain from the program and may hinder others from benefiting as well. It is also important to exclude those individuals who are a threat to themselves or others. A brief observation period can help to maintain the safety and integrity of the group to minimize critical incidents or predictable negative or hazardous behaviors in the field.

Assigned readings and bibliotherapy prior to group work helps participants understand the general concepts of REBT and includes the expectations and process of the adventure program. This may alleviate initial stressors and anxiety and prepare participants to ask questions relevant to the treatment. Along with the program presentation, participants complete standardized pretest questionnaires and background information, including relevant medical, psychiatric, and psychosocial histories. Questions relevant to contraindications of outdoor adventure activities (e.g., allergies, injuries, specific phobias, current medications, etc.) are covered.

Individual treatment planning, goal setting, and predicting behaviors for interventions constitute a standard procedure used by all staff prior to the expedition or initiative course. A collaborative effort in goal setting with the clients is encouraged. Treatment plans rely on observable and measurable behaviors so that progress can be readily assessed.

Group REBT therapy is then introduced as the principle method of processing group and individual experiences, and the Full Value Behavior contract is reviewed and agreed upon before further progression in treatment can occur. The "challenge by choice" philosophy is explained, and the initial principles of the ABCs of REBT begin. In addition to the processing groups (briefing and debriefing) of adventure activities, group initiatives, problem solving, trust activities, and an average of two psychoeducational groups per day are scheduled. Daily postactivity journal writing and REBT self-help forms are assigned and discussed to enhance therapeutic insight and education.

The goals of the therapy, adventure experiences, and experience as a whole for the participants are to decrease irrational beliefs and stress symptoms; increase unconditional self-acceptance; increase frustration tolerance; specify symptom relief based on individual treatment plans; and increase philosophical outlook on individual's responsibility in creating their own discomfort. The REACT program stresses that the empowerment of participants is not in taking control over the events in their lives, but in perceiving events in such a way as to make them manageable. With continued practice, clients can adopt a more healthy lifestyle and more rational ways of thinking and behaving. These overall goals are then tested by postexperience follow-up and further group or individual work as needed. Need for additional bibliotherapy or support groups determined by participants and therapists in collaboration.

As more adventure-based counseling programs emerge, it becomes more apparent that it is not the experience alone that effects change: change comes from the application of counseling-oriented processes applied to experiential activities within the context of a group. Therefore, it is no longer sufficient for one to be trained in outdoor-related fields, or to be paired up with a therapist to run adventure programs; instead, cross-training models are needed for proper implementation of therapeutic guidelines (Berman, 1995).

LIMITATIONS AND FUTURE RESEARCH

Research is necessary to foster the successful application of adventure-based programs. One of the main limitations of the REACT program is that it should not be used as a stand-alone treatment, but as an adjunct to more traditional therapies. It is also imperative to discover how to foster retention in adventure-based therapy programs. Any benefits gained by the adventure or wilderness experience can be lost without follow-up procedures (Priest & Lesperance, 1994). It is hoped that the integration of the adventure-based programs within a more stabilized and theoretically sound treatment modality such as REBT may alleviate some of these limitations.

Issues concerning treatment effectiveness, integration of adventure-based therapy with other modalities, clear definitions of program terminology, and how adventure activities fit in with *DSM-IV* diagnostic and symptom criteria need to be addressed (Gass, 1993). Other questions requiring further research include:

(1) How does the adventure process vary for clients with particular diagnoses? (2) What are contraindications for adventure experiences (e.g., should survivors of sexual abuse perform the trust fall)? (3) What influence does medication have on the adventure process? (4) What influence does the composition of a group have on the effectiveness of treatment during adventure experiences? (5) Should there be a database of information identifying certain activities as being most effective with a particular population or specific problem area? Issues of professionalization, evaluation approaches, program monitoring, retention and follow-up, experimental studies, safety information, leader effectiveness, feedback from participants, and effectiveness of treatment continue to be addressed.

SUMMARY AND CONCLUSIONS

The advantages of using a cognitive-behavioral approach, specifically REBT, in concert with adventure-based therapy are seen in the basic similarities in and principles shared by the two approaches. Treatment effectiveness would be truly enhanced by maintaining internal consistency of theory and process throughout the program. With this in mind, positive outcomes and increased effectiveness would likely occur with other theoretical approaches, including reality, psychodynamic, client-centered, systemic, multimodal, and other therapies, as long as the process could be verified and replicated.

REBT may be best suited to this format because it is brief, empirical, reliable, and usually easily explained to participant groups. REBT keeps the focus on the client, is present-oriented, and empowers participants with the responsibility for their own wellness and learning. Future sessions in individual or booster groups are available, as well as self-help books that are an inexpensive follow-up to maintain therapeutic gains that transform participants from being clients into being their own therapist.

REACT can serve as a brief and powerful adjunct to traditional REBT when there are indications that more effective approaches are needed for particular individuals or groups who are resistant to or less able to benefit from office therapy. Additionally, REACT may be a first choice for treatment in cases where low frustration tolerance or the need to build unconditional self-acceptance is indicated.

REACT does not deny the presumed therapeutic effects of wilderness therapy and the particular environment, but by maintaining a consistent theoretical framework, strives to stack the deck in favor of therapeutic uniformity when considering the overall effectiveness of combined treatment. I believe that, in theory, adventure-based therapy programs will benefit from the highly structured and down-to-earth approach of a REBT regimen. Having counselors trained in this process will lead to consistency of results and make for more sound outcome research. Clients will benefit from the ease and transition of generalizing wilderness situations to real-world problems with the assistance of outside REBT therapy follow-up sessions. If the client has had REBT sessions prior to the wilderness experience (as in the REACT program), then the main focus would be on the task at hand, and processing critical events would be readily understood within those terms. Counselors would be both adventure wilderness and REBT trained, and the facilitating of client learning and relevant critical events such as irrational beliefs, disputational strategies, and blocks to goals would take on a more clinical focus.

REFERENCES

Bacon, S. (1988). Paradox and double binds in adventure education. In M.A. Gass (Ed.), *Adventure therapy: Therapeutic applications of adventure programming* (pp. 259–282). Dubuque, IA: Kendall/Hunt.

Banaka, W., & Young, D. (1985). Community coping skills enhanced by an adventure camp for adult chronic psychiatric patients. *Hospital and Community Psychiatry, 38*(7), 745–748.

Bandura, A. (1977). Self-Efficacy: Toward a unifying theory of behavioral change. *Psychological Review, 84*, 191–215.

Berman, D.S. (1995, August). Adventure therapy: Current status and future directions. *Journal of Experiential Education, 18*(2), 61–62.

Berman, D.S., & Anton, M. (1988). A wilderness therapy program as an alternative to adolescent psychiatric hospitalization. *Residential Treatment for Children and Youth, 5*, 41–53.

Bernard, M.E. (Ed.). (1991). *Using rational-emotive therapy effectively: A practitioner's guide*. New York: Plenum Press.

Bisson, C., & Luckner, J. (1996, August–September). Fun in learning: The pedagogical role of fun in adventure education. *Journal of Experiential Education, 19*(2), 108–112.

Bunting, C. (1995, May). Physiological measurements of stress during outdoor adventure activities. *Journal of Experiential Education, 18*(1), 5–11.

Cason, D., & Gillis, H.L. (1994). A meta-analysis of outdoor adventure programming. *Journal of Experiential Education, 17*(1), 40–47.

Castellano, T.C., & Soderstrom, I.R. (1992). Therapeutic wilderness programs and juvenile recidivism: A program evaluation. *Journal of Offender Rehabilitation, 17*(314), 19–46.

Clagett, A.F. (1989). Effective therapeutic wilderness camp programs for rehabilitating emotionally disturbed, problem teenagers and delinquents. *Journal of Offender Counseling, 11*(1), 79–86.

Clagett, A.F. (1992). Group-integrated reality therapy in a wilderness camp. *Journal of Offender Rehabilitation, 17*(314), 1–18.

Clapp, C.L., & Rudolph, S.M. (1990). Building family teams: An adventure-based approach to enrichment and intervention. In M.A. Gass (Ed.), *Adventure therapy: Therapeutic applications of adventure programming* (pp. 111–121). Dubuque, IA: Kendall/Hunt.

Cole, E., Erdman, E., & Rothblum, E.D. (1994). *Wilderness therapy for women: The power of adventure.* New York: Haworth Press.

Davis-Berman, J.L., & Berman, D.S. (1989). The wilderness therapy program: An empirical study of its effects with adolescents in an outpatient setting. *Journal of Contemporary Psychotherapy, 19*(4), 271–281.

Davis-Berman, J.L., & Berman, D.S. (1993). Therapeutic wilderness programs: Issues of professionalism in an emerging field. *Journal of Contemporary Psychotherapy, 23*(2), 127–134.

Davis-Berman, J.L., Berman, D.S. (1994). *Wilderness therapy: Foundations theory, and research.* Dubuque, IA: Kendall/Hunt.

Davis-Berman, J.L., Berman, D.S., & Capone, L. (1994). Therapeutic wilderness programs: A national survey. *Journal of Experiential Education, 17*(2), 49–53.

Dillenschneider, C.A. (1983). *Wilderness adventure programming for the mentally retarded: A rationale and therapeutic basis for program development.* (ERIC Document Reproduction Service, ED238216).

Dryden, W. (1995). *Brief rational-emotive behavior therapy.* New York: Wiley.

Ellis, A. (1972). *Executive leadership: The rational-emotive approach.* New York: Institute for Rational-Emotive Therapy.

Ellis, A. (1974/1991). *Experiential therapy vs. rational-emotive therapy* (Rev. ed.). New York: Institute for Rational-Emotive Therapy.

Ellis, A. (1991). Using RET effectively: Reflections and interview. In M.E. Bernard (Ed.), *Using rational-emotive therapy effectively: A practitioner's guide* (pp. 1–33). New York: Plenum Press.

Ellis, A. (1994). *Reason and emotion in psychotherapy: Revised and updated.* New York: Carol.

Ellis, A. (1996). *Better, deeper, and more enduring brief therapy: The rational-emotive behavior therapy approach.* New York: Brunner/Mazel.

Ellis, A., & Dryden, W. (1997). *The practice of rational-emotive behavior therapy* (2nd ed.). New York: Springer.

Ellis, A., & Grieger, R. (1977). *Handbook of rational-emotive therapy.* New York: Springer.

Ewert, A. (1989). *Outdoor adventure pursuits. Foundations, models, and theories.* Ohio: Publishing Horizons.

Finkenberg, M.E., Shows, D., & DiNucci, J.M. (1994). Participation in adventure-based activities and self-concepts of college men and women. *Perceptual and Motor Skills, 78,* 1119–1122.

Friedberg, R.D., Fidaleo, R.A., & Mikules, M.M. (1992, Summer). Inpatient cognitive therapy: Detours, potholes, and road blocks along the routes of progress. *Journal of Rational-Emotive & Cognitive-Behavior Therapy, 10*(2), 83–93.

Gall, A.L. (1987, March). You can take the manager out of the woods but . . . *Training and Development Journal,* 54–58.

Gass, M.A. (Ed.). (1993). *Adventure therapy: Therapeutic applications of adventure programming.* Dubuque, IA: Kendall/Hunt.

Gass, M.A., & Gillis, H.L. (1995a, May). CHANGES: An assessment model using adventure experiences. *Journal of Experiential Education, 18*(1), 34–40.

Gass, M.A., & Gillis, H.L. (1995b). Focusing on the "solution" rather than the "problem": Empowering client change in adventure experiences. *Journal of Experiential Education, 18*(2), 63–69.

Gass, M.A., & McPhee, P. (1990). Emerging for recovery: A descriptive analysis of adventure therapy for substance abusers. *Journal of Experiential Education, 13*(2), 29–35.

Gillett, D.P., Thomas, G.P., Skok, R.L., & McLaughlin, T.F. (1991, Spring). The effects of wilderness camping and hiking on the self-concept and the environmental attitudes and knowledge of twelfth graders. *Journal of Experiential Education, 22*(3), 33–44.

Gillis, H.L., & Bonney, W.C. (1986). Group counseling with couples or families: Adding adventure activities. *Journal for Specialists in Group Work, 11*(4), 213–220.

Gillis, H.L., & Bonney, W.C. (1989). Utilizing adventure activities with intact groups: A sociodramatic systems approach to consultation. *Journal of Mental Health Counseling, 11*(4), 345–358.

Gray, S., & Yerkes, R. (1995). Documenting clinical events in adventure therapy. *Journal of Experiential Education, 18*(2), 95–101.

Grieger, R.M. (1985, Fall/Winter). The process of rational-emotive therapy. *Journal of Rational-Emotive & Cognitive-Behavior Therapy, 3*(2), 138–149.

Harris, P.M., Mealy, L., Matthews, H., Lucas, R., & Moczygemba, M. (1993). A wilderness challenge program as correctional treatment. *Journal of Offender Rehabilitation, 19*(3/4), 149–164.

Hazelworth, M.S., & Wilson, B.E. (1990, Summer). The effects of an outdoor adventure camp experience on self-concept. *Journal of Environmental Education, 21*(4), 33–37.

Herbert, J.T. (1996, October-November-December). Use of adventure-based counseling programs for persons with disabilities. *Journal of Rehabilitation, 3*–9.

Huber, C.H., & Baruth, L.G. (1989). *Rational-emotive family therapy: A systems perspective.* New York: Springer.

Hughs, A., & Dudley, H. (1973). An odd idea for a new problem: Camping as a treatment for the emotionally disturbed in our state hospitals. *Adolescence, 8,* 43–50.

Jenkins-Hall, K. (1994). Outpatient treatment of child molesters: Motivational factors and outcomes. *Young Victims, Young Offenders,* 139–150.

Kimball, R.O. (1979). *Wilderness experience program: Final evaluation report.* Santa Fe: State of New Mexico Forensic System, Health and Environment Department.

Kjol, R., & Weber, J. (1993). The 4th fire: Adventure-based counseling with juvenile sex offenders. In M.A. Gass (Ed.), *Adventure therapy: Therapeutic applications of adventure programming* (pp. 103–121). Dubuque, IA: Kendall/Hunt.

Kushnir, T., & Malkinson, R. (1993, Winter). A rational-emotive group intervention for preventing and coping with stress among safety officers. *Journal of Rational-Emotive & Cognitive-Behavior Therapy, 11*(4), 195–205.

Lange, A. (1986). *Rational-emotive therapy: A treatment manual.* Unpublished manuscript, Florida Mental Health Institute, Tampa.

Larson, J.D. (1990). Cognitive-behavioral group therapy with delinquent adolescents: A cooperative approach with the juvenile court. *Journal of Offender Rehabilitation, 16*(1/2), 47–63.

Laws, D.R. (Ed.). (1989). *Relapse prevention with sex offenders.* New York: Guilford Press.

Leaf, R.C., Krauss, D.H., Dantzig, S.A., & Alington, D.E. (1992, Winter). Educational equivalents of psychotherapy: Positive and negative mental health benefits after group therapy exercises by college students. *Journal of Rational-Emotive & Cognitive-Behavior Therapy, 10*(4), 189–205.

Levine, D.V. (1978). Experiencing the city. *Journal of Experiential Education, 1*(2), 13–19.

Long, J.W. (1987, March). The wilderness lab comes of age. *Training and Developmental Journal,* 30–59.

Maguire, R., & Priest, S. (1994, August). The treatment of bulimia nervosa through adventure therapy. *Journal of Experiential Education, 17*(2), 44–48.

Marx, J.D. (1988, November-December). An outdoor adventure counseling program for adolescents. *Social Work,* 517–520.

Mason, M.J. (1987, Spring/Summer). Wilderness family therapy: Experiential dimensions. *Contemporary Family Therapy, 9*(1/2), 90–105.

McPhee, P.J., & Gass, M.A. (1993). A group development model for adventure therapy programs. In M.A. Gass (Ed.), *Adventure therapy: Therapeutic applications of adventure programming* (pp. 171–178) Dubuque, IA: Kendall/Hunt.

Miles, J.C. (1987, Winter). Wilderness as a learning place. *Journal of Environmental Education, 18*(2), 33–40.

Mitten, D. (1995). Building the group: Using personal affirming to create healthy group process. *Journal of Experiential Education, 18*(2), 82–90.

Nadler, R.S. (1995). Edgework: Stretching boundaries and generalizing experiences. *Journal of Experiential Education, 18*(1), 52–55.

Nadler, R.S., & Luckner, J.L. (1992). *Processing the adventure experience: Theory and practice.* Dubuque, IA: Kendall/Hunt.

Neely, M.A., & Kling, E.B. (1987). Effects of leadership training during wilderness camping. *Small Group Behavior, 18*(2), 280–286.

Nottingham, E.J., & Neimeyer, R.A. (1992). Evaluation of a comprehensive inpatient rational-emotive therapy program: Some preliminary data. *Journal of Rational-Emotive & Cognitive-Behavior Therapy, 10*(2), 57–79.

Parker, M., & Stoltenberg, C.D. (1995). Use of adventure experiences in traditional counseling interventions. *Psychological Reports, 77,* 1376–1378.

Priest, S. (1995, August). The effect of belaying and belayer type on the development of interpersonal partnership trust in rock climbing. *Journal of Experiential Education, 18*(2), 107–109.

Priest, S., & Lesperance, M.A. (1994). Time series trends in corporate team development. *Journal of Experiential Education, 17*(1), 34–39.

Ringer, M., & Gillis, H.L. (1995). Managing psychological depth in adventure programming. *Journal of Experiential Education, 18*(1), 41–51.

Rogers, C. (1973). A theory of personality. In T. Millon (Ed.), *Theories of psychopathology and personality* (pp. 217–230). Philadelphia: W.B. Saunders. (Reprinted from "A theory of therapy, personality, and interpersonal relationships as developed in the client centered framework" in *Psychology: A study of a science* (Vol. 3), by S. Koch, Ed., 1973, New York: McGraw-Hill.)

Sachs, J.J., & Miller, S.R. (1992). The impact of a wilderness experience on the social interactions and social expectations of behaviorally disordered adolescents. *Behavioral Disorders, 17*(2), 89–98.

Schoel, J., Prouty, D., & Radcliffe, P. (1988). *Islands of healing: A guide to adventure-based counseling.* Hamilton, MA: Project Adventure.

Stich, T.F. (1983). Experiential therapy. *Journal of Experiential Education, 6*(3), 22–30.

Stich, T.F., & Gaylor, M.S. (1983). Risk management in adventure programs with special populations: Two hidden dangers. In M.A. Gass (Ed.), *Adventure therapy: Therapeutic applications of adventure programming* (pp. 161–169). Dubuque, IA: Kendall/Hunt.

Vincent, S.B. (1995). Emotional safety in adventure therapy programs: Can it be defined? *Journal of Experiential Education, 18*(2), 76–81.

Walen, S.R., DiGiuseppe, R., & Dryden, W. (1992). *A practitioner's guide to rational-emotive therapy* (2nd ed.). New York: Oxford University Press.

Walsh, V., & Gollins, G. (1976). *The exploration of the Outward Bound process.* Silver Springs: Colorado Outward Bound School.

Webb, P.J. (1993). The use of a three-day therapeutic wilderness adjunct by the Colorado Outward Bound School with survivors of violence. In M.A. Gass (Ed.), *Adventure therapy: Therapeutic applications of adventure programming* (pp. 95–102). Dubuque, IA: Kendall/Hunt.

Whitford, R., & Parr, V. (1995). Uses of rational-emotive behavior therapy with juvenile sex offenders. *Journal of Rational-Emotive & Cognitive-Behavior Therapy, 13*(4), 273–282.

Yalom, I. (1985). *The theory and practice of group psychotherapy* (3rd ed.). New York: Basic Books.

PART THREE

TECHNOLOGY-BASED TECHNIQUES

CHAPTER 7

Biofeedback with Children and Adolescents

TIMOTHY P. CULBERT

> Every change in the physiologic state is accompanied by an appropriate change in the mental-emotional state, conscious or unconscious, and conversely, every change in the mental-emotional state is accompanied by an appropriate change in the physiological state.
>
> —Green, Green, and Walters (1970)

THIS QUOTE sets the stage for understanding the important relationship between cognition/behavior/emotion and physiologic change. While engaging an individual in behavioral and/or psychological therapies of any variety, the therapist may or may not be aware of profound physiologic changes in the client that can be therapeutic, be countertherapeutic, and can guide the therapist in facilitating therapeutic change in a positive direction for the client. Although observation can provide clues as to a client's physical state and emotional experience, it is primarily subjective and, therefore, unreliable. Similarly, client self-report can be inaccurate. For example, clients may state they feel subjectively "relaxed" when they are, in fact, experiencing a state of high sympathetic nervous system arousal. The use of biofeedback training, physiologic monitoring, and related techniques can lend precision to this process, opening up a wide range of effective and creative options to enhance psychotherapeutic progress in ways that traditional "talk" therapies cannot offer.

There is increasing recognition within the pediatric medical and mental health fields that many childhood disorders and symptoms have equal psychologic and biologic components (Haggerty, Roughman, & Pless, 1993; Murphy, 1992). Biofeedback offers the child psychotherapist an ideal tool to assist children in understanding and addressing the mind-body connection inherent in many complex pediatric psychophysiologic problems, including acute and chronic pain, anxiety and stress-related symptoms, sleep disorders, school performance problems, and disorders of elimination, to name just a few.

INTRODUCTION AND DEFINITIONS

Biofeedback refers to the use of electronic or electromechanical equipment to measure and then feed back information about physiologic functions. Information about these physiologic functions may be utilized by individuals to assist them in enhancing awareness of their body and then to modulate the physiologic function in a desired direction. Feedback can be provided in either auditory, visual, or multimedia formats, whichever a client finds most appealing and understandable (Schwartz & Associates, 1995).

The physiologic functions most commonly measured with biofeedback equipment include peripheral (finger) temperature, breathing pattern and gas exchange, muscle activity, electrical brain activity, skin conductance, and heart rate (see Table 7.1a–7.1f). For more technical detail about specific modalities and for general background about the field of biofeedback, the reader is referred to texts by Schwartz and Associates (1995), Basmajian (1989), Criswell, (1995), and Andreassi (1995). Recently, this area has been designated broadly as applied psychophysiology or behavioral physiology.

Table 7.1a
Biofeedback Modalities: Peripheral (Finger)
Temperature (Thermography)

Abbreviation:
TMP

Description:
Peripheral temperature is generally a good indirect indicator of autonomic nervous system (ANS) balance. Generally, the more aroused your sympathetic nervous system (SNS)—as in stress, anxiety, anger states—the lower your finger temperature. In certain disorders, such as migraine and Raynaud's, the mechanisms governing baseline finger temperature and temperature change are more complex. For most subjects, with relaxation and lowering of SNS activity, peripheral temperature generally increases as peripheral blood flow improves. There is no strict goal for temperature training with pediatric clients, but an upward trend (increasing temperature) and achieving /maintaining a finger temperature above 92° F is desirable.

Placement/Setup:
Secured on nondominant index or second finger with paper tape or Velcro strap.

Clinical Notes:
Inexpensive home-training temperature devices are useful and include biodots, dermatherms, and small alcohol thermometers. Temperature training is particularly useful for children with migraine headache, Raynaud's disorder, and anxiety disorders.

The importance of understanding the links of physiology to behavior, emotions, and cognitions cannot be understated. The contribution of stress to childhood pathophysiology is also increasingly evident (Gagnon, Hudnall, & Andrasik, 1992; Rutter, 1998). Ongoing research suggests increased evidence for specific psychophysiologic patterns that occur with a variety of common presenting problems, including anxiety, panic attacks, headaches, sleep disturbance, ADHD, functional or somatoform pain syndromes, irritable bowel syndrome, enuresis, and encopresis (Culbert, Reaney, & Kohen, 1994; Gagnon et al., 1992;

Table 7.1b
Biofeedback Modalities: Electromyography

Abbreviation:
EMG

Description:
Measurement of muscle activity. Values depend somewhat on placement of sensors and the sensitivity of the equipment being used. For the purposes of relaxation training, one is usually looking for a value of less of 3 microvolts as being reflective of a "relaxed muscle."

Placement/Setup:
Can be used in wide-area measures for general relaxation training or very specific localized placements for muscle reeducation. Common training sites for relaxation purposes are bifrontal and across the trapezia muscles. Placed on the skin with small adhesive pads.

Clinical Notes:
For introductory purposes early in biofeedback training with children, a forearm placement is useful because it is quickly controlled and mastered by most children and therefore facilitates easy understanding of mind-body links as well as building confidence and enjoyment of the experience. Evidence for muscle relaxation in a specific set of muscles does not imply more generalized relaxation nor does it reliably correlate with SNS arousal. EMG training is particularly helpful in tension-type headache, rehabilitation work, and encopresis, as well as being incorporated into diaphragmatic breathing training as a way to monitor thoracic activity.

Murphy, 1992; Steptoe, 1991). In addition, interesting research in mapping the somatic signature for emotions is also ongoing (Cacioppo, Klein, Bernston, & Hatfield, 1993; Ley, 1994), as well as work in psychophysiologic stress profiling, which provides insight into an individual's autonomic nervous system (ANS) balance, reactivity, and recovery ability (Murphy, 1992). Further elucidation of findings in these areas of inquiry could have a major impact on how therapeutic change is facilitated in psychotherapy, identifying the distinct interplay of physiologic and psychologic components necessary in managing behavioral and emotional problems of childhood.

Table 7.1c
Biofeedback Modalities: Heart Rate

Abbreviation:
HR or PPG (photoplethysmography).

Description:
Can show heart rate increases and decreases. Heart rate commonly increases in states of emotional arousal (anger, fear) and decreases with relaxation. Norms vary quite a bit depending on age of the patient but are always reported as number of beats per minute.

Placement/Setup:
Placed on fingertip with Velcro band or elastic band.

Clinical Notes:
There has been a lot of recent interest in evaluating and retraining of the normal heart rate variations seen with breathing in and out called respiratory sinus arrhythmia (RSA). In some persons with chronic stress-related conditions (anger, hypertension), RSA is lost. The patient's symptoms tend to improve when normal RSA is retrained utilizing heart rate and breathing biofeedback techniques.

THE RELATIONSHIP OF BIOFEEDBACK TO BEHAVIORAL AND PSYCHOLOGICAL THERAPIES

In their 1998 article, Moss and Lehrer point out that the notion of a biological perspective on psychology and the integration of "body work" with psychotherapeutic techniques is not a new one. Freud utilized a reclining position on a couch during psychoanalysis and observed that this posture helped the patient to assume the "evenly hovering attention" he sought for self-exploration. Sandor Ferenczi, a student of Freud's, observed in 1925 that relaxation exercises were useful in overcoming physical inhibitions and resistances to awareness in psychotherapy (Moss & Lehrer, 1998). Early psychoanalytic practice sometimes utilized relaxation practices to facilitate emotional expression. Wilhelm Reich identified the concept of "muscular armor," which he characterized as patterns of muscular tensing and bracing that block

Table 7.1d
Biofeedback Modalities: Electrodermal Activity (Skin Conductance)

Abbreviations:
EDA, SCL (skin conductance level), GSR (galvanic skin response).

Description:
Measures how much conductance the skin has to a low amount of electrical current passed across its surface. This is a function of how many sweat glands are open in the skin, which is controlled by an individual's level of SNS activation. With more SNS activation or arousal, there is increased conductivity of the skin surface, and therefore higher values if conductance is measured and lower readings if resistance is measured. In terms of conductance values, a reading of 5 micromhos or below is considered reflective of a desirable state of lowered SNS arousal.

Placement/Setup:
Velcro band is used to apply sensors to two fingers on one hand.

Clinical Notes:
EDA is a very sensitive modality reflecting SNS arousal with quick and sometimes dramatic changes, which can be elicited with emotional reactions of the patient. EDA is not always highly consistent across sessions, but the general trend in activity is useful. EDA can be very good for modality for anxiety, phobia issues, stress, and sleep disorder work. It can also be very helpful for disorders of ANS dysregulation. It is commonly used as part of a psychophysiologic stress profile to look at acute response and speed of recovery.

---

emotional expression. He developed a body therapy that included massage and muscle pressure to help patients release this tension, which he postulated would then facilitate psychotherapeutic work (Reich, 1949). Beneficial responses noted from these techniques included improved posture, warm skin with enhanced blood flow, muscular flexibility, and deep respiration with free and easy movement of the chest (Raknes, 1970). Frederick Alexander popularized the idea that the body "speaks" and that body language can be a key to understanding emotional disorders (Moss & Lehrer, 1998).

Table 7.1e
Biofeedback Modalities: Breathing

Abbreviations:
PNG (pneumography), a way to measure abdominal and thoracic movement during the breathing cycle.

CAP (capnometry), refers to the measurement of exhaled carbon dioxide gas (CO_2) from the lungs.

Respiratory rate, measured as number of breaths per minute and varies somewhat with age.

Description:
PNG: Measures abdominal and thoracic movement with stretch sensors.

CAP: Currently, it is becoming increasingly popular and helpful to measure exhaled CO_2 content as another way to look at proper breathing versus hyperventilation and other dysfunctional breathing patterns as reflected in actual gas exchange. With CAP, an exhaled CO_2 in the range of 38 to 42 Torr is the usual goal of training.

Respiratory rate: With relaxed breathing, most patients can develop an inhalation:exhalation ratio of 2:1; for children, this usually means breathing in to the count of 3 to 4 seconds and breathing out to the count of 6 to 8 seconds with a resulting respiratory rate of 6 to 8 breaths/minute.

Placement/Setup:
PNG and Respiratory rate: Velcro straps with stretch sensors embedded in them are placed around the abdomen and chest.

CAP: Small piece of flexible plastic tubing positioned with tape so that the tip is in the nostril; the tubing is then attached to either a handheld CAP unit or, with newer equipment, connected directly to a computerized biofeedback hardware interface and then displayed.

Clinical Notes:
There is excellent support for breath control training in anxiety, particularly panic attacks, asthma, and a variety of stress management applications. The desired breathing pattern is called diaphramatic or belly breathing and involves a relaxed, freely moving abdomen with a slow, rhythmic pace. This facilitates better oxygenation and better CO_2 release and often fosters sense of deep relaxation. Patients with anxiety and panic disorders commonly subtly engage in more thoracic breathing patterns and hyperventilate or overbreathe. This may lead to the development of lower CO_2 levels, which in turn changes the blood's acid/base balance, which can negatively effect cerebral blood flow. Information about breathing pattern can be linked with HR measurement as described above to look at the normal, desirable pattern of heart rate variation with breathing (RSA).

Table 7.1f
Biofeedback Modalities: Electroencephalography (Neurofeedback)

Abbreviation:
  EEG

Description:
  Sensors measure type of different brain wave frequencies and intensity of electrical brain activity in different areas of the brain. Different ratios of activity and amplitudes of specific brain wave frequencies (alpha, theta, and beta waves) are evaluated and then trained to specific criteria.

Placement/Setup:
  Electrodes placed on scalp with electrode paste or gel. Various locations on the head (called montages) are used to capture electrical functioning in different parts or lobes of the brain. Specific placement is determined by the disorder being assessed or type of treatment protocol being used.

Clinical Notes:
  Neurofeedback is increasingly popular as a nonpharmacologic treatment option for a variety of neurophysiologic disorders, including ADHD, seizure disorders, and learning disabilities.

Other pioneers in this area include Ida Rolf and Moshe Feldenkrais, who embraced the need for various physical therapies and attention to muscular tension, posture, and movement as a way of influencing behavioral change (Moss & Lehrer, 1998). Edmund Jacobsen's progressive relaxation (Jacobsen, 1938) and Schultz and Luthe's autogenic training (Schultz & Luthe, 1969) are also well-known examples of relaxation and body awareness techniques that can positively enhance a patient's receptivity to psychotherapy. An early use of physiologic monitoring is seen in Carl Jung's work between 1902 and 1910, in which he observed patient changes in galvanic skin response and breathing to determine which words elicited strong reactions potentially indicative of a psychological complex (Mars, 1998).

As early as 1958, Wolpe and others were identifying psychophysiological links in behavior therapy as their work on anxiety disorders progressed. Particular interest was focused on the "peripheral manifestations " of anxiety as measured in heart rate and skin conductance. In 1960, a group of psychologists organized the Society for Psychophysiological Research, which was followed by the publication of the group's newsletter, *Psychophysiology*, in 1964 (Johnston & Martin, 1991).

Biofeedback is the next link in this chain, bringing much finer precision and sophistication in measuring, recording, analyzing, and feeding back physiologic information during therapy, with benefits for both therapist and client. Biofeedback technology and methods began their evolution in the 1950s and early 1960s with the convergence of several areas of inquiry, including surface electromyography (EMG) studies, operant conditioning of ANS functions in curarized rats, computer science, cybernetics, stress research, and the development of the field of behavioral medicine (Schwartz, 1995). Biofeedback is most commonly used to train relaxation in a variety of ways, as manifest by decreased muscle tension, markers for lowered sympathetic nervous system (SNS) arousal (such as lower heart rate, decreased skin conductance, and increased peripheral temperature), and diaphragmatic breathing patterns. It is also used increasingly as a component in comprehensive behavioral assessment and for correcting specific pathophysiologic elements of mind-body problems (Johnston & Martin, 1991; Sussman & Culbert, 1998).

In 1979, the Biofeedback Society of America (now the Association for Applied Psychophysiology and Biofeedback) published the results of a study on the topic of biofeedback as an adjunct to psychotherapy. The report concluded that biofeedback-assisted psychotherapy may be very beneficial for a variety of problems and that it seemed particularly useful in (1) establishing a therapeutic alliance, (2) breaking a therapeutic impasse, (3) reaching severely disturbed patients, and (4) facilitating psychophysiologic exploration (Rickles, Onoda, & Doyle, 1979).

In the past 20 years, a number of psychologists including Toomin, Mars, Green, Moss, and Shellenberger, have described their work in this area combining psychotherapy with biofeedback and physiologic monitoring in an integrated approach for a variety of problems (Johnston & Martin, 1991; Mars, 1998).

The American Psychological Association has recently identified biofeedback as a "proficiency" under APA guidelines. In addition, there are now master's- and doctoral-level training programs in clinical psychophysiology and biofeedback and behavioral physiology being offered at graduate psychology programs in the United States.

A number of journals—*Psychophysiology, Applied Psychophysiology and Biofeedback,* and *International Journal of Psychophysiology*—cover research in this area. In addition, there are two excellent general biofeedback texts (Basmajian, 1989; Schwartz & Associates, 1995) and a number of other helpful texts that examine similar topics (Andreassi, 1995; Coles, Donchin, & Porges, 1986). It should be pointed out that none of these are specific to the use of biofeedback or related psychophysiologic procedures with children and adolescents. There is, however, an excellent review chapter by Olness and Kohen in their 1996 text and several journal review articles on this topic (Andrasik & Attansio, 1985; Culbert, Kajander, & Reaney, 1996; Finley & Jones, 1992; Smith, 1991).

BIOFEEDBACK WITH CHILDREN AND ADOLESCENTS

Biofeedback is one technique within a category that has been described as "self-regulation skills" for children (Sussman & Culbert, 1999). Self-regulation techniques facilitate a child's natural drive for autonomy and mastery. Learning a self-regulation skill empowers pediatric patients to focus their mind in a way that positively affects their body. This process encourages children to take ownership and control of their problem and actively participate in its resolution. This category describes strategies that identify and cultivate a child's innate abilities to achieve a desired level of health and wellness. The techniques are commonly integrated in the therapeutic milieu and include biofeedback, self-hypnosis and hypnotherapy, cognitive-behavioral therapy, breath control training, and related relaxation strategies (see Table 7.2).

Children and adolescents make excellent biofeedback subjects (Andrasik & Attansio, 1985; Culbert et al., 1996). From the standpoint of physiologic control, children are very capable of

Table 7.2
Self-Regulation Skills for Children and Adolescents

Biofeedback.

Self-Hypnosis (RMI).

Breath control training.

Progressive muscle relaxation.

Autogenic training.

Cognitive/Behavioral therapy.

modulating finger temperature, electrical brain activity, breathing, muscle tension, and other modalities in desired directions as demonstrated in several studies, and generally do this with greater proficiency than adults (Attansio et al., 1985; Dikel & Olness, 1980). Studies also demonstrate the remarkable ability of pediatric subjects to control selected aspects of immune system function, including salivary immunoglobulin content and natural killer cell activity (Hall, Minnes, & Olness, 1993; Olness, Culbert, & Uden, 1989).

For children, the developmental norm of an active and intense fantasy life suggests a special relationship between physiologic control and mental imagery. Imagery is often used during biofeedback training to facilitate relaxation and also to engender certain emotional responses. Lee and Olness (1996) have shown that the type of imagery utilized by a child (active versus passive) will determine the type of physiologic change experienced, as reflected in heart rate, peripheral temperature, and electrodermal activity (EDA) measurements. Studies also demonstrate that athletes using active imagery, even while muscularly relaxed, will show physiologic changes in heart rate and blood pressure that approximate those of actual exercise experience (Wang & Morgan, 1992). This research highlights the importance of careful attention to the cognition suggestions and imagery utilized during the biofeedback process with pediatric patients, because these elements can play such a crucial role in creating the desired behavioral and physiologic change.

Along these lines, it is also important to note the relationship among hypnosis, altered states of awareness, and biofeedback training with children. Children naturally, quickly, and frequently shift between alternative states of awareness in their daily life experience. Listening intently to music, quietly reading a good book, passionately playing a challenging video game, going to the doctor's office after an injury—these situations can all entail a shift in the state of conscious awareness a child is experiencing and these shifts may occur many times a day (Olness & Kohen, 1996).

Hypnosis with children has been defined as the cultivation of specific, desirable alternative states of awareness for the purpose of positive therapeutic change. In hypnotic or trance states, persons are more susceptible to suggestion. During biofeedback training, when attention is highly focused and there is increased awareness of internal body events and sensations, it is arguable that pediatric clients are in an altered state of awareness and are therefore, by definition, highly suggestible (Culbert et al., 1994; Olness, 1997). It is important for the therapist to be attuned to this special condition: language must be carefully chosen and images and messages conveyed that are congruent and appropriate for a given child in a given situation. Detailed attention to this type of therapeutic communication is very important in devising successful self-regulation strategies for pediatric patients and must be tailored to the developmental level, personal interests, and experiences of each child (Marino & Kohen, 1996). Karen Olness, a pioneer in pediatric hypnosis and biofeedback research, points to the fact that many of the techniques used in biofeedback training with children are similar to hypnotic induction and deepening strategies (Olness, 1997). The link between mental imagery, hypnotic trance or altered states, and subsequent physiologic changes needs further clarification. One thing is for certain: biofeedback can play a powerful role in mind/body education for children by illustrating that a change in one's thinking causes a change in one's body in a very immediate, concrete fashion. For example, as a child imagines a favorite place or special activity, he or she can observe the related changes in temperature, EMG activity, breathing, and EDA, which often leaves a lasting impression.

Biofeedback training for children *is not* the same process as it is for adults. Children require a highly flexible, customized, creative treatment approach. Of course, developmental considerations play an important role in treatment planning. Unlike the case with adults, it is not always helpful or necessary to train to absolute physiologic standards (such as finger temperature greater than 95°F or skin conductance level [SCL] less than 3.0 micromhos). Attention span, learning style, and sensory preference must also be considered when devising biofeedback strategies for young clients. Different types of feedback (auditory and visual), game displays, practice strategies, and adjunctive strategies must be tested and agreed upon to optimize engagement and motivation.

One unique aspect of biofeedback training that makes it tremendously popular and appealing for children is the availability of videogame-like formats the therapist can utilize as a treatment "hook." In the author's clinical experience, a number of hardware and software devices have been reviewed and tested with children of all ages. This allows for optimum flexibility, variation, and choice of appropriate format and challenge presented at each biofeedback training session. Children often do best when the therapist can choose the biofeedback task carefully to tap into the developmental drive for fantasy, curiosity, and challenge that children seek in play activities. When these intrinsically motivating features are purposefully designed into biofeedback-based treatment strategies for pediatric clients, the results are often quite remarkable. Children absolutely love returning to the office to play their favorite "videogame for their body" in subsequent sessions.

REVIEW OF BIOFEEDBACK LITERATURE

Current childhood problems for which biofeedback is indicated as either a primary or adjunctive treatment are listed in Table 7.3.

Strong literature support exists for biofeedback-based strategies as first-line treatments for childhood tension-type and migraine headache. A number of good controlled studies including meta-analyses identify the efficacy of biofeedback as a first-line approach (Burke & Andrasik, 1989; Duckro & Cantwell-Simmons, 1989; Labbe & Williamson, 1983), with peripheral temperature training and bifrontal EMG training as the most commonly used

Table 7.3
Applications of Biofeedback to Pediatric Disorders

Disorder	Biofeedback Modalities
Pain	
Headache	EMG, TMP, PNG
RAP	EMG, TMP, PNG
Acute	EDA, PNG
Anxiety Disorders	PNG, CAP, TMP, EDA
Panic	
GAD (Generalized anxiety disorder)	
PTSD (Posttraumatic stress disorder)	
OCD (Obsessive-compulsive disorder)	
Stress management	
Performance anxiety	
Phobias	
Sleep	EMG, TMP, PNG
Enuresis	Conditioning alarm
Encopresis	Anorectal EMG & manometry
ANS Dysfunction	EDA, HR, TMP
Raynaud's	
RSD	
Hypertension	
Neuromuscular rehabilitation	EMG
ADHD	EEG
Learning disabilities	EDA, EEG
Seizures	EEG
Habit disorders/impulse control problems	EMG, PNG
Tics/Tourette's	EMG, EDA, PNG
Chronic illness	PNG, CAP, TMP, PNG
Asthma	
CA	
Hematologic disorders	
Peak performance training	Various

modalities. Biofeedback and related self-regulation skills can also be very helpful in working with children with acute and chronic pain (including procedural pain, needle phobia issues, and postoperative pain) by facilitating relaxation, teaching controlled breathing, and building a child's confidence in self-regulatory pain control ability (Kajander et al., 1998; Kuttner, 1996; Lambert, 1996; Zeltzer & LeBaron, 1982).

Child psychologists are collaborating with physical therapists and other professionals in utilizing surface EMG biofeedback training for children and adolescents as part of pediatric neuromuscular rehabilitation. This has become a well-developed area and has potential benefits for children with spina bifida, cerebral palsy, and head injury as well as those with brain tumors, recovering burn victims, and children with genetic disorders. In this context, biofeedback can be used for patients requiring proprioceptive awareness and muscle reeducation, patients in need of strength and endurance training, and those in need of muscle down training (Bolek, 1998; Brundy et al., 1974; Flodmark, 1986; Nash, Neilson, & O'Dwyer, 1989).

Children with disorders of elimination clearly benefit from biofeedback-based strategies. In the case of primary nocturnal enuresis, the use of conditioning alarms is well established as the most cost-effective choice (Fordham & Meadow, 1989; Schwartz & Associates, 1995). Urodynamic biofeedback techniques and other specialized biofeedback-based approaches for bladder control are also evolving (Combs, Glassberg, Gerdes, & Horowitz, 1998; Killam, Jeffries, & Varni, 1985; Parker & Whitehead, 1982; Sugar & Firlit, 1982). Children with encopresis that is secondary to neuromuscular abnormalities (spinal dysraphism, Cerebral Palsy, sacral agenesis) or postsurgical intervention often benefit from anorectal EMG biofeedback (Iwai, Nagashima, Shimotake, & Iwata, 1993; Wald, Chandra, Gabel, & Chiponis, 1987; Whitehead, Parker, & Masek, 1988). Children with encopresis (functional megacolon) that is refractory to traditional medical management may also have specific issues with dysfunctional defecation dynamics that can be corrected with EMG and manometric biofeedback training procedures (Loening-Baucke, 1990; Olness, McParland, & Piper, 1980).

Children, adolescents, and adults with various forms of anxiety (panic attacks, generalized anxiety disorder) and somatization disorders that are likely anxiety- or "stress"-related are a group for which promising biofeedback-based treatment possibilities are evolving. These include breath control training (via capnometry [CAP] and pneumography [PNG]), EDA-based desensitization procedures, as well as instruction in heart rate variability and peripheral temperature modulation (Beck & Emery, 1985; Gagnon et al., 1992; Kajander & Peper, 1998; Mars, 1998; Timmons & Ley, 1994).

Cutting-edge pediatric applications for biofeedback technologies include sleep disorders, impulse control problems including anger management, and problems related to ANS dysregulation such as Raynaud's disorder, reflex sympathetic dystrophy, irritable bowel syndrome, and hypertension (Barowsky, Moskowitz, & Zweig, 1990; Culbert & Bonfilio, 1998; Ewart, Harris, & Iwata, 1987; Lightman, Pochaczevsky, & Ilowite, 1987; Rose & Carlson, 1987).

Biofeedback and self-regulation skills training can also be used to promote optimal functioning in musicians, athletes, performers, and students. Performance enhancement at all levels is an area with great future promise within the field of applied psychophysiology, and children are of course logical subjects for such intervention at early ages (Kall, 1997; Olness & Kohen, 1996).

Electroencephalographic (EEG) biofeedback applications are advancing at a rapid rate, with promising evidence accumulating that children can alter their EEG amplitudes and maintain this learning for reasonably long time frames. Current research is beginning to support the use of neurofeedback in the treatment of pediatric neurobiologic problems as a way of improving functioning for children with ADHD, learning disabilities, and seizure disorders. Research with EEG biofeedback for children with PTSD, anxiety, depression, enuresis, and immunomodulation is also ongoing but inconclusive to date (Faber, 1998; Finley & Jones, 1992; Linden, Habib, & Radojevic, 1996; Lubar, Smartwood, Smartwood, & O'Donnel, 1995; Seifert & Lubar, 1975; Tansey, 1984).

A number of studies clearly support the benefits of biofeedback-based relaxation and breath control training for children with asthma (Kotses et al., 1991; Lehrer, 1998). Other promising areas of potential clinical application for applied psychophysiologic therapies involve the use of biofeedback and relaxation training for children with psychological and behavioral problems related to their adjustment to chronic illnesses such as diabetes, cancer, and autoimmune disorders.

CLINICAL APPLICATIONS

Biofeedback can be utilized in several different paradigms in conjunction with psychotherapy, behavioral modification strategies, and behavioral counseling. Biofeedback is being used by a variety of pediatric health care and educational professionals in a number of settings. For the purposes of this chapter, the focus is on applications of biofeedback in clinical behavioral and psychological therapy.

Most children can be taught or "coached " in biofeedback techniques across six to eight 40-minute biofeedback sessions that are spaced one to two weeks apart. It is usually helpful to schedule the first three or four sessions about one week apart and then move to a two-week interval for subsequent sessions. Children are expected to practice the techniques learned in the office at home and at school. A minimum of two 5-minute practice sessions per day are recommended, although more are encouraged. Children are asked to keep a daily log or symptom diary describing practice progress and symptom descriptions, typically utilizing a Visual Analogue Scale (VAS) rating system for symptom severity.

In the first one or two sessions, parents are often invited to observe to get a general sense of how the process works, what practice expectations are, and how they might help in home coaching their child. After that, children are usually invited to participate alone so that therapists have their full attention and also to emphasize their responsibility, choice, and sense of partnership in the therapeutic process.

Each client typically is taught several different biofeedback-related techniques and then subsequent sessions are tailored to clients' interests and preferences. Different visual screen displays and auditory feedback options are explored to make the experience optimally engaging and appropriately challenging for each individual. The therapist may choose one specific modality to train in a given session or, as patients' progress, may choose to train two or more modalities simultaneously. Throughout this process, we often describe biofeedback to our young clients as a "videogame for your body." It is clear that biofeedback with its computer-based, high-tech, multimedia format is very appealing and culturally syntonic with today's high-tech computer-literate youth.

One helpful model in clinical biofeedback training follows a hierarchical structure of tasks: *discern–control–generalize*. This organizational scheme flows logically across sessions, and a given pediatric client cannot efficiently move to the next phase until the tasks in the current phase are mastered.

In the *discern* phase of training, clients are taught about mind-body links and physiologic control and assisted in learning to discriminate differences between states of relaxation (low SNS arousal) and tension or anxiety (high SNS arousal). For example, for the child with anger management difficulty, one might work on early recognition of emotional arousal as manifest in specific physiologic changes (increased muscle tension, rapid breathing, pounding pulse). In general, patients can be taught better awareness of their response patterns to a variety of triggers, environmental and interpersonal. It is important to note that for children, normative baseline values for clinical and nonclinical values at different ages and for different modalities don't completely exist. Baseline values across sessions can also vary, particularly for EDA and peripheral temperature.

Early in biofeedback therapy, many patients benefit from completing a psychophysiologic stress profile. This can help clients identify their unique pattern of ANS reactivity (an individual's ANS "fingerprint") to different types of stressful stimuli and their ability to recover from such stress. During this procedure, the patient is attached to various sensors (temp, EMG, EDA, PPG, and breathing) and a two- to four-minute baseline is recorded. The patient is then instructed in a two- to four-minute "eyes open" relaxation condition followed by an "eyes closed" period of equal length. The patient is then led through a set of different standardized stressors (e.g., cognitive stressor: doing a rapid series of age-appropriate math calculations; physical stressor: running in place or placing an extremity in an ice water bath), with each stress condition lasting two to four minutes. After each stress condition, patients are once again led into an "eyes open" and then "eyes closed" relaxation period to record how rapidly they "recover" from the stress condition. The profile can then be reviewed with the client. Information about preferred response modality can be helpful in determining which modality to train in subsequent sessions. For example, it is clear that some children will be sensitive temperature responders with rapid and large changes across each condition in the profile. Other individuals respond much more dramatically in another modality such as heart rate or EDA. Time to recovery is also an important element to examine and can be an important outcome to train, particularly with problems such as anxiety and anger management.

In the *control* phase of training, children are coached to master specific skills and achieve certain trends or threshold goals in training a specific physiologic function. For example, they might be helped to consistently maintain a bifrontal EMG reading below 3 microvolts, an EDA below 5 microvolts with directed relaxation, or a finger temperature of 93°–95° F (all of these would be common goals for children and reflect a desirable level of lowered SNS activity). With diaphragmatic breathing, children master the ability to relax chest and thoracic musculature, achieve good abdominal movement, breathe at a slow pace, and maintain an inhalation time of 3 to 4 seconds with an exhalation time of 6 to 10 seconds.

If capnometry is added to measure actual CO_2 exhalation, the patient is asked to target 38 to 42 Torr (a measure of the partial pressure of gases) as a normal value. Breath control training is a favorite of many pediatric patients and offers a relatively quick way to relax and control anxiety in many settings. We begin with a home practice recommendation of twice a day for five minutes to foster comfort, confidence, and experience with these techniques. It is important to note that it is not clear that it is necessary for children to achieve rigidly defined, predetermined goals for any given modality, although general trends in certain modalities are indicative of the desired trend in or magnitude of physiologic change, as described in Table 7.1(a–f). In this phase of training, many children find that specific mental imagery enhances the rapidity with which they can regulate their level of change for a given modality. A common example would be a child utilizing mental imagery about warmth and relaxation-related experiences as a way to facilitate his or her own peripheral temperature change.

Helping clients to *generalize* their skills and apply them successfully in appropriate real-life situation or environment (without the "machine" or the therapist) is often the most challenging part of biofeedback training. Most children enjoy quick success in the discern and control sessions, and within three to five sessions most are achieving the desired physiologic control goals in the biweekly office-based sessions. For transfer of skill to the appropriate setting to take place, the therapist must then move into helping the children or adolescents to identify triggers and cues that will help them to know when to apply their self-regulatory skills. We encourage parents and teachers to help with cuing in ways that are agreed upon with clients as a way to remind them to use their biofeedback skills. We also encourage the relevant adults to reward/reinforce children for evidence that they are cooperating and putting forth effort in applying their self-regulation skills in the relevant situation. Role playing certain situations to elicit emotional arousal and/or imaginal rehearsal techniques are very helpful in preparing for the real-life stimulus.

Usually, one or two long-term follow-up sessions or refresher sessions are set up two to four months out from the initial cluster to check up on long-term progress and to offer any support and adjustments needed to the plan.

Biofeedback techniques can be used alone or in conjunction with a variety of psychotherapy techniques. A few paradigms are described next.

Biofeedback and Self-Awareness Teaching

One clear benefit of biofeedback training for children and adolescent clients is that it offers an immediate and often dramatic way to demonstrate the connection of mind and body phenomena. For example, in children with anxiety-related symptoms, the therapist uses the EDA and breathing modalities in early sessions to quickly demonstrate how these modalities change when the child thinks differently. When children are asked to imagine an anxiety-provoking situation, they usually note that EDA increases and that breathing rate may increase; they may also move into a more pronounced thoracic breathing pattern. Conversely, when children imagine being in a calm, happy place, they often note a decrease in EDA and slowing and deepening of respiration. EMG is also an excellent and entertaining way to introduce a child to biofeedback and self-regulation. With the EMG sensor attached to their forearm, one can work with children as young as age 5 years and show them the difference between a tense and a relaxed muscle. By the use of various colorful displays, children can be led through a progressive muscle relaxation exercise and play "games" while really engaging in and enjoying the process in a very nonthreatening way. EMG training is also often a very easy way to build confidence and awareness of a child's self-control ability with quick and convincing results. This early success is very reinforcing and can build enthusiasm and rapport in the treatment relationship. It can really demonstrate to kids of all ages the idea that a "change in your thinking causes a change in your body"!

PSYCHOPHYSIOLOGIC MONITORING

Beyond its value in providing information to pediatric patients about their body, biofeedback equipment can provide physiologic monitoring data that are quite helpful for the therapist. Some psychotherapists routinely monitor physiologic changes during therapy sessions but do not initially share the information with the client in real time. Watching SNS activity and changes when talking about certain sensitive or uncomfortable topics can give the therapist helpful information in determining what themes, topics, and life experiences are particularly distressing, stimulating, or affecting for a given person. Physiologic monitoring can also be used to evaluate progress with specific strategies such as relaxation training or to ascertain response to certain types of thematic material or mental imagery. The therapist may choose to review certain recorded data at a later time with the client or even with parents as a way to help them understand certain behavioral patterns, to reinforce progress, and to facilitate the child's interest in possibilities for change.

INTEGRATED APPROACHES

It is evident that biofeedback can be used to facilitate traditional psychotherapy in a number of ways. First of all, biofeedback can be a comfortable, nonthreatening, and quite "playful" way to begin the psychotherapy process, build rapport, and elicit a sense of curiosity. In addition, relaxation can enhance emotional comfort and willingness to communicate. As described previously, biofeedback can play a role similar to that of induction techniques used in hypnosis and hypnotherapy. Watching the visual feedback and listening to a monotonous auditory feedback tone tend to narrow attention and increase awareness of internal body events and sensations, which open the door to further discussion of these phenomena. There is also evidence that states of deep relaxation enhance access to unconscious material and facilitate fantasy and imagery. With development of an alternative state of awareness during biofeedback training, the child may be more available to therapeutic suggestion.

We employ a number of techniques in any one session and across sessions. Mental imagery is commonly employed to provide the opportunity for imaginal or in vitro rehearsal, to enhance physiologic change, and to deepen the relaxation experience. Cognitive-behavioral therapies are particularly helpful in assisting the client in generalizing these skills to other settings and in crafting a plan of how and when to use these skills in real-life settings. Reframing the problem in manageable terms and with an emphasis on daily function (as opposed to limitations created by the symptom) is also helpful, as is the development of a positive self-talk repertoire.

In the author's experience and opinion, biofeedback therapy should be deliberately designed to enhance each child's sense of mastery and control, thus promoting a shift from a more external to a more internal locus of control, which in and of itself can be a critical step in any psychotherapeutic process.

CONTRAINDICATIONS

Biofeedback is of course not a panacea, and care must be taken to understand its indications, contraindications, and limitations in therapy. For example, biofeedback training is not typically suitable for children who are severely depressed or psychotic and should be undertaken with extreme caution in children with PTSD and other severe emotional problems. It is advisable to be clear that some scientific literature supports the use of a specific biofeedback modality for a specific disorder. Pediatric professionals should always seek supervision and case consultation when in doubt.

Therapists should only utilize biofeedback training with clients with presenting complaints/diagnoses that are well within their usual scope of training, expertise, and interest. It is not advisable for adult therapists to "dabble" in pediatric biofeedback without appropriate formal training, supervision, and experience. Professionals should be honest with parents and with patients about the expected length of therapy and reasonable expectations for the biofeedback training process.

In a 1987 study, Olness and Libbey found that 20% of children referred for self-regulation training (primarily hypnosis) had a previously undiagnosed biologic etiology for their condition. This study points to the fact that all children presenting with psychophysiologic symptoms require thorough medical and neurologic evaluation to rule out organic conditions that may contribute to the presenting symptom. For example, children with headaches and abdominal pain need specific medical and neurologic evaluation to rule out tumor, infection, and metabolic problems that can cause recurrent pain. Children with anxiety symptoms need thorough evaluation to exclude thyroid dysregulation, cardiovascular abnormality, and neurological disorders. Children with school performance problems, sleep disturbance, and disorders of elimination may also need comprehensive psychological, educational, or medical assessment before biofeedback training is initiated.

Concurrent use of psychotropic medication is not a contraindication to biofeedback and/or relaxation training but needs to be carefully reviewed on a case-by-case basis. Certain psychotropic agents will change ANS responsivity and so may affect baseline measurements and the child's ability to modulate certain modalities such as peripheral temperature, heart rate, and skin conductance. Some children can reduce or even eliminate the need for certain medications when biofeedback training is successful (e.g., analgesic use in juvenile migraine), but of course this should be carefully coordinated with the prescribing physician.

CASE STUDIES

Case 1

Judy is a 12-year-old girl referred by her psychotherapist for biofeedback therapy to help her anxiety symptoms. Judy's family described a one-and-a-half-year history of "panic attacks," which Judy was experiencing with increasing frequency in a number of specific situations, including prior to and during car rides, while being a server at church, and when taking tests at school. Judy described the physical sensations that accompanied these experiences as including feeling hot or flushed, getting cold fingers, and becoming slightly nauseated. She wasn't sure whether she was breathing harder or faster during these episodes but did notice her heart beating rapidly. On two occasions, she had gotten so upset that she actually fainted.

The working diagnosis from her therapist was that of Anxiety Disorder NOS (not otherwise specified) because these symptoms did not have a classic panic attack pattern. An interesting and possibly related note was a history of autonomic nervous system dysregulation in the family. Judy's mother stated that Judy and her father had been diagnosed at some point with a "vasovagal syndrome," suggesting ANS hypersensitivity and a tendency to faint. Judy's father described a long history of panic attacks and anxiety symptoms as well as obstructive sleep apnea. He admitted to being irritable and negative with family members but felt this was improving with treatment. Of note, the family did describe experiencing a significant car accident when Judy was age 8 years, although no one was badly injured.

Judy was otherwise described as a pleasant girl who did well academically. She was also described as being successful socially. Judy's own individual therapy was felt to be going well.

After the initial interview, all parties were in agreement that Judy may well benefit from physiologic control training designed to help her identify her anxiety symptoms early and then learn to control them with appropriate relaxation-based strategies. It was also hoped that a better sense of internal control would strengthen Judy's self-confidence in her ability to help herself with these symptoms.

At the first biofeedback session, Judy was taught about SNS activity and instructed in a basic progressive relaxation technique. Baseline bifrontal EMG reading was in the range of 4 to 5 microvolts consistently with a decrease to the desired 2 to 3 microvolt range with relaxation training. Baseline skin conductance (EDA) measurement was 7 to 11 micromhos with a subsequent reduction to the 3 to 4 micromho range with relaxation. Practice strategies for daily regular relaxation of 5 minutes at least twice each day were agreed upon. Judy was also encouraged to track her symptoms and "comfort" ratings daily on a calendar.

At the second biofeedback session, a psychophysiologic stress profile was performed to help Judy and her biofeedback therapist understand how her body responded to certain types of stress. Baseline readings showed relatively high skin conductance response in the range of 14 to 17 micromhos. Baseline heart rate was normal for age with an average of 94 beats/minute and evidence for good heart rate variation with breathing (respiratory sinus arrhythmia). During an initial eyes-open relaxation baseline, her skin conductance level dropped to the 5.5 to 8 micromhos with a drop in heart rate to 84 beats/minute, both good indicators of decreased SNS arousal. Judy was asked to perform a set of rapid math calculations as a cognitive "stress" condition. She became noticeably more muscularly tense, and during this cognitive stressor her skin conductance increased to the 14 to 15 micromho range with an increase in heart rate to 90 to 91 and slightly decreased RSA. She was able to recover to baseline reading levels within approximately three minutes. These physiologic arousal patterns were reviewed with Judy.

By the third session three weeks after her first session, Judy was experiencing good symptom control and tolerating medium-range car rides with no discomfort. In addition, she was feeling much more in control while being a server at church, where she was participating regularly again. In subsequent sessions, peripheral temperature training and diaphragmatic breathing techniques were also explored as new ways to add to Judy's self-control, and she demonstrated good proficiency with these. She was provided with home temperature training bands to reinforce her success at home. Capnometry during relaxed breathing revealed Judy's CO_2 at

36 to 37 consistently, still a little low and indicative of overbreathing. This was corrected with breath control work.

Judy completed three more biofeedback sessions spaced two to three weeks apart and continued to do well with other symptoms including her test-taking anxiety and also some sleep onset issues. She felt quite pleased and confident about her self-regulatory abilities and was discharged from biofeedback treatment back to her regular psychotherapist to continue treatment around family issues. The biofeedback therapist and Judy's regular therapist stayed in contact throughout this time to coordinate their approaches.

Case 2

Ricky was a 12-year-old-girl presenting with diagnoses of recurrent abdominal pain, depression, school avoidance, and short stature. At the time of referral from her child psychiatrist for biofeedback training, Ricky described a nine-month history of depressive symptomatology being treated with a selective serotonergic reuptake inhibitor (SSRI) antidepressant, with reasonable improvement in mood. Ricky had experienced a stomachache approximately six months earlier as part of an acute viral gastrointestinal illness. During that illness, she had missed a few days of school. After the other signs of acute infectious illness subsided, Ricky continued to complain of recurrent, diffuse lower abdominal pain and was consistently absent from school because of it. At the time of referral, she had missed virtually all of the second half of the school year.

Medical workup had not revealed any identifiable organic contribution to her pain. She had been participating in ongoing psychotherapy and described a good relationship with her therapist. Despite school ending a few weeks earlier, Ricky continued to complain of daily, unvarying stomachaches, which she rated as about a 7 on a VAS of 0 to 10. She stated at one point that if she couldn't get rid of these stomachaches, she "would just rather die."

At the first biofeedback visit, mind-body connections were discussed and Ricky was told about different self-regulation techniques she might learn to help herself with the stomachaches. Ricky was asked what she thought was the cause of her stomachaches, but she stated that she wasn't sure. However, she actively agreed with the idea that her stomach had retained a "pain memory or tracing" from earlier that winter, when she was acutely ill, despite the fact that her body had otherwise recovered. We agreed that she needed to "reprogram" the pain circuits and pathways between her stomach and brain to shut the "pain gate" so that message was no longer being sent. To emphasize and reinforce this idea of mind-body linkages, Ricky was then coached through some initial muscle awareness work with good result. When asked the question "Who is the boss of your pain?" she clearly responded that she was. We emphasized the notion that with regular practice, she would soon feel more in control of her comfort level.

At the second session, diaphragmatic breathing was taught and integrated with mental imagery about a healthy stomach and body, decreasing her pain sensation and allowing her to enjoy a state of deep comfort and relaxation. We also began reframing her pain experience away from a focus on the abdominal discomfort and toward a focus on her successful functioning day-to-day in not allowing that pain to interfere with what she decided she wanted to do.

By the third and fourth sessions, it was clear to Ricky's mother that Ricky was not talking about the pain nearly as much as she used to and that she was enjoying a number of activities with her friends over the course of the summer. Ricky stated that although she didn't necessarily feel that her pain rating had changed much, she was choosing to ignore and work through it. Ricky demonstrated good control of various physiologic modalities with lowered heart rate, decreased EDA, and increased temperature consistently evident in office sessions. Her mastery of these physiologic functions provided a powerful metaphor for her ability to control her pain as well. We continued to explore mind-body links, strengthen her sense of self-control, and develop helpful self-hypnosis strategies around the stomachache issue.

Ricky was discharged back to the care of her ongoing therapist with improved functioning and clear direction as to how to reengage in the coming school year and to continue to self-regulate her pain.

Discussion

In both of the cases, biofeedback training added a dimension to the therapeutic process that served to reinforce the notion that one's mind and body are connected, and therefore a change in one's thinking can cause a change in one's body.

With the understanding that "you are the boss of body," each client was assisted in identifying and mastering the self-regulation skills best suited to manage their problem. Different biofeedback modalities were utilized at different times to increase body awareness, decrease emotional arousal, and facilitate eventual transfer of skill into appropriate situations. Teaching of lowered SNS activity was of particular relevance to Judy, where emotional arousal was playing a role in her symptoms. For Ricky, establishing a clear mind-body link and development of a strong self-control metaphor seemed important in highlighting her ability to reprogram her pain perception.

EQUIPMENT

A number of hardware and software options for computer-based biofeedback setups are currently available and generally range in cost from $1,500 to $15,000. Stand-alone devices, which are generally less expensive, are also available. Home training items such as temperature dots and bands are appealing to pediatric clients and quite affordable. Information about the larger biofeedback manufacturers and distributors can be obtained from the Association for Applied Psychophysiology and Biofeedback.

A number of biofeedback hardware and software companies produce a variety of different software graphical interface displays, although there are not many that are truly game-like or that were designed specifically for children and adolescents. The exception to this is seen in EEG applications software and equipment for which the technology is evolving rapidly and for which an extensive review is beyond the scope of this essay.

Favorite displays currently available include games such as biofeedback baseball, basketball, and golf, which are EMG controlled and pit the child against the computer (CMM BioGames Pack). Traffic Light, River Rafting, Kaleidoscope, and a catching game are also popular with young children (J and J Engineering). Images of sunsets, animals, flowers, beautiful geometric "mandala" designs, and games employing colorful dots and movement available on new software are also intriguing to pediatric patients (Bio Research Institute). Figure 7.1 depicts a few of these visual displays. The products mentioned above do not represent the entire range of what is available nor do they represent an endorsement. They are however, software applications for which the author has fairly extensive familiarity in use specifically with pediatric clients.

TRAINING

Training in biofeedback is required for the clinician to develop skills and the flexibility to utilize these skills creatively, effectively, and in a developmentally appropriate way. Use of biofeedback requires very specific technical expertise, understanding of basic anatomy and physiology, background in ANS function, and, ideally, some familiarity with computer hardware and software. Increasingly, there are more technical applications including applied respiratory physiology and neurofeedback that require even more specialized training.

In Figure 7.1, the Bio Integrator provides not only graphical kinds of feedback, such as line graphs and fill graphs, but offers

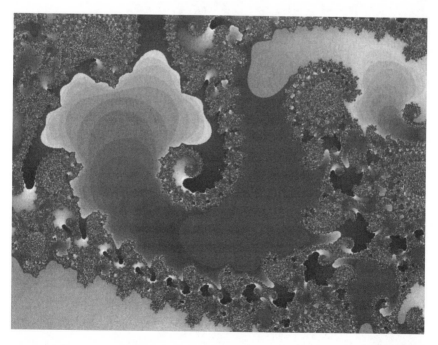

(continued)

Figure 7.1 Visual Biofeedback Displays: A Sampler. (Bio Integrator images courtesy of Steve Wall, Bio Research Institute, 331 East Cotati Ave., Cotati, CA 94928.)

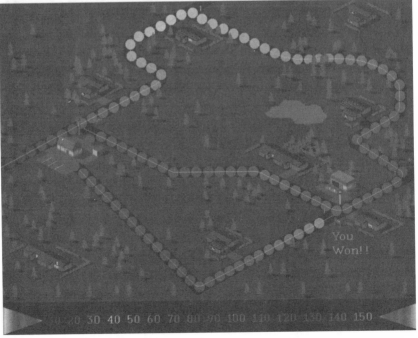

Figure 7.1 *(Continued)*

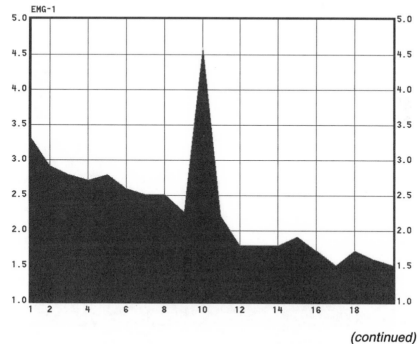

(continued)

Figure 7.1 *(Continued)*

Heart Rate

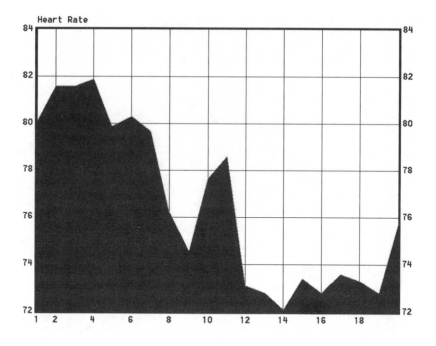

Left Temperature

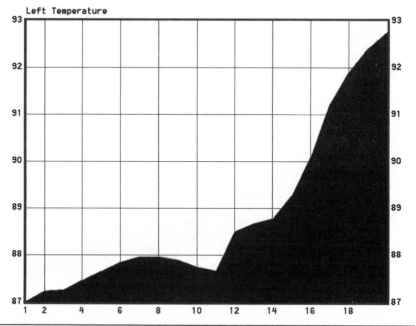

Figure 7.1   *(Continued)*

an image library where nature scenes, games, and mandalas may be animated in direct proportion to physiological changes occurring in the body. The first four images are Biofeedback displays. The next three are graphs that illustrate the positive effects of the relaxation response. As can be seen from the data, as the clients practiced their relaxation skills learned in biofeedback, heart rate and EMG came down and hand temperature rose.

Generally, a clincian is expected to be trained first within a child health discipline (psychology, nursing, pediatrics, child life, social work) and then go on to acquire proficiency in biofeedback as an additional therapeutic tool. Biofeedback is best considered an added area of clinical expertise and a useful tool within the clinician's professional treatment armamentarium, as opposed to a field or profession of its own, although that is changing (Glaros, 1998). It is often very helpful, even advisable, for pediatric clinicians to complete some training in hypnosis and hypnotherapy with children in addition to or even prior to biofeedback training, as many of the techniques learned in hypnosis training are very helpful and important in biofeedback therapies for children.

Training in biofeedback is available through a variety of sources, and further information is available through the Association for Applied Psychophysiology and Biofeedback (see Table 7.4).

Table 7.4
Training Opportunities Organization/Resource Guide

Society for Developmental and Behavioral Pediatrics
19 Station Lane
Philadelphia, PA 19118

Association for Applied Psychophysiology and Biofeedback
10200 West 44th Avenue, Suite 304
Wheat Ridge, CO 80003

Biofeedback Certification Institute of America
10200 West 44th Avenue, Suite 304
Wheat Ridge, CO 80003

Certification of training in biofeedback is available through the Biofeedback Certification Institute of America and represents the highest professional standard currently available in this area. Certification requires a specified number of formal course work hours, clinical supervision, and case experience, followed by a written and practical examination. Training specific to biofeedback and hypnosis with children is available through the Society for Developmental and Behavioral Pediatrics.

CONCLUSIONS

The child's inner world is a place of imagination, fantasy dreams, and inner sensations. Biofeedback techniques increase and cultivate the potential of this inner world, acting as a bridge between psyche and soma to the place within the child where therapeutic change can and does occur. Those that work with children in health care, school, and related settings must recall that the child's inner world is an ever changing place, profoundly influenced by developmental stage, life experience, and capabilities. Training via biofeedback and related self-regulation strategies provides concrete, immediate evidence of the mind-body connection for children and facilitates their appreciation of self-control and self-mastery, key steps in the process of therapeutic change.

Increasingly, there is awareness in pediatric health care of a comprehensive approach with children in all aspects of care that considers mind and body in an integrated biopsychosocial model. The need for the widespread and immediate integration of mental health into pediatric primary medical care clinics on a daily basis is increasingly evident based on surveys of parents and professionals. With up to 20% of children experiencing psychophysiologic symptoms at some point in development, the humanitarian and economic incentives are there as well (Starfield & Borkowf, 1980).

Biofeedback serves as an ideal bridge between biomedical and mental health paradigms. For pediatric biofeedback as a field, the need has been established, the training is becoming available, the research base is strengthening, and the interest among patients is evident. The evolution in psychophysiologic therapies parallels the emerging evidence of psychosocial morbidities in clinical pediatric practice. New pediatric health care supervision guidelines have strongly identified a mandate for child health professionals to assist children in coping with stressful life experiences and in developing a sense of self-efficacy. The need for training of more pediatric health care professionals in biofeedback, hypnosis, and related techniques is evident, and efforts are underway to begin this process (Sugarman, 1996). Some experts feel that training in applied psychophysiologic techniques should become mandatory for those in the primary care fields (Wickramasekera, 1996).

A recent survey of 100 consecutive children who completed biofeedback training suggests that the majority found these strategies very enjoyable and effective and completed training with an enhanced sense of self-control (Kajander, Culbert, & Reaney, 1998). Like many psychological/behavioral interventions, the actual mechanisms of therapeutic change with biofeedback training are speculative at best. The question of whether it is the general effects of biofeedback training (relaxation, increased sense of internal locus of control, positive expectancy) or specific effects (changes in ANS balance, changes in brain wave patterns, specific suggestions, perceptual shifts) that result in positive change and symptom control remains unanswered.

One of the glaring needs in the field of applied psychophysiology as applied to pediatric populations is for a larger normative data set for various ages and subpopulations of children. For the field to continue to move forward, we of course need to supply colleagues, third-party payers, and our clients clear evidence that these techniques are cost-effective and truly helpful. Clinical outcome studies on pediatric populations would best be served by first establishing what in fact a normal baseline psychophysiologic state is for a variety of commonly utilized biofeedback measures (EMG, Temp, EDA) at different ages in healthy populations. Investigators could then compare those same measures in clinic-referred samples for problems like ADHD, anxiety, headache, and so on. It would also be helpful to create and standardize a developmentally appropriate psychophysiologic stress profile for use as a baseline assessment tool for all children and adolescents undertaking biofeedback training.

As microelectronics and software options improve, we imagine a future with easy access to inexpensive home-based and school-based biofeedback devices as well. One might hope that personal handheld biofeedback game-format devices for kids will become as ubiquitous as the Nintendo or Sega videogames. If designed with the same level of multimedia sophistication as current video and computer games, biofeedback games should be at least as appealing and rewarding—with the payoff being each child/adolescent's improved physical, educational, and emotional functioning.

It is exciting to imagine the possibilities for biofeedback and self-regulation skills training for children in the next 15 to 20 years. The impact on cost savings and reduced morbidity in pediatric health care by just implementing what we know already about biofeedback training benefits would likely be substantial. It is hoped that this chapter will encourage child health professionals to become interested in and trained in these techniques so that we can better treat the emerging "new morbidities" for children and adolescents as we move into the twenty-first century.

REFERENCES

Andrasik, F., & Attansio, V. (1985). Biofeedback in pediatrics: Current status and appraisal. In M. Wolriach & D. Roth (Eds.), *Advances in developmental and behavioral pediatrics*. Greenwich, CT: JAI Press.

Andreassi, J. (1995). *Psychophysiology: Human behavior and physiological response*. Hillsdale, NJ: Erlbaum.

Attansio, V., Andrasik, F., Burke, E., Blake, D., Kabela, E., & McCarran, M. (1985). Clinical issues in utilizing biofeedback with children. *Clinical Biofeedback and Health, 8*, 134–141.

Barowsky, E., Moskowitz, J., & Zweig, J. (1990). Biofeedback for disorders of initiating and maintaining sleep. *Annals of New York Academy of Science, 602*, 97–103.

Basmajian, J. (1989). *Biofeedback: Principles and practice for clinicians* (3rd ed.). Baltimore: Williams & Wilkins.

Beck, A.T., & Emery, G. (1985). *Anxiety disorders and phobias: A cognitive perspective*. New York: Basic Books.

Bolek, J. (1998). Surface EMG applications of pediatric biofeedback in rehabilitation settings. *Biofeedback, 26*(3), 21–23.

Brundy, J., Korein, J., Gordon, L., Grynbaum, B., Lieberman, K., & Friedman, L. (1974). Sensory feedback therapy as a modality of treatment in CNS disorder of voluntary movement. *Neurology, 24,* 925–932.

Burke, E., & Andrasik, F. (1989). Home vs. clinic based biofeedback treatment for pediatric migraine: Results of treatment through one year follow-up. *Headache, 29,* 434–440.

Cacioppo, J., Klein, D., Bernston, G., & Hatfield, E. (1993). The psychophysiology of emotion. In M. Lewis & J. Haviland (Eds.), *Handbook of emotions*. New York: Guilford Press.

Coles, M., Donchin, E., & Porges, S. (1986). *Psychophysiology: Systems processes and applications*. New York: Guilford Press.

Combs, A., Glassberg, A., Gerdes, D., & Horowitz, M. (1998). Biofeedback therapy for children with dysfunctional voiding. *Urology, 52,* 312–315.

Criswell, E. (1995). *Biofeedback and somatics*. Novato, CA: Freeperson Press.

Culbert, T., & Bonfilio, S. (1998). Biofeedback and cognitive/behavioral therapy for children with anger management problems: An integrated approach. *Biofeedback, 26*(3), 27–29.

Culbert, T., Kajander, R., & Reaney, J. (1996). Biofeedback with children and adolescents: Clinical observations and patient perspectives. *Journal of Developmental and Behavioral Pediatrics, 17,* 342–350.

Culbert, T., Reaney, J., & Kohen, D. (1994). Cyberphysiologic strategies with children: The clinical hypnosis/biofeedback interface. *International Journal of Clinical Experiential Hypnosis, 42,* 97–117.

Dikel, W., & Olness, K. (1980). Self-hypnosis, biofeedback and voluntary temperature control in children. *Pediatrics, 66,* 35–40.

Duckro, P., & Cantwell-Simmons, E. (1989). A review of studies evaluating biofeedback and relaxation training in the management of pediatric headache. *Headache, 29,* 428–433.

Ewart, C., Harris, W., & Iwata, M. (1987). Feasibility and effectiveness of school based relaxation in lowering blood pressure. *Health Psychology, 6,* 399–416.

Faber, S. (1998). EEG biofeedback for children and adolescents: A pediatrician's perspective. *Biofeedback, 26*(3), 18–20.

Finley, W., & Jones, L. (1992). Biofeedback with children. In E. Walker & M. Roberts (Eds.), *Handbook of clinical child psychology* (pp. 809–827). New York: Wiley.

Flodmark, A. (1986). Augmented auditory feedback as an aid in gait training of cerebral palsied children. *Developmental Medical Child Neurology, 28,* 147–155.

Fordham, S., & Meadow, M. (1989). Controlled trial of bell alarm against mini-alarm for enuresis. *Archives of Disease of Childhood, 64,* 651–656.

Gagnon, D., Hudnall, L., & Andrasik, F. (1992). Biofeedback and related procedures in coping with stress. In A. La Greca, L. Siegel, J. Wallander, & E. Walker (Eds.), *Stress and coping in child health* (pp. 303–326). New York: Guilford Press.

Glaros, A. (1998). Is biofeedback a profession? Some methods for answering the question. *Biofeedback, 26,* 4–7.

Green, E., Green, A., & Walters, E. (1970). Voluntary control of internal states: Psychological and physiological. *Journal of Transpersonal Psychology, 2,* 1–26.

Haggerty, R., Roughman, K., & Pless, I. (1993). *Child health in the community* (2nd ed.). New Brunswick, NJ: Transaction.

Hall, H., Minnes, L., & Olness, K. (1993). The psychophysiology of voluntary immunomodulation. *International Journal of Neuroscience, 69,* 221–234.

Iwai, N., Nagashima, M., Shimotake, T., & Iwata, G. (1993). Biofeedback therapy for fecal incontinence after surgery for anorectal malformations. *Journal of Pediatric Surgery, 28,* 863–866.

Jacobsen, E. (1938). *Progressive relaxation.* Chicago: University of Chicago Press.

Johnston, D., & Martin, P. (1991). Psychophysiologic contributions to behavior therapy. In P. Martin (Ed.), *Handbook of behavioral therapy and psychological science: An integrative approach* (pp. 383–409). New York: Pergamon Press.

Kajander, R., Culbert, T., & Reaney, J. (1998). *A survey of pediatric biofeedback participants.* Unpublished manuscript.

Kajander, R., & Peper, E. (1998). Teaching diaphragmatic breathing to children. *Biofeedback, 26*(3), 14–17.

Kajander, R., et al. (1998). Applied psychophysiology of pain management in children. *Biofeedback, 26*(3), 24–26.

Kall, R. (1997). Optimal functioning training. *Biofeedback, 25,* 8–10.

Killam, P., Jeffries, J., & Varni, J. (1985). Urodynamic biofeedback of urinary incontinence in children with myelomeningocele. *Biofeedback and Self-Regulation, 10,* 161–171.

Kotses, H., Harver, A., Segreto, J., Glaus, K., Creer, T., & Young, G. (1991). Long-term effects of biofeedback-induced facial relaxation on measurements of asthma severity. *Biofeedback and Self-Regulation, 16,* 1–21.

Kuttner, L. (1996). *A child in pain.* Vancouver: Hartley and Marks.

Labbe, E., & Williamson, D. (1983). Temperature biofeedback in the treatment of children with migraine headaches. *Journal of Pediatric Psychology, 8,* 317–326.

Lambert, S. (1996). The effects of hypnosis/guided imagery on the post-operative pain course of children. *Journal of Developmental & Behavioral Pediatrics, 17,* 307–310.

Lee, L., & Olness, K. (1996). Effects of self-induced mental-imagery on autonomic reactivity in children. *Journal of Developmental & Behavioral Pediatrics, 17,* 323–327.

Lehrer, P. (1998). Emotionally triggered asthma: A review of research literature and some hypotheses for self-regulation therapies. *Applied Psychophysiology and Biofeedback, 23,* 13–41.

Ley, R. (1994). Breathing and the psychology of emotion, cognition, behavior. In B. Timmons & R. Ley (Eds.), *Behavioral and psychological approaches to breathing disorders* (pp. 81–91). New York: Plenum Press.

Lightman, H., Pochaczevsky, R., & Ilowite, N. (1987). Thermography in childhood reflex sympathetic dystrophy. *Journal of Pediatrics, 11,* 551–555.

Linden, M., Habib, T., & Radojevic, R. (1996). A controlled study of the effects of EEG biofeedback on the cognition and behavior of children with attention deficit disorders and learning disabilities. *Biofeedback and Self-Regulation, 21,* 35–49.

Loening-Baucke, V. (1990). Modulation of abnormal defecation dynamics by biofeedback treatment in chronically constipated children with encopresis. *Journal of Pediatrics, 116,* 214–222.

Lubar, J., Smartwood, M., Smartwood, J., & O'Donnel, P. (1995). Evaluation of the effectiveness of EEG neurofeedback training for ADHD in a clinical setting as measured by changes in TOVA scores, behavioral ratings and WISC-R performance. *Biofeedback and Self-Regulation, 20,* 83–89.

Marino, R., & Kohen, D. (1996). The power of words: Communicating effectively with young patients. *Journal of the American Osteopathic Association, 96,* 10–13.

Mars, D. (1998). Biofeedback-assisted psychotherapy using multimodal biofeedback including capnography. *Biofeedback, 26,* 12–14.

Moss, D., & Lehrer, P. (1998). Body-work in psychotherapy before biofeedback. *Biofeedback, 26,* 4–7.

Murphy, J. (1992). Psychophysiological responses to stress in children and adolescents. In A. La Greca, L. Siegel, J. Wallander, & E. Walker (Eds.), *Stress and coping in child health* (pp. 45–71). New York: Guilford Press.

Nash, J., Neilson, P., & O'Dwyer, N. (1989). Reducing spasticity to control muscle contracture in children with cerebral palsy. *Developmental Medicine and Child Neurology, 31,* 471–480.

Olness, K. (1997). Clinical applications of biofeedback and hypnosis. *Hypnosis, 24,* 70–78.

Olness, K., Culbert, T., & Uden, D. (1989). The self-regulation of salivary immunoglobulin A by children. *Pediatrics, 83,* 66–71.

Olness, K., & Kohen, D. (1996). *Hypnosis and hypnotherapy with children* (3rd ed., pp. 319–328). New York: Guilford Press.

Olness, K., & Libbey, P. (1987). Unrecognized biologic basis of behavioral symptoms in patients referred for hypnotherapy. *American Journal of Clinical Hypnosis, 30,* 1–8.

Olness, K., McParland, F., & Piper, J. (1980). Biofeedback: A new modality on the management of children with fecal soiling. *Behavioral Pediatrics, 96,* 505–509.

Parker, L., & Whitehead, W. (1982). Treatment of urinary and fecal incontinence in children. In D. Russo & J. Varni (Eds.), *Behavioral pediatrics: Research and practice* (pp. 143–174). New York: Plenum Press.

Raknes, O. (1970). *Wilhelm Reich and orgonomy.* New York: St. Martin's Press.

Reich, W. (1949). *Character analysis.* New York: Orgone Institute Press.

Rickles, W., Onoda, L., & Doyle, C. (1979). *Biofeedback as an adjunct to psychotherapy* (Task Force Section Report). Wheat Ridge, CO: Biofeedback Society of America.

Rose, G., & Carlson, J. (1987). The behavioral treatment of Raynauds': A review. *Biofeedback Self-Regulation, 12,* 257–272.

Rutter, M. (1998). Stress, coping and development: Some issues and some questions. In N. Garmezy & M. Rutter (Eds.), *Stress, coping and development in children* (pp. 1–42). Baltimore: Johns Hopkins University Press.

Schultz, J., & Luthe, W. (1969). *Autogenic therapy: Autogenic methods* (Vol. 1). New York: Grune & Stratton.

Schwartz, M., & Associates. (1995). *Biofeedback: A practitioner's guide.* New York: Guilford Press.

Seifert, A., & Lubar, J. (1975). Reduction of epileptic seizures through EEG biofeedback training. *Biological Psychology, 3,* 157–184.

Smith, M. (1991). Biofeedback. *Pediatric Annals, 20,* 126–131.

Starfield, B., & Borkowf, S. (1980). Psychosocial and psychosomatic diagnosis in primary care of children. *Pediatrics, 66,* 159–167.

Steptoe, A. (1991). Psychobiological processes in the etiology of disease. In P. Martin (Ed.), *Handbook of behavioral therapy and psychological science: An integrative approach* (pp. 383–409). New York: Pergamon Press.

Sugar, E., & Firlit, C. (1982). Urodynamic biofeedback: A new therapeutic approach for children with incontinence. *Journal of Urology, 128,* 1253–1258.

Sugarman, L. (1996). Hypnosis in a primary care pediatric practice: Developing skills for the new morbidities. *Journal of Developmental & Behavioral Pediatrics, 17,* 300–306.

Sussman, D., & Culbert, T. (1999). Self-regulation skills training. In M. Levine, A. Crocker, & W. Carey (Eds.), *Developmental/behavioral pediatrics* (3rd ed., pp. 843–850). Philadelphia: Saunders.

Tansey, M. (1984). EEG sensorimotor rhythm biofeedback training: Some effects on the neurologic precursors of learning disabilities. *International Journal of Psychophysiology, 1,* 163–177.

Timmons, B., & Ley, R. (Eds.). (1994). *Behavioral and psychological approaches to breathing disorders.* New York: Plenum Press.

Wald, A., Chandra, R., Gabel, S., & Chiponis, D. (1987). Evaluation of biofeedback in childhood encopresis. *Journal of Pediatric Gastroenterology and Nutrition, 6,* 554–558.

Wang, Y., & Morgan, W. (1992). The effect of imagery perspectives on the psychophysiologic responses to imagined exercise. *Behavioral Brain Research, 52,* 167–174.

Whitehead, W., Parker, L., & Masek, B. (1988). Treatment of fecal incontinence in children with spina bifida: Comparison of biofeedback and behavioral modification. *Archives of Physical Medicine and Rehabilitation, 67,* 218–224.

Wickramasekera, I., Davies, T., & Davies, S.M. (1996). Applied psychophysiology: A bridge between the biomedical model and the biopsychosocial model in family medicine. *Professional Psychology: Research and Practice, 27,* 221–223.

Wolpe, J. (1958). *Psychotherapy by reciprocal inhibition.* Stanford, CA: Stanford University Press.

Zeltzer, L., & LeBaron, S. (1982). Hypnosis and nonhypnotic techniques for reduction of pain and anxiety during painful medical procedures in children and adolescents with cancer. *Journal of Pediatrics, 101,* 1032–1035.

CHAPTER 8

Therapeutic Applications of Computers with Children

LOUIS L. AYMARD

THE EXPLOSIVE growth of digital electronics in the last two decades of the twentieth century is tantamount to what occurred with the invention of the printing press or the onset of the Industrial Revolution. This phenomenon is a consequence of rapid technological advances in the space and electronics industries. It has impacted every segment of modern society, from the complex systems that protect national security to the toys found in the households of America. Children born in the past two decades are comfortable with virtual pets, Laser Tag, Game Boy, and electronic toys driven by integrated circuits that would have been beyond the ken of electronic engineers in the 1950s. They are the progeny of the Digital Generation, who expect games to be fast-paced, multisensory experiences. They push buttons or manipulate joysticks for instantaneous responses in a virtual world.

In the late 1970s, the personal computer (PC), one of the marvels of the Digital Age, made an entrée into the homes and businesses of America. The PC has assumed a premiere place in the cornucopia of children's electronic playware. Seymour Papert (1993), a visionary mathematician at Massachusetts Institute of Technology, refers to the computer as the children's machine. He presents a scholarly exposition of children's love of computers in his book, *The Connected Family: Bridging the Digital Generation Gap.*

> Across the world there is a passionate love affair between children and computers. I have worked with children and computers in Africa and Asia and America, in cities, in suburbs, on farms and in jungles. I have worked with poor children and rich children; with children of bookish parents and with children from illiterate families. But these differences don't seem to matter. Everywhere, with very few exceptions, I see the same gleam in their eyes, the same desire to appropriate this thing. And more than wanting it, they seem to know that in a deep way it already belongs to them. They know they can master it more easily and more naturally than their parents can. They know they are the computer generation. (1996, p. 1)

A unanimous consensus about which toys are appropriate for play therapy does not exist among clinicians. Ginott (1960) believed "a treatment toy should (1) facilitate the establishment of contact with the child; (2) evoke and encourage catharsis; (3) aid in developing insight; (4) furnish opportunities for reality testing; (5) provide media for sublimation" (p. 243). Recent clinical studies (Allen, 1984; Bosworth, 1994; Canter, 1987; Casey & Ramsammy, 1992; Clarke & Schoech, 1984; Favelle, 1994; J. Gardner, 1991; Johnson, 1984, 1987; Kokish, 1994; Margolies, 1991; Oakley, 1994; Resnick, 1994; Sherer, 1994; Sisson, Mayfield, & Entz, 1985) have shown that the computer meets those criteria. It is interesting to note that whereas child therapists use puppets, board games, sand play, doll houses, and other traditional play materials, the children with whom they work come to their offices with electronic gadgets and virtual toys. Therefore, it is timely for school counselors and child therapists to bridge the digital generation gap and to innovate with computers in their work with children of the Digital Age. To help with that mission, this chapter will review the clinical studies published in the professional literature; suggest a methodology for getting started, with computer neophytes in mind; describe practical therapeutic applications of computers with children and adolescents; and recommend directions for future developments in this field.

HISTORICAL BACKGROUND

As digital technology reduced the size of computers from huge mainframes to diminutive desktop machines in the 1980s, a group of pioneers began exploring the value of the PC in child psychotherapy. David H. Allen was one of the first clinicians to report the successful use of computers in child therapy. He recounted the experience using Ultima, a Dungeons and Dragons fantasy game, with 7- to 14-year-old children on the Apple II+ computer (Allen, 1984). Action in Ultima commences with the players creating and naming a character who is a fighter, a wizard, a cleric, or a thief. Each persona has unique powers as well as handicaps. At the start of the game, the character is armed with weapons, food, armor, and hit points, which are lost when he is struck in battle. The object of play is to free a princess who is incarcerated in a dungeon of the king's castle. As Allen's patients were absorbed with the game, he served as a mentor, offering suggestions to them about salient choices. He provided support and empathy when children's errant choices produced frustration. Also, Allen processed the content and action of the game, applying outcomes to critical issues in the children's lives. Although Ultima is a complex game requiring months to complete, Allen concluded that "children who have completed therapy with the game appear to have more self confidence, a sense of mastery, more willingness to accept responsibility for themselves, and less stigma about having been in therapy" (1984, p. 333).

Clarke and Schoech (1984) developed a psychotherapeutic computer game for impulsive adolescents. The text-based fantasy game was written in BASIC programming language for a DEC-20 computer and Teletype printing terminal. The authors note that "a CRT (cathode ray tube, a TV-like screen) was not available at the testing facility" (p. 341). (The contrast between that system and today's multimedia computers illustrates the enormous technological advances in electronics over two decades in this century.) Clark and Schoech hypothesized that their game would engage the adolescents' attention, and thereby obviate anger and resentment about coming to counseling. They sought to teach problem solving and to enhance their clients' self-esteem through the mastery of complex situations. The computer invited players to start the game with the greeting "What is your name?" After typing a name, the machine responded "Hello. *Name*, do you need instructions? Yes or no?" Players were introduced to the Adventure of Lost Loch, a game in which they were offered 5,000 gold pieces by King Tripoli if they found and returned his crown from the dreaded Cave of Darkness. As the game unfolded, players accrued points for good choices and lost points for poor choices at critical decision points. The game, a research prototype, was used successfully with four adolescents for a period of one month. Only one therapy session was missed among all subjects during the course of the research. The adolescents looked forward to coming for counseling sessions. The patterns of responding to episodes in the game afforded the therapists a rich source of clinical data about the participants' respective interpersonal styles. Clark and Schoech contrasted the adolescents' favorable responses to the computer therapy to the acrimonious reactions of 12 colleagues at the mental health agency. Some were outraged that mental health professionals would consider the computer an adjunctive therapeutic medium. Others pejoratively dismissed the project as ludicrous or a fad. Those who supported the idea often qualified it with the assertion "*You* do it and I'll support you" (Clark & Schoech, 1984, p. 349, italics added).

An article published in the *Journal of Reading, Writing, and Learning Disabilities* describes how a broad range of commercially available children's software was used for helping children with behavioral problems and special learning needs (Sisson et al., 1985). Fantasy games, diary keeping, biofeedback, role-playing games, and educational software were the focus of individual and group counseling sessions with latency-age children. For example, an angry adolescent, Sam, used database software to make electronic cards of his enemies, graphically describing the recompense he wished for them. This allowed the therapist to process Sam's feelings by reviewing recurrent themes in his writing, thus showing Sam that aggression and verbal assaults are destructive in peer relationships. Sisson et al. also successfully used group computer play with adolescent girls traumatized by sexual abuse. Rapport strengthened among group members as the therapists introduced a variety of competitive, cooperative, and didactic games. Subsequent to challenging each other and the therapists in group computer play, the girls began to trust each other. They disclosed intimate details about their personal histories. The insights gained about their traumas were of inestimable value to the young women. They became energized by these personal discoveries and parlayed them into community service activities, such as speaking to women's groups and helping parents shelter their children from sexual exploitation.

By the end of the 1980s, the Macintosh computer, with creativity software, became an integral tool in the effective treatment of young inpatients (Canter, 1987). The children and adolescents participating in the research produced computer artifacts that enhanced their therapeutic experiences. Some of the behavioral gains observed by the treatment staff in the young patients were an increase in attention span, the development of visuospatial expression, enhanced self-confidence and creativity, and refined interpersonal communication.

In the 1990s, other clinical studies documented the value of the computer in psychotherapy with children and adolescents. Margolies (1991) described MacTherapy, a series of HyperCard-based programs used to "form a natural bridge for psychoeducational tasks, facilitating both therapeutic (social) and educational interventions for resistant or disabled learners" (p. 70). The Mac-Mentoring Project was designed to recapture the educational interests of disenfranchised youth (Casey & Ramsammy, 1992). Under the supervision of a counselor, adolescents were paired with elementary school children in a mentoring program. The teens were at risk because of poor school attendance, problems with self-esteem, and disruptive classroom behavior. Their mandate was to teach computer literacy to younger children by using Macintosh games in the public domain. As the adolescents became more invested in the program, they took pride in their accomplishments. They were responsible for all facets of the work, including personal demands, such as being punctual for tutoring sessions. The forthright exchanges between the adolescents and the counselors assigned to them as supervisors led to increased trust and self-disclosure between the parties. This interpersonal outcome differed markedly from a control group who participated in traditional counseling sessions.

Electronic arcade games and computer fantasy games are useful as adjunctive techniques in psychotherapy with children and adolescents. J. Gardner (1991) successfully used the Nintendo game, Super Mario Bros., in play therapy with 5- to 10-year-olds. He found that processing the strategies that the children employed in playing Super Mario Bros. enabled them to perceive subtle cues in interpersonal situations, to displace aggression, to deal with success and failure, and to develop metacognitive problem solving. Kokish (1994) discovered that the computer had dual utility in his private practice as an office system and as a toy in play therapy. He skillfully used his office PC, loaded with a paint program, a word processor, and role-playing games, as a psychotherapeutic toy with children who were victims of physical and sexual abuse. Favelle (1994) used adventure-fantasy software with adolescents at an inpatient treatment center to help them deal with their aggressive urges in socially appropriate ways. He found that role-playing software, simulating real-life situations, allowed the adolescents to develop personal insights and to explore experiences they may not encounter in group therapy sessions.

In recent years, some clinicians have undertaken the ambitious enterprise of developing therapeutic software. SMACK (Oakley, 1994) is a program that allows teens to make their own decisions about drug use and to experience a simulation of the consequences of those decisions. It is an attempt to introduce the negative consequences of drug use without the lecturing tone usually associated with antidrug materials. Other successful projects created interactive software to raise the level of moral reasoning in distressed youth (Sherer, 1994) and to educate adolescents about health issues such as smoking, drugs, and sexuality (Bosworth, 1994).

Resnick (1994) is a pioneer in developing interactive electronic technology and digital tools for social work education and practice. His contributions include producing interactive electronic media for children and adolescents, surveying the use of computers in human services, and encouraging professional networking through online exchanges.

A summative review of the literature published to date about computer use in child therapy reveals several common themes across a diverse group of studies. First, none of the authors reported that the computer is therapeutically contraindicated with children or adolescents. Most therapists found ways of skillfully integrating computer play into the fabric of the child's therapy with talking, game playing, storytelling, and other traditional psychotherapeutic techniques. And the presence of a computer in the therapist's office (for playing games) significantly lessened initial resistance to the therapy. The authors cited copious examples of how play therapy with computers affected personal insight, behavior change, and catharsis in their young clients. Most important, regarding the issue of psychotherapeutic outcomes, there was resolution of the presenting problem(s) in all cases.

USING THE COMPUTER IN CHILD THERAPY: GETTING STARTED

Developments in American digital technology are progressing at a rapid pace. This phenomenon has implications for therapists who purchase electronic equipment for their practices. Personal computers become obsolete almost as quickly as they are shipped from a manufacturer. Dispensing advice about acquiring a computer system is dicey business; nevertheless, the following guidelines may be helpful to counselors and therapists who want to innovate with this technological medium. They are not intended to be prescriptive or proscriptive.

DECIDING ON THE APPLICATIONS

When child therapists decide to acquire a computer, they frequently ask what type of *hardware* they should buy. The approach outlined here offers a different perspective on the matter, which may make it seem odd. Before investing in computer hardware, software, or peripherals, therapists should carefully examine *how* and *with whom* the system will be used. For example, those who work with developmentally disabled or violent children may decide computer use in their work is countertherapeutic. If the clinical population is comprised of preschoolers, a traditional keyboard and monitor will be less inviting to the child than the more colorful kiddy keyboards and monitors with decorative frames. Young children who see a computer on an office desk rather than among the toys in the play therapy room may experience transference of the parental admonition that "the computer is Mommy's/Daddy's machine; children shouldn't touch it."

Irrespective of the setting in which they work, most therapists usually opt for the three basic applications of word processing, drawing, and playing games. Word processing software is useful for recording children's stories and therapy journals. Computer drawings are made with paint programs that produce colorful pictures by manipulating the mouse or an electronic sketchpad. Word processors and paint programs can be used conjointly to produce arts and crafts that stimulate the child's creative process through the course of therapy. Naturally, therapists' needs will evolve over time; however, the rule of thumb applicable to any electronic device is true here: more "bells and whistles" mean more expense.

Child therapists are accustomed to working with budget constraints. They are well acquainted with hand-me-downs, yard sales, and buying toys at discount stores. The well-honed skill of resourcefulness in finding playthings for children will be an indispensable asset when they shop for computer hardware and software. With patience, resourcefulness, and luck, they can assemble an excellent system that will be a source of enjoyment for children and will enhance the psychotherapeutic mission.

The question of whether specific psychotherapeutic approaches lend themselves to computer applications is a salient, albeit unanswered, question in the professional literature at this juncture. Hypothetically, computers should be ideally suited for cognitive-behavior play therapy, but contraindicated in filial therapy. Further discussion of this matter, beyond posing the question, is beyond the scope of this chapter. The philosophy of treatment, level of comfort with technology, and willingness to try new approaches are the critical factors in determining whether to use the computer in psychotherapy with children and adolescents. The review of studies to date reveals that clinicians are reporting favorable outcomes when computers are an ancillary medium in child psychotherapy. Child therapists at local, national, and international conferences regale the author with enchanting stories about serendipitous experiences when using computers with children. It appears the child therapy community will not dismiss the computer as a juggernaut of the twentieth century. Rather, a cadre of professionals is coalescing and is harnessing the multidimensional facets of digital technology for psychotherapeutic purposes.

SELECTING THE SOFTWARE

Purchasing children's software is an enormous undertaking. The choices are staggering. A recently published book, *The Elementary Teacher's Sourcebook on Children's Software*, reviews 2,961 programs appropriate for preschool, elementary, and middle school children (Wolock, Orr, & Buckleitner, 1998). Children's software is usually produced on 3½-inch floppy diskettes or CD-ROMs. Newer titles that incorporate sound, 3-D graphics, and animation cost approximately $20 to $70. Purchasing a drawing program and a couple of games will require an investment of $100 or more in just software. Less expensive options for building a library of children's software are discussed below.

Shareware is software based on the marketing concept "try before you buy." Some titles are truncated versions of the full-featured program. Others allow the consumer to try the software for a limited period of time, after which it becomes inoperable if it is not upgraded. In either case, the user pays the author's asking price for unlimited access to the upgraded version of the program. Shareware is reasonably priced when compared with comparable titles sold in computer stores. Because shareware developers do not have to pay for marketing, packaging, and distributing their products, they can transfer those savings to the consumer. Where is shareware found in the computer world? Some companies advertise online. A quick search on the Internet will produce several Web sites that feature children's shareware. Some software firms specialize in marketing new shareware titles; these companies advertise in computer and technology magazines. Some offer club memberships; joining the club allows a member to try several titles for a few dollars each.

Freeware is a handout, software given away at no cost and with no conditions. It is an excellent way to obtain programs for child therapy. Some freeware titles are demos, developed in hopes that the user will want to purchase future upgrades of the product. Because some programmers realize there will not be a considerable demand for or profits from their work, they release the software to the public domain. An example of freeware is a program that the author downloaded from an American Sign Language web site. It introduces children to the manual alphabet used by deaf Americans. When children type a message on the keyboard, the letters are translated into fingerspelling that scrolls across the computer screen. This program is very popular with children. A word of caution about freeware is imperative for neophytes: Unsavory characters exist in the computer field as they do elsewhere; a particular admonition is to beware of dreaded computer viruses that can dismantle or destroy a system. When downloading or otherwise acquiring freeware, newcomers to the computer field should seek the help of someone who can determine if the freeware is virus-free or if the company producing it is a reputable one.

When major software companies discontinue titles, these become available at very reasonable prices. Computer and office supply stores have specials bins filled with bargain software. The programs are liquidation items. If the graphics and features are not too arcane, bargain software is a thrifty way to collect children's programs. Used software is plentiful at yard sales and computerfests. Acquiring software this way requires an act of faith: if the product is not in the original shrink-wrapped package, buyers cannot be certain if it has been contaminated by a virus or was modified by its owner. Computer buffs buy impulsively, as does everyone else; later, they are encumbered with hardware or software they'll never use, so they are delighted to dispose of it for a fraction of what it originally cost.

Selecting the Hardware

Advances in the design and manufacture of computer hardware have been astounding in the past decade. Personal computers for home and office are equipped with massive storage capacities, digital audio processing, full-motion video, animation, and a host of other features. New computer systems come on the market at an exponential rate, so the decision about which system to purchase is an overwhelming undertaking. The selection process is confounded when friends try to cajole colleagues into quickly buying the latest/greatest deal that has just come on the market. Computer magazines are not always helpful either; although they publish advertisements and reviews of the newest systems, readers are relegated to digesting hundreds of pages of complex technical data. Books about purchasing computers often become outdated before they reach the consumer.

With the aforementioned as a backdrop, how can anyone proffer advice about purchasing computer hardware? The purpose of this section is not to recommend the purchase of a specific system, but to suggest a decision tree that will assist the reader in approaching the problem with clarity and structure. Deciding which computer is best for the clinical office is a more manageable process if it is reduced to answering four questions: Does the clinician prefer a new or a used system? Is portability essential, or will a desktop model suffice? Does the user prefer the Windows or the Apple platform? Will the computer be used exclusively in play therapy, or will it double as an office machine?

The first question involves a trade-off between cost and technology. As is commonly the case with any equipment, new computers are more expensive than used ones. Naturally, new computers incorporate current digital technology. They operate recently published versions of multimedia software that resemble the arcade games that appeal to children. Purchasing a new computer obviates guesswork about how the system has been used. No computer is a sound purchase if an electronic hobbyist modified its circuit boards or if a computer hacker reprogrammed the software. As the trend toward upgrading to newer computers continues, experts estimate that by the year 2000 there will be more than 50 million obsolete computers in America. Many of those systems will be quite adequate for child therapists. Holzberg (1995) provides an insightful analysis of the used computer market, although the article is dated. The reader may wish to search the Internet for more current information on the topic.

The second question deals with the issues of portability and price. Laptop computers afford users more portability and flexibility than desktop systems. This feature alone may be critical for therapists who must travel to several sites. Also, a portable computer can be moved easily within a play therapy room. When used with a battery pack, it can be placed in a favorite spot with the child and therapist huddling around it. Some companies manufacture docking stations for laptop computers. The docking station is an electronic "shell" with external ports for a monitor, a keyboard, a printer, and other peripherals; when the computer is inserted into the docking station, one enjoys the comforts of desktop computing and the convenience of a laptop system. Because laptop computers store data and programs on an internal hard drive, if the computer is taken on the road, the data or programs go with it. In terms of cost, laptops generally cost more than comparable desktop systems with identical features. One reason is the high cost of miniaturization of the microcircuits in portable computers.

The issue of whether to run the Apple or Windows platform is a major one. Devotees of the respective platforms are staunch supporters of them, and newcomers to the computer world will be bamboozled by the pejorative rhetoric that surrounds this matter. Some sales personnel direct prospective buyers away from purchasing Macintosh computers because "Apple is a dying company." That contention has been around for more than 10 years. Conversely, Apple advocates soundly denounce the DOS/Windows platforms as complex at best, user-hostile at worst. Several years ago, a member of a local Apple club proudly displayed the bumper sticker "Friends don't let friends drive DOS." Resolving the dilemma—buy an Apple computer or buy a Windows computer—may be a simple matter if the applications chosen will run only on one of the machines. Fortunately, software companies are publishing programs on CD-ROMs that will run on both the Macintosh and Windows-based computers; therefore, one does not have to abandon a favorite software title because it is incompatible with a specific platform.

The answer to the question of whether the computer will be dedicated to therapeutic work or double as a business system carries significant clinical implications. If a therapist uses the computer for both purposes, precautions must be taken (such as password protection) to ensure that sensitive files and confidential information are not accessible to the children who use it. If the system is not secure, the therapist may behave in countertherapeutic ways, such as anxiously restricting the child's freedom to explore the games and programs on the computer. Also, a computer that is positioned next to a phone and books on a business desk will not look like another toy in the playroom. Forethought and planning are imperative if the computer is to take its place among the array of toys and games in the play therapy room.

With so many questions to answer and issues to resolve, deciding which computer to acquire may sound like an interminable process. But if word processing, drawing, and playing games are entry points, then almost any PC that works is adequate for starters. The drawback is personal image: older systems, with text-based menus and crude graphics, are a "turn-off" for some children. But if the system is functional, the work can begin. That's a better alternative than reading about colleagues who are doing great things with children and computers.

Learning the System before Using It

Child therapists take pride in mastering clinical or counseling techniques before using them in sessions. An important caution about the therapeutic application of computers is that clinicians should be thoroughly comfortable with the hardware and software before introducing the technology to a child. The best computer tutor is a 7-year-old child. That assertion may be a hyperbole, but many adults have neighborhood children as their computer mentors. Asking a child to guide the way when learning about the computer is a viable possibility. Other opportunities to learn about computers are abundant. Neighbors and friends who are computer literate are often willing to help. Local community colleges and universities offer noncredit, self-edification courses on a variety of computing topics. Virtual computer courses are available from commercial online service providers. Local computer clubs have instructional programs and videotapes for new members. The International Society for Technology in Education (ISTE) is an interdisciplinary group of professionals who are committed to supporting the integration of computer-based technology into classroom instruction. Although ISTE is principally pedagogic in focus, it provides books, periodicals, distance education courses, and special interest groups (SIGs) that are invaluable to anyone who uses computers with children.

A wealth of information technology is available to child therapists through the Internet. Accessing the online resources requires a computer, a modem (an electronic device that connects the computer to the telephone line), telecommunications software, and an Internet service provider (ISP). Getting started requires an investment of time and money; however, therapists who effectively use the Internet discover that the World Wide Web, with its graphic user interface, has a number of sites devoted to child and adolescent psychotherapy. Electronic mail, newsgroups (Usenet), and listservers are other exciting ways for professionals to share the latest information and resources in their respective fields. Usenets and listservers are online discussion groups on a wide range of topics; thousands of them are available online at no cost. Subscribing to these services usually requires users to leave an e-mail message expressing their intent to join the group with the site coordinator. A common message used for that purpose is (subscribe <listserver or discussion group name><your name>). Once a member, bulletins or messages posted about a topic become available immediately to all members enrolled in the service.

PRACTICAL MATTERS

Safety First

Conceal electrical cords and cables safely behind your system and away from children's touch. Dangerous voltages are usually shielded safely within the housing of the computer; however, power strips and AC cords are shock hazards if children come in contact with them. Because several cables are necessary to make connections between peripherals and the computer's central processing unit, children can become entangled in them if they are exposed. Hiding cables and physically securing the monitor so it can't be knocked over by active children will make the playroom safe and allow the therapist to concentrate on the important business of relating to the child. Family computer magazines have been publishing excellent, detailed articles about child-proofing systems.

Good Housekeeping

Counselors and clinicians are accustomed to saving the drawings, stories, cartoons, diaries, and figures that children fabricate in psychotherapy. The artifacts produced by children with computers are usually stored on electromagnetic media. Good computer housekeeping involves creating a file structure with directories and subdirectories in which to store children's special projects so they are safe and easily retrievable. When saving files created by children in therapy sessions, the issues of privacy and confidentiality are critical. Storing documents with filenames like SMITH.DOC, SMITH.ART, or even MARY.DOC will compromise the identity of a patient. One solution to this problem is to provide each child with his or her own diskette. Colored 3½-inch floppy diskettes are ideal for this purpose. These should be safely stored in the office. The diskette serves two purposes: it evokes a sense of belonging, because children will have left a product from the therapy hour in the playroom, and it eliminates children's access to confidential materials created by other young clients.

Environmental Contaminants

For all their sophistication, computers are sensitive devices. Their innards contain delicate electronic circuits. System failures, which are costly to repair, can occur without any apparent reason. A therapist who set up her computer near sand trays discovered the system was inoperative the very day she planned to introduce a new computer game to a child. Over time, the powdery dust from sand play therapy damaged contacts on the motherboard. Computers in playrooms should be in safe places, away from water, sand trays, paints, and other potentially damaging materials. Environmental factors that are dangerous to computers are dust, heat, humidity, magnetic fields, and electrical storms. Dust, heat, and humidity damage internal circuits; electrical storms produce power surges with dangerously high voltages, which can fry computer circuits. In areas that have a high frequency of electrical storms, a power-strip with surge protection is a necessity. A safer but more expensive course of action is to obtain an uninterruptible power source (UPS) that protects equipment from power surges and keeps it running safely for short periods during a power outage. The UPS permits the computer operator to close out applications that are active without losing data or disrupting the software. Electromagnetic fields have the potential to erase data from diskettes. Magnets are used in many objects (e.g., speakers, paper clip dispensers, toys) commonly found in the therapist's office or playroom; although removing every magnet in the immediate surroundings is unnecessary, toys containing magnets should not be proximate to the diskettes that store programs or children's computer projects.

The 30-Minute Rule

The brainchild of a colleague of the author, the 30-minute rule is an operating principle for computer users at any level of expertise. The rule states that one should devote no more than 30 minutes to solving complex hardware or software problems. Debugging computers can consume an enormous amount of time. Although it may be intriguing to ferret out that elusive cyberbug, such an undertaking is often a waste of a busy professional's valuable time. After 30 minutes of computer sleuthing, referring the matter to a technician or a friend with computer expertise is a better course of action.

THE COMPUTER AS A PSYCHOTHERAPEUTIC TOY

Teachers have been trailblazers in discovering pedagogical applications of computers with children. They use them for the delivery of course content, drill-and-practice, online data collection, cultural exchanges, composition, speech therapy, and special education projects. Conversely, the therapeutic use of the computer with youngsters has been slow to develop. Margolies (1991) wrote, "the computer's role as an agent of socialization is just beginning to be explored" (p. 70). Preliminary survey research conducted with play therapists in Maryland sheds light on this phenomenon. Kepner and Thompson (1995) designed a two-page questionnaire to request information about computer use in therapy sessions. The questionnaire was mailed to 88 play therapists in the Baltimore-Washington metropolitan area. The response rate was 58% with 51 surveys returned. Of all the respondents, 12% reported using the computer in child therapy. The most frequently reported reasons for nonuse were the lack of technical knowledge (37%) and the expense of the setup (35%). However, more than half the respondents (65%) indicated they would consider using the computer in play therapy if they had the opportunity for training in how to use the system. Many of those surveyed reported difficulty in determining exactly how computers could be incorporated effectively into counseling and play therapy. Using computers in child therapy does not have to be a complex or ponderous process. With a modicum of ingenuity, any clinician can transform the computer into an electronic easel, a gaming machine, a craft factory, a desktop publisher, a music maker, a behavior management system, or a medium for therapeutic telecommunications. The following discussion describes those applications in detail.

PAINT PROGRAMS

Most personal computers built in the past 15 years include paint software. The Apple II computer features Mouse Paint. Macintosh computers are bundled with MacPaint, and computers running Microsoft Windows include MS Paint. The screen layout in paint programs will differ depending on the model and age of the computer; however, most of them will resemble the one found in Figure 8.1.

The left side of the screen usually displays the drawing tools; the bottom of the screen contains a palette of colors or patterns. The mouse is used to select different tools or features of the program. Using a click-and-drag action, lines, shapes, and other artistic effects are made on the screen with the mouse. Usually, text can be typed in the drawing area on paint programs. Other tools allow the operator to erase, color the screen, change visual perspectives, delete the drawing, save the file, and print the artwork.

Adults who try paint programs complain that they are difficult to use. Drawing on a horizontal surface while the output appears vertically on a screen can be perceptually confusing. Children do

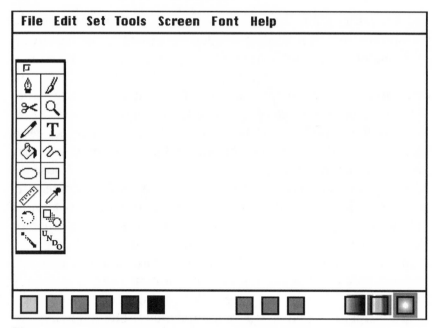

Figure 8.1 Sample of Initial Screen in Paint Programs.

not seem to have that problem. They are comfortable using the mouse to draw and freely experiment with all the features of paint programs. In a comparative study of the graphic representations of 2- and 3-year-old children, Matthews and Jessel (1993) found that preschoolers employed similar mark-making strategies independent of whether they used traditional art media such as pencils, crayons, and markers or the mouse with an electronic paint program.

Counselors working with young children in a learning clinic at Michigan State University found that paint software produced catharsis, ventilation of feelings, and personal insight (Johnson, 1984). They used the Apple IIe computer, equipped with an electronic graphics tablet and LOGO (Papert, 1980), a drawing program that allows children to depict figures and designs on the computer screen by moving a small triangular object called a turtle. Johnson found that "computer art is a way of enhancing communication between the child and the counselor and offers a projective assessment tool as well as a medium for looking at new ways of perceiving the self and exploring new and more adequate coping behaviors" (p. 130). Subsequently, Johnson (1987) described the course of therapy with a 10-year-old passive dependent boy who used "feeling paintings" to work through an overdependence on his mother following the sudden death of his father.

Inexpensive art supplies are available in craft stores. So why use a costly, cumbersome machine like the computer for drawing pictures? Three features of paint programs that make them ideal for child art are interactivity, flexibility, and storage. First, computers produce a variety of visual and/or sound effects when children manipulate the drawing tools of paint programs. Second, many paint programs contain an undo command that cancels the last feature drawn in the picture. This command allows children to change their artwork immediately, making the computer a more forgiving art medium than traditional media. Finally, computer art may be stored in an electromagnetic format, permitting a therapist can save the child's work in stages as it is being produced. When the respective files are retrieved and displayed in serial order, they give an uncanny overview of the psychodynamic process underpinning the production of the art. Drawings created by children during the course of therapy can be stored in files that are easily converted into a computer slide presentation that depicts the child's therapeutic journey. Also, some adolescents who refuse to draw with traditional art media because "it's for little kids" are enthusiastic about using paint software.

Thematic and pictorial representations in children's computer art are just being explored. Although no large normative studies of computer art exist in the literature, clinicians who use this expressive medium find that children draw nature, people, animals, favorite objects, vehicles, and other themes commonly found in artwork produced with pencils, crayons, markers, and finger paint.

Clinicians are finding a variety of uses for paint software. Aymard (1997) describes the Computer Family Drawing (CFD) technique. Following the basic instructions developed by Burns and Kaufman (1970), he asks children to *paint* a computer picture of their family doing something. The word *draw* is omitted from the directions so that children are free to use all the features of the software; also, asking children to draw with paint programs places on them the burden of creating art that looks like traditional drawings. Nevertheless, the CFDs were remarkably similar in appearance and theme to the Kinetic Family Drawings (KFDs) drawn with paper and pencil. Production time taken for CFDs ($M = 15.6$ minutes) compared favorably with the time ($M = 9.3$ minutes) required for children to complete KFDs in an outpatient clinic setting. Gamson (1997) used computer art as a cathartic technique in group therapy with children 7 years and older. The children became more articulate about discussing the types of abuse they experienced after representing it on the computer screen. The children's drawings projected powerful themes of verbal, physical, and sexual abuse.

As computers are used more frequently in child therapy, clinicians are likely to find that their young clients serendipitously devise marvelous ways of using them for therapeutic gain. The following case illustrates this point. Lisa's therapist had a computer on his desk primarily for business purposes. It had not occurred to him that the computer was useful for counseling children. One day, Lisa recognized the icon for drawing software and suggested they play the game "Secret Messages." She went over to the computer, started the paint program, and used the spraycan to scrawl the message "I hate school" on the screen. Each week, Lisa began her session by spray-painting graffiti about family, friends, or teachers on her "brick wall" (the computer screen). She insisted on erasing the message at the end of the session so that it would remain a secret between her and her therapist.

Transforming Software into Playware

Traditional games are easily adapted for psychotherapeutic purposes with children. Two child analysts (R. Gardner, 1986; Loomis, 1957) believe that the game of checkers has therapeutic utility for children with a variety of presenting problems. Schaefer and Reid (1986) proposed that childhood games are valuable as projective techniques, help establish a therapeutic alliance with children, and are a means of ego enhancement. Because games are rule-governed activities of childhood, they are an important way for children to practice cognitive skills and an opportunity for socialization. If traditional childhood games are adaptable for psychotherapeutic purposes with children, can children's software have clinical utility as well? Several clinical studies (Allen, 1984; Casey & Ramsammy, 1992; Favelle, 1994; J. Gardner, 1991; Kokish, 1994; Margolies, 1991; Oakley, 1994; Resnick, 1994; Sisson et al., 1985), as well as the experiences of other child therapists, suggest that the answer to that question is a resounding yes.

The following example illustrates how an inexpensive shareware game, Funny Face, was adapted to "playware" for use in child therapy. Funny Face resembles an electronic Mr. Potato Head. Its author describes the program as "software that stimulates creativity!" (Zamora, 1992, to obtain a demo version, see the web site: http//www.zware-usa.com). When the program loads, the initial screen appears with the title at the top; the center of the screen flashes with a display of the various kinds of faces one can create with the program. After clicking the mouse, the child enters the program and sees the screen displayed in Figure 8.2. (The DOS version of the program is displayed for readers who have older computers. Funny Face is also available in

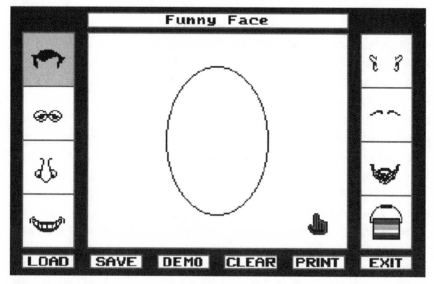

Figure 8.2 Funny Face Software Opening Screen (DOS Version). (Used with permission.)

a Windows version.) By selecting certain facial features, children create a face of their choosing. The paint bucket in the box on the lower right of the screen allows children to color the face they have drawn. If a printer is connected to the system, the face can be printed as well as saved on diskette for future use.

Funny Face, like any well-designed children's software, is an excellent way of building rapport with youngsters who are coming into therapy for the first time. When children enter the office or the playroom, they are immediately attracted to the faces flashing furtively on the screen. With a simple click of the mouse, they begin the game and start conversing with the therapist about the program's features or about the face they plan to draw.

Children's software can be a powerful projective technique. While the child is absorbed in playing on the computer, the therapist is free to observe his or her problem-solving strategies, dialogue, visual-motor coordination, and interpersonal processes. The artifacts children create with the computer give the clinician insights into their unique ways of perceiving the world. The following cases are examples of the projective nature of computer play.

Tommy had a disastrous early educational history. He was withdrawn, inattentive, slow in school, and rejected by peers. In the third grade, a psychological evaluation revealed that he had a serious learning disability. Tommy's parents were urged to remove him immediately from public school and enroll him in a local private institution for children with learning problems. Play therapy was recommended. Tommy loved computers; he sat in front of them for hours playing games. Naturally, he was surprised and delighted to discover a computer in the therapist's office. When he came in the playroom and saw the funny faces flashing on the screen, he wanted to play the computer game. As Tommy played with Funny Face, he laughed and said, "I'll make a face you won't forget." After pasting features on the face, he erased them quickly, as though it was aversive for him to look at a full face. He tried a variety of colors but decided on a monochromatic scheme. Tommy completed the face shown in Figure 8.3 and called it "Vanished." As rapport built between Tommy and his therapist, he expressed the chagrin he felt about his failures in

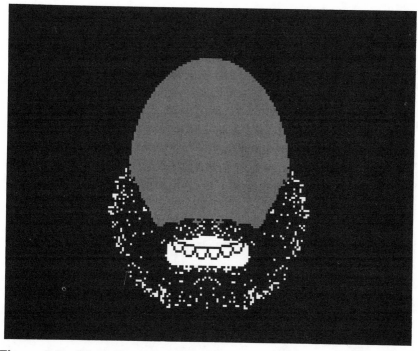

Figure 8.3 "Vanished." Face Produced with Funny Face Software by a 9-Year-Old Learning-Disabled Boy. (Used with permission.)

the classroom and the teasing he endured on the playground when classmates called him "Tommy the Dummy."

When Paul was 8 years old, his parents suspected that he had been sexually abused. His naturally gregarious manner gradually disappeared, and he spent long hours in his room; he lost interest in sports and was failing school; he began making suggestive comments to his younger sister and other girls in the neighborhood. Paul came to the psychologist for an evaluation. He thought drawing was for little kids and resisted any paper and pencil tasks. When he spotted Funny Face displayed on the computer, he asked what it was; the therapist explained that it was a computer game and asked if he wanted to play it. After spending some time experimenting with the program, Paul created the haunting face in Figure 8.4. He colored the whites of the eyes red as though they were bloodshot, then chose a zipper for

Figure 8.4 A Haunting Face Made with Funny Face Software by a Sexually Abused Boy. (Used with permission.)

the mouth. Several sessions later, Paul disclosed that during summer vacations, his maternal grandmother, a widow, often fondled him when he visited her home. Children express powerful feelings through electronic media just as they do with paints, clay, sand play, drawing, and other therapeutic materials.

Not only is Funny Face excellent for establishing rapport with children, but it can also be used for making masks. The faces children make are saved as PCX or picture files; graphics software, desktop publishing programs, and some word processors import PCX files. The pictures can be sized (shrunk or enlarged) and printed on white or color sheets. Slots for the eyes are cut with scissors or a hole-puncher. Clear contact paper or transparent paper laminate will make the masks durable if children want to use them for role playing in subsequent sessions.

The Make-A-Feelings-Face is another therapeutic application of Funny Face. Children may not be able to verbalize their feelings about daily experiences or their reactions to traumatic situations. When they are comfortable playing Funny Face, the therapist can invite them to make a face that shows how they are feeling that day. Often, after the face is created, children name the feeling or discuss the troublesome experience. If the drawing is saved on a diskette, the file can be opened in future sessions. The image of the face is an evocative stimulus to continue discussions with children about the issues dealt with in the previous session. Faces made by children across several therapy sessions can be captured by graphics software and printed as cameos on a single sheet. Presentation graphics programs create beautiful slide shows that display the faces in the sequence in which the children created them.

Funny Face was written for IBM-compatible computers, and it is affordable in any budget. Thousands of programs, like Funny Face, exist in shareware and freeware libraries. The clinical utility of the software comes not from its content, but from the creative ways children use it for therapeutic purposes. As clinicians become more comfortable using computers, they are certain to discover myriad ways of adapting therapeutic techniques to cyberspace. When those are published in books, journals, or online dialogues, therapists will have an impressive armamentarium of computer-based applications for use with children and adolescents.

COMPUTER ARTS AND CRAFTS

Arts and crafts actively engage children in play therapy. Personal computers, equipped with crafting software, are excellent tools for producing therapeutic artifacts. Software companies frequently publish these programs under the title of creativity software. They incorporate the drawing and publishing features of their predecessors, transforming the computer into a desktop craft shop. Notepaper, stickers, cards, banners, and other supplies are often furnished in the package. It is not necessary to have the latest creativity software to explore computer crafts with children;

word processing software is sufficient to start the process. Kuntz and Kuntz (1994) describe more than a dozen creative activities for children using Microsoft Word, word processing software available in Macintosh and Windows versions. Their book, *Computer Crafts for Kids*, has colorful illustrations and stepwise instructions for computer novices. Computers stimulate creativity, so therapists can create craft projects from the following ideas as well as from those presented in the book.

Decorative diskette labels are very popular with children. Assorted labels with bright colors and playful designs can be made for children to use with their diskettes. Many word processors have templates that make it easy to create labels. The process can be accomplished in three simple steps:

1. Use a decorative font that is easy to read and appealing to children. At the top of the label, type an appropriate title in uppercase, such as MY SPECIAL COMPUTER DISK. A horizontal line may be inserted two spaces below for the child's name.
2. Import a graphics file to decorate the label. Children take pride in decorating crafts with their own computer drawings.
3. Print the label on a color printer.

Stickers of any size can be produced without label-making software. Use the shape tool in the word processor to make a square graphics or text box. Import a picture inside the box, then add a slogan and a border so the sticker can be cut out later. The copy command is a useful way to duplicate the design on the page. When the page is filled with the designs, glue it to the front side of contact paper; after the glue dries, the custom stickers are ready to be cut out and used. Some paper distributors sell 8½″ × 11″ white sheets with sticky backs for laser and inkjet printers; this is an easier, albeit more expensive, way to create sheets of children's stickers.

Finger puppets and paper dolls are best made with word processors that include graphics programs. Use the shape tool to draw a horizontal rectangle four inches long and one half inch wide. This shape will be the base of the puppet or paper doll.

Duplicate the shape once or twice on the page with the copy command. Then import and resize a clipart figure, a child's drawing, or a photographic image to fit directly on top of the rectangle. Cut around the image and on the perimeter of the rectangle. If the figure is to be a finger puppet, connect the ends of the paper with a piece of tape or glue, sizing the diameter of the base for an adult's or child's finger. If the figure is a paper doll, folding the base in thirds will make the doll freestanding.

Certificates that acknowledge and reward children for their accomplishments can be made with any word processor. Certificate-making software for use with older computers is reasonably priced but may be hard to find. Word processors that come with newer computers often have templates for making certificates. After users choose a pleasing design, the program gives prompts to enter a name, if appropriate, and a message for the certificate.

Customized notepads with therapeutic messages are fun to make with children. Youngsters with attention deficit disorders are often reminded by parents and teachers to "think before you act." Desktop publishing a notepad with that kind of slogan is easy to do with any word processing software. Enter the slogan anywhere on the page; alongside it, place an appropriate image, such as a cartoon figure in a pensive pose. Dividing an 8½" × 11" sheet (portrait orientation) into quarters, the image and slogan are copied in each quadrant of the paper. When the printed sheets are cut into quarters and stapled at the top, children have notepads to use at home or at school.

Calendar templates for weeks, months, or years, are commonly found in many popular word processors. Some have options for printing the text in foreign languages. Calendar making is enhanced for children if the product is printed on colorful, decorative paper such as that found in office supply and computer stores. Text on the calendar may be a reminder to the child or special messages of encouragement for particular days or weeks.

Origami and paper airplane patterns are available in special software packages. The desired pattern is selected from several displayed on the screen. Often, the program asks if the user wishes to print a set of instructions for folding the papercraft. Some desktop publishing software may include a few origami and paper airplane patterns among the templates that are provided with them.

Making game boards requires some ingenuity, and the designs will vary depending on the complexity of the game. When creating game boards, children and therapists should experiment with all the graphic features of word processors or desktop publishing programs. Because pages can be joined with tape, the size of the finished product does not need to be restricted to a single sheet of paper.

T-shirts for any occasion or with special inscriptions are made with software developed specifically for that purpose. After the design is created, it is printed on T-shirt transfer paper. The software has a feature that instructs the printer to flip, or reverse the image on the transfer paper. Usually, a hand iron applies the decal to the T-shirt. Child therapy groups may focus on a particular theme or life issue. Group members may be invited by the therapist(s) to pool their collective efforts and design a T-shirt that embodies the experience. This project is probably best suited for school counseling projects, inpatient settings, and summer camps where the appropriate equipment is available and participants are not under the time constraint of the traditional therapy hour.

Digital cameras, scanners, and monochromatic or color videocameras are peripherals that enhance creativity and make computer crafting an intriguing endeavor. These are expensive acquisitions. They work best with newer computers that have advanced central processing units with large amounts of memory or RAM. With these powerful tools and the proper software, therapists who work with children and adolescents in any psychotherapeutic setting can fabricate personalized crafts like at no other time in the history of the field.

ADAPTING TRADITIONAL CHILD THERAPY TECHNIQUES TO THE COMPUTER

The notion of adapting a traditional child therapy technique to the computer was advanced by Olsen-Rando (1994). He presented a theoretical proposal for developing a computerized version of the Talking Feeling and Doing board game. Although no progress has been made on this proposal, his suggestion should be an incentive for child therapists to use their ingenuity for adapting traditional child therapy techniques to the personal computer.

Winnicott (1971) describes a paper-and-pencil game in which the therapist and child take turns making lines that are used to draw a picture. Cybersquiggles is an adaptation to computers of Winnicott's technique that can be introduced to children as a game of imagination. With the paint program loaded, the therapist asks the child if he or she would like to play a computer imagination game. The therapist makes a random scribble (squiggle) in the blank portion of the screen. The squiggle is immediately saved as a file (e.g., SQUIG1). The child is encouraged to imagine what the squiggle might become and to make a picture using any of the tools or colors on the screen. Upon completion of the drawing, the child's production is saved as a second file (e.g., SQUIG2). In the third phase of the game, the child tells a story about the imaginative creation. Cybersquiggles is very popular with latency-age children and adolescents. Also, the game may be played in traditional fashion, as Winnicott conceived of it, using only the black pen in the paint program. This version of the game requires therapist and child to take turns making squiggles on the screen. The following case illustrates how Cybersquiggles was incorporated into a termination session with an 11-year-old girl.

Sara came to play therapy because her parents were concerned that she had few friends, struggled with homework, lacked organizational skills, and forgot to do chores at home. Her mother and father were successful business executives who had unreasonable expectations for their daughter. They thought Sara's struggles were due to laziness; they couldn't fathom why she didn't use initiative in resolving problems at home and in school. After a parent training program, Sara's parents became less demanding and more affectionate toward her. As she developed strength and self-assurance from play therapy, Sara began to express her emotional needs at home and was more assertive in the classroom. In her last session, she wanted to play the computer squiggle game. She transformed the vertical squiggle drawn by the therapist into a fox's nose, completing the animal's face with eyes and ears. Sara then used the spray can to paint red fur on the animal's face. Her story, "The Fox," marvelously captures Sara's youthful journey in search of a peaceful family life:

> Once upon a time there was a fox and he woke up one morning and decided to go out and find a treasure. He didn't know where to start looking. He checked under a cherry tree but there was no treasure. Next he went to the stream and jumped in the water to see if there was any treasure in the water but there was none. Now he decided to go to his friend the owl and see if there was a treasure with the owl up in the tree. His friend, the owl, said "I haven't seen any but if I do see a treasure I'll tell you." Now the fox is getting frustrated. He looked high and low for treasures and couldn't find any. He decided to go home and tell his brother and sister and maybe they could help him. He told his brother and sister and they set off to look for treasures with the fox in the woods. They were walking and talking and the fox with his big nose ran into a tree. They were all laughing, even the fox, that ran into the tree. He had found his treasure. The moral of the story is the fox didn't need a treasure. He had already found one by being with his family.

STORYTELLING WITH COMPUTERS

For centuries, myths and stories have captured the imagination of people of all cultures. Storytelling has been the mainstay of child psychotherapy since its inception. Mills and Crowley (1986) provide an insightful analysis of the use of stories as a therapeutic medium in working with children and their parents. Because storytelling is such an interpersonal phenomenon, how can the computer even be remotely helpful in this endeavor? Three possibilities have been explored in clinical practice. The first technique uses the computer as a printing press to publish children's writings as picture storybooks (The Computer Make-A-Picture Storybook). The second option employs "movie-making" software to create animated stories (The Animated Theater). The third possibility is for the therapist to use presentation graphics software to script a favorite therapeutic story or metaphor. After editing the story for content and effects, the therapist can present it to children on the computer at the appropriate time. If a therapist is just becoming familiar with digital technology, the first application is the easiest of the three.

The Computer Make-A-Picture Storybooks allows children to use the paint program and a word processor to produce their own drawings and story. The first step is to ask the child to produce a drawing or set of drawings with the paint program. After the pictures are drawn, they can be printed and displayed in full view of the child. The child then closes the paint program and opens a word processor to record the story. Some children like to type the story themselves. For younger children or for those who do not type, the therapist can function as a scribe, typing the story as the child tells it. If the therapist doesn't type, another possibility is to have the child dictate the story on a tape recorder for later transcription. In essence, this technique is not different than storybook making with children using construction paper and crayons. However, the fun in producing a computer storybook is enhanced by the editing capabilities of modern computers. Most computers come with colorful clip art that can be used to decorate the pages. If the therapist has a small hand scanner, children's favorite drawings, pictures, and symbols can be scanned into the work. Some ambitious children even create web sites on the Internet to publish their stories and poetry. Charles the Turtle, shown in Figure 8.5, is the central character in the following story. A 10-year-old girl, who loved to make computer storybooks, is the author.

The Turtle and the Lucky Flower

Once upon a time there was a turtle named Charles. Charles was afraid to cross the street. His mother always told him that there is nothing to worry about, that she will always be there for him. One day, Charles was going to go out for a walk and pick some berries for supper. He was walking but he noticed the berries were on the other side of the street. So the sun said that he would give Charlie a special flower so he wouldn't be scared. Charlie started to cross the street with the special flower. Then the wind came and just blew the flower right out of his hand. The sun was there so he said "don't worry, just finish crossing the street." So that is what Charlie did. When he got there, he was so happy he

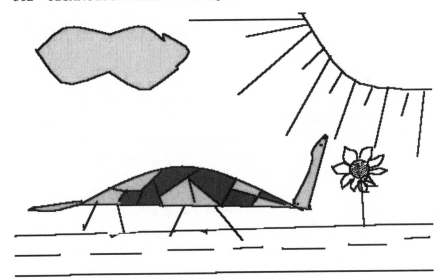

Figure 8.5 "Charles the Turtle." A Picture from a Therapeutic Story Created Using the Computer. (Used with permission.)

didn't need a lucky flower. From that day forward, Charlie was never afraid to cross the street. The End.

The Animated Theater is a novel therapeutic application of computers with children. It requires movie-making software, which is the computer analogue of therapeutic games such as The Storytelling Card Game (R. Gardner, 1988). Some patience and practice are required to master these programs; nevertheless, they are an outstanding means of animated storytelling for children and adolescents. Three features are common to movie-making software. First, there are a series of backgrounds or familiar scenes (a classroom, a home, a street) from which players select. Some of the backgrounds are plain colors. Second, several male and female characters are available from "central casting." Finally, children direct the characters' movements, dialogue, and expressions. Most of this is accomplished with menus or by clicking and dragging the mouse to produce special effects. The script is typed in using the keyboard. When the story is completed, children feel a tremendous sense of pride as they watch the production with their therapist. Sometimes, children retrieve the file containing their story and edit it. It is interesting to observe the changes they make in a story over time as they progress through the stages of play therapy. One method of using The Animated Theater is to ask if the child would like to produce a movie that will teach a special lesson to other children. The therapist may suggest a theme that is relevant to the child's life, such as making friends. After a little coaching about the basic features of the software, the therapist is able to observe the production as it unfolds. The process sounds complicated and time-consuming; however, if the therapist is familiar with the software, it is possible to produce a simple story (one minute in length) within a 50-minute session and a more detailed one (three to five minutes) in two or three sessions.

Therapy journals and autobiographical stories for adolescents are other ways to use the computer. Therapists who employ cognitive behavioral techniques may invite clients to compose a small paragraph about the principal theme discussed in a session. The date/time stamp on most word processors is a way to follow the progress over time. A more ambitious project is to use all features of multimedia computers to assist children and adolescents in creating an animated production of their life stories.

Creating therapeutic stories with multimedia software brings an exciting dynamism to the psychotherapeutic process for children and adolescents. Presentation graphics programs and multimedia authoring software are ideal tools for creating metaphors and stories. Presentation graphics programs often come bundled with many office software suites. They include templates, graphic images, and special transition effects for creating slide shows. The serial nature of their output—frame by frame—is the feature that makes them useful for storytelling. A therapist can arrange the sequence of slides so that the story unfolds in cartoon fashion. Although some investment of time is required to learn the software, the skills acquired are useful not only for making therapeutic stories but also for designing professional presentations. A language arts teacher in a rural Nebraska school district taught his eighth-grade students to create computer interactive storybooks for the first- and second-graders in the school. The article that reviews this project (Fredrickson, 1997) contains directions for designing interactive storybooks.

THERAPEUTIC TELECOMMUNICATIONS

American children are going online in record numbers. Telecommunications professionals project that the number of children online will rise from approximately 3 million in 1998 to 20 million in 2002. Because telecommunications lends itself to interactivity, is it possible for this virtual medium to have therapeutic applications? At first glance, the term therapeutic telecommunications seems like an oxymoron. Lead stories appear in print and electronic media about pedophiles, pornography, and other perils of going online. Chatrooms are depicted as places waiting to ensnare unsuspecting young kids. Sherry Turkle (1995) proffers an insightful sociological analysis of virtual communities in her book *Life on the Screen: Identity in the Age of the Internet.* She posits that telecommunications has spawned a new culture of simulation. Global connectivity has enabled people from all cultures to inhabit virtual worlds and to establish new identities within the amorphous structure known as the Internet. Online personas afford denizens of the Internet opportunities to enter into new roles, thus reinventing the self. Turkle believes that children are taking the lead in this sociocultural revolution and that adults are anxiously trailing behind them.

A fascinating, albeit dated, account of the psychotherapeutic value of telecommunications for children appeared not in the clinical literature, but in the *Washington Apple Pi Journal,* an Apple Computer Club newsletter (Kercher, 1990). Kercher describes the Tele-Foster Grandparent Program that introduced children in 12 special education classrooms to 48 senior citizens in nursing homes in Michigan, Canada, and Hawaii. The project, designed by educators in the Genesee Intermediate School District in Flint, Michigan, was widely publicized and lauded in the local press. At that time, telecommunications was in its infancy, and modems were just emerging on the electronic market. Computer aficionados, eager to communicate with each other online, established electronic meeting places known as bulletin board systems or BBSs. Computer bulletin boards were sources for downloading simple programs, posting information, and retrieving electronic announcements. Many had an e-mail service for members who subscribed.

The Tele-Foster Grandparent Program was a tremendous success. Children with learning disabilities who approached school composition exercises with diffidence were writing lengthy electronic letters to their tele-foster grandparents. Teachers found that the children took pride in their work, checking spelling and grammar before uploading the message to the BBS. And seniors found a link with the outside world; daily, they eagerly awaited any communication from their children. Self-esteem is reported to have improved in both populations. Most important, intergenerational communications of a therapeutic nature appeared in the online dialogues. The following excerpts from the online dialogues illustrate this point:

"My gerbil died—can anybody help?" . . . The senior citizen responded: "You're feeling sad because your gerbil died. Losing something that you love really does make a person sad. Once when somebody I loved died, I felt lost and lonely too. I think the thing that helped me the most was trying to remember the good times, the fun times, more than I remembered the loss. As long as I can carry those happy memories, it's as though part of that person I loved is still with me." (Kercher, 1990, p. 66)

"Dear Jenny" (a child wrote to her Tele-Foster Grandparent), "Yesterday I lied to my teacher Miss Phillips that I had my reading done. I got it done today! Did you ever lie to your teacher about getting your work done? Shauna."

Teacher's comments: "Shauna's letter was another of these true confessions that I would not have gotten were it not for Genkids. The fact that she had lied to me had bothered her all day but it was not until she wrote her letter that I knew what the problem was." (Unpublished data provided to the author by Mary Kercher)

Starbright World is a multimillion-dollar commercial telecommunications program for hospitalized children. The founders, Hollywood director Stephen Spielberg and Hollywood producer

Peter Samuelson, invited leading authorities in digital technology to construct the interactive network that allows real-time video-conferencing in 3-D virtual worlds. Many of the children who use the system have pernicious illnesses or have undergone surgical procedures such as bone marrow transplants that require isolation in sanitary rooms for weeks. Computers used in the network are state-of-the-art: they feature a variety of telecommunication modalities such as message exchange, audio streaming, and video-conferencing. The most intriguing is the use of avatars, animated characters chosen by the children to represent themselves in the virtual world. Avatars permit anonymity, particularly for young oncology patients who have lost their hair or are anxious about their physical appearance. When children log on to the system, they search for playmates from other participating hospitals. Once found, the children meet, play games, or discuss their respective illnesses on virtual, 3-D playgrounds. They may also choose real-time videoconferencing as a means of meeting each other as well as any visitors who are in the room. Controlled studies are underway to examine the impact of Starbright World on hospitalized children's experiences of loneliness, pain, and anxiety during protracted hospital stays (Stephenson, 1995). Pediatric oncologists anticipate that the program will have an unequivocally positive effect on the children's self-esteem as well as improve their socialization skills and coping behaviors.

The Tele-Foster Grandparent Program and Starbright World should inspire members of the child therapy community to invest their creative energies into developing telecommunication projects that are innovative and therapeutic for young people. An example is Virtual Dyadic Child Counseling. The concept involves linking two children and their counselors from different school districts through online dialogues. The pairs go online, with the supervision of their counselors, and share common experiences, or solutions to mutual problems. Text of the dialogues can be printed out to review the content and the process of the therapy. One might inquire, Why not put the children in a therapy group? If the children are geographically proximate, the interpersonal exchange is preferable. But in rural areas of the country where people are separated by great distances, travel to a common site for group counseling is impractical. Telecommunications will provide sufficient interpersonal distance, at first, to make the project successful; as the level of trust grows among the participants, videoconferencing could be added; and in those instances where travel is not prohibitive, the dyads could meet. The project may produce unanticipated interpersonal and psychotherapeutic outcomes, such as those derived from the Tele-Foster Grandparent Program and Starbright World.

ADDITIONAL APPLICATIONS

Making music with musical instrument digital interfaces (MIDIs) is an unexplored technological vista for child therapists. The components in the MIDI allow musical instruments to interface with the computer's central processing unit. A common instrument used with MIDIs is the piano keyboard. With proper software, the computer and the keyboard can make, record, and play musical selections. The simplest way to make music with the computer in the playroom is to use audio CDs of children's music, available in retail stores almost everywhere. This will work only if the computer has a dedicated CD drive, a sound board, and speakers. Older systems can be retrofitted with these components. Multimedia systems, manufactured within the past few years, have these components built into the system.

Behavior management software is beginning to appear on the market, and it will be a welcome tool for child behavior therapists. Tickle Box (1994) and The Self-Controlled Classroom (1996) are two examples of child behavior management software. The latter is available only for Macintosh computers. Both programs require children to work with parents, teachers, or counselors to plot behavioral baselines and establish target behaviors. The programs keep track of progress, provide reinforcing consequences, and allow results to be plotted in graphs or charts. Therapists may augment the reinforcing qualities of these programs by designing certificates and/or stickers as secondary reinforcers for children.

Children's storybooks on interactive CD-ROMs have become quite popular in recent years. Some publishers feature a range of titles that address child therapy issues. One of the first titles to appear was the popular children's story about a fledgling fruit bat, Stellaluna, who is separated from her mother and adopted by a family of robins. Storybooks on CD-ROM incorporate interactive, multimedia effects that delight children. Children may choose to follow the story or to click on an area of the screen that interests them and explore it further.

Simulation gaming software taxes the problem-solving skills of children and adolescents. The design of this software is quite a programming feat. The common feature across all these programs is that the user is able to construct, from ground zero, an ecosystem, such as a city or a colony of ants. The decisions the player makes about the system have consequences. Success requires the player to exercise forethought and good judgment; if the approach to designing and developing the ecosystem is haphazard, negative consequences are incurred. Bart, a 12-year-old dyslexic boy in a private school, loved to play SimCity every day when he came home from school. Asked why he liked the game, Bart responded, "I get to be in charge and, if I do a good job, the people in my city cheer and have a parade for me." Simple games of strategy come loaded on many new computers; they are easy to master, and children love the challenge they provide. While a child is busy solving the problems presented by a computer game, the therapist can gain valuable insights into the child's worldview and problem-solving skills.

Fantasy, mystery, and war games (shoot-to-kill) also have proven useful in therapeutic work with youth. The shelves of computer stores are filled with them, and each therapist will have a favorite one. The intrigue generated by this genre of software may result in *cybergenic hyperfocus,* a term playfully used by the author to describe the compelling way that computer games totally absorb children (and, of course, some adults). Several clinical studies (Allen, 1984; Favelle, 1994; J. Gardner, 1991; Kokish, 1994; Margolies, 1991; Resnick, 1994; Sisson et al., 1985) support the contention that computer games do not have a deleterious effect on the psychotherapeutic relationship. Nevertheless, therapists must monitor the work carefully to be certain the game is truly helping children confront and resolve the life issues that brought them into therapy.

SUMMARY AND CONCLUSIONS

PRINCIPAL POINTS IN REVIEW

Clinical studies published during the past 15 years demonstrate that the personal computer is a dynamic, powerful psychotherapeutic medium for children and adolescents. Educators have seized the opportunity to use computers for pedagogic and remedial purposes. Psychotherapeutic applications of computers with children have evolved more slowly. Preliminary survey research (Kepner & Thompson, 1995) supports the notion that, although child therapists acknowledge the clinical utility of the PC, their lack of training, technophobia, and ignorance about cogent ways to employ the technology are hindrances for them. Symbolic interactionist theory explains the sociocultural basis for the digital generation gap: adults use computers for productivity; children play with computers like toys.

A growing number of psychotherapists are discovering creative uses for computers in their work with children and adolescence. Paint programs allow children to draw pictures, make cartoons, and write storybooks. Computer fantasy games, simulation games, and war games permit the displacement of aggression and gratification of unconscious fantasies. Children's interactive CD storybooks are a new medium for bibliotherapy. Telecommunications has spawned videoconferencing, avatars, and virtual playgrounds that link chronically ill children in pediatric units. Elementary software can transform the computer into a desktop publishing system or a craft workshop. The MIDI, with appropriate peripherals, brings music therapy into the playroom. Finally, traditional child therapy techniques are being adapted for use on computers by innovative therapists.

Child specialists who wish to retrofit the playroom or counseling office with a computer don't have to spend a fortune. Many affordable options for acquiring computer hardware and software are available today. Getting started is a six-step process: (1) consider the age and specific needs of the population with whom the computer will be used; (2) decide on the specific applications appropriate for the work; (3) select the software that will run those applications; (4) acquire the system, including a computer, monitor, printer, and peripherals; (5) practice with the system before using it in sessions; and (6) explore all opportunities for professional development in the computer field and in the therapeutic applications of computers.

DIRECTIONS FOR THE FUTURE

Opportunities for research and publishing are legion in this burgeoning field. Psychotherapy outcome studies, reviews of children's software, and articles describing new ways of adapting digital technology to special populations are needed. Controlled empirical studies should contrast traditional play therapy techniques with computer play therapy. Although many of the articles in the clinical literature extol the merits of computers in child therapy, the evidence cited to support that assertion is often anecdotal in nature.

Software development will ensue when therapists learn the multifaceted nature of computers and begin dialogues with professionals in digital technology. If computers have unlimited therapeutic potential for children and adolescents, that potential will reach critical mass only when clinicians give impetus to the development of hardware and software that is inherently therapeutic. Commercial software developers, who know little about child therapy, are forging ahead in this field; their work is impressive, but child/adolescent therapists have an important consultative role to play in collaborating with software engineers. They should be proactive in generating ideas for children's therapeutic software. Therapists who have experience writing code from previous employment may choose to create their own programs. Any expert in child development should be a welcome member of a team that is producing electronic products for young people.

Technology is pushing the design of computer hardware to unprecedented heights. Microprocessor speeds have reached astronomical levels: years ago, it was a technological marvel if a computer chip performed a million operations in a second; today, electronic firms are ready to unveil microprocessors that complete a billion operations per second. The machines of the future may look very different from the desktop or laptop computers of today, but they will continue to be tools for ensuring that children attain an optimum level of cognitive, social, and emotional adjustment.

An online professional community will be crucial for networking and for avoiding duplication of effort. This will develop in three forums: through online exchanges on listservers, at professional conferences devoted to the topic of computers and child therapy, and in professional journals in print and electronic media.

Computers are not therapeutic per se. Kokish (1994) sagaciously argues that "a computer is no more inherently therapeutic than a crayon or a paper bat. It is the use the therapist makes of the tool, in the context of the therapeutic relationship that makes the difference for each child" (p. 149). Computer play therapy is not an elixir, nor is it *the* treatment modality of the twenty-first century; computers are another way to reach children. A self-imposed mandate of child therapists is to meet children in their world. Building rapport is a sine qua non for the psychotherapeutic process to blossom. Play therapists have explored every possible avenue of working with children and adolescents; they use every imaginable toy or game that appeals to their young clients. If Papert's (1993) assertion is accurate, and the computer is the children's machine, then children will invite their therapists to play with them in cyberspace. Cyberspace is a virtual playground, but it is where the children are playing. Therapists who join them there may be uncomfortable at first in this unfamiliar territory. Once they become acclimated to it, they have an unprecedented opportunity to accompany children on an odyssey of self-discovery in that new frontier: the journey from cyberspace to inner space.

REFERENCES

Allen, D.H. (1984). The use of computer fantasy games in child therapy. In M.D. Schwartz (Ed.), *Using computers in clinical practice: Psychotherapy and mental health applications* (pp. 329–334). New York: Haworth Press.

Aymard, L. (Speaker). (1997). The magic of cyberspace: Computers and play therapy (Cassette Recording Tapes 13–14). Miami, FL: Convention Tapes International.

Bosworth, K. (1994). Computer games and simulations as tools to reach and engage adolescents in health promotion activities. *Computers in Human Services, 11*(1/2), 109–119.

Burns, R.C., & Kaufman, S.H. (1970). *Kinetic family drawings (KFD): An introduction to understanding children through kinetic drawings.* New York: Brunner/Mazel.

Canter, D.S. (1987, March). The therapeutic effects of combining Apple Macintosh computers and creativity software in art therapy sessions. *Art Therapy,* 17–26.

Casey, J.A., & Ramsammy, R. (1992). *MacMentoring: Using technology and counseling with at-risk youth.* Ann Arbor, MI: ERIC Clearinghouse on Counseling and Personnel Services. (ERIC Document Reproduction Service No. ED 344 179)

Clarke, B., & Schoech, D. (1984). A computer-assisted therapeutic game for adolescents: Initial development and comments. In M.D. Schwartz (Ed.), *Using computers in clinical practice: Psychotherapy and mental health applications* (pp. 335–353). New York: Haworth Press.

Favelle, G.K. (1994). Therapeutic applications of commercially available computer software. *Computers in Human Services, 11*(1), 151–158.

Fredrickson, S. (1997). Interactive multimedia storybooks: Integrating technology into the language arts curriculum. *Learning and Leading with Technology, 25*(1), 6–10.

Gamson, M. (1997). *The spring of Tampa Bay children's services Web page* [On-line]. Available: http://www.springkidsteam.org.

Gardner, J.E. (1991). Can the Mario Brothers help? Nintendo games as an adjunct in psychotherapy with children. *Psychotherapy, 28,* 667–670.

Gardner, R.A. (1986). The game of checkers in child therapy. In C.E. Schaefer & S.E. Reid (Eds.), *Game play: Therapeutic use of childhood games* (pp. 215–232). New York: Wiley.

Gardner, R.A. (1988). *The storytelling card game.* Cresskill, NJ: Creative Therapeutics.

Ginott, H.G. (1960). A rationale for selecting toys in play therapy. *Journal of Consulting Psychology, 24,* 243–246.

Holzberg, C.S. (1995, May/June). The second time around: Used computers can be a good deal—if you know the facts. *Electronic Learning,* 55–59.

Johnson, R.G. (1984). High-tech play therapy. *Journal for Remedial Education and Counseling, 1,* 128–133.

Johnson, R.G. (1987). Using computer art in counseling children. *Elementary School Guidance & Counseling, 21*(4), 262–265.

Kepner, T., & Thompson, D. (1995). *Use of the computer as a psychotherapeutic toy: A survey of play therapists in Maryland.* Unpublished raw data.

Kercher, M. (1990). Tele-foster grandparent program. *Washington Apple Pi Journal, 66.*

Kokish, R. (1994). Experiences using a PC in play therapy with children. In H. Resnick (Ed.), *Electronic tools for social work practice and education* (pp. 141–150). New York: Haworth Press.

Kuntz, M., & Kuntz, A. (1994). *Computer crafts for kids.* Emeryville, CA: Ziff-Davis Press.

Loomis, E.A. (1957). The use of checkers in handling certain resistances in child therapy and child analysis. *Journal of the American Psychoanalytical Association, 5,* 130–135.

Margolies, R. (1991). The computer as social skills agent. *T.H.E. Journal, 18*(6), 70–71.

Matthews, J., & Jessel, J. (1993). Very young children use electronic paint: A study of the beginnings of drawing with traditional media and computer paintbox. *Visual Arts Research, 19,* 47–62.

Mills, J.C., & Crowley, R.J. (1986). *Therapeutic metaphors for children and the child within.* New York: Brunner/Mazel.

Oakley, C. (1994). SMACK: A computer driven game for at-risk teens. *Computers in Human Services, 11*(1), 97–99.

Olsen-Rando, R.A. (1994). Proposal for development of a computerized version of the Talking, Feeling, and Doing Game. *Computers in Human Services, 11*(1/2), 69–80.

Papert, S. (1980). *Mindstorms: Children, computers and powerful ideas.* New York: Basic Books.

Papert, S. (1993). *The children's machine: Rethinking school in the age of the computer.* New York: Basic Books.

Papert, S. (1996). *The connected family: Bridging the digital generation gap.* Atlanta, GA: Longstreet Press.

Resnick, H. (Ed.). (1994). *Electronic tools for social work practice and education.* New York: Haworth Press.

Schaefer, C.E., & Reid, S.E. (Eds.). (1986). *Game play: Therapeutic use of childhood games.* New York: Wiley.

Self-Controlled Classroom [Computer software]. (1996). Secaucus, NJ: Childswork Childsplay.

Sherer, M. (1994). The effect of computerized simulation games on the moral development of youth in distress. *Computers in Human Services, 11*(1/2), 81–95.

Sisson, L.H., Mayfield, S.A., & Entz, S. (1985). Reaching students through computers: A new therapy for learning and playing. *Journals of Reading, Writing and Learning Disabilities International, 1,* 61–83.

Stephenson, J. (1995). Sick kids find help in a cyberspace world. *Journal of the American Medical Association, 274*(24), 1899–1901.

Tickle Box [Computer software]. (1994). Atlanta, GA: Adaptive Learning Company.

Turkle, S. (1995). *Life on the screen: Identity in the age of the Internet.* New York: Simon & Schuster.

Winnicott, D.C. (1971). *Therapeutic consultations in child psychiatry.* New York: Basic Books.

Wolock, E., Orr, A., & Buckleitner, W. (Eds.). (1998). *The elementary teacher's sourcebook on children's software.* Flemington, NJ: Active Learning Associates.

Zamora, B. (1992). *Funny Face user manual: Installation and operations.* Antioch, CA: Z-WARE.

CHAPTER 9

Video Self Modeling and Related Procedures in Psychotherapy

PETER W. DOWRICK

INCREASING NUMBERS of people see themselves on video every year. The opportunity for *unintended* video self modeling becomes more common. Most often, the effects are benign; sometimes, they are moderately beneficial. By contrast, properly *planned self modeling* can be powerful.

This chapter offers some background on the technique and enough practical information to get started. First, there is a general overview of video self modeling and related interventions, focusing on clinical applications with children and youth. Then the chapter guides clinicians step-by-step through a video self modeling intervention. Finally, a few technical tips are offered

This chapter is dedicated to the students, colleagues, and families who have taken enthusiastic interest in self modeling in its various forms and in the principles of feedforward. I thank John Anderson for his help in proofing and suggestions on this manuscript. Material for this chapter was drawn, in part, from a review article (Dowrick, 1999) and a procedure manual (Dowrick, Meunier, & Connor, 1998).

315

that cover the basics of camera operation, editing, and so on. Forms and protocols are included to simplify the process.

Self modeling is an intervention procedure using the observation of *images of oneself* engaged in adaptive behavior (Dowrick, 1999). Most commonly, these images are captured on video, edited into two- to four-minute vignettes, and repeatedly reviewed to learn skills or adjust to challenging environments as part of a therapy or training protocol (Benson, 1995; Dowrick, 1991; Meharg & Woltersdorf, 1990). Audiotapes, still photographs, stories in print, and individuals' imaginations are also used for self modeling. Researched interventions exist for a wide variety of applications: disruptive behavior, selective mutism, depression, anxiety, sports, social skills, personal safety, self-control, physically challenging situations, the training of service providers, and others. A full range of ages (toddler to grandparent) and diverse developmental conditions (autism to Olympic athletics) have been addressed (see review by Dowrick, 1999). The vast majority of reports claim to demonstrate the effectiveness of self modeling in a variety of research paradigms: case studies, pre-post, multiple baselines, active controls, and inactive controls.

The first use in the literature of the term self modeling was by Creer and Miklich (1970) in a brief report of a hospitalized asthmatic boy with serious social deficits. Independently, Hosford (Hosford, 1980; Hosford, Moss, & Morrell, 1976) developed applications with adults, dubbed "self-as-a-model." My interest began with the exploration of different methods to create mastery images on video of clinically relevant skills otherwise not attainable (Dowrick, 1978, 1979; Dowrick & Raeburn, 1977). I subsequently focused on *types* of self modeling (e.g., distinctions of "feedforward" and "positive self-review"; see below) and in finding its place in learning theory (Dowrick, 1983, 1991, 1999).

The most effective form of self modeling uses *feedforward,* a term coined to refer to video images of mastery not yet achieved, created by editing together components from the skill repertoire as available. For example, a teen who is immobilized by the thought of inviting a schoolmate over to his house can enact the elements: pick up a phone, dial a number, say the words, and so on; these elements can be videotaped separately and edited together into a novel action, showing competence in a developmentally appropriate way.

A simpler strategy is *positive self-review*, which refers to selectively compiling the best recorded examples of skills already manageable but infrequently achieved. Thus, a tennis player is followed by a video camera during a tournament or extensive practice. After selective editing, she gets to review her best service, overhead volley, and so on, after a full day of many attempts. In either form, self-modeling tapes are typically two to three minutes long and are reviewed every one or two days, about six times, for maximum effect. Sometimes, they are reviewed again every two months or when a maintenance booster is desirable.

There are several other, more familiar ways that video can be used to enhance learning. The most common of these is *video feedback*. It is clear after 30 years of research findings that simple video feedback has mixed, sometimes deleterious, effects (see Dowrick, 1991, Chapter 6). Feedback provides an *assessment* of behavior, not intervention; skills training or therapy occurs, if at all, from coaching or other intervention based on the assessment information. Unless the direction of personal change is self-evident or provided by the therapist, feedback is emotionally damaging and behaviorally unproductive. It has recently been realized, but not widely understood, that images of future mastery are much more effective than those of past errors (Bandura, 1997). All creatures learn from the observation of their successes; what sets humans apart is their ability to learn from the observation of successes they have *not yet had.*

A case example illustrates it well. Chance, a 9-year-old boy with Asperger's autism, panicked after a fire alarm sounded without warning at his school, then asked obsessive questions about whether the alarm would sound again. He did not respond to reassurances, being ignored, or contingency management. Chance was so disruptive to his class that he was suspended. I was consulted by the primary clinician, and we used a simple approach. At home, following discussion about the alarm being set and some rehearsal, it was possible to videotape Chance sitting on the sofa, the alarm sounding, followed by he and his mother reacting calmly and leaving the house. This footage was edited to about two minutes. Chance reviewed it three days in a row, returned to school, and did not express concern about an alarm again (Bline & Dowrick, 1992).

There are many other examples of using this technique with people whose disorders seriously interfered with community activities (e.g., Dowrick & Ward, 1997; Kehle, Owen, & Cressy, 1990; Krantz, MacDuff, Wadstrom, & McClannahan, 1991; Shear & Shapiro, 1993). The brevity of the tape and economy of intervention (in Chance's case, three days of viewing, two minutes of tape) are common features of reported interventions.

Applications of self modeling have been so diverse, it seems most useful to recognize seven procedural categories as guides of when and how to use this intervention (Dowrick, 1999; see Table 9.1).

INCREASING ADAPTIVE BEHAVIOR CURRENTLY INTERMIXED WITH NONDESIRED BEHAVIORS

This category is listed first because it is the most common. A number of studies report that this approach decreases disruptiveness (e.g., Davis, 1979; Dowrick, 1978; Dowrick & Raeburn,

Table 9.1
Seven Categories of Self-Modeling Applications

1. Increasing adaptive behavior currently intermixed with nondesired behaviors.	PSR*
2. Transfer of setting-specific behavior to other environments.	Feedforward
3. Use of hidden support for disorders that may be anxiety-based.	Feedforward
4. Improved image for mood-based disorders.	PSR
5. Recombining component skills.	Feedforward
6. Transferring role play to the real world.	PSR, Feedforward
7. (Re)Engagement of disused or low-frequency skills.	PSR

*PSR refers to positive self-review.
Source: Dowrick, 1999, Reprinted with the permission of Cambridge University Press.

1977; Greelis & Kazaoka, 1979; Kehle, Clark, Jenson, & Wampold, 1986; Shear & Shapiro, 1993; Woltersdorf, 1992). Other applications include parenting (Meharg & Lipsker, 1991), basketball (Melody, 1990), job interviews (Batts, 1978), classroom teaching (Hosford & Brown, 1976), work skills for people with disabilities (Dowrick & Hood, 1981), and stuttering (Bray & Kehle, 1998).

This approach requires videotaping in vivo and is most suited to high-frequency events. Conditions may be maximized (reduced distractions, incentives for trying hard, etc.), but essentially the technique is to videotape a sample of behavior and to edit onto a (new) positive self-review tape just the pieces that looked effective.

TRANSFER OF SETTING-SPECIFIC BEHAVIOR TO OTHER ENVIRONMENTS

Self modeling has been used occasionally with dramatic effect to enable a skill or activity in new, challenging settings. The best examples are found in the treatment of selective mutism (Kehle, Root, Spackman, & Bray, in press). In the self-modeling approach, we record the child's speech in a favorable environment (usually at home with parents) and edit it *into the context* of a teacher's questions or conversation at school. Examples reported by Dowrick and Hood (1978), Holmbeck and Lavigne (1992), and Pigott and Gonzales (1987) have shown positive results, with size effects from 0.8 to 6.2 (Pionek, Kratochwill, & Sladeczek, 1996). The approach has been extended to audio (Blum et al., 1998).

USE OF HIDDEN SUPPORT FOR DISORDERS THAT MAY BE ANXIETY-BASED

Using video, a person can be seen to cope with a normally threatening situation by providing a hidden support. That is, physical or emotional support is planned so that it is not evident in the recording or it can easily be edited afterwards. Examples include Dowrick and Dove (1980), Dowrick and Raeburn (1995), and Holman (1991). Although most research studies are of physical skills, case studies suggest the use of this approach for clients whose anxiety level interferes with role playing. It may be helpful for children or adolescents who have been victimized or exploited.

Improved Image for Mood-Based Disorders

Most studies emphasize skill acquisition, but self modeling can directly affect mood. Dowrick and Jesdale (1990) used self modeling for women (18 to 50 years), most of whom were mildly depressed and/or anxious. Kahn, Kehle, Jenson, and Clark (1990) reported a school-based study for clinically depressed adolescents. Attention was given to makeup, dress, posture, and camera angles to maximize a positive appearance, as well as to social skills.

Recombining Component Skills

Some of the foremost exemplars of feedforward are to be found in challenging sport skills (Dowrick, 1989), particularly figure skating, kayaking, and powerlifting (Franks & Maile, 1991). Other studies report positive but not dramatic results (Boyer, 1987; Bradley, 1993; Melody, 1990; Scraba, 1989; Winfrey & Weeks, 1993). Some interventions have been applied to language development (e.g., Andersson, Melin, Scott, & Lindberg, 1995; Bolivar, 1993; Haarman & Greelis, 1982), including the acquisition of new grammatical forms in preschoolers (Buggey, 1995).

In these examples, a piece of a behavior (e.g., saying a few words) is prompted and then performed by the subject. The pieces are combined into a meaningful discourse. The idea connects well to the strategy of using role plays, which are larger pieces, or sequences that have a context, a behavior, and an outcome (see below).

Transferring Role Play to the Real World

Early studies (Creer & Miklich, 1970; Hosford, 1979; Hosford et al., 1976) used this strategy. With modern equipment, good use can be made of partial role plays, in which a new skill is so tenuous that any rehearsal requires intense support, and it remains incomplete or partially accurate and infrequently performed. Partial role plays are edited into the context of a challenging situation and a positive outcome. This approach was used in personal safety training for young adults with cognitive disabilities (Dowrick, 1986, 1991; Perry, 1989).

(RE)ENGAGEMENT OF A DISUSED OR LOW-FREQUENCY SKILL

Learning a skill such as personal safety is highly vulnerable to lapsing before it is needed. Skills such as impulse control or problem solving have frequent opportunities for practice. The teens and young adults in our personal safety training program taught us a method of maintaining skills needed in very low-frequency situations. They contrived to keep their self-model tapes and look at them, at their own initiative, every month or two. Two years later, Sara was accosted by a man wanting money. Sara was appropriately assertive and eventually went to a store manager for support. When asked by her house parent why she behaved as she did, Sara said, "That's how you're supposed to deal with strangers. It's on my safety tape."

The video reminder does not have to originate from self modeling; it can be a recording of any interaction or skill. For example, as a personal library for medical equipment technicians, a U.S. Army trainer developed positive self-review videos at the end of learning each new repair procedure. Thus, the technicians, called at 2 A.M. months after training, could quickly review their tapes and remind themselves of the correct procedures. In a year, the trainer saved the army an estimated $10,000—and probably some lives (Dowrick, 1991).

MECHANISMS

SELF-EFFICACY

In 1977, Albert Bandura published his seminal article on self-efficacy as a unifying contribution in behavior change. At about that time, independent analyses of self modeling described its mechanisms as *skill acquisition* and *motivation* (Dowrick, 1976;

Hosford et al., 1976), ideas that fit well with self-efficacy. Some studies have found correlations between self-efficacy and skills learned in self modeling (Bradley, 1993; Holman, 1991; Kelley, 1986; Schunk & Hanson, 1989). Other studies have noted a self-evident relationship (Dowrick & Hood, 1981; Meharg & Lipsker, 1991; Pigott & Gonzales, 1987).

Bandura (1997) described self modeling as providing the essential elements of self-efficacy, noting that the advantage of seeing oneself perform successfully is that it "provides clear information on how best to perform skills, and it strengthens beliefs in one's capability" (p. 94). Observing an image of oneself produces a different reaction from observing someone else in the identical context: a self-image secures more attention and provides a better source of self-belief; by contrast, an image of someone else produces less attention and is a weaker source of self-efficacy.

LEARNING BY OBSERVATION OF ONE'S SUCCESSES

Contributing factors to personal well-being include:

- Clarification of goals and outcome.
- Reminders of previous competence.
- A positive self-image.
- Repeated observation of (apparently) competent role play.
- Observation of one's skills applied to a new setting.
- Anxiety-free behavior, or successful outcomes despite anxiety.
- Demonstrations of new skills composed of preexisting subskills (Dowrick, 1999).

The self-image in the "success mode" can be attractive and fun. Thus, the participant can be engaged in learning and doing. It is parsimonious to consider the *observation of one's behavior* to be a *learning mechanism in its own right,* not a special case of observational learning from others with some positive reinforcement and cognitive restructuring thrown in. That is, we may recognize that *the observation of one's adaptive or valued behavior increases the future likelihood of that behavior.* Self modeling remains innovative and underrepresented in psychotherapy because of widespread preoccupations with feed*back* and response learning. The cited research indicates the value of learning from images of *future* behavior. The *related procedures* below add weight to these conclusions, as well as indicating nonvideo alternatives that embody the same principles and spirit.

RELATED PROCEDURES

The term self modeling was coined in the context of video. But as noted, the self-image can be used to model adaptive behavior in other ways. The most obvious comparison is imaginal self modeling, or mental rehearsal, as it is usually called. As with other imaginal-only procedures, reviews of mental rehearsal outcome studies find overall positive but modest effects (Druckman & Bjork, 1991). Imaginal self modeling requires less effort from the teacher/trainer/therapist. It can be engaged in without access to a video player, but it is much less vivid and reliable. However, Mulcahy and Schacter (1982) reported an exceptionally thorough examination of cognitive self-modeling and compared its effects favorably with group counseling and role play to teach interpersonal skills to adolescents.

Another related procedure is labeled picture prompts (Steed & Lutzker, 1997)—also called photo activity schedules (Krantz, MacDuff, & McClannahan, 1993) or pictorial self-management (Pierce & Schreibman, 1994). This procedure uses a sequence of still photographs to lead a person through the key elements of an activity. For example, when Sione arrives home from school he is reminded what to do by looking at a series of pictures of himself, including taking off his shoes, putting his school books on the table, and getting a glass of water—rather than relying on directions from adults. The number of photos for a given set of instructions depends on how many elements are pivotal, which in turn depends on individual characteristics such as developmental age and experience. Some children may need five pictures when others need only one. (If we extrapolate to 25 or

30 pictures a second, shown on a monitor, we have video self modeling.)

Other ways in which the self-observation of adaptive behavior may take place are in vivo and in print. Selective attention to successful classroom behavior, for example, can be promoted by self-monitoring (Kern et al., 1995). Or adopting a new role (cf. Kelly, 1955; fixed roles in personal construct theory), if the role is suitably selected and maintained, can lead to a self-modeling effect. Self-in-print or biblio self modeling makes the reader the key character of self-guiding texts (Embry, 1995; Kojian, 1992). For example, a story of a latchkey girl coming home after school, and the precautions she takes, has blanks for the reader to write in names of self, family, and so on.

APPLICATION TO PSYCHOTHERAPY

This section offers a guide to some types of applications with descriptive vignettes, which illustrate how self modeling uses positive self-images to help children and youth to learn, to relate, to succeed, and more. Here are some of the prime purposes:

- Develop specific coping skills.
- Increase self-confidence.
- Improve self-image.
- Apply role-play skills to the real world.
- Reduce fear of failure.

The positive self-imagery of successful accomplishment builds the needed confidence to empower children and youth to perform at their highest potential. Video self modeling can help in many ways, such as to:

- Learn a new skill, to help individuals do better and feel better.
- Increase the frequency of a skill they have but do not use very often.
- Transition to a new situation.
- Find purpose in life.

HELPING CHILDREN LEARN A NEW SKILL

Some of the best examples use video to show a child performing a skill he or she is not currently capable of performing or does not have the confidence to perform independently. The video is recorded and edited to create an image of a child doing something that is not part of his or her repertoire. This type of video self modeling is referred to as *feedforward*.

Although the following case is fictitious, it illustrates a method that has quite often been used successfully with very shy individuals (e.g., Kehle et al., in press):

> Junnita is a shy girl with a mild cognitive disability. She gets very nervous when she needs to talk to adults outside her immediate family. She converses happily with her friends. Junnita and her clinician make a tape showing her in conversation with a friend. Then a neighbor is videotaped speaking the same phrases as Junnita's friend. The neighbor's speaking is edited into the context of Junnita's part of the conversation. The self-modeling video creates an image of Junnita speaking to the neighbor (someone Junnita is too nervous to talk to). Junnita watches the tape every day for two weeks. This image helps Junnita literally recognize her potential, and she loses much of her nervousness. She begins to make conversation, first with the neighbor, then with other adults.

INCREASING THE FREQUENCY OF AN INCONSISTENT SKILL

At times, a child has the skill to perform a certain behavior, but his or her performance is inconsistent. In this case, it is useful to videotape the child doing his or her best and make a video simply by editing together the more successful parts. This strategy is an example of *positive self-review*.

Again, this case is fictional but based on many examples from practice and research (e.g., Gipson, McKenzie, & Lowe, 1989):

> Jason is impulsive and distractible (he has an attention deficit, hyperactivity diagnosis). In basketball, he sometimes catches and passes very well; at other times, he does not watch the ball or passes to the wrong person, contributing to his ridicule by other

students and a major source of low self-esteem. Jason's clinician takes a camcorder to a game and videotapes 15 minutes of it. The missed balls and miffed passes are edited out of the video and Jason watches only his good plays. After watching this tape for a week, Jason's game improves and he begins to feel better about himself.

HELPING CHILDREN TRANSITION TO A NEW SITUATION

Many fears in childhood arise around transitions: moving to a new town, a new school, even a different classroom. A video can be made in the new situation with the assistance of a trusted individual. There are no new skills to be learned, but a new environment in which the child sees himself coping well. He gains confidence and feels less anxious about the changes. These are called *transitions videos.*

> Ronnie is a child with autism. He is advancing from a small middle school to much larger high school. Environmental changes make Ronnie very apprehensive. Ronnie goes with his sister to the high school to videotape his likely routines in the new lunchroom and classroom. Because his sister is there for the video, Ronnie stays calm and feels confident. Ronnie watches the video of himself in his new school whenever he feels like it over the summer. At the next school year, he settles in quite quickly, with feelings of familiarity. (cf. Fitzgerald & Dowrick, 1995)

HELPING CHILDREN FIND PURPOSE IN WHAT THEY DO

Sometimes, children and youth find it difficult to see beyond today; in such cases, it may be useful to make a video exploring the future. First, have the young person express her dreams of what she might be or do in the future. Then make a video of these futures with her in it. Reviewing such videos can give purpose and motivation for the present. These *video explorations* do not show skills that will necessarily ever be learned, but they are related to self modeling by the use of the positive self-image.

Asimal is a depressed teenager. At 17, she has no motivation for the present. When asked about her future, she says it is "a void." But after three weeks of brainstorming with Asimal and her parents on the topic of "what might you be doing at age 22," she developed a list of where she would live (an apartment with one roommate), a job (news researcher), relationship with family (phone calls and monthly visits), and owning a small car for transport and recreation. With an action plan from the clinician, Asimal's father made a six-minute video of all these scenes, with Asimal acting as her 22-year-old future self. She now found reason to complete high school. With immediate reengagement at school, she became active and social, thus improving her mood. (cf. Dowrick & Wiedle, 1995)

SELECTIVE USE OF SELF MODELING

Self modeling is successful with a wide range of individuals and issues. Potential interventions for clinicians working with children and adolescents have been indicated above. Often, the choice to use video self modeling is a practical one, for which the list of seven categories of intervention in the introduction provide some guidance.

Forms of self modeling other than video should also be considered. Whatever the form, there are three guiding principles. First, a child's well-being will benefit from attention to past successes. Second, progress will be further inspired by successes not yet had. And third, most benefit will be gained by images that have personal *future relevance;* that is, the behavior and implied or explicit outcomes have value for the individual. In the next part of this chapter, the example of Javonna demonstrates in more detail how to make a self-modeling video.

SELF-MODELING INTERVENTIONS: STEP-BY-STEP

The practice of video self modeling may be identified in six steps. These steps will be described by way of a case study—a fictionalized composite from several interventions. Other (nonvideo) self-modeling techniques can follow a set of comparable steps.

Intervention Illustration

Javonna is 13 years old. She has a short attention span, avoids doing her homework, fights with her younger brother, and is frequently in social battles with her peers at school. Some of the peers she calls friends, but she has no close friendships. Her internalizing mood often keeps her from being noticed in family and school settings, but it also contributes to her unpopularity.

Javonna's unhappiness and poor history of success in social problem solving have led to an attitude of not wanting to try to improve anything about herself. Self modeling has the potential to restore some belief in herself and to teach her some skills pivotal to her progress.

Six Steps in Self Modeling

It is useful to consider the self-modeling process in six steps (see Figure 9.1). The self-modeling intervention will capture potential solutions as images. These images show adaptive skills that illustrate challenges *and* the mastery to overcome them. Effective self-modeling tapes are only two minutes long, so it is necessary to find specific, pivotal images.

Conceptualization: Identifying the Issues and the Outcomes

The task of conceptualization is *to identify potential solutions*. Javonna presents many issues, which is often the case in psychotherapy settings. The selection of issues, in terms of importance, may reveal a *pivotal* skill; that is, a behavior that may enable others to occur naturally. Potential solutions will be precise images that can be recorded on video.

Javonna's Issues and Goals. Javonna and her clinician, with help from parents, teacher, and others, sort through the issues. She decides that her most important goal is "to do nicer reactions to people"—to learn social interactions that improve her relationships while maintaining her dignity. That will reduce her sibling rivalry (Goldenthal, 1999), improve school friendships (Dowrick, 1986), and predictably improve her mood (Clarke, Hops, & Lewinsohn, 1992). Incidentally, assessments revealed third-grade reading levels, for which she was assigned a community tutor in hopes of improving grades, school bonding, and attitude toward homework.

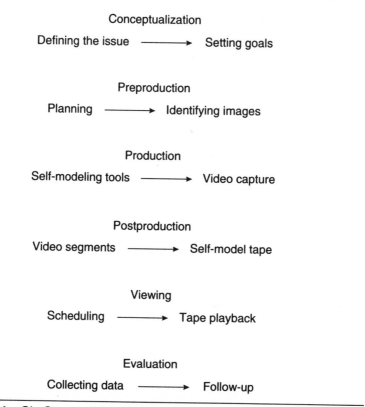

Figure 9.1 Six Steps of the Self-Modeling Procedure.

Although reading can be assisted with self modeling (Dowrick, Power, Manz, & Ginsburg-Block, in press), the social behavior was considered pivotal for purposes of the main intervention.

Javonna and her clinician brainstormed potential solutions to achieve her goals. Fabricio used a flip chart on which to draw each solution, and knowing that the selected solution(s) would be videotaped, helped the solutions become *tangible and visual.* They come up a long list, including positive coping with being teased at school or by her brother, asking a classmate over to her house, and telling the truth to her teacher about not doing her homework. Javonna and Fabricio decided to try the first one because her brother could be brought in as a collaborator, and some success may generalize to the school.

Documenting the Issue. Information concerning the typical situations leading to confrontations between brother and sister and their frequency is important. It enables a better video and it creates a baseline against which to measure future skill acquisition. Fabricio also arranged for baseline data on all the other issues.

Motivation to change and belief in the intervention to produce change are also important. These can both be assessed on 5-point scales, as indicated in Figure 9.2. Most children are very receptive

---

Motivation can be assessed with a rating scale:

Circle the number on the scale below to show how much you want to change—1 if you don't at all want to change, 5 if you *really* want to change.

    1   2   3   4   5
no desire to change   really wants to change

Then, measure the child's perception of how successful the video self-modeling intervention will be, using a similar method.

    1   2   3   4   5
video self-modeling will not help   video self-modeling will help a lot

With children for whom this task is too abstract, include the following instructions:

1------------ 2------------- 3 ------------4 ------------5

I want you to show me how much you like your mother [known that she adores her mother]. Please mark the line here (5) if you like her absolutely very much. Mark here (1) if you don't like her *at all*. Mark somewhere else on the line if you like her in between. Proceed similarly with a known strong *dislike* (e.g., broccoli) to get a mark at the other end of the line.

1------------ 2------------- 3 ------------4 ------------5

Then try for a response of "well, maybe, maybe not" for the experience of an in-between rating. It should now be possible to get a meaningful rating on *desire to change* and *expectation* of the intervention to support change.

1------------ 2------------- 3 ------------4 ------------5

The assessment of motivation to change gives the clinician a better understanding to make decisions with regard to future interventions.

Figure 9.2   Useful Forms.

to a video self-modeling intervention, finding fun in the idea of "being on TV" or "starring in a sci-fi movie" about themselves. But sometimes, not making a video is an easy way to avoid (scary) change. Older teens may be skeptical but willing to try. If the child or youth is opposed to video self modeling, consider another type of intervention.

Documenting the issue for Javonna showed that she had serious arguments with her brother almost once a weekday and more than five times a day on weekends, usually over conflicts of space. She rated herself a 5 (*really* wanting to change) and a 4 (somewhat confident the video would help).

Preproduction

Planning the Video. The video is by planned by writing a script and drawing a storyboard. Consider the video in three parts: the setting or event the child usually finds challenging; the adaptive response; a positive outcome. Then plan a series of visual (and auditory) scenes within each part. Keep the script straightforward with as many scenes as necessary. This written documentation provides a *script*. A *storyboard* can put the script into a pictorial medium. Self-modeling videos generally are made from a good script *list* to incorporate the originality of the client. A more or less full storyboard is recommended to transfer a skill across settings, or for video explorations.

Javonna's script included the following sequence of the scenes:

1. Title, with Javonna in a proud but pleasant pose.
2. Harry on the family computer.
3. Javonna looking annoyed, then calming herself.
4. Javonna negotiates with Harry.
5. Harry refuses.
6. Javonna strikes a deal.
7. Harry agrees.
8. Javonna on the computer, congratulated by Mom.
9. Credits, over Javonna's smile.

Notice how the script allows for ad lib by the actors, more in the form of outcome objectives than line-by-line directives. The scenes were role-played in the office with Fabricio on the camera. He filmed Javonna's initial reaction in two separate shots: a long shot of looking upset, with computer in view; a close-up of Javonna looking calm (recorded earlier). Fabricio knew that Javonna could not make the transition of emotions, even in acting. For "Javonna negotiates," there were several trials, videotaped with over-the-shoulder shots, close-ups, and different angles. When Fabricio was satisfied that he had a negotiation in Javonna's own words, he proceeded to the next scene. Earlier, when he had less experience, he did practice runs on scenes like negotiation before picking up the camera to reduce unnecessary editing. But part of the point of self modeling is that intact role plays are *not required*—only the pieces that can be edited into a useful image are needed.

Production

Video Capture. This section describes how to use coaching, prompting, camerawork, and props—self-modeling tools—to capture the required images on videotape. The technical processes of camera operation, sound, lighting, and so on, are covered later.

Production Tools of Self Modeling. Some of the self-modeling tools that can support Javonna are:

> *Coaching:* Fabricio frequently coached Javonna with statements like "Take a deep breath and say it again more casually, as if you were speaking to me, not Harry."
>
> *Prompting:* When Javonna did not know what to do when asked "to look calm," Fabricio prompted her to look at a picture of Madonna he had hung on his wall, at which she gave a little sigh and a smile.
>
> *Camera Angles and Zoom:* Examples here include varying camera angles to improve editing and zooming in on Javonna's smile to create a bigger effect.
>
> *Props:* Fabricio did not use any, but sometimes cue cards are helpful. Often, props are used to create a location (there already was a computer in the office), such as a bus stop or a locker room.

Anticipated Editing: Editing is an essential part of postproduction (see below). It is just as essential to anticipate during the production phase exactly what can and cannot be achieved by editing.

A self-modeling tape requires creativity and some competent editing. First, the psychotherapist identifies the skill the child does not have in his or her repertoire, recognizes its importance developmentally, and describes it. The next step is to *stop* thinking as a clinician and plan the video as would a *movie director.* That is, think in terms of how to get a final image on tape, rather than how to produce the outcome behavior (see Table 9.2). The product will show a positive image, often beyond the individual's current mastery. Different techniques are used to accomplish the image of adaptive skills in challenging situations. Of course, self modeling has limits and does not teach skills outside the individual's capacities.

Postproduction

Postproduction, as with other forms of editing, is the selection, trimming, and rearrangement of existing material. The insertion of new material, unlike in manuscript editing, is onerous and avoided if possible. Editing is a significant skill in the self-modeling process. Once the images are recorded, they are logged, ready for selection and rerecording. First, look for the skills demonstrated on the tape that meet the script list objectives (think as a clinician). Second, arrange the sequence of tape segments that gives the preferred image (think as a movie director).

Fabricio uses tape-to-tape *crash editing:*

1. He connects the video and audio outputs from his camcorder to the inputs of his video cassette recorder (VCR), and the outputs from his VCR to the TV.
2. He rewinds the tape in the camcorder and resets the counter to 0.
3. He reviews the tape two or three times to log the sequences he wants, with in and out (beginning and ending) points,

Table 9.2
A Few Technical Tips

1. Use a tripod whenever possible to keep the camera *steady* and also *horizontal.*

2. Practice the handheld camera, too: lean against something to steady yourself; triangulate your hands and elbows; breathe slowly/steadily. Invest in an image-stabilized camera.

3. Zoom slowly—and very seldom.

4. Pan (move the camera across the scene) a bit more often but just as slowly.

5. Zoom in tight for a smile, a signature, a detailed movement that you know you're going to *cut* to in the editing.

6. Use a camera with a *manual exposure* (or at least "back light" feature). Increase the exposure if there is a window behind your subject, if the faces are dark-skinned or in shadows. Special lighting is not necessary for self-modeling.

7. Always take a spare battery. Put red rubber bands around empty batteries (green = full).

8. "Memory" is a myth, but nonetheless invest in "memory-free" batteries: they have higher capacitance, enabling them to recharge and to hold their charge better.

9. Whenever you put a new tape in the camera, record half a minute of the carpet or other neutral surface. The very beginning of a tape is hard to edit and prone to technical flaws.

10. The best sound with versatile camerawork is achieved with clip-on microphones and remote transmission. Get advice on the best types and the pitfalls; be prepared to pay at least $200. If you plan to document your work, good microphone sound is essential.

11. Most often, the built-in microphone will give adequate, reliable sound.

12. Always use a (cheap) headset, to monitor sound while recording. A loose connection, errant radio broadcasts, or flat batteries can make a beautiful picture worthless.

synopses of content, and the final sequential order to appear on the edited tape (see Figure 9.3).

4. He then searches for and copies each of these sequences in turn onto a new tape in the VCR. First, he records 20 seconds of blank and sets the VCR on record-pause. Then he

In (Begin #)	Out (End #)	Beginning Cue	Ending Cue	Content/ Comments	Edit Seq. #
0:30	0:50	Change to blue	Elapsed time	Blue lead-in/ "Titles" tape	1
1:04	1:10	Begins second smile	Count 2 after last word	"Hi, welcome to J . .'s Negotiation Video"	3
1:22	1:27	"Javonna!"	Say the word, short pause	Handscripted on white board	2
1:58	2:02	Sharp focus on computer	4 secs later	Harry at the computer	4

Figure 9.3 Video Editing Plan. The first four rows are filled in to illustrate the use of this form.

selects the beginning of the title sequence on the camcorder and sets it in play-pause mode.

5. Then Fabricio takes the camcorder and VCR off pause simultaneously. At the end of the title sequence, he quickly hits the pause button on the VCR. He then stops the camcorder and searches for the next component to be recorded, repeating the process. *Note:* If the VCR is paused too late at the end of the selection, it can be backed up and repaused in record mode. If it is paused too early, the selection needs to be redone. Although these steps are tedious using current technology, the original is always preserved. Also note that VCRs and camcorders vary in how they start rolling from the pause mode. Some experimentation is required to anticipate the delays and to know how to synchronize the machines. (For an excellent book with more detail, see Kyker & Curchy, (1994, especially pp. 94–97).

6. After all the pieces are assembled, they are reviewed. Javonna watches her tape and approves (fortunately; otherwise, Fabricio would have to reedit, which is why he kept such good editing logs and notes).

There are different editing methods available, but they all accomplish the same result. The identified images have to be sequenced and put together in a way that achieves the objectives of the script list.

Viewing

Javonna watches her tape every day for two weeks, then occasionally after that. Her parents document the viewing using the viewing log (see Figure 9.4).

Scheduling.   A viewing schedule specifies the following:

How often and how many times the tape should be watched. The minimum viewing schedule is three times a week for two weeks. Once a day, as for Javonna, is common because it can be part of a regular routine. More often is recommended for lower developmental abilities.

Where the tape will be watched and who else may watch it.

Child _____ Clinician _____

    Referring Issues _____

    Positive Behavior for Acquisition _____

    Other Notes _____

Recording Date _____ Editing Date _____

VIEWING		OUTCOMES
Date; Person present; Other conditions	Child's reactions	Rate: 1 lowest, 5 highest, or Frequency of adaptive change
Example: 11/2/97, Mom; Viewed twice.	Pleased; Javonna said "Cool—can we see it again?"	Kinder to Harry, no other change.
1.		
2.		
3.		
4.		
5.		
6.		
7.		
8.		
9.		
10.		

Figure 9.4 Video Log (Plan and Viewing Schedule).

Guidance appropriate to comments during viewing: always positive, generally limited to redirecting attention to the (positive aspects of) behavior on the screen.

Use of the viewing log to record the time and the date of each viewing, with comments.

The clinical staff can then follow up by phone.

Evaluation

Goal-Oriented Data
What progress was achieved toward the goal stated in the planning phase?

Were any new behaviors or skills observed?

Was there a change in the frequency or consistency of behaviors or skills?

Follow-Up.   Javonna's progress was evaluated after one, three, and six months. She showed immediate improvement in the relationship with her brother and subsequently did better with her peers at school, getting into fewer fights and less coercion. She improved in measures of self-esteem and self-efficacy related to peer and family interactions. Her relationships with teachers and other adults did not significantly improve, so these were targeted for the next self-modeling intervention. These issues of *timing* of follow-up and *subsequent* intervention are typical considerations, not unique to self modeling.

CONCLUSIONS

Video self modeling helps children achieve their larger goals through the emphasis on potential *solutions*. Tangible, visually effective reactions to challenging situations provide self-observational learning opportunities to develop and progress. Behavior change occurs through skill building and self-efficacy. Thus, the likelihood of generalization is improved. The behavior change from these videos tends to be "context-independent": one video can support new skills in a range of contexts.

REFERENCES

Andersson, G., Melin, L., Scott, B., & Lindberg, P. (1995). An evaluation of a behavioral treatment approach to hearing impairment. *Behaviour Research and Therapy, 33,* 283–292.

Bandura, A. (1977). Self-efficacy: Toward a unifying theory of behavior change. *Psychological Review, 84,* 191–215.

Bandura, A. (1997). *Self-efficacy: The exercise of control.* New York: Freeman.

Batts, C.L. (1978). *The effects of modeling with contingent reinforcement, self-modeling, and role-playing on developing interviewee skills in ex-offenders within the employment interview.* Doctoral dissertation, American University.

Benson, B.A. (1995). Psychosocial interventions update: Self-modeling. *Habilitative Mental Healthcare Newsletter, 14,* 110–113.

Bline, C.A., & Dowrick, P.W. (1992, May). *Video feedforward in the treatment of autistic behavior.* Paper presented at annual Pathways Conference on Developmental Disabilities, Anchorage, AK.

Blum, N.J., Kell, R.S., Starr, H.L., Lloyds Lender, W., Bradley-Klug, K.L., Osborne, M.L., & Dowrick, P.W. (1998). Audio feedforward treatment of selective mutism. *Journal of the American Academy of Child and Adolescent Psychiatry, 37,* 40–43.

Bolivar, C. (1993). *The use of video self-modeling to teach social-communication skills to adults with mental retardation.* Master's thesis, University of Alaska Anchorage.

Boyer, B.L. (1987). *Using the self-as-a-model with video editing in athletic performance.* Master's thesis, University of the Pacific, Stockton, CA.

Bradley, R.D. (1993). *The use of goal-setting and positive self-modeling to enhance self-efficacy and performance for the basketball free-throw shot.* Doctoral dissertation, University of Maryland, College Park.

Bray, M.A., & Kehle, T.J. (1998). Self-modeling as an intervention for stuttering: A replication. *School Psychology Review, 27,* 587–598.

Buggey, T.J. (1995). An examination of the effectiveness of self-modeling in teaching specific linguistic structures to preschoolers. *Topics in Early Childhood Special Education, 15,* 434–458.

Clarke, G., Hops, H., & Lewinsohn, P. (1992). Cognitive-behavioral group treatment of adolescent depression: Prediction of outcome. *Behavior Therapy, 23,* 341–354.

Creer, T.L., & Miklich, D.R. (1970). The application of a self-modeling procedure to modify inappropriate behavior: A preliminary report. *Behaviour Research and Therapy, 8,* 91–92.

Davis, R.A. (1979). The impact of self-modeling on problem behaviors in school-age children. *School Psychology Digest, 8,* 128–132.

Dowrick, P.W. (1976). *Self modelling: A videotape training technique for disturbed and disabled children.* Doctoral dissertation, University of Auckland.

Dowrick, P.W. (1978). Suggestions for the use of edited video replay in training behavioral skills. *Journal of Practical Approaches to Developmental Handicap, 2,* 21–24.

Dowrick, P.W. (1979). Single dose medication to create a self model film. *Child Behavior Therapy, 1,* 193–198.

Dowrick, P.W. (1983). Self-modelling. In P.W. Dowrick & S.J. Biggs (Eds.), *Using video: Psychological and social applications* (pp. 105–124). Chichester, England: Wiley.

Dowrick, P.W. (1986). *Social survival for children: A trainer's resource.* New York: Brunner/Mazel.

Dowrick, P.W. (1989). Videotraining strategies for beginners, champions, and injured athletes. In A.A. Turner (Ed.), *Proceedings of American College of Sports Medicine, Alaska Regional Conference, Oct. 1987.* Anchorage: University of Alaska.

Dowrick, P.W. (1991). *Practical guide to using video in the behavioral sciences.* New York: Wiley Interscience.

Dowrick, P.W. (1999). A review of self modeling and related interventions. *Applied and Preventive Psychology, 8,* 23–39.

Dowrick, P.W., & Dove, C. (1980). The use of self-modeling to improve the swimming performance of spina bifida children. *Journal of Applied Behavior Analysis, 13,* 51–56.

Dowrick, P.W., & Hood, M. (1978). Transfer of talking behaviours across settings using faked films. In E.L. Glynn & S.S. McNaughton (Eds.), *Proceedings of New Zealand Conference for Research in Applied Behaviour Analysis.* Auckland: Auckland University Press.

Dowrick, P.W., & Hood, M. (1981). Comparison of self-modeling and small cash incentives in a sheltered workshop. *Journal of Applied Psychology, 66,* 349–397.

Dowrick, P.W., & Jesdale, D.C. (1990). Effets de la retransmission vidéo structurée sur l'émotion: Implications thérapeutiques [Effects on emotion of structured video replay: Implications for therapy]. *Bulletin de Psychologie, 43,* 512–517.

Dowrick, P.W., Meunier, R., & Connor, M.E. (1998). *Video futures: A user's guide to video self modeling and related procedures.* Unpublished procedure manual, Center on Disability Studies: University Affiliated Program, University of Hawaii, Honolulu.

Dowrick, P.W., Power, T.J., Manz, P.H., & Ginsburg-Block, M. (in press). Creating futures in under-resourced communities: Response to schools. *Journal of Prevention and Intervention in the Community.*

Dowrick, P.W., & Raeburn, J.M. (1977). Video editing and medication to produce a therapeutic self model. *Journal of Consulting and Clinical Psychology, 45,* 1156–1158.

Dowrick, P.W., & Raeburn, J.M. (1995). Self-modeling: Rapid skill training for children with physical disabilities. *Journal of Developmental and Physical Disabilities, 7,* 25–37.

Dowrick, P.W., & Ward, K.M. (1997). Video feedforward in the support of a man with intellectual disability and inappropriate sexual behaviour. *Journal of Intellectual and Developmental Disability, 22,* 147–160.

Dowrick, P.W., & Wiedle, J. (1995, August). *Video futures: Strategies for transitions and other challenges for children and youth.* Continuing education workshop, American Psychological Association annual convention, Toronto.

Druckman, D., & Bjork, R.A. (Eds.). (1991). *In the mind's eye: Enhancing human performance.* Washington, DC: National Academy Press.

Embry, D. (1995, November). *Using cognitive social competence research for a large scale approach to reduce youth violence.* Paper presented at Association for Advancement of Behavior Therapy annual convention, Washington, DC.

Fitzgerald, K., & Dowrick, P.W. (1995). *Video feedforward for children with autism and other disabilities.* Invited workshop, annual Pathways Conference on Developmental Disabilities, Anchorage, AK.

Franks, I.M., & Maile, L.J. (1991). The use of video in sport skill acquisition. In P.W. Dowrick & associates (Eds.), *Practical guide to using video in the behavioral sciences.* New York: Wiley Interscience.

Gipson, M., McKenzie, T., & Lowe, S. (1989). The sport psychology program of the USA Women's National Volleyball Team: Delivering sport psychology services to the 1988 Olympic athletes [Special issue]. *Sport Psychologist, 3,* 330–339.

Goldenthal, P. (1999). *Beyond sibling rivalry.* New York: Henry Holt.

Greelis, M., & Kazaoka, K. (1979). The therapeutic use of edited videotapes with an exceptional child. *Academic Therapy, 15,* 37–44.

Haarman, B.S., & Greelis, M.T. (1982). The therapeutic use of edited videotapes as a primary means of behavioral intervention in the shaping of appropriate grammatical and contextual use of language. *Journal of Special Education Technology, 5,* 52–56.

Holman, L. (1991). *Self-efficacy and video feedforward: A new technology applied to teaching beginning swimming.* Master's thesis, University of Alaska Anchorage.

Holmbeck, G.N., & Lavigne, J.V. (1992). Combining self-modeling and stimulus fading in the treatment of an electively mute child. *Psychotherapy, 29,* 661–667.

Hosford, R.E. (Producer). (1979). *Self-as-a-model* [Video]. Washington, DC: American Personnel and Guidance Association.

Hosford, R.E. (1980). Self-as-a-model: A cognitive, social-learning technique. *Counseling Psychology, 9*(1), 45–62.

Hosford, R.E., & Brown, S.D. (1976). *Using social modeling procedures to improve undergraduate instruction* (Tech. Rep. Contract No. 8-407674-07427). Santa Barbara: University of California Innovative Teaching Project.

Hosford, R.E., Moss, C.S., & Morrel, G. (1976). The self-as-a-model technique: Helping prison inmates change. In J.D. Krumboltz & C.E. Thoresen (Eds.), *Counseling methods* (pp. 487–495). New York: Holt, Rinehart and Winston.

Kahn, J.S., Kehle, T.J., Jenson, W.R., & Clark, E. (1990). Comparison of cognitive-behavioral, relaxation, and self-modeling interventions for depression among middle-school students. *School Psychology Review, 19,* 196–211.

Kehle, T.J., Clark, E., Jenson, W.R., & Wampold, B.E. (1986). Effectiveness of self-observation with behavior disordered elementary school children. *School Psychology Review, 15,* 289–295.

Kehle, T.J., Owen, S.V., & Cressy, E.T. (1990). The use of self-modeling as an intervention in school psychology: Case study of an elective mute. *School Psychology Review, 19,* 115–121.

Kehle, T.J., Root, M.M., Spackman, V.S., & Bray, M.A. (in press). Augmented self-modeling as a treatment for children with selective mutism. *Journal of School Psychology.*

Kelley, M.A. (1986). *Three mediums of practice and the maintenance of pursuit rotor proficiency, self-efficacy, and imagery ability: A comparative study.* Master's thesis, University of Alaska Anchorage.

Kelly, G.A. (1955). *The psychology of personal constructs: Clinical diagnosis and psychotherapy* (Vol. 2). New York: Norton.

Kern, L., Wacker, D.T., Mace, F.C., Falk, G.D., Dunlap, G., & Kromrey, J.D. (1995). Improving the peer interactions of students with severe emotional and behavioral disorders through self-evaluation. *Journal of Applied Behavior Analysis, 28,* 47–59.

Kojian, H.J. (1992). *The use of biblio self-modeling in the reduction of dental anxiety in children.* Doctoral dissertation, Fuller Graduate School of Psychology, Pasadena, CA.

Krantz, P.J., MacDuff, G.S., & McClannahan, L.E. (1993). Programming participation in family activities for children with autism: Parent's use of photographic activity schedules. *Journal of Applied Behavior Analysis, 26,* 137–138.

Krantz, P.J., MacDuff, G.S., Wadstrom, O., & McClannahan, L.E. (1991). Using video with developmentally disabled learners. In P.W. Dowrick & associates (Eds.), *Practical guide to using video in the behavioral sciences.* New York: Wiley Interscience.

Kyker, K., & Curchy, C. (1994). *Television production for elementary and middle schools.* Englewood, CO: Libraries Unlimited.

Meharg, S.S., & Lipsker, L.E. (1991). Parent training using videotape self-modeling. *Child and Family Behavior Therapy, 13*(4), 1–27.

Meharg, S.S., & Woltersdorf, M.A. (1990). Therapeutic use of videotape self-modeling: A review. *Advances in Behaviour Research and Therapy, 12,* 85–99.

Melody, D.W. (1990). *The influence of self-modeling on free-throw shooting.* Doctoral dissertation, University of Connecticut, Storrs.

Mulcahy, G.A., & Schacter, J.G. (1982). Cognitive self-modeling, conventional group counselling, and change in interpersonal skills. *Genetic Monographs, 106,* 117–175.

Perry, S.A. (1989). *The development of self-modeling for social safety skills with the developmentally disabled.* Master's thesis, University of Alaska Anchorage.

Pierce, K.I., & Schreibman, L. (1994). Teaching daily living skills to children with autism in unsupervised settings through pictorial self-management. *Journal of Applied Behavior Analysis, 27,* 471–481.

Pigott, H.E., & Gonzales, F.P. (1987). The efficacy of videotape self-modeling to treat an electively mute child. *Journal of Clinical Child Psychology, 16,* 106–110.

Pionek, B.C., Kratochwill, T.R., & Sladeczek, M. (1996, August). *Selective mutism: A meta-analysis of intervention outcomes.* Paper presented at annual convention of American Psychological Association, Toronto.

Schunk, D.H., & Hanson, A.R. (1989). Self-modeling and children's cognitive skill learning. *Journal of Educational Psychology, 81,* 155–163.

Scraba, P. (1989). *Self-modeling for teaching swimming to children with physical disabilities.* Doctoral dissertation, University of Connecticut, Storrs.

Shear, S.M., & Shapiro, E.S. (1993). Effects of using self-recording and self-observation in reducing disruptive behavior. *Journal of School Psychology, 31,* 519–534.

Steed, S.E., & Lutzker, J.R. (1997). Using picture prompts to teach an adult with developmental disabilities to independently complete vocational tasks. *Journal of Developmental and Physical Disabilities, 9,* 117–133.

Winfrey, M.L., & Weeks, D.L. (1993). Effects of self-modeling on self-efficacy and balance beam performance. *Perceptual and Motor Skills, 77,* 907–913.

Woltersdorf, M.A. (1992). Videotape self-modeling in the treatment of attention-deficit hyperactivity disorder. *Child and Family Behavior Therapy, 14,* 53–73.

PART FOUR

OTHER TECHNIQUES

CHAPTER 10

Hypnotic Techniques for the Treatment of Children with Anxiety Problems

RICHARD B. GRIFFIN

HYPNOSIS AND hypnotic techniques can be effective in the treatment of children who have anxiety problems (Gaffney, 1993; Griffin, 1996, 1997; Kohen & Olness, 1993; Nath & Warren, 1995; Olness & Kohen, 1996; Sapp, 1991; Schultz, 1991; Stanton, 1994). As an adjunct or ancillary technique to an ongoing therapy, hypnosis has the potential to help children develop mastery and control over their anxiety and the problems associated with it. With adequate training in general hypnosis and specialized hypnosis training with children, clinicians can use this effective technique within their areas of competency. Hypnotherapy has a demonstrated efficacy with many types of childhood problems, and it can also offer children a high-interest treatment approach that directly addresses their problems. At the same time, hypnosis provides clinicians with a strategic tool for creative therapeutic interventions.

HISTORICAL BACKGROUND

Hypnotic phenomena have been reported from cultures around the world and from all periods of recorded history (Wickramasekera,

1988). Hypnosis with children has deep historical roots, and references to its use can be found in sources dating back many centuries. Biblical accounts make reference to children being exposed to healing methods that utilized suggestion and faith (Olness & Kohen, 1996). In the modern era, the first documented cases of using hypnotic techniques with children date back to Mesmer in the late eighteenth century. Reports about hypnosis with children were made by French and English clinicians in the nineteenth century as well. Baldwin (1891) produced the first journal article, "Suggestion in Infancy," devoted to child hypnotherapy. It is interesting to note, however, that there were virtually no reports of hypnotherapy with children during the first half of the twentieth century. Ambrose published a book entitled *Hypnotherapy with Children* in 1961, and the trend began to shift. It was not until the 1960s and 1970s that reports documenting the use of hypnosis with children began to appear in American literature. It was also during this time period that workshop training for hypnosis in general and hypnosis with children in particular began to be offered on a wide scale (Olness & Kohen, 1996).

During this same period, standardized hypnotic susceptibility tests for children and adolescents were developed. Their introduction provided instruments that allowed for further study of hypnotic phenomena and stimulated research in this area. The development of standardized susceptibility tests for children and adolescents provided researchers with empirical data on developmental issues in hypnotic responding. Eventually, there was an increase in interest in the clinical efficacy of hypnotic interventions with children. Reports were forthcoming that described how hypnosis could be useful in treating a variety of children's problems and disorders.

THE NATURE OF HYPNOSIS AND HYPNOTIC RESPONDING

There is debate over the nature of the hypnotic state and how to define it. Some theorists and clinicians maintain that the hypnotic state is not inherently different from the waking state. This position, called the social learning view, was introduced in the

1960s and maintains that contextual cues, environmental factors, and situational demands are responsible for a person's response to the hypnotic situation. The social learning theory emphasizes that "hypnotizability does not reflect an underlying trait but is a function of learning history and environmental influences" (Bates, 1993, p. 41). The opposing view is one that was prominent for a hundred years before the social learning theory was introduced. This position, called the trait view (sometimes called the state theory), holds that people vary in their ability to experience hypnosis. This capacity, or hypnotizability, tends to remain stable throughout the individual's lifetime. Theorists and clinicians who subscribe to this view regard hypnosis as an altered state of awareness or consciousness that is fundamentally different from a normal waking state. The experience of certain types of higher-level hypnotic phenomena (e.g., hallucinations and amnesia) requires a rare talent that cannot be taught (Kirsch & Lynn, 1995).

Just as there are different views of hypnosis, there are numerous definitions of hypnosis. A few select definitions are noted here. Kohen and Olness (1993) define hypnosis as "an alternative state of awareness and alertness characterized by heightened and focused concentration that is achieved in order to actualize a particular goal or a latent potential" (p. 359). Wickramasekera (1988) defines hypnosis as "a form of information processing in which voluntarily initiated suspension of peripheral awareness and critical analytic mentation can readily lead in some people to major changes in perception, memory, and mood that have important behavioral and physiological consequences" (p. 55). He also notes that a sense of involuntariness is a hallmark of the hypnotic state. This writer views hypnosis as an altered state of consciousness that involves absorption, suggestibility, and focused attention that can produce noticeable changes in sensations, thoughts, feelings, and behavior. Notable changes in attitude and motivation can also occur.

The terms hypnotizability, hypnotic susceptibility, and hypnotic responsiveness refer to a mental ability or capacity a person has to enter into and experience hypnotic phenomena. This mental ability, or hypnotizability, appears to be very stable. Susceptibility tests administered to subjects in late adolescence and again

10 years later produced a test-retest correlation of .82 (Piccione, Hilgard, & Zimbardo, 1989), which suggests that hypnotic ability is about as stable a trait as intelligence. Hypnotizability appears to be a complex personality characteristic that has both a learned and a genetic component. It has a general heritability index of .64 (Morgan, Higard, & Davert, 1970). Hypnotizability is measurable on well-standardized tests such as the Stanford Hypnotic Susceptibility Scales (forms for adults and children) and the Harvard Group Scale of Hypnotic Susceptibility (for adults). It has a roughly normal (bell curve) distribution in the general population: about 10% to 15% of the adult population would be considered highly hypnotizable and about 10% to 15% have very little hypnotic ability (Wickramasekera, 1988). About 2% of the general population is nonhypnotizable, and the reasons for this are unknown. Those in the middle range have a moderate degree of hypnotizability. Most people are hypnotizable enough to benefit from clinical hypnosis (Brown & Fromm, 1986). Hypnotizability has not been found to be strongly related to any single personality trait. It may be best conceptualized as a metatrait (Palsson, 1997). There are no gender differences, and a modest correlation with intelligence exists (Olness & Kohen, 1996).

DEVELOPMENTAL CONSIDERATIONS

Several studies have demonstrated that children are more hypnotically responsive than adults (Barber & Calverley, 1963; Morgan & Hilgard, 1973). Hypnotizability tends to increase with age beginning at about age 5 years. However, this anchor (5 years old) may be an artifact due to the unavailability of test instruments for children younger than 4 years of age. It is generally agreed that hypnotic responsiveness before age 3 is limited (Plotnick & O'Grady, 1991). This chapter addresses hypnotic interventions for children aged 6 years and older. However, a brief discussion of hypnotic or hypnoticlike experiences that occur in children younger than 6 years is presented.

Josephine Hilgard (Hilgard, 1979; Hilgard & Morgan, 1978) introduced the concept of protohypnosis to describe hypnotic responsiveness in children younger than 6 years. In her view, the protohypnotic state appeared to be fundamentally different from the hypnotic states that older children experienced. A young child may be "better able to be distracted by listening to a story or by participating in a verbal game with a friendly adult than by removing himself from the scene through his own fantasy or through reliving an earlier game or experience of his own" (Hilgard & Morgan, 1978, p. 286). Children may not be able to determine the difference between what is voluntary and what is involuntary behavior on their part. Added to this is the observation that very young children are able to move easily between reality and fantasy and may not always reliably distinguish between the two. It is the opinion of this writer that hypnotic responding in children younger than 6 years is qualitatively different from hypnotic responding that occurs in older children.

After age 5 years, hypnotizability in children increases and peaks between 9 and 12 years of age. From that point, hypnotizability appears to decrease slightly, levels off in late adolescence and early adulthood, and remains very stable during adulthood (Morgan & Hilgard, 1973). The normative data available in this area come from test results provided by standardized susceptibility tests. One of the most widely used susceptibility tests for children is the Stanford Hypnotic Clinical Scale for Children (SHCS-C). This test, developed by Morgan and Hilgard (1978/1979), has several versions, but each is similar in that each includes a standardized induction script and a standardized administration of a series of tasks that the subject is required to perform. The subject's performance on each task is scored and an overall score is obtained for the entire test. The test takes about 20 minutes to administer and consists of seven items. It comes in two forms, one for children aged 6 to 16 years and a modified form for children aged 4 to 8 years.

Differences in Hypnotic Responding among Age Groups

In general, there are a number of differences in the way children respond to hypnotic interventions when compared with adults. The concept of protohypnosis was described earlier to explain how children under the age of 6 years appear to respond. Because the term children can apply to anyone under the age of 18 years, a commonsense view will be adopted to define the terms children and adolescents according to age range. For the sake of discussion, youngsters aged 6 to 12 years will be referred to as *children* and those 13 years and older will be regarded as *adolescents*. Even children in the 6 to 12 years age group demonstrate a wide degree of developmental variation.

Children younger than 6 years usually do very well with storytelling and situations that pull for their active participation in imaginative involvement. Formal trances are typically not necessary and may not be that effective. Adolescents (aged 13 years and over) often respond in ways that are similar to adults in the hypnotic state. They frequently do well with adult-style inductions. Of importance here is the child's developmental level. It is possible for a 14-year-old to operate on a developmental level that is emotionally and cognitively commensurate with that of the average 9-year-old; the converse could be true as well. The key to determining which approach or induction style is appropriate for a particular child is that child's developmental level. This, of course, is determined through the clinical interview, assessment activities, and direct observations and interactions with the youngster.

Several features describe how children differ from adults. Children are often very active in trance; they may move around, squirm, and adjust their position in the chair. Frequently, their movement is acting out the imaginal scenes that have been suggested to them by the therapist. Sometimes, their squirming is an indication of the awkwardness of the situation as they perceive it; they may laugh and giggle due to feeling conspicuous. This is in dramatic contrast to most adult hypnotic subjects, who typically sit or lie motionless for long periods of time during the hypnosis session. Children's movements can also be used to help them become more involved in the imagined situations. It is often advantageous to utilize their affinity for movement in developing inductions and imaginal situations that emphasize physical movement. Action scenes can be very effective in helping many children enter into a hypnotic state.

Sometimes, children insist on keeping their eyes open during inductions and occasionally during the entire trance situation. They may close their eyes initially but then open them to look around. This seems to happen frequently with younger children.

It is usually best to let them do this and even tell them that it is acceptable to do whatever feels comfortable. At about age 11 years, most children (90%) will prefer to close their eyes during the induction (Morgan & Hilgard, 1978/1979). Compared with adults, children tend to be more receptive to using all of their senses (Linden, 1995). They tend to do best with imagery and suggestions that utilize a variety of sensory modalities. Inductions and imaginal scenes that include the combined use of tactile, auditory, and even olfactory cues in addition to visual suggestions are likely to be well received by children. The use of multiple sensory modalities tends to enrich the experience and may make the imagined scene or situation appear more genuine and realistic. Children appear to have a heightened receptivity to sensory stimulation.

Children also have an enhanced capacity for imaginative involvement. They tend to become easily and intensely absorbed in the present moment. However, present reality can become suspended as they enter into "here and now" fantasy experiences (Kuttner, 1991). This can provide a natural opening for hypnotic interventions that use magic, fictional characters, or action hero figures. Children look at reality in a different manner from adults and are more open to experimentation (Linden, 1995). Improbable situations can be created in which the child or other people are transformed or altered in magical ways. Youngsters are able to move easily between reality and fantasy and can often combine elements of the two. Most children like to deal with primary process and enjoy imagination and supernatural events. Intensity of feelings and emotional states appears to be higher in children; some children can become very excited, happy, or sad while dealing with images and mental pictures.

DEVELOPMENTAL DIFFERENCES IN INDUCTIONS

As mentioned previously, cognitive development, as well as emotional maturity, clearly influences how children respond to hypnotic interventions and what type or style of intervention is appropriate. It should be noted, however, that the modified form of the SHCS-C uses the same induction for children in the 4 to 8-year age range regardless of whether the child is 4 or 8 years old.

Similarly, one induction is also used on the standard form of the SHCS-C for children in the 6 to 16-year age range. Of course, the fact that these are standardized tests necessitates the use of identical instructions or inductions for all subjects. The point is that, although it is not recommended, a single induction can be used for children of widely differing ages. However, the most effective inductions are those that are individually tailored to the child's developmental level and his or her unique interests.

Just as there is disagreement about how to define hypnosis, there is also some debate about when first hypnosis occurs. Some experts maintain that hypnosis begins as soon as the child becomes interested in the interactional process between the therapist and the child. It is considered hypnosis "if it engages the child's interest, focuses the child's attention, and achieves the desired result of making a personal connection with the child" (Kohen & Olness, 1993, p. 360). Kuttner (1988) noted that children frequently lack distinct boundaries between fantasy and reality and move easily and naturally from fantasy to reality-based cognitive activities. In this view, natural spontaneous hypnosis states are occurring all the time. Examples include focusing one's attention on TV, reading a book, watching a movie, or daydreaming. For the purpose of this chapter, however, the position is taken that except for very young children, aged 5 years or younger, hypnosis initiated by a therapist involves some type of formal induction.

There are no hard and fast rules governing which induction is best for a given child. The developmental level of the child is clearly the best guide to use; for example, immature adolescents may respond well to techniques that younger children would find appealing. The following suggestions concerning types of inductions are made as general guides to facilitate and enhance the child's capacity to respond hypnotically. Hypnotic techniques and approaches vary, and the ones suggested below are based more on general knowledge about children's interests and activities at different developmental age levels than they are on empirical findings.

For early childhood (2 to 4 years of age), blowing bubbles, use of pop-up books, and storytelling are effective ways to induce trance. Using the child's favorite activity, speaking to the child through a doll or stuffed animal, and using floppy Raggedy Ann or Andy dolls are also recommended. Children in the preschool and early school grades (4 to 8 years of age) might respond best to inductions that include a favorite place, storytelling, a flower garden, coin watching, bouncing ball imagery, a playground activity, or a finger lowering exercise (Olness & Kohen, 1996). For this age group, Linden (1995) recommends the use of pretend roles (such as those of a princess, a pilot, or a rag doll) and pretend situations. Puppets and animal metaphors are also considered effective at this age.

During the middle childhood period (8 to 12 years of age), imagery involving a favorite place, a favorite activity, favorite music, cloud gazing, a flying blanket, playing video games, and riding a bike are considered appropriate. Arm lowering, coin watching, arm rigidity, eye fixation, and hands moving together are also recommended (Olness & Kohen, 1996). Other inductions for this age group include learning and controlling metaphors, using adventure imagery (heroes and heroines), drawing, using controls and switches, and watching movies (Linden, 1995). For adolescents (13 to 18 years of age) favorite place and sports activities, playing computer games (actual or imagined), driving a car, and playing or hearing music are suggested. Other recommended inductions for this age group include the use of hands coming together as magnets, progressive relaxation, eye fixation, and hand levitation (Linden, 1995; Olness & Kohen, 1996). For this age range, many adult inductions are often effective.

ANXIETY IN CHILDHOOD

Attempting to conceptualize anxiety problems and anxiety disorders in childhood and adolescence is not an easy task. There is no widely accepted definition of anxiety, and there is not a clear distinction between fear and anxiety (Schultz, 1991). The intensity of the anxiety, the frequency of its occurrence, and the manner in which it is expressed are considered when determining if the anxiety problem requires clinical intervention. Anxieties and fears are common in children and are viewed as normal occurrences within the sequence of developmental stages. Anxiety may be beneficial in that it has survival value and may signal dangerous and threatening situations. At lower levels, anxiety tends to enhance performance. At higher levels, it tends to interfere with and impede optimal performance (Allen, 1980; Hill, 1984). If it is disruptive and its debilitating effects become pronounced, high levels of anxiety may become maladaptive and even pathological.

DIAGNOSTIC CLASSIFICATION AND PREVALENCY RATES

After the publication of the *DSM-IV* (American Psychiatric Association [APA], 1994), anxiety disorders in children and adolescents were defined differently. Separation anxiety disorder is the only diagnosis remaining in the classification of "Disorders Usually First Diagnosed in Infancy, Childhood or Adolescence." The overanxious disorder diagnosis is now subsumed under the generalized anxiety disorder diagnosis. The social phobia diagnosis has largely replaced avoidant anxiety disorder. This classification probably has advantages for researchers, who can now narrow the developmental gap between childhood and adult anxiety disorders (Bernstein, Borchardt, & Perwien, 1996).

Anxiety problems that appear in childhood seem to have important clinical implications for the occurrence of anxiety problems later on in the individual's life. Over half the adults suffering from generalized anxiety disorder reported its onset in childhood or adolescence (APA, 1994). Longitudinal studies support the notion that anxiety may be an enduring personality feature. In a 12-year longitudinal study, Caspi, Henry, McGee, Moffitt, and Silva (1995) found that 5-year-old boys and girls described as confident and eager to explore novel situations were less likely to manifest anxiety in adolescence. Those 5-year-old children who were described as shy, passive, fearful, and avoidant were more likely to exhibit anxiety disorders as they grew up. Ialongo, Edelsohn, Werthamer-Larsson, Crockett, and Kellam (1995) conducted a longitudinal study with children and found the occurrence of anxiety symptoms in the first grade significantly predicted anxiety problems in the fifth grade.

Prevalency rates for anxiety disorders in childhood are variable and depend on the particular study and the anxiety diagnoses that were used. Several studies (Albano & Chorpita, 1995; Anderson, Williams, McGee, & Silver, 1987) found the most common anxiety disorder in children to be separation anxiety disorder, which had prevalency rates between 2% and 4%. One of the problems in anxiety disorder research and in clinical practice is distinguishing between "normal" anxiety and fears and those that would constitute psychiatric disorders. Bernstein et al. (1996) found prevalency rates for isolated subclinical anxiety disorder symptoms in nonreferred children of between 10% and 30%. For subclinical phobias the prevalency rates were between 11% and 23%.

CLINICAL HYPNOSIS AND ANXIETY PROBLEMS

Hypnosis is not a treatment by itself and is always adjunctive to a primary therapeutic framework. Regardless of the particular framework used, respect for the patient and sensitivity to his or her problems should be paramount. The therapist's ability to establish rapport, project empathic understanding, and create an atmosphere of safety and trust is an essential component of the hypnotic intervention. Optimal conditions are those in which the child is open to new experiences and motivated to seek change and work toward achieving his or her goals. It is best to go slow and lay the groundwork for a trusting therapeutic relationship that will help promote motivational and attitudinal changes in the hypnosis sessions. Conveying a genuine sense of encouragement and offering positive reinforcement during and following the hypnosis sessions helps ensure that the intervention will be successful. The decision to use hypnosis with a child or adult is not something that should be casually or hastily decided. Children and their parents are entitled to a thorough explanation of what hypnosis is and how it will be used.

CLINICAL TREATMENT OF CHILDREN WITH ANXIETY PROBLEMS UTILIZING HYPNOTIC INTERVENTIONS

Traditional treatment approaches for children with anxiety problems include psychodynamic psychotherapy, behavioral and/or cognitive-behavioral treatment, and pharmacological interventions. As mentioned earlier, the role of the hypnotic intervention is an adjunctive one. The nature of the presenting problem, the child's social history, and the therapist's orientation are just a few of the factors that determine the type of therapeutic framework within which the hypnotic intervention is integrated. When relationship and attachment issues are prominent, a psychodynamic approach is usually warranted. Especially when there is evidence of trauma or abuse, exaggerated dependency needs, or a dysfunctional family system, a strong emphasis on family-of-origin issues through a psychodynamic approach is recommended. Parental involvement is usually very important in these kinds of cases and family therapy can be very beneficial.

Hypnosis can be introduced into almost any therapeutic framework. Cognitive-behavioral therapy (CBT) approaches are frequently used in conjunction with hypnosis. CBT approaches are symptom-focused and can be utilized as a primary treatment approach or as a supplement to an ongoing psychodynamic therapy. CBT approaches have empirically demonstrated efficacy with anxiety problems in children (Kendall & Southam-Gerow, 1996). Hypnosis may be introduced into an ongoing CBT treatment program, or specific CBT techniques may be included within a given hypnotic intervention regardless of the primary therapeutic approach utilized. Hypnosis and CBT share common techniques: relaxation activities, rehearsal, imagery, and desensitization are employed in both (Golden, 1994).

Hypnotic interventions for the treatment of anxiety rely heavily on desensitization. In a typical intervention, the child is helped through hypnosis to enter into a relaxed, comfortable state. The therapist typically suggests that the child can acquire new coping skills or view the situation from a different perspective. Changing the attributes of the situation is also helpful in decreasing or alleviating anxiety. Imaginal exposure is then suggested and the child is asked to imagine being in the anxiety-producing situation while accessing and utilizing the new coping skills and the modifications in perception. CBT techniques involving relaxation, coping self-statements, cognitive restructuring, self-reinforcement, modeling, and imaginal exposure can be included in a hypnotic intervention. Kendall et al. (1996) found that children as young as 9 years of age can benefit from cognitive strategies.

ASSESSMENT OF ANXIETY

A good clinical interview should be the first step in the assessment process. The interview should focus on acquiring as much information as possible about the onset, history, and relevant details of the anxiety problem. Consideration should be given to developmental issues and the degree to which the type, intensity, and frequency of the anxiety reaction deviates from accepted norms for that age or developmental period. Physical problems, if present, should be carefully explored, and a thorough medical history should be obtained. Social histories are very useful, and attention should be given to the existence of anxiety problems or affective disorders in the immediate family or in members of the preceding generations. School performance, both academically and behaviorally, is very important. Input from teachers in the form of informal, anecdotal information is helpful; teachers' input provided by standardized rating scales that assess anxiety is useful as well.

There are a number of clinical instruments that measure anxiety in children (see Bernstein et al., 1996, for a comprehensive listing) and are helpful in determining the severity of the anxiety problem. Parents and sometimes children may complete these rating scales. It is recommended that children and adolescents be referred for a medical examination if symptoms of anxiety are severe or seriously restrict the client's functioning. Antidepressant medication might be warranted, at least initially. Many medical conditions can produce nervousness and anxiety in individuals who have no emotional difficulties. Hypertension, hyperthyroidism, hypoglycemia, anemia, and hypoxia are among disorders that can produce multiple symptoms, as can side effects from certain medications (Wilson, 1996).

The initial sessions begin with time spent with the child establishing rapport and building a therapeutic alliance. Encouraging the child to talk about personal interests and favorite activities is an important way to establish rapport. This also provides a counterpoint to the serious work that is the focus of the therapy session: the child's problem. Eventually, it becomes necessary to deal with the clinical problem at hand. It is helpful to ask the child directly, "Do you know why you are here?" or "Why did your parent(s) bring you in to see me today?" The child might respond with "Because I'm afraid of getting shots" or "Because I need to learn to relax." If the child does not know, it is appropriate to eventually supply the answer and say, "Your mother (or father or parents) told me you were afraid of getting shots." It is important to encourage the child to work with the therapist and form an alliance. The therapist might ask the child, "How can I help you with this?" or "How can we work together to take care of your problem?" Sometimes, the child will volunteer that he or she came to see the therapist to do hypnosis. This creates a natural opening to introduce the topic of hypnosis.

Although single-session hypnosis interventions are possible, this is not recommended. It is important to establish a therapeutic alliance with the child. Hypnosis will serve as an adjunctive technique to an ongoing therapeutic framework that might involve psychodynamic or supportive therapy or CBT approaches. A careful assessment will help determine whether a hypnotic intervention is appropriate. There are a number of contraindications that should be considered. Hypnosis should not be used when (1) it could lead to physical endangerment for the child, (2) it could aggravate existing emotional problems or create new ones, (3) its purpose is simply to have fun experimenting with hypnosis, (4) the problem is more effectively treated by some method other than hypnosis, or (5) the diagnosis is incorrect and the real problem should be treated some other way (Olness & Kohen, 1996).

THE PRESENTATION OF HYPNOSIS TO THE PARENT(S) AND THE CHILD

There are several points to consider when presenting hypnosis to the parent(s) and the child. The presentation should be done in a straightforward manner, and it is recommended that the actual term hypnosis be used with the parent(s). There are authors who prefer that hypnosis be described in terms of natural events and occurrences and use terms such as "using your imagination" and "learning to relax" (Kohen & Olness, 1993). There are clear advantages to this approach: it makes it easier to convince the child that hypnosis is a natural and easily attainable state or condition, and it also tends to demystify the phenomenon when hypnosis is described in everyday terms such as imagination or daydreaming.

The use of these and similar terms to explain to children and parents what hypnosis is can be very effective. However, this writer makes a point to refer to the hypnotic intervention as hypnosis. This is done for several reasons. The term hypnosis and the accompanying procedures are likely to produce a placebo effect; generally, the more a therapy or approach is viewed as special or distinct, the more likely the client will attach added importance to it and its potential to help with his or her problem. Another reason is that the word hypnosis itself may not only represent a misunderstood concept but may also conjure up negative associations for some people. If parents or children do have concerns about hypnosis, it is best to know about them and address them early, before the hypnotic interventions are even attempted. A parent who does have such objections to the use of hypnosis (e.g., for religious reasons) may become upset to learn later that the therapist was employing hypnosis without the parent's consent.

It is sometimes surprising to learn of the faulty beliefs and misconceptions many adults as well as children have concerning hypnosis. With the parent, it is recommended that the hypnotic intervention be referred to as hypnosis; with the child, it depends on developmental level and vocabulary. Usually, for children who are at least at the 7-year-old developmental level, use of the word hypnosis is appropriate. With younger children, the hypnotic intervention may be described as magic or as a time when fun things can happen. Younger children are usually far more concerned about the activity itself than the word(s) used to describe it.

Adults who are educated and otherwise present themselves as knowledgeable and sophisticated often hold misconceptions about hypnosis; children, of course, frequently have very strange ideas about hypnosis as well. Any inaccuracies or misconceptions that parents or children bring forth should be addressed and corrected.

It is important to ask children if they know anything about hypnosis or if they have ever been hypnotized. Frequently, children have obtained information about hypnotic states from TV or the movies. Common misconceptions include what a therapist or hypnotherapist can or cannot make you do; these concerns may involve the therapist's putting the subject under a spell and commanding the subject to do silly or embarrassing things. The classic examples are "barking like a dog" or "quacking like a duck." A standard response to these misconceptions is to tell children that they would not do anything in a hypnotic state that they would feel uncomfortable doing in a normal, waking state. Other questions might involve the nature of the trance state and how one comes out of this state. Any opportunities that occur to inform and educate the parents and the child should be utilized.

It is important to help the child see that hypnotic states or trance states are natural and occur in everyday life. Examples can be offered that involve daydreaming, being lost in thought, and becoming absorbed in a TV show, a song, a book, a game, or a physical activity. It is important to suggest to the child that everyone has this ability. The child may be asked to recall similar personal experiences involving absorption that he or she has had in the past. The therapist may ask, "Have you ever been watching a movie and you forgot you were in a movie theater?" The therapist should also let children know that he or she is there to help them move into this special but entirely natural state. It should be emphasized that the therapist will help them use their natural abilities to do this. The therapist might say, "You already know how to do this. You already have the ability. I'm just going to help." Children might be given the suggestion that the more they want to do this (enter trance), the better it will work. A further suggestion might be that the child remains relaxed and "Just let whatever happens happen." It might be a good idea to add, "This is going to be fun."

The concept of the mind-body connection is important to convey to children, although age level, cognitive development, and vocabulary may exclude some children from comprehending this information. Children that can grasp the concept are told, "You and I are going to work together to help you use your mind to control your body." Common examples of this are given, and children are told that they do this every time they think about raising an arm and the arm rises. Another example might be, "Whenever you think about reaching for a pencil and your hand begins to move toward the pencil, your mind and your body are working together." It is also important to talk about how the children's thoughts can affect their body or produce physical reactions. Blushing is a good example of this (Olness & Kohen, 1996). It is suggested to the child that "Your mind realizes that you did something embarrassing and your body responds to that in a physical way." These ideas have direct applications to anxiety reactions and anticipatory apprehension. They also help the child understand how thinking about being afraid can produce physical reactions (e.g., sweating and increased heart rate).

For anxious children, their anxiety is often pervasive and easily generalized. This certainly applies to anxieties about the hypnotic experience itself. Care should be taken to explore any fears or concerns that the children or parents have about hypnosis. Concern about losing control is common with anxious children. Sometimes, there is concern about loss of control as it relates to the depth or the length of the trance (e.g., "What if I don't wake up?"). Fear of the dark and reluctance to close one's eyes are common and should be addressed; children should be given permission to keep their eyes open if this is a concern. It is important to reassure children that nothing will be done during the hypnotic session to intentionally surprise or scare them.

Issues may arise about whether the parent(s) should be present in the office during the child's hypnotic session. This occurs frequently with children suffering from separation anxiety disorders and with overprotective parents. Unless it is clear that the parent's presence will be disruptive, often it may be beneficial to allow the parent to remain in the office and observe, at least during the initial session. This tends to promote an open atmosphere and may result in the parent's becoming more supportive of the child's use of hypnosis. Later, it may be suggested that the parent allow the child and the therapist to work together by themselves.

Once all questions and concerns have been addressed and children and parents have agreed to the use of hypnosis, it is recommended that the parent or guardian sign an informed consent form. It should be explained to the parent why the hypnotic procedure is indicated and what possible risks are involved in the procedure. Of particular importance during the informed consent process is educating the parent about the legal ramifications of using hypnosis and the possible inadmissibility of hypnotically refreshed or enhanced material in courtroom proceedings; laws pertaining to this vary from state to state. To avoid the risk of legally contaminating future testimony in court, it is strongly recommended that hypnosis not be used if the child has a history of abuse. Some state statutes hold that the use of hypnosis may permanently contaminate the subject's future testimony in court (Scheflin & Shapiro, 1989). Any therapist who chooses to use hypnosis with children should become familiar with the legal implications of using hypnotic techniques in the state in which he or she practices. This is particularly important when the child has a history of being abused or abuse is suspected in the present situation.

HYPNOTIC TECHNIQUES

There are numerous hypnotic techniques that can be used with children with anxiety problems. In their simplest forms, hypnotic interventions tend to have two main purposes. The first is to explore and possibly determine the origin of present symptoms, such as fears, phobias, or anxious reactions. The collective grouping of hypnotic approaches used to accomplish this is referred to as uncovering techniques. Some type of regressive approach is typically used in this approach; open-ended situations may be presented in trance, and these situations may involve requests for answers to questions or solutions to problems. The second general purpose for the use of hypnosis aims at symptom control or reduction and self-regulation. This approach frequently involves direct suggestions that clients will be able to see themselves as more confident in the anxiety-producing situation and/or better able to accomplish a difficult task. In this type of intervention, when symptoms arise, specific coping skills or techniques will be activated to eliminate or reduce the symptoms. Projective techniques can be used for both uncovering the origin of symptoms and for symptom control; these techniques tend to form the basic framework for desensitization work. Ideomotor finger signals represent another method that is extremely useful during hypnotic interventions. These techniques and others will be briefly discussed.

Age Regression

In this technique, suggestions are made for the patient to go back in time to an earlier point in life. The purpose is to determine if present difficulties are associated with an earlier event. There are several techniques that can be used to produce age regression. The main objective is to allow the child access to past experiences and influences that may play a part in the current problem. Related to age regression is the hotly debated area of repressed memory (sometimes referred to as false memory) that is usually associated with recovered memories of trauma or abuse. This topic is beyond the scope of this discussion, but it does suggest an issue that requires some clarification. It is important to know that information retrieved hypnotically, whether from adults or children, should never be considered 100% accurate. Distortions, confusion between fantasy and reality, and even outright fabrications can occur during hypnosis. What is important is the usefulness of the material retrieved and its symbolic relevance to the problem.

Age Progression

This involves an imaginary movement or excursion into a future time for the purpose of seeing a different outcome or conclusion. Typically, the child is asked to imagine a scene in which he or she is able to master a problem, such as anxiety. A specific outcome may be suggested that involves the child's being able to handle a previously stressful situation in a calm and composed manner. Suggestions may be given to help children picture themselves behaving calmly while performing a specific task or activity. Reactions from others can also be suggested in the outcome. Suggestions can also be made for the children to see how their lives will be different in the future once their symptoms have subsided.

Projective Techniques

Projective techniques can incorporate a wide variety of imaginary situations and props (e.g., movie theaters, picture frames, dreams), typically, movie screens, blank walls, TV screens, and remote controls are used. At a given cue, images, messages, or scenes can be projected onto a screen. The therapist might say, "I am going to count to three and when I reach three, information related to your problem will appear on the screen. One, two, three." Then the therapist may ask the child what he or she saw and request that the child describe this orally. Variations of this technique are common, and the answers or information received may not be restricted to a visual representation; the suggestion may be given that the message may be received in the form of words or sounds or as a sense of knowing. The developmental level of the child frequently determines how the therapist describes this situation. Elaborate setups can be created in which a movie theater is the backdrop and a curtain rises to reveal pertinent information. The therapist may suggest that the child have a waking dream (while in trance) that will provide helpful information about the child's problem.

During projective techniques, children may be given the instruction to watch themselves on a movie screen or on a TV set performing a particular activity. Children can be further instructed to watch themselves as if they were watching a TV or a movie about someone else; the children are thereby able to distance themselves from the negative affect the scene or situation might produce. Controls can be offered that allow the child to regulate the feeling level of the projected scene. The controls can be set at zero so the child does not experience any emotion (no anxiety); the controls can be gradually increased based on the child's comfort level and coping ability. Split-screen techniques can be used so that children can see their current performance on one screen and their future, successful performance (with the positive outcome) on the other screen. Projective techniques can also be used to determine answers to open-ended questions, such as "What would help you deal with this problem?" "Is there anything else we should consider about this problem?" and "Is there anything in your past that is associated with your current problem?"

Sensory Distortions

A frequently used sensory distortion is the suggestion for numbness or the absence of feeling in a given part of the body. Glove anesthesia, a technique frequently used for pain control, can often accomplish this. The suggestion is given that the hand will feel completely numb. When this occurs, the numbness can be transferred to other areas of the body. This is sometimes helpful for children who have hypodermic needle phobias.

Ideomotor Signals

Ideomotor signaling is a powerful technique that uses finger signals. Although this can be presented to the child in many different ways, a typical explanation involves telling the child that it is fun and interesting to talk with your fingers. This is done while the child is in a hypnotic state. "Talking with the fingers" is also a way to stay in a comfortable state of relaxation. Using finger signals avoids analytical, language-based responding with the accompanying complexities of verbal communication. Ideomotor approaches also tend to keep children and adults in a stable trance state with minimal disturbance. It tends to be a technique that appeals to older children and is often used with adults, but younger children can utilize it as well. For some clinicians, ideomotor signaling is viewed as a way to gain access to unconscious conflicts and their accompanying symptoms; for others, there is nothing particularly abstract or mysterious about the process. The ideomotor signals represent a simple and direct way for the subject to communicate. Regardless of the significance attached to it, ideomotor signaling is simple to set up and initiate.

The child is asked to focus attention on one hand, which should be stretched out flat with the palm against the chair or sofa. The child is told that using the fingers to talk is fun and interesting. Then suggestions are given that might include, "Think of the word 'yes,' and as you think of the word 'yes,' your index or pointer finger will slowly rise in the air." As it does, the child is told, "That's good, now let the finger down slowly." Next, the child is told, "Think of the word 'no,' and as you do so, let your middle finger rise in the air." Finally, the child is told, "Think of the phrase 'not ready to say,' and as you do, your thumb will rise in the air." Reinforce the child for allowing this to happen. There are many variations on this. For example, the therapist might say, "As you think of the word 'yes,' one of your fingers will rise in the air, and I wonder which one will rise in the air?" This writer's preference is to tell the child which fingers to use because it is easier for the therapist to remember which finger corresponds to which response or word(s).

A few simple practice exercises might then be attempted. The therapist might ask the child questions such as "Do we have permission to do something about your problem?" It is always important to offer the child a sense of control over what he or she is experiencing. Sometimes, the child will respond with the finger that indicates "not ready to say" or even "no." At this point, the therapist might say, "Will you think about it?" or "Will you be ready to answer soon?" The child may indicate a reluctance to proceed; however, eventually, the therapist will attempt to encourage further progress toward the goal of using hypnosis to help the child with his or her problem. If the child is adamantly against moving forward in a certain direction, the issue should be dropped and the resistance should be explored in waking state therapy.

Another important use of ideomotor signals has to do with determining the depth of trance. Because there are few outward physical signs that reliably indicate the depth of trance the child is experiencing, it is always helpful to ask the child directly. By using finger signals, this can be accomplished by asking, "Are you in the right level of trance for us to do the work we need to do today?" If the "no" finger rises, then the therapist might ask, "Should we go deeper?" If the "yes" finger rises, the suggestion can be made that the 'yes' finger will rise again when we are in the right level of trance." The child is given a minute or so to allow these adjustments to occur and to eventually respond with the finger signal.

THE HYPNOTIC INTERVENTION

Endless possibilities exist for hypnotic interventions. For the sake of simplicity, this process is described in rather discrete stages. Although the hypnosis session itself is typically a fluid and continuous activity, for the purpose of illustration, five separate stages will be discussed: (1) the induction, (2) deepening and expanding the trance state, (3) the learning stage, (4) imaginal exposure to the anxiety-producing situation, and (5) assimilation and preparation for the future. In actual practice, some stages overlap and some are condensed or eliminated. This depends on how the child is responding to the hypnotic intervention at a given time; it also depends on the child's previous experience with hypnosis and whether ongoing hypnotherapy is occurring with the child.

THE INDUCTION

As mentioned earlier, the age of the child and his or her developmental level should largely determine the type and style of induction that is used. Hypnotic interventions typically involve some form of personal imagery. Physical relaxation is frequently used as well, but relaxation is not considered an essential component of the induction or of the trance state itself. For younger children, storytelling is almost synonymous with hypnosis. Younger and older children as well may be somewhat restless and move around during the induction; active inductions, especially those that incorporate movement, may be very effective in those cases.

Although not essential, the administration of a standardized susceptibility scale such as the SHCS-C is a good way to begin the initial hypnosis session. It provides the clinician with an accurate measure of the child's level of hypnotizability, and it allows the child to experience a trance state under neutral, nonthreatening conditions. In addition, it gives the child an opportunity to experience a wide range of hypnotic phenomena. The clinician is able to gain some insight into how readily the child responds to certain types of suggestions or hypnotic tasks as compared to others.

It is possible to incorporate various psychomotor techniques in the induction. These techniques represent physical movement tasks that are found on susceptibility scales. They are typically outside the normal range of the child's experience. Activities such as arm lowering or raising (levitation), arm rigidity, arm catalepsy, and hands moving together (magnetic hands) are examples. Although not a physical technique, counting (by the therapist) from 1 to 10 can be used to promote a trance state. These activities can be incorporated into inductions with many children. The degree to which the child complies with these suggestions is usually indicative of whether the child is responding to the hypnotic induction. These activities can also be used as deepening techniques.

A fundamental characteristic of hypnosis with children is their controlled use of imagination and imagery. It is important to find out about the child's interests, favorite activities, and pastimes, as these are easily incorporated into the induction. Interests that are based on fantasy and imagination are especially useful; storybook characters and superheroes can also be included in the induction. Inductions that incorporate all the senses are particularly appealing to children. The therapist should encourage the child to describe his or her favorite activities. Spending time with the child in play activities before the hypnosis session is attempted is a good way to gather this kind of information. Questions about the child's favorite TV show, favorite comic books, favorite music, and hobbies often provide useful material that can be incorporated into inductions.

The details the child provides about his or her interests are important, especially ones that allow the therapist to verbally suggest or create a scene or situation. Details of the child's favorite place and the visual, auditory, tactile (warm, cool, breezy, soft) and even olfactory stimuli associated with it are important in creating inductions. Because the therapist usually does not know exactly what a particular place is like, it is best to qualify suggestive descriptions and make them open-ended. An example might be, "I don't know what you'll find most interesting about your favorite place. Perhaps it will be the color of the sky, or maybe it will be a pleasant smell, or perhaps you will notice the way the sunlight reflects off the leaves as the branches sway in the gentle breeze." Pacing, rhythm, and voice tone are obviously important factors in the induction.

It is relatively easy to combine various scenes and activities. The child may skate down a winding road with smooth asphalt until arriving at a beach, where he or she takes the skates off and walks along a sandy path and hears the sound of the surf and the seagulls calling in the background. Any physical activity that has a rhythmic quality to it has the potential to be useful in inductions. These include skating, swinging, swimming, running, and riding a bike, to mention a few. Children and adults often have particular dislikes and fears, and it is important to ascertain what they are before the imagery is suggested; common fears or dislikes are stairs, elevators, heights, the dark, and closed spaces.

The relaxation response is important to induce and cultivate at some point in therapy. This is particularly important for children with anxiety problems. Relaxation is a competing response to anxiety; theoretically, if the child maintains a state of relaxation, anxiety cannot occur. Relaxation is also important in desensitization activities. Whether to encourage relaxation at the beginning of the induction or at a later point may depend on how receptive the child is to moving into a relaxed state. With especially active children, physical relaxation may be difficult to achieve; in such cases, they should be allowed to move about in trance if they wish to do so. Some children become more anxious as they relax, especially if control issues are prominent; sometimes, this type of child responds well to progressive muscle relaxation, which involves alternately tightening and relaxing specific muscle groups.

It is sometimes appropriate to begin the hypnotic session with suggestions to relax. The child may be told, "Give yourself permission to relax." A technique can be initiated in which "a wave of relaxation begins to move smoothly and gently from the top of your head" and into the child's face, head, and neck and then proceeds systematically through the various muscle groups. The therapist suggests that specific muscle groups will "let go of the tension and just relax." The wave of relaxation continues throughout the body until it reaches the child's feet. At that point, the process begins again in a continuing cycle as the therapist repeats the suggestions and the child continues to experience the waves of relaxation.

Specific training in diaphragmatic deep breathing activities can be given to the child in a waking state. Breathing is very important in promoting the relaxation response. It not only has a direct effect on producing physical relaxation quickly and easily, but it also can serve as a cue to prompt a coping skill in real-life, anxiety-producing situations. Later, in the trance state, the child can receive suggestions such as "You will remember to breathe" or "You will remember to practice breathing when you encounter a feared situation."

After the child comes out of trance, it is important to ask what he or she remembers about the session and especially what worked well in the induction. Therapists are often surprised to learn that the child is not responding in verbatim fashion to their suggestions; the therapist might have been describing a waterfall and the child decided to climb a tree instead. It is always important to ask after the hypnosis session if there was anything about it that the child did not like or if anything happened that made the child feel uncomfortable. These problems can be modified or corrected in the next session.

DEEPENING AND EXPANDING THE TRANCE STATE

Once the initial stages of the induction have been completed and it appears that the child is responding with at least a mild hypnotic response, it is then advisable to consider whether to deepen the trance state. A deep trance is not a necessity, and mild trance states are effective for the majority of problems that hypnosis addresses. If a deeper hypnotic level is considered useful by the therapist, there are numerous ways to help the child accomplish this; walking down stairs, counting, or climbing up or down a ladder are just a few techniques that can be used to deepen the trance state.

Helping the child create an imaginary special place or a safe place encourages trance deepening as well. It can also help enhance the relaxation response. Suggestions for a special place imagery might begin by suggesting that the child is opening a door and entering a room that will become his or her special place, and that the child is the only one who can go to this place. Once inside the special place, the child can be encouraged to set up and decorate the room anyway he or she wants. It can have windows or no windows; hardwood floors, tile, or carpeting; the walls can be painted or wallpapered in any color that the child likes; there can be posters and pictures on the walls.

The child is given permission to spend time deciding what he or she would like in the room and how to decorate it. The child is then told, "While you are thinking about all these possibilities, there is something that is already in the room. It is a big, soft, fluffy couch." The child is instructed, "Go over to the couch, sit down, and notice you begin to sink deeper and deeper into the softness, into the fluffiness, deeper and deeper." The therapist might continue to provide more suggestions for relaxation and peacefulness. The child is then told, "This is your special place and you can come here anytime you want, anytime you need to relax or feel calm and in control."

The child may also be told that favorite activities can occur in this place and special guests can be invited to visit. In such open-ended situations, it is often helpful to ascertain what the child is experiencing while this is occurring. For example, the child might be asked, "Can you see your friend?" or "Is Spiderman there with you?" This information can be elaborated on to further help the child expand the trance experience. The child's friend might be asked to offer advice on how to deal with a particular problem. Spiderman's presence might be used to promote confidence and courage in future situations.

Most children and adolescents can benefit from the use of ideomotor finger signals to indicate the depth of trance (discussed previously) or to help deepen trance levels. Other deepening techniques can make use of psychomotor responses such as arm levitation or magnetic hands. When using arm levitation as a deepening technique, it is suggested that the child focus attention on the right or left hand; he or she is then told to notice that the hand and arm are beginning to feel very light. It is further suggested that the "hand is becoming so light, in fact, that it will begin to lift off the arm of the chair." As the arm rises, another suggestion is made that the arm will move toward the child's face. The child is then given the suggestion, "Your hand will gently touch your cheek, and when this happens you will move even deeper into trance."

A similar technique involves the use of "magnetic hands." Children are instructed to hold their arms out in front of them with the palms facing inward. The suggestion is made that both hands have powerful magnets attached to them and will begin moving closer and closer toward each other. The child is then told, "When your hands touch, you will go into an even deeper state of trance."

THE LEARNING STAGE

In this stage, new coping skills are taught and different ways to perceive situations are suggested. The emphasis is usually on promoting the relaxation response and increasing self-confidence. Ego-strengthening techniques are also helpful, and children can be reminded of difficult situations they faced and mastered in the past. It is important to emphasize the child's strengths and enhance them as much as possible. Most children have mastered some difficult and anxiety-producing situation in the past, such as learning to ride a bicycle or attending the first day of school. These experiences can be useful to highlight. Opportunities to draw on the child's strengths should be utilized whenever possible.

Modeling can be introduced in imaginal situations when the child is in trance. It is helpful to ask in a waking state if the child can imagine someone else successfully dealing with the particular anxiety-producing situation that is causing him or her distress. The therapist might say, "I wonder how (your older sister, your best friend) would handle this situation?" and "Can you see him or her doing that now?" Superheroes can serve as models as well; such symbolic models can be very effective, especially if the child already has an interest in or identifies with a particular action figure or superhero. They tend to enhance the child's capacity for imaginative involvement and help create an atmosphere conducive to transformation and dramatic change.

Superheroes can be brought forward on command. A signal can be suggested to the child, such as "When you tug on your ear or tap your forehead with your index finger, Wonderwoman will be at your side to protect and guide you." Attributes of the superhero can also be called into play and utilized by the child. The child can be told, "When you snap your fingers, you will turn on a switch that will give you the courage of a Power Ranger." Tangible objects can also be helpful, such as a plastic angel, a small stuffed animal, or a Batman figure. The child can be told, "When you need to relax or when you need more confidence, you will remember to hold or touch or rub the figure."

There are numerous techniques the child can be taught that are designed to produce and enhance a coping response. An example of a very simple technique involves exhaling or "blowing out" the breath. This can be an effective technique because it employs a physiological mechanism that helps produce the relaxation response by releasing tension. The child may be given the suggestion, "When you feel frightened, you will remember to blow out slowly, and when you do, you will relax." Related to this is diaphragmatic or deep breathing; as mentioned previously, this is an excellent coping skill that produces a quick and reliable calming response. The child can be given the suggestion, "When you feel anxious or scared, you will remember to take a deep breath (or several deep breaths), and with every breath you take, you will feel calmer and more confident."

Ideomotor signals can be useful to gauge the child's current confidence level. Children can also be asked to predict how confident they would be if required to deal with the anxiety-producing situation right now. Ideomotor signals can also be used to measure increases in the confidence level. Children can be asked to visualize their confidence level on a 10-point scale, which could resemble a thermometer or be a digital display. Suggestions are then given for the child's confidence to grow and increase. Children can be given the suggestion that thinking about their confidence level can help make it grow. They might be told, "Concentrate on your confidence level, and when it moves from a seven to an eight, let me know by raising the 'yes' finger." This can be repeated and the child can be asked, "Is it possible for your confidence level to go even higher?" If the answer is yes, the same procedure is repeated until the confidence level reaches 10 or cannot go higher.

Other ways to improve the child's ability to cope with anxiety-producing situations include suggesting that the child perceive the situation differently and in less threatening ways. Negative thoughts can be restructured to become more positive and goal-directed. Self-coping statements can be learned and rehearsed in the trance state. Children can help supply statements based on what they typically think or say to themselves in anxious situations. Negative self-statements that stress the child's sense of inadequacy or incompetence can be turned around to emphasize the opposite. Repetition of positive self-statements such as "I know I can do this" and "I've got all the confidence I need right now" help the child overlearn these more adaptive statements.

IMAGINAL EXPOSURE TO THE ANXIETY-PRODUCING SITUATION

In this stage, children are reminded of their innate strengths, the coping skills they have learned, and the new perspectives or "new ways of looking at things" they have acquired. Strength and confidence are called into play. Assistance from any special helpers (images of favorite stuffed animals, favorite superheroes, or lucky charms) may be invited. Children may have a superhero that will appear on cue or a favorite animal or stuffed toy that they can focus on and rub or pet for added confidence. Imaginal exposure may be graduated in various ways according to the length of time of the exposure, the intensity of the exposure, or even the proximity of the child to the anxiety-producing situation.

Successive approximation becomes important as the child learns to tolerate increasing degrees of imaginal exposure in the trance state. For example, the child may have a fear of public speaking. A suggestion might be made that the child begin by entering the classroom where the oral presentation is to be given and to imagine that it is the actual day and time for which the presentation is scheduled. Feelings of relaxation and confidence are cued and activated by whatever means the child has previously chosen (a switch, a breath). The therapist then instructs the child to imagine walking into the classroom and being able to remain calm and confident.

The therapist may provide a detailed description of the imagined situation to help the child get into the scene. The therapist may then ask a series of questions that include "Can you see yourself in the class?" "Can you see the other children and the teacher?" and "Are you still calm and confident?" Further questions may focus on the child's confidence level: "What is your confidence level now?" and "Does it need to go higher?" The child can stop the scene anytime he or she wants. The therapist may ask, "Can we continue with the scene?" If the child indicates yes, the therapist might ask, "Can you see yourself walking up to the front of the class?" and "Are you ready to give the presentation?"

Any additional aides or coping devices can be elicited at this point, confidence switches can be turned on, and superheroes can be summoned to assist. The therapist may ask, "Have you turned on your confidence switch?" or "Can you see the Power Ranger there with you?" Additional techniques employ the use of controls or gauges to decrease the anxiety or feeling level. Children can be instructed to use a projection technique, such as watching themselves perform the feared task on a movie screen or TV. Suggestions can be made for them to use a remote control that allows them to turn down the feeling or intensity level. They can watch themselves perform the task with the feeling level on zero; with successive repetitions of the scene, the feeling level can be raised until it is at a full or normal level. A split-screen can be utilized whereby the children can see themselves at the beginning of the scene on one screen while the other screen shows them at the end of the scene being successful.

Further embellishment of the imaginal scene can help the child experience a positive outcome to the anxiety-producing situation. For example, the child may be told:

> Now imagine that you have just given a wonderful presentation and you were not anxious at all. As you finish your presentation, you notice that all of your classmates are looking at you with admiration and they really seem to have enjoyed your talk. You can tell by the looks on their faces that they found your talk to be interesting and entertaining. The teacher smiles at you and thanks you for your talk. Later, you receive a piece of paper from the teacher with your grade on it. You got an A for your presentation. Not only that, but you feel very good about yourself. You feel relieved and happy and you tell yourself you did a great job. Can you see this? Can you see your classmates and your teacher? Can you see your grade?

Whether it is accomplished in a single session or in several sessions, eventually the child reaches a point of full imaginal exposure and contact. Upon successful completion of this, the child is encouraged to give himself or herself positive reinforcement and make positive self-statements, perhaps congratulating himself or herself on doing a good job.

ASSIMILATION AND PREPARATION FOR THE FUTURE

In this stage, the most effective components of the previous stage should be verbally reinforced through repetition. It is also suggested to the child during the close of the hypnotic session that the coping skills and perceptual changes that have been learned can be used in the real-life, anxiety-producing situation. It is helpful to inform children that all of these newly acquired skills get better with practice. Suggestions that they will be able to remember to allow themselves to relax, even during routine situations, is important. At this point, the trance ends and the child returns to a waking state.

Although technically not a part of the hypnotic experience, but still an important part of the overall process, is the stage immediately following the return to a waking state. It is important to ask children about their experiences and reactions during the hypnotic state. Frequently, children will have had experiences that the therapist did not know were taking place. It is important that any negative experiences are revealed so that they can be prevented in the future. Positive experiences, especially ones that the therapist was not aware were taking place, are important and can be incorporated into future sessions. For example, the child may not have responded to the therapist's suggestion to go to a special room but instead entered a large field where he or she could run and skip; during the next session, the field may be incorporated into the trance experience.

It is important to provide positive reinforcement to children for what they achieved in the session, even if their hypnotic responsiveness appeared to be minimal. It is also important to repeat and reinforce, in a waking state, what was suggested and created in trance. Encouragement should be provided to continue to practice these skills. Expressing to children the belief that the therapist has confidence in them and their ability to master the stressful situation can be very powerful.

Of importance at this point is to encourage children to use and practice self-hypnosis at home. Simple instruction can be provided and children can be encouraged to practice self-hypnosis in therapy sessions until they feel competent with it. Suggestions can be made, such as "The more you practice self-hypnosis, the better you will be at doing it." It appears most effective when children perform self-hypnosis on their own without parental encouragement or reminders. Parents tend to view self-hypnosis in much the same way they do homework, and so power struggles can develop around it. The goal, of course, is to encourage self-hypnosis so it will become a primary coping skill or activity for the child that can be generalized to any stressful or anxious situation in the future.

Occasionally, a single session is all that is required to deal with a specific situation or problem, but frequently more sessions and further reinforcement are needed. The ultimate goal, of course, is to see how the child handles the actual anxiety-producing situation. A test situation is usually necessary to see if the child has improved and can now demonstrate mastery and control over the anxiety and the anxious reaction. Sometimes, improvement comes in small increments. The cognitive-behavioral aspects of treatment are frequently emphasized at this point, as gradual and progressive steps may be required before actual mastery is achieved. When success is achieved, the therapist should provide ample praise and reinforcement. It is important to help children feel good about themselves. The goal is to help children internalize self-confidence and apply it in future situations. Follow-up sessions are usually scheduled to ensure that children have maintained their gains.

SUMMARY

Hypnosis is effective in the treatment of children and adolescents with anxiety problems. Children have a natural affinity for hypnosis; they thoroughly enjoy fantasy and have a heightened capacity for imaginative involvement. Hypnotic techniques can be very engaging and even fun for children, and hypnosis can have a direct impact on their ability to acquire a sense of mastery and gain control of their problems. Children as a group make very good hypnotic subjects. There are differences in the way children respond to hypnosis as compared with adults, and it is important to be aware of these developmental differences. Hypnotic interventions, especially inductions, should be tailored to the individual child's developmental level and his or her particular interests. A sensitive yet straightforward approach is recommended when presenting hypnosis to children and their parents.

In developing and conducting hypnotic interventions, the therapist should be proficient in selecting appropriate inductions, deepening the trance level, and creating imaginative ways to enhance coping and expose the child to imaginal scenes for mastery of the anxiety-producing situation. Competency in these skills is derived directly from training, clinical supervision, and experience with hypnosis. Clinicians who wish to use hypnosis with children should be competent in child health care fields and have completed training in general hypnosis and specialized training in hypnosis with children. Hypnosis organizations, comprised of licensed health care professionals, can often offer excellent training opportunities. The American Society of Clinical Hypnosis is one such organization with an active training program. Clinicians who conduct hypnosis with children are typically assuming primary responsibility for the ongoing treatment of the child.

Because hypnosis utilizes relaxation and imagery, it is well suited for interventions that deal with anxiety. Although it can be integrated into many different therapies, its combination with CBT appears to be a good clinical match. CBT approaches and hypnosis can be combined to present desensitization activities involving imaginal exposure, rehearsal, and cognitive restructuring. Coping skills involving relaxation techniques, activation of confidence switches, and assistance from real or imaginary helpers can be included as part of the desensitization work. Eventually, self-hypnosis is taught and can become an effective coping skill for children to use outside of the therapy setting. Hypnosis has considerable potential as an effective, strategic intervention to help children overcome their fears and anxieties.

REFERENCES

Albano, A.M., & Chorpita, B.F. (1995). Treatment of anxiety disorders. *Psychiatric Clinics of North America, 18,* 767–784.

Allen, G.J. (1980). The behavioral treatment of test anxiety: Theoretical innovations and emerging conceptual changes. In M. Herson, R. Eisler, & P. Miller (Eds.), *Progress in behavioral modification.* New York: Academic Press.

Ambrose, G. (1961). *Hypnotherapy with children* (2nd ed.). London: Staples.

American Psychiatric Association. (1994). *Diagnostic and statistical manual of mental disorders* (4th ed.). Washington, DC: Author.

Anderson, J.C., Williams, S., McGee, R., & Silver, P.A. (1987). DSM-IV disorders in preadolescent children. *Archives of General Psychiatry, 44,* 69–76.

Baldwin, J.M. (1891). Suggestions in infancy. *Science, 17,* 113–117.

Barber, T., & Calverley, D. (1963). "Hypnotic-like" suggestibility in children and adults. *Journal of Abnormal and Social Psychology, 66,* 589–597.

Bates, B.L. (1993). Individual differences in response to hypnosis. In J.W. Rhue, S.J. Lynn, & I. Kirsch (Eds.), *Handbook of clinical hypnosis.* Washington, DC: American Psychological Association Press.

Bernstein, G.A., Borchardt, M.P., & Perwien, D.A. (1996). Anxiety disorders in children and adolescents: A review of the past ten years. *Journal of the American Academy of Child and Adolescent Psychiatry, 35,* 1100–1119.

Brown, D.P., & Fromm, E. (1986). *Hypnotherapy and hypnoanalysis.* Hillsdale, NJ: Erlbaum.

Caspi, A., Henry, B., McGee, R., Moffitt, T., & Silva, P. (1995). Temperamental origins of child and adolescent behavior problems: From age three to age 15. *Child Development, 66,* 55–68.

Gaffney, S. (1993). Hypnosis in the alleviation of anxiety. *Australian Journal of Clinical and Experimental Hypnosis, 21,* 19–25.

Golden, W.L. (1994). Cognitive behavioral hypnotherapy for anxiety disorders. *Journal of Cognitive Psychotherapy, 8,* 265–273.

Griffin, R.B. (1996). Hypnosis in the treatment of children with phobias. In F. Culbertson (Chair.), *Hypnosis with children: Science and practice.* Symposium conducted at the Annual Convention of the American Psychological Association, Toronto, Canada.

Griffin, R.B. (1997). Hypnotic techniques for children with anxiety problems. In F. Culbertson (Chair.), *Hypnotherapy with children and adolescents.* Symposium conducted at the Annual Convention of the American Psychological Association, Chicago.

Hilgard, J.R. (1979). *Personality and hypnosis: A study of imaginative involvement* (2nd ed.). Chicago: University of Chicago Press.

Hilgard, J.R., & Morgan, A.H. (1978). Treatment of anxiety and pain in childhood cancer through hypnosis. In F.H. Frankel & H.S. Zamansky (Eds.), *Hypnosis at its bicentennial: Selected papers.* New York: Plenum Press.

Hill, K.T. (1984). Debilitating motivation and testing: A major educational problem, possible solutions and policy applications. In R. Ames & C. Hines (Eds.), *Research on motivation in education.* New York: Academic Press.

Ialongo, N., Edelsohn, G., Werthamer-Larsson, L., Crockett, L., & Kellam, S. (1995). The significance of self-reported anxious symptoms in first grade children: Prediction to anxious and adaptive functioning in fifth grade. *Journal of Child Psychology and Psychiatry, 36,* 427–437.

Kendall, P.C., & Southam-Gerow, M.A. (1996). Long-term follow-up of a cognitive-behavioral therapy for anxiety disordered youth. *Journal of Consulting and Clinical Psychology, 64,* 724–730.

Kirsch, I., & Lynn, S.J. (1995). The altered state of hypnosis: Changes in the theoretical landscape. *American Psychologist, 50,* 846–858.

Kohen, D.P., & Olness, K. (1993). Hypnotherapy with children. In J.W. Rhue, S.J. Lynn, & I. Kirsch (Eds.), *Handbook of clinical hypnosis.* Washington, DC: American Psychological Association Press.

Kuttner, L. (1988). Favorite stories: A hypnotic pain-reduction technique for children in acute pain. *American Journal of Clinical Hypnosis, 21,* 148–169.

Kuttner, L. (1991). Special considerations for using hypnosis with young children. In W.C. Wester & D.J. O'Grady (Eds.), *Clinical hypnosis with children.* New York: Brunner/Mazel.

Linden, J. (1995). *The integration of hypnosis and psychotherapy with children and adolescents.* A workshop conducted for the Virginia Hypnosis Society, Richmond.

Morgan, A.H., & Hilgard, E. (1973). Age differences in susceptibility to hypnosis. *International Journal of Clinical and Experimental Hypnosis, 21,* 78–85.

Morgan, A.H., Hilgard, E.R., & Davert, E.C. (1970). The heritability of hypnotic susceptibility of twins: A preliminary report. *Behavior Genetics, 1,* 213–224.

Morgan, A.H., & Hilgard, J. (1978/1979). The Stanford hypnotic clinical scale for children. *American Journal of Clinical Hypnosis, 21,* 148–155.

Nath, S., & Warren, J. (1995). Hypnosis and examination stress in adolescence. *Contemporary Hypnosis, 24,* 119–124.

Olness, K., & Kohen, D.T. (1996). *Hypnosis and hypnotherapy with children* (3rd ed.). New York: Guilford Press.

Palsson, O. (1997). *An introduction to clinical hypnosis.* Workshop conducted at Eastern Virginia Medical School, Norfolk.

Piccione, C., Hilgard, E.R., & Zimbardo, P.G. (1989). On the degree of stability of measured hypnotizability over a 25-year period. *Journal of Personality and Social Psychology, 56,* 289–295.

Plotnick, A.B., & O'Grady, D.J. (1991). Hypnotic responsiveness in children. In W.C. Wester & D.J. O'Grady (Eds.), *Clinical hypnosis with children.* New York: Brunner/Mazel.

Sapp, M. (1991). Hypnotherapy and test anxiety: Two cognitive-behavioral constructs on the effects of hypnosis in reducing test anxiety and improving academic achievement in college students. *Australian Journal of Clinical Hypnotherapy and Hypnosis, 12,* 26–31.

Scheflin, A.W., & Shapiro, J.L. (1989). *Trance on trial.* New York: Guilford Press.

Schultz, J.R. (1991). Anxiety in children. In W.C. Wester & D.J. O'Grady (Eds.), *Clinical hypnosis with children.* New York: Brunner/Mazel.

Stanton, H.E. (1994). Self-hypnosis: One path to reduced test anxiety. *Contemporary Hypnosis, 11,* 14–18.

Wickramasekera, I.E. (1988). *Clinical behavioral medicine: Some concepts and procedures.* New York: Plenum Press.

Wilson, R. (1996). *Don't panic: Taking control of anxiety attacks.* New York: HarperCollins.

CHAPTER 11

Focusing as a Therapeutic Technique with Children and Young Adolescents

BART SANTEN

WE ARE all born with the capacity of organismic knowing and internal evaluating called focusing. However, as a consequence of life's demands, our access to that bodily wisdom tends to get lost. Eugene Gendlin, who introduced the concept of focusing in the field of psychotherapy (Gendlin, 1981; Gendlin, Beebe, Cassens, Klein, & Oberlander, 1968), described it as a skill that can be reconstituted by means of specific therapeutic interventions. He developed the focusing technique to enrichen other therapeutic methods and modalities with this facilitator of bodily experiencing.

Initially, focusing was taught almost exclusively to adults. It demonstrated its effectiveness in psychotherapy with cancer patients (Grindler, 1984), psychosomatic clients (Fuhrmann, 1992), incarcerated domestically violent men (Bierman, 1997), and others. Combinations with imagery (Olsen & Gendlin, 1970) and with dreamwork (Gendlin, 1986b) have been explored. However, the use of focusing in child and adolescent psychotherapy lagged behind. In 1988, Neagu concluded that "this experiential

384

procedure has been largely untried with children and adolescents" (p. 266). Today, the literature is still limited. The purpose of this chapter is to call attention to this technique to stimulate others to explore its effects in the context of other methods of child psychotherapy.

HISTORICAL ROOTS AND RESEARCH

Gendlin's (1962, 1964) thinking about personality change was inspired by the phenomenological and existential philosophers Husserl, Sartre, Buber, and Merleau-Ponty. His contribution to psychotherapy is historically rooted in humanistic psychology (Gendlin, 1994). In the fifties, Gendlin was trained by Carl Rogers. Rogers and Gendlin worked together closely for many years. Gendlin gave Rogers full credit for his influence. He described focusing as a special kind of client-centered psychotherapy (Gendlin, 1984).

Gendlin (1986a) learned from Rogers that

> if every bit of a client's expression is taken by the therapist, checked, verified, and then left to stand as it is, without editing, without "correcting" and "improving" and "interpreting," then this inner relief and space lets more and more come from inside until a self-propelled change rises in the client. (p. 10)

However, although still convinced that such a nondirective therapist attitude of accurate listening and responding is important as a baseline, Gendlin began to emphasize that the presence or absence of a *bodily* response in the client determines the success or failure of psychotherapy. Without that kind of resonance, the client stays stuck in "mere talking" and in repeating "the same old feelings." A research project on client-centered psychotherapy with schizophrenics (Rogers, Gendlin, Kiesler, & Truax, 1967) confirmed that a specific kind of teaching is necessary when a client is stuck or far from experiencing change. The Experiencing Scale was developed (Klein, Mathieu, Kiesler, & Gendlin, 1973) to predict success or failure from listening to the client's manner of talking—an expression of level of experiencing—during the first psychotherapy sessions. Gendlin began to develop focusing instructions to help clients with low levels of experiencing to improve that capacity. He made that skill of inner reference teachable.

THEORY

Focusing theory emphasizes the importance of bodily felt experiencing. Experiencing (Gendlin, 1962, 1964) is the reaction of a person's body to all that comes to it from either the outside world or the inner world. The body reacts to those stimuli with a constantly changing feeling quality, to be distinguished from sheer emotions and physiological sensations because it encompasses all felt aspects of a particular problem or situation. It is a bodily sensation with meaning. Most of the time, this bodily felt process does not get our attention; although basic to our psychological functioning, it operates at the edge of awareness. When someone experiences bodily, he or she connects with a vague—but clearly immediate—feeling. Gendlin calls this the felt sense of that problem or situation.

When a person is able to welcome a felt sense and to keep it company just the way it is, it will be ready to express itself. But frequently, people are unable to do this. Their structure-bound manner of experiencing makes them behave in a structure-bound way. Their crudely directive conscious self stands in the way. They need to learn how to connect with the edge of awareness, where the felt sense can be noticed. Focusing-oriented psychotherapy stresses and teaches this crucial distinction—between the usual conscious self and the felt sense—at every point of the therapeutic interaction.

Gendlin speaks of psychological health in terms of the quality of the interaction between a person's experiencing and current symbolizations (e.g., words, gestures, images). Health presupposes that preconceptual experiencing is in continuous interaction with those symbolizations. This enables felt senses to change and new facets of meaning to unfold. On the other hand, to the extent that experiencing is structure-bound it is curtailed: the interaction between perceptions, thoughts, verbal utterances, and actions on the one hand and their experiencing has been disturbed. Certain cues tend to trigger "the same old feeling" and the same habitual behavior, without doing justice to the complex reality of the situation. In a case of extreme structure-boundness, persons will not perceive their feelings and actions as "owned." They find themselves watching the movie of what just happens to happen. The absence of a feeling process coincides with the lack of a sense of self. Just as occurrences in the outside world may lack an interpretation based on bodily experiencing, this bodily felt process may lack a relationship with the self. The case examples in this chapter illustrate how a decrease of structure-boundness coincides with the recovery of the sense of self.

Focusing is the mental activity that leads to the reconstitution of experiencing (Gendlin, 1981, 1997; Santen & Gendlin, 1985). Focusing-oriented psychotherapy facilitates clients' acknowledgment of troublesome experiences at the depth of bodily sensing. To achieve this, clients need to be helped to stop being directive and coercive with themselves. They are helped to help their inner critic stop preventing their inward client (their felt sense) from speaking:

> Some people talk all the time, either out loud or at themselves inside, and they don't let anything directly felt form for them. Then everything stays a painful mass of confusion and tightness. . . . It is necessary for the person to keep quiet, not only outwardly, but also not to talk inside, so that a feeling place can form. (Gendlin, 1974, p. 231)

Clients are encouraged to become client-centered with their felt sense. All interpretations and interferences in the client's head are welcomed with respect, but shelved, given a separate space. This allows felt senses to form, open up, and speak. Focusing instructions enable the client to receive it all, including what comes from a felt sense (e.g., words, images, memories), "to stand next to it, to stand it, to bear it, to give it space, to be with it, to let it be, to maintain himself/herself next to it, to let it come more into focus if it will, but not to push it" (Gendlin, 1984, p. 91). This facilitator of change is reminiscent of a mechanism described by Franz Kafka (1935):

You could think: you must dispose of yourself, and yet—without contradicting that statement—stand your ground, in the awareness that you have acknowledged that. That would really mean pulling yourself out of the swamp by your own hair. (p. 55)

The case examples in this chapter illustrate how this can be guided.

PROCEDURE

Gendlin compares focusing with a motor. You wouldn't have a motor running without something (an avenue or method of psychotherapy) that it runs. It is the combination that makes sense.

The use of focusing in psychotherapy sessions—ranging from a minor focusing suggestion by the therapist to an emphasis on formal focusing teaching—can reconstitute a process once stopped. Gendlin (1997, p. 276) assumes that "the body has implied the next steps ever since, and will enact them if the interaction makes it possible." Conditions are shaped to release this enactment. The therapist can sharpen his or her sensitivity as to when such "next steps" could be facilitated. He or she may notice that clients talk (or play) round a subject without going into their feelings of it, although it seems obvious to the therapist that it is meaningful to them. Clients may say (or play) all they can say (or play) clearly, without knowing how to go on. They may tell/show nothing meaningful, though they seem to want to. They may mention bodily symptoms that indicate their structure-boundness. Or their bodily posture may show it.

When clients are stuck in such a way, focusing instructions can help them to get into their body "at the edge of not-yet-knowing what this is" (Weiser Cornell, 1996, p. 30) and unlock their feeling process. Gendlin teaches this in six steps (Durak, Bernstein, & Gendlin, 1997):

The teaching of the first step begins after checking if the focuser has the ordinary capacity for inwardly sensing the middle of his body. He is invited to sit straight and relax a bit. If he wants to, he can close his eyes.

(1) The focuser begins with learning a certain relation to a problem—neither swamped by its intensity, nor avoiding it. This is called "clearing a space"—inwardly making a place to stand clear of the problem, but still feeling it at its edge. "There" the focuser feels the whole problem, but he does not enter it or work on it. He sorts out the various problems he is carrying at the moment, and he adopts this relation to each of them.

(2) The focuser chooses a specific problem. It's "felt sense" is enabled to come. The "felt sense" differs from the familiar intense emotions. It is a holistic bodily quality, often slight in comparison. It is how the problem as a whole affects the middle of the body, usually an uneasy sense, unclear as to content but distinct in quality.

(3) The focuser finds a phrase or an image to express this bodily quality, for example: "heavy," "tight," "jumpy," "fluttery," or "a picture of stormy clouds"—some quality words, a phrase or an image.

(4) The resonance between felt sense and words or image is checked several times, to get a confirming bodily response.

(5) The "felt sense" is then directly "asked" by the focuser—much as one might ask another person—what is it about the problem that makes this quality? Another kind of question is: What does this felt sense want or need? The focuser learns ways to maintain this asking-contact with the unclear bodily quality of the problem, or to return to it if it is lost. If that can be done for a minute or so, there is often a "felt shift," a release, and along with it a small step of change in the problem.

(6) What comes at such a step needs to be quickly protected from the focuser's usual attitudes, thoughts, and self criticism. Feelings are distinguished from action choices. Such a step is not final—further focusing usually changes it further. It is important for the focuser to keep what came at such a step, so that further steps ensue. (p. 9)

INSTRUCTING CHILDREN AND YOUNG ADOLESCENTS ON FOCUSING

The kind of stepwise teaching of focusing just described cannot be used without modifications in therapy with children and young adolescents, because of the less abstract and conceptual nature of their thinking. Research on such unmodified teaching of focusing to children 10 to 14 years old (Heintz, 1997) shows that they get lost along the road. They are able to differentiate their bodily felt sense and to clear a space, but they appear to be overtaxed by the time they go to the rest of the focusing process. They cannot sustain their attention. They need more active ways.

Children need more anchors than most adults do. They respond better if they don't sit in the rather passive focusing posture adults use. More than adults, they should be taken by the hand. They can be invited to stand, walk, talk, listen to their own voices, write, or paint. They can record what they say and listen to their words. Their art can concretize and document the felt sense for them. The physical act of drawing can help their felt sense to move. Visual images thus created can remind them where the focusing process began and where it ended. These images can function as a tangible reference point to return to in later focusing sessions. Bodily felt images, experienced in the child's body, can be treated like a felt sense (Rappaport Friedman, 1988; Weiser Cornell, 1996). Equipped with such anchors, children and young adolescents can improve their focusing ability as well as older adolescents and adults can. The literature concerning such modifications with children (Iberg, 1997; Marder, 1997; Neagu, 1988; Santen, 1990; Santen & Koopmans, 1980; Yuba & Murayama, 1988) and with adolescents (Barba, 1985; Santen, 1988, 1993) explores these possibilities.

INFANTS: FOCUSING THROUGH MEDIATION

As mentioned before, newborn infants have full access to their felt senses. The sustainment of this experiential process presupposes empathic relating by parents, usually the mother. Through bodily and verbal reflection of feelings, nurturant acts, and attention focus, the mother can carry forward the infant's experiencing. She symbolizes the process of experiencing implicit in the infant's rhythms; when the infant withdraws, she retains a silent focus and allows the infant to experience himself or herself. Also, she verbalizes the infant's felt experience (Coyle, 1987).

The natural process may be disrupted if the mother gives structure-bound responses. Parents can learn to recognize their structure-boundness as reflected in their experiencing and their parental behavior. Improvement of their ability to attend to their felt sense of the parent-infant relationship can improve the quality of their empathic relating with their child. In this way, the child's focusing ability can be repaired (Boukydis, 1990).

PRESCHOOLERS AND LATENCY CHILDREN: FOCUSING BY PLAYING

As children grow older, many influences put their focusing ability under pressure. On the other hand, most children's focusing is nourished by their nonverbal play through metaphor. Play provides them a relatively safe way of symbolizing, without too much concern for external realities and judgments. When we see children switching to different toys and playing out another scenario with a slightly different theme, they are probably resonating by themselves. In this way, the child "gets at the 'all that,' the felt sense, going deeper into it" (Huebert, cited in Lou, 1997, p. 91).

By giving their children the opportunity to play, parents give them opportunities to carry their experiencing forward. If children have enough support and safety in daily life, and if their parents basically accept the right of their feelings to exist, there probably won't be any need for psychotherapy.

If play therapy is indicated, the therapist should always keep the following question in mind: "Will whatever I want or do help the inward sensing, make the safety or space for it, or will it crowd, impose, distract from the child's own track"(Gendlin, 1986a, p. 11). In most instances, explicit focusing instructions would disturb the child. Then the therapist can trust "that 'the body knows' and that it will bring along the suitable solutions if it gets the right space to clarify itself" (Meurs & Leijssen, 1997, p. 245). The therapist—with a safe and steady presence, therapeutic rules and materials—follows and reinforces the direction and meaning that presents itself in the child's play and in the other ways the child expresses himself or herself. The child moves on into whatever he or she needs to explore, and that is therapeutic because "those feelings that are acknowledged can

move to a better place, those that are denied get stuck and cause
all sorts of problems" (Lou, 1997, p. 91).

However, some children in play therapy need to be introduced
to focusing. During their therapy sessions, we can see them depict their emotion in a structure-bound way: anxious, swamped,
or avoidant, caged in repetitive play themes and/or repetitious
verbalizations. There seems to be no movement into a forward
direction:

> The lives of these children seem to be filled with difficult feelings
> that they dare not attend to or they would be completely over-
> whelmed, because they experience their outside world as unsafe.
> They do not have a safe place inside. Helping these children find
> or create such a place would be a crucial first step in their ther-
> apy. (Marder, 1997, p. 79)

When we provide such children with the safe structure of focusing interventions and help them to disengage somewhat from
what bothers them, without denying that it bothers, they can find
a sufficiently safe place for themselves and learn a way of self-
relating that initiates change.

MESSAGES TO CONVEY

Whenever the therapist introduces focusing, he or she should
communicate several characteristics of the process that the child
is asked to engage in.

The teaching of focusing has a directive element. It adds structure, and it interferes with the child's habitual ways. This cannot
be done without asking the child to invite some unpredictability.
The process has its own direction, its own reasons. Children are
invited to stop reasoning with it, although they might discover
the emotional reasons behind this reasoning or attacking. They
must counteract some of their own ways of keeping control. Although invited to keep their own pace, they are helped to get out
of their own way. On the other hand, they should experience that
focusing has a nondirective element as well. Nothing but the
child's own experiencing is facilitated. The therapist does not

oppose or comment on feelings/longings that the child's "own body center coming from himself" (Gendlin, 1979, p. 2) expresses, whatever those feelings/longings may say.

The therapist helps children to experience that focusing brings ego strength. At children's own pace, they are alternately encouraged to maintain and then let go of ego control. What comes at the edge of awareness can be used constructively by the child's ego. The therapist tries to make the child experience that, although a deep process is involved, it need not be hard and overwhelming work. The therapist does no pushing into the contents of "heavy stuff."

Focusing is the child's own process. Most of all, children need to learn a new way of self-relating. The therapist should communicate to children that they have both the freedom of sharing and the freedom of silence, as long as they share this one goal of their concerted action: the decrease of inner muteness within the child.

THE STEPS WITH CHILDREN

A child, focusing during therapy, is involved in one or more of the following mental acts: clearing a space, welcoming a felt sense, getting a handle on that felt sense, asking that felt sense questions, and/or protecting the change focusing brings by receiving that change in a welcoming way.

CLEARING A SPACE

At the beginning of focusing work, there are two possibilities: children begin to work on something they deliberately choose, or they await what demands their attention. In the second case, again there are two possibilities: one specific issue comes to the front, or all troublesome experiences the child's body carries clot together. If children seem to be stuck, but find no specific concern, they can do a first step of clearing a space: welcome and acknowledge each of the bothersome issues their body carries, by giving each of them a space of its own without going into it. Preschool and latency children are able to do this, but until children are about 10 years old, they cannot rely just on their imagination to achieve this. The younger the child, the more he or she needs to act, for example, actually put each "bad" feeling into a stuffed animal, or actually empty his or her pockets of all problems. Children can put their problems on the therapist's desk as if they were real objects, or they can draw themselves, surrounding their picture with cloud shapes. Each of these cloud shapes can be filled in with words for "one of the things that are happening." Children older than 10 years have other possibilities to clear space. They can play Complaint Department, putting each complaint on tape. Or they can find out what stands between themselves and their good feeling at the other side of the playroom by giving each troublesome experience size and shape by cutting it out on paper and putting all the pieces somewhere on the floor.

CASE ILLUSTRATION

Patsy (14 years old) mentions that it bothers her that she never feels cheerful. She is invited to sit on a chair. The therapist asks her to look at the bench on the other side of the room, and to imagine that the cheerfulness she misses is over there. She is asked to find out what bothers her that interferes with cheerfulness. When she looks at the bench and checks inside, "not belonging anywhere . . . feeling alone" appears to be the bodily "no, not fine" response. She writes this down on a piece of paper and puts that note on the floor on a place where it somehow feels right to put it right now. Then she asks herself, "If this were somehow all right, how would I feel inside?" She waits and sees how she would feel. Then a second package comes up connected with "feeling inferior," as she says. When she puts a note about this concern on the floor in the same way, she looks at both, then chooses to focus on the first feeling she mentioned (Santen, 1990, p. 784).

Whatever method has been chosen, children should respond with some bodily release. If no sense of free space results, children may need to find their "background feeling" (always a bit sad; always . . .). When space has been cleared for that background feeling as well, a bodily release is likely to result.

When all this has been done, the child can choose one "package" to welcome its felt sense. Most often, there is no general round of clearing a space. Children may struggle with a specific problem or situation. The therapist joins them right there. Children are helped to make a place to stand clear of that problem as a first step toward the welcoming of its felt sense. The therapist helps them to disidentify somewhat from the "something" inside their body that might want to say something. This enables children to be with their feeling from a somewhat different perspective. They can witness their feeling without having to deny its intensity (Weiser Cornell, 1996).

If children's structure-boundness is not too invalidating, they can clear a space easily when they turn their attention inside. The therapist makes them understand that they can attend to a place in their body that can speak and be listened to.

CASE ILLUSTRATIONS

Sarah (6 years old) is very upset about being teased by a friend. That bad feeling doesn't seem to go away. The therapist asks her if she can find that bad feeling inside. Sarah does this easily. The therapist suggests to her a different way of relating to it: to listen to it in a welcoming way and see if it has anything to tell Sarah from its newly cleared space (Marder, 1997, p. 76).

James (10 years old) doesn't want his parents to help him with a problem he has. He doesn't know why. He just doesn't feel like doing it. That feeling is cleared as a place that can speak and be listened to. "You don't know why," the therapist says, "but you can feel it that you don't want them to come, right?" When James confirms this, the therapist continues: "You can just keep your mind on that feeling, and it will probably tell you more about why" (Iberg, 1997, p. 70).

If children's structure-boundness boxes them in too much, they need additional anchors to achieve disidentification.

CASE ILLUSTRATIONS

Ronald (12 years old) notices that he has short flashes in his head. Thoughts reach awareness, but they are repressed so fast inside that, until now, he has never given it particular attention. What he refers to as "the devil" is short cut by "the angel" immediately. The therapist asks Ronald to write a story called "The Devil and the Angel." He asks Ronald to record it on a tape recorder, to listen to it silently and to wait for a bodily response. Hearing himself through his ears makes it easier for Ronald to check inside and stay concentrated (Santen, 1990, p. 791).

Hester (14 years old) complains that she has "a stone" in her head. The therapist asks her to draw that bodily felt image, welcome it, and show it to her body to wait for a bodily response. Looking at it, Hester begins to talk about "dark territories" and "a kind of labyrinth." The therapist asks her to close her eyes to enable herself to imagine that stone at a distance that feels right for her. A feeling process, until now inhibited by frozen rage, can start from this point (Santen, 1990, p. 787).

When children need more anchors in the beginning, they usually also need more structure during following steps, until their feeling process becomes more self-propelling.

WELCOMING A FELT SENSE, GETTING A HANDLE ON THAT FELT SENSE, RESONATING THAT HANDLE

The child now stands clear of his or her problem. The therapist helps the child welcome its bodily felt sense. The child can welcome fresh words or images originating from this bodily felt sense. Whatever handle word or handle image comes will be matched with the feeling inside once again to see if it fits. New words or a changing image might be the result. If the child's inner critic interferes inside with critical comments or with "feelings about feelings," these are welcomed in a friendly way and shelved to a separate space. The feeling place must keep its freedom to breathe.

CASE ILLUSTRATIONS

Excitedly and fearfully, Ronald listens to his own story on tape. The story includes no reference to feelings. Ronald's sentences ("You must kick a child," the devil says; "don't do it," says the angel.") function as a handle, awakening the bodily felt sense of this ongoing struggle. They resonate from the outside with the felt sense, stirring a bodily talking-back. When Ronald begins to write again, this writing shows that his experiencing has been carried forward. The new handle words refer increasingly to a felt process.

Hester imagines looking at her stone. The therapist helps her find a bodily response by inviting her to ask inside how she feels when she thinks of the existence of that stone. Hester attends inwardly. The stone functions as a handle. It changes, becomes lighter. Little flowers appear around the edge. Hester goes back and forth between looking at the handle and turning her attention to the middle of her body. The body responds with new handle words: "An island, surrounded by boiling tar . . . a whirling mass." The unfreezing of a feeling process has begun.

ASKING

Children can be invited to ask open questions to the felt sense ("What's the crux of this?" "What needs to happen?" "Where does this get me the worst?"). This can help them to get to the "more" that might be there. This kind of curious asking-followed-by-waiting can help them maintain their respectful inner attitude. However, as can be seen in the case illustrations in this chapter, a merely verbal way of asking doesn't meet the child's needs. To deframe their habitual pattern, children may ask their felt sense if there is an image that represents it in some way. If the child already painted a bodily felt image of a felt sense, he or she can be invited to paint "the heart" of it, or to paint it "a thousandfold enlarged"; when the child has painted "the black," he or she can be invited to paint what is called "into the black." Such new images may resonate with the felt sense and initiate a felt shift with new handle words, new insights.

This waiting for a bodily talking-back needs time. Any interference by the child's mind (quick answers, criticism, feeling on top of feelings) is traced by the therapist, guided apart; the waiting is for a bodily answer.

RECEIVING

Children should get time to shelter what has come from their deep source. They should neither run away from it, nor go into it. There is no need to act on what has become clear now, no need to criticize it, no need to rush to the next thing. Gendlin (1979) compares this with pitching a tent, preparing to stay for a while.

Neagu (1988) calls this "a new biointegrative way of living with the problem" (p. 272). The therapist protects the child against any inclination to hurry on, inviting the child to write some of the newfound words on paper, to walk or sit with them for some days by keeping them in a pocket. Thus, the child's body gets the time, space, and protection to adapt to what's new.

CASE ILLUSTRATIONS

Sarah: Play Therapy Combined with Focusing

The following case illustration was prepared by Marder (1997), who conducted the play therapy.

In many ways, Sarah (6 years old) was a well-functioning child, relatively at home in the world of feelings. However, after a difficult period including a custody battle between her parents, who had divorced two years earlier, she was displaying many symptoms of anxiety: she wet the bed, "played with herself" a great deal, had a difficult time making decisions, and seemed to feel that she needed to be perfect. Most of all, she was reluctant to express negative feelings or anger.

The therapist saw Sarah for a total of 29 sessions; four of these were focusing sessions. The therapist described them as pivotal in the psychotherapeutic process.

From the beginning, Sarah fluctuated in her ability to tolerate her more difficult feelings. When Sarah first entered the playroom, she focused on a poster of children displaying many different emotions. The therapist asked her to point to a picture "that you sometimes feel like," and she pointed to a sad face, saying, "I felt sad when Mommy and Daddy got divorced." When the therapist asked her to draw a picture of this, however, she drew a bright, happy picture before talking about her sad, frightened feelings. After some time, apparently tired of all this emotion, Sarah asked to play. She played creatively and with great energy; one could see the health and vitality that existed side by side with her struggles.

During the next eight sessions, the therapeutic medium was individual play therapy. The therapist soon realized that Sarah was struggling with both angry, aggressive feelings and a desire to be coddled and babied. She alternated between expressing these aggressive and regressive feelings and retreating to the safer although highly creative artistic play that she so much enjoyed. Sarah's true self seemed to be struggling to break through her protective identity of a "cute little girl."

During the next few weeks, Sarah seemed to retreat slightly from dealing openly with her feelings, and the techniques the therapist regularly used in therapy to elicit feelings from children didn't seem to be sufficiently effective. However, she was clearly grappling with aggressive feelings: she made pretty little objects out of Play-Doh, finished a Play-Doh man, and at the end of the session smashed it with her fist, saying, "You're dead." Outside of the play therapy situation, her experiencing was becoming slightly less structure-bound; her mother reported she was more open emotionally. However, she continued the by now familiar pattern of aggression followed by retreat.

The following week, the tenth session, the therapist introduced focusing instructions. Sarah was very upset about being teased by a friend at school. The therapist asked Sarah if she'd like her to show Sarah something the therapist sometimes did when she had a bad feeling that wouldn't go away. She asked Sarah if she could find the bad feeling inside; Sarah did this easily. Then the therapist suggested to her a different way of relating to that troublesome experience, by listening to it in a welcoming way and seeing if it had anything to tell her. The words that followed ("He didn't mean it") may have reflected blocking by an inner critic, but her lightened, changed demeanor suggested the possibility of a genuine experiential shift. She seemed done with the issue and wanted to play.

The next two sessions, Sarah absorbed herself in playing again. Then came a session that was critical in terms of her use of focusing to free up some of her stuck feelings. Sarah's mother reported that Sarah had been clingy and tearful recently. The therapist tried to teach a different way of self-relating again. "Sarah," she said, "can you find that bad feeling inside you?" "It's hiding," Sarah replied after a moment. The therapist handed her a stuffed animal and tried to help her find a way of relating to the feeling from a comfortable distance. "Can you see if it will hide in the teddy bear?" Sarah did try. She placed the bear next to the bad feeling in her stomach and then up to her ear. She was able to find a handle for the feeling: "It's about too many things happening." However, she seemed unable to move further; it stayed tight. When the therapist asked what these many things were, Sarah replied that she forgot.

The therapist then began teaching clearing a space. She reached over for a drawing pad and some magic markers. She drew a person with a sad face, glanced at Sarah, and began to sketch the pattern of her clothes. Intrigued, Sarah grabbed the markers and began energetically coloring the person. The therapist quickly drew six cloud shapes in a circle around the person and said, "These are for all the things that are happening." Sarah filled in the circles, almost all on the theme of "not enough time." The therapist asked her mother whether there was any way of doing anything about these problems. She readily agreed and found a solution, and Sarah took the initiative in making some suggestions.

Sarah seemed to be gaining a stronger sense of herself; her mother reported that she seemed less invested in pleasing people lately. Sarah also demonstrated this during her play time; she made hundreds of Play-Doh "worms" and then gleefully informed the therapist that she was a witch and therefore would have to eat all the worms. She evidently was feeling a little freer inside.

Another crucial focusing session came the following week. Sarah reported that she had been clearing a space at home. "It took six animals to take out all the bad feelings," she explained. That day, however, she felt nervous, sad, and scared, because a friend had encouraged her to play with matches. Sarah said that the nervous feeling was very deep inside and would not talk. Again, a focusing intervention was used to facilitate the process. Sarah was asked to draw a picture of the nervousness. She drew a large picture of a sad-faced little girl and drew four dark spots on her body, which represented the feelings. The therapist drew some circles for her. Sarah took a toy gun, put it to her body, shot the gun into her hand, then held her hand up to her ear. She did this four times, filling in the circles with her problem feelings, but she was still caught up. The scared feeling about her friend was still deep inside and would not come out. The therapist invited her to keep that feeling company in its hiding place, and ask it every now and then if it wanted to say anything.

A lot of change was reported between these focusing sessions. Sarah became more assertive. Angry feelings about her mother clarified themselves and were expressed directly toward her. Sarah's increasingly messy but still creative play suggested another step toward being freer inside.

Several weeks later, another focusing session took place. Sarah was in a bad mood and didn't want to talk about it. In the following conversation, the therapist continued teaching her the focusing attitude of noncoercive inward attending and receptivity toward whatever was stirring inside. Thus, Sarah was helped to allow herself to be more receptive to her own feelings.

THERAPIST: Sarah, you can let the feeling talk just to you; you don't have to tell me and your mother if you don't want to. How about that?

SARAH: Okay. (quiet for a minute, then pointing to her stomach)

THERAPIST: What does it feel like?

SARAH: Jumpy and angry; it's mad and it doesn't want to talk to anyone.

THERAPIST: Can you try being very nice and friendly to it?

SARAH: No, I'm mad at it.

Sarah was then helped to realize and accept that she could make room for both the "jumpy and angry" feeling and the "mad," nonaccepting feeling that seemed to be on top of it. The therapist explained that there was plenty of room inside to have both feelings and that the jumpy, angry feeling probably had a good reason for feeling that way. By separating out the "mad at it" part of herself, she allowed room for the feeling underneath to breathe and speak, and this carried her experiencing forward. Her jumpy and angry feeling expressed itself more fully now. "It sure does have a good reason for feeling jumpy and angry! People have been bugging me and pushing me on the playground all day." Then Sarah reported an exciting discovery: "I think that part of the reason I'm so mad is that I didn't get to say good-bye to Mom in the morning." She turned to her mother, who had been asleep that morning, and told her that her stepfather didn't allow her to wake her mother up. Sarah's mother promised that she would tell Sarah's stepfather that it was okay for Sarah to come in and say good-bye in the morning. After this, Sarah insisted that her mother come into the playroom, where Sarah engaged in more witch-stomping. Outside of therapy, Sarah continued expressing anger more frequently than before.

Things seemed to be winding down. Few difficulties remained to report. Sarah's focusing ability had improved considerably. She seemed to be more client-centered with her bodily felt sense. Her mother reported that Sarah was in touch with a 3-year-old child inside herself, a child much angrier and sadder than the Sarah she had known up to now. During the twenty-eighth session, Sarah reported that when she was playing a game with her family, her 3-year-old was sad that she wasn't winning. Sarah had talked to the 3-year-old, she said, and had told her "I know you feel sad, but maybe you'll win the next game." Then she felt better. The 3-year-old also wet the bed whenever Sarah took off her absorbent underwear. When the therapist suggested that Sarah ask the 3-year-old what she could do to help, the 3-year-old said that she was scared and that Sarah couldn't help. The therapist asked her what she would like to say to her 3-year-old now. Sarah told her that she felt sad and wanted her to stop. The 3-year-old replied that she would try. Sarah was satisfied.

At this point, the therapist felt that Sarah, with the assistance of her mother, was becoming her own therapist. She no longer needed psychotherapy.

Roger: Imagery Combined with Focusing

When Roger was 9 years old, his grandfather died. Roger, who lived in Austria at that time, attended the funeral in the Netherlands. Three months later, the family settled in Holland again.

Roger's inability to cope with these overwhelming situations caused a considerable increase of his structure-boundness. He got caught up in obsessive-compulsive thinking and ritualistic behavior. Although desperately trying to keep control, he became the impotent observer of his free-floating aggressive thoughts. As time passed, Roger sank into a depression.

When Roger was 12 years old, I was one of the people who advised his admission to a clinic for psychiatric treatment. Roger knew that. When I became his individual psychotherapist several months later, he told me that he hated me. I listened to his strong emotions and we talked about what had happened to him in the far and recent past. But Roger seemed disconnected from what he said. He was caught up in arousal and the sheer emotion of fury. Week after week, his words kept reinforcing his narrowed emoting that ran off with him. Roger seemed detached from a feeling process. He habitually oriented himself toward my presence instead of sensing inwardly. His outer talking needed to be interrupted and replaced by a way of self-relating. I decided to introduce focusing instructions to promote such reorientation.

During the seventh session, I asked Roger to try a way of clearing a space by means of painting: to paint how he was feeling in the middle of his body. Because his head might interfere, I stressed that there was only one but crucial criterion: a bodily felt stirring that signaled "yes, that's how it feels like" when he stepped back after painting and went back and forth between looking at what he had painted and letting that brush along the meaning place in the middle of his body.

Roger chose to paint what he called "feeling unsafe." But he didn't paint that feeling. Instead, he stayed in his head and painted what he saw as a cause of that feeling. So I asked him to shelve all inner talking ("I want to smash something," "I am homesick," "Why am I ill?," "I want to be with my grandfather and also with my grandmother," "What time is it?"), to write each of these thoughts down on a separate piece of paper as soon as it appeared, and go on painting. For a moment, this brought Roger closer to his felt sense: he painted a constricted bird. But after this apparent symbolization of a felt sense of constrictedness, censorship took over again. Roger wrote: "The free bird who doesn't need to worry about anything. Maybe he doesn't have friends, but he is happy."

In spite of that, Roger gave his next painting the name "Sensitive." He painted a smiling boy who had a small, sad-looking boy in the middle of his body. The small boy cried and looked at his crying heart. Roger referred to his painting as follows: "A second person inside has the same heart as he himself. Their heart cries. But only the second person shows it. The big person is 15. The small person is 9 years and 15 years at the same time. For 6 years already the big one plays puppetry, while the small one does the crying inside."

In the following sessions, I asked Roger to paint "the crying inside." He painted a big crying heart, partially grounded in a black basis. He enlarged that black basis in his next painting, which was followed by another one which he called "the anger in the black." When he checked in the middle of his body how this "anger in the black" felt, the phrase "anger like a hard stone" came up as a new handle. This anger apparently protected him against what might await him in the black. Meanwhile, experiencing was carried forward. The act of verbalizing the existence of that stone seemed to crack that shield a little.

Roger became more frightened. He reported that images were running in his head. One of these concerned "people who are dear to me dying." "The button switches it off," he explained, "so that I cannot see this picture." Although he didn't allow himself to keep that picture company, he began to reveal why he needed to run away from what could be found inside: "When I feel miserable I try to distract myself. And then I come here. Then that shield seems to be gone. Without that shield I feel lonely. Feeling that you are alone is one of the most dreadful feelings. I feel a bit guilty when I feel that I am alone. The picture of my parents keeps me upright."

Getting closer to experiencing his "disloyal" feelings toward his parents, Roger felt panic. He told his parents that he wanted to terminate therapy. His parents encouraged him to go on, which gave him more space to receive what would come, whatever it would be. He went on with his introspection: "Somehow, there is no talent for trying out what you say. There's a wall in between. I resist without knowing that I do it."

Roger had sorted out something inside resisting next to his "I" that wanted to carry on. His "I" seemed to be ready to explore his resisting wall, which should be done with a truly accepting (client-centered) and welcoming attitude. I decided to ask Roger to be with that wall and welcome its felt sense. Focusing was combined with imagery to make it easier for him to turn his attention to a level of bodily talking-back. The imagined wall would function as a handle, like a base camp from where Roger would be able to make his trips toward welcoming the felt sense. Because I let him know that he could always return to the front of the wall, his openness to receiving whatever these trips would bring was facilitated.

Gendlin might have used the following metaphor: "Make a door. Keep your hand on the doorknob. You can later open it a little or not. You know where it all is. It can wait." I asked Roger to stand upright, to close his eyes, to imagine the wall somewhere in front of him, and to be with it for a while in a welcoming way. From his separate standpoint—the wall there, Roger here—Roger cleared a space. He saw a red wall, surrounded by black. He got in touch with his felt sense. "It is silent there. I feel lonely," he sighed. Roger stepped toward the imaginary wall, touched it with his hands. I asked him to go back and forth between being with the wall this way and being with that sense of "lonely." With eyes closed, Roger stepped to the right. He waited close to the black. It felt "even more lonely now." He stayed with it for a minute.

The next week, Roger stood in front of the wall again. He stepped aside till he had the surrounding black in front of him. Pictures referring to the past began to run "like a movie." Roger stopped that film by bowing his chin downward, turning his attention to the middle of his body. He began to talk. It seemed that a hurtful place was opening up: "A man is running across the street . . . I see my grandfather . . . My grandmother is sitting in her chair."

Roger began to breathe heavily. He continued: "I see a brown burning cross in the church . . . My grandfather committed to the flames, the day when he died . . . My brother and I have to step ahead . . . We have to stand in front of the coffin . . . My grandfather is wearing black shoes . . . All people are crying . . . Me too."

Repeating a deeply felt spot quietly and slowly can be helpful to discover the broader bodily sense from where it comes. So I reiterated sentences Roger said while he was crying. They resonated with his feeling place.

ROGER: Grandfather's eyes are closed.
THERAPIST: His eyes are closed.
ROGER: It seems that he sleeps.
THERAPIST: It seems that he sleeps.
ROGER: I touch his leg.
THERAPIST: You touch his leg.
ROGER: I touch his right leg.
THERAPIST: It is his right leg that you touch.

Roger began to speak more fluently from his hurt place. He addressed the image of his grandfather, told him that he wanted him to live. He repeated it over and over. Each time, I reiterated what he said. Gradually, Roger became more peaceful. "I really wish I could be with you," he sighed. "I wish you were here. That is what I want."

Roger returned to the front of the wall. He checked inside and looked at the wall. He noticed a change. The lower part of the red wall had turned gray.

The next session, Roger met the wall again. This time, the provided structure made him connect with his anger. The anger was locked up in a "bowl." When he released some of that anger in his imaginative space, he realized how frightened he was of all that anger inside.

During this process of unraveling, Roger encountered what he called "lots of strings, like tangled snakes." I used these bodily felt images as a handle to let him clear a space again. He addressed each of these snakes separately, put each one somewhere in front of him, in a space of its own. He checked each one inside to find out if it was on the right place right now. He took some time and reported: "It is quiet . . . As if everything is fine . . . well ordered . . . As if I have done very well . . . Just as if I have no worries . . . I feel a bit set free . . . as if all thoughts have been taken out of my head."

The fact that he entered this good space for a while helped him to become aware that "loose fears, piled up and pounding together, give a heavy feeling in my stomach . . . All black . . . Just like: once there was something, and more and more added to it without me noticing it . . . It just clotted together."

The following week, Roger wanted to clear a space toward each of the snakes again. He addressed one of them, looked at it, and turned his attention inside to ask if what the snake represented was connected with any part of his (Roger's) life. The body said back that the snake reminded of "Austria." When Roger kept these words company for a moment—"snake Austria . . . snake Austria"—to see if there would be a bodily stirring, a sense of "some sadness" came, "a very special feeling that I almost never have: a feeling of goodbye." Because Roger's inner critic made him hasten to add that this feeling was "impossible" and "far-fetched," I helped him to shelve these feelings by asking them kindly to go aside and let the felt sense be. Roger returned to his fragile spot: "I ended up there . . . And suddenly everything was gone . . . I was forced to leave Austria."

Roger realized that he had truly felt at home there. He stayed with that understanding and waited, until he resumed his talking from that feeling place: "It hurts . . . I was feeling fine there, and then suddenly displaced . . . Suddenly I had to start all over . . . I wish I could live here peacefully also, but I have to be a little tense all the time."

Roger cried. His anger grew: "I feel fucked up that I had to leave there . . . I am angry that I—goddammit—had to leave there."

Roger had begun to acknowledge this other "disloyal" hurt. The self-propelling of his feeling process had come to the point where he could share these feelings with his parents. "I didn't know that all that anger was there," Roger commented two weeks later. "This week I told my mother that I was angry at my parents. I felt a bit ashamed about it, but my mother said that she understood." This new action step coincided with a fundamental inner change. "Formerly," Roger said, "it was as if a feeling kept biting at me, nagging, sticking to me. It wouldn't go away. As if I was sitting in a bowl. It made me depressed and, goddammit, go away!" Roger described that formerly he had found himself to be either stuck in the "quicksand" of "bad feelings" or in the "arrestment," because he locked himself up to prevent being swamped: "Now there is a quiet position in myself. Sometimes that bad feeling tries to get me, but I don't sink away anymore. Now a feeling can stand above that bowl.

I don't have to arrest myself anymore and think: 'I am stuck'; now I can think and feel: 'I can go anywhere.' "

Roger's experiencing had developed beyond the former structure-bound state of obsession and depression. As he reported, he actively protected his "quiet" space at moments when he felt more vulnerable.

Some weeks later, Roger's parents confirmed recent considerable changes. They said that Roger became more authentic. He took more responsibility for his feelings. The gloomy cloud around him was gone. When Roger was asked what therapy had meant to him, his answer confirmed "the actual continuation of processes that once were stopped" (Gendlin, 1997, p. 276): "It has become easier to say goodbye," he summarized. "When I was with that wall I learned how to deal with that. When I am at home on Sundays now, it has become easier for me to say goodbye and return to the clinic."

Rachel: Art Work Combined with Focusing

When Rachel was 13 years old, she was sent for psychiatric residential treatment because of severe conversion symptoms. Most of her past had been colored by fear and social invalidation. Increasingly, Rachel stayed in bed. She became anorectic. Chronic somatic complaints and extreme fatigue kept her away from school since she was 11.

Soon after her admission to the clinic, individual therapy started. Back then, Rachel didn't realize that she had been abused sexually for a number of years.

During our first therapy sessions, Rachel seemed distracted (Santen, 1993). She was evidently caught up in a state of self-alienation. At first, when she mentioned the existence of an "impervious cloud of real feelings," I tried to guide her in finding handle words referring to that experience. But she could not break through the fog.

Because of Rachel's severe state of dissociation, during the following months, I introduced several ways of clearing a space as entrances for her to reconnect with her felt sense.

To provide her with an anchor to let her find handle words, I offered her pages with quotations I had selected from Franz Kafka's diaries and letters, quotations referring to Kafka's own struggle with self-alienation and dissociation. I asked her to read them and to underline phrases, if any, that felt familiar to her. This way of clearing a space, reading a symbolization out there, followed by checking inside if anything stirs in response, enabled Rachel to get in touch with her frightening world in a bearable way. "I try to tell about something located in my bones, which can only be experienced in my bones," Rachel marked. "Maybe it is nothing but that fear. Fear extended to everything. Constricting fear of using a word. This fear is maybe not just fear, but also a longing for something which is more than all that's frightening" (Kafka, 1985, p. 189). Rachel searched for contact. Apparently, behind her fear a longing was hidden. "The road I want to go I cannot go on my own feet" (p. 188). She marked that sentence as well, and that seemed to be another signal. Besides that, she let me know that I threatened her weak identity. "When I'm alone I'm still alive," she underlined, "but when someone comes to visit me he literally kills me" (p. 177).

A few weeks later, Rachel was mentally distracted again. For that reason, I introduced another way of clearing a space. I asked her to "disappear" behind herself by moving to another chair, behind the one she was sitting on, so that she could actually be more distant from me, in order to find a more suitable relationship toward her felt sense. When she moved, I asked her to check inside to see if anything was coming up. "I scream," she said, but she couldn't scream. To help her stay in touch, once again I switched to another way of clearing a space. I asked her to paint in a focusing way: to paint that scream, and to take some steps backward to enable herself to check inside to see if what she had painted really fit in with her felt sense (Santen, 1988, 1990).

Rachel painted: red and black scratches, blue dots. She wrote THE SCREAM above that picture. When I asked her, she took some steps backward again. She was here, and all that concerning the scream was out there. She looked at what she had made, waited silently for any handle words referring to the felt quality of what she had visualized. "It is the scream of all that distress," she said. "It is located in that wall . . . in that cage." I let her taste these handle words—"wall" and "cage"—out loud, to let them resonate with her feeling place inside. She found that "cage" fit the best. So she wrote "I cry in the cage" above her painting and completed it with a frame in red and black.

A week later, Rachel painted the scream again. To promote an attitude of "asking," to evoke the question "Where does all this distress get me the worst?" I asked Rachel to enlarge the painting. She pointed to the blots she made and called them tears. She mentioned that her inner "voices" kept her from crying. When I guided her in putting these interfering critics slightly aside—by letting her write down each statement of a voice on a separate paper as soon as it came up—this made room for her felt sense connected with those tears. Something got released. She verbalized a felt shift. "A collapsed world," Rachel said, and when she had said that she noticed that her feelings had shifted. What she had painted, she said, didn't fit any longer with what she experienced right now. So she painted again, and this evoked new verbalizations. "An injured flower treaded by a foot," she added. An aggressor treading her had entered the scene. Rachel took some time to receive what had shifted along with the picture she had drawn. She created some distance again, and noticed: "My life has been treaded under foot . . . I just don't know who has done it." Some self-propelling of her feeling process manifested itself. When Rachel had written down these last words, she added the word "destroyed" to clarify what she meant. Simultaneously, as in a trance, she eliminated the word "I" from her text. Evidently, the flaring up of feeling took turns with censoring interventions.

Once again, I asked Rachel to clear a space and welcome her felt sense. She took steps backward and looked at her painting. This time, censorship didn't defeat her emerging ability to feel. Instead, censorship gave way to an authentic sigh: "I know that I shouldn't say it, but I find it unfair. I am almost fourteen and I don't know yet what living means. I only looked. I also want to live myself."

Immediately, this expression of Rachel's self was responded to by interfering "voices." She wrote down what they said on the space reserved for those expressions. Their echo resounded in what she wrote: "finds it unfair" and "also wants it herself."

During the two months that followed, I helped Rachel to sustain basically the same pattern. Each time when we met, I let her start with painting a bodily felt image as a handle; she let that resonate with her felt sense and cleared a good space to receive whatever came up in response. I showed her her last painting, asked her to pick up the handle word(s) that had come up subsequently, and let her use them as a point of reference for a new painting. In this way, a sequence of emotionally related explications originated. Each one was processed in a focusing way. The self-propelled feeling process began to flow.

Rachel and I looked at her last painting. "Destroyed," I said, to evoke that handle for her. "Would you mind painting that?" Initially, something inside Rachel made her object. Then she took her brush. Up to now, her red stripes had been painted stiffly; from now on they were brushed in more vividly. Rachel almost couldn't bear looking at what she had visualized: "Just imagine: when it's like that in your body it is frightening. Destroyed in my thinking; horrible, like an earthquake in the head. Bang! Suddenly everything is gone."

Rachel discovered that this destruction of awareness had taken place many years ago. She tried to capture how she had suffered from self-alienation. By doing that, she took another step in the gradual process of restoring her sense of self: "I am fed up with . . . that when I do something I don't know what I say, that I cannot be myself. Then I say totally different things, things that don't belong to me. That makes one desperate; anyway, it does to me. I am just fed up with being mentally in pieces."

A few days later Rachel added: "It is as if I'm bursting. I try to let it come out, but I don't succeed. I am utterly phoney. I am just like a doll. It is as if you are not there, as if something else presses the button and then you start to talk."

Once again, Rachel painted the scream with an "asking" approach. This time, she painted a thousandfold enlarged how "terrifying-and-beyond-description" it was inside. She painted a big black mass. Red and blue stripes whirled around. But when Rachel had gone several steps backward to welcome her felt sense, she became aware of an another felt shift. Reality appeared to be even more heavy now. Rachel painted again. The whole painting appeared in black, framed in a red cage. Rachel stepped back. She checked inside, looked at her painting, and got in touch with her felt sense of all that seemed to be beyond description. The handle word "apathetic" came up. But when she tasted that word out loud, to let it resonate with the feeling in the middle of her body, she began to realize that this so-called lack of sensitivity was her defensive reaction to a burden heavier than she could bear: "It is so much that I can't bear it anymore, but I have no choice, so I try to make myself a little bit indifferent."

Rachel was desperate. She didn't know how to cope with this situation. However, the reconstitution of her feeling process and her increased ability to verbalize what she felt paved the way for a frightening but crucial discovery. The next time Rachel entered my office, she indicated another felt shift. She stated that she hated herself. I asked her to write down "I hate myself" at the top of a new big piece of paper. A few moments later, without noticing it herself, she hid the word "I" behind a black arrow. At the same time, Rachel revealed her inner reality at a new level, with far-reaching consequences. By painting "I hate myself," Rachel succeeded in clarifying the deadlock of the self-alienated state she found herself in. Two identical females—only the color of their skirts distinguished them from each other—appeared tied together. Their backs were sticking in a pie. Handcuffs chained their wrists as well as to each other. Their thoughts were merging continuously. Their black hearts were broken, their bellies winced. A cross all over the painting indicated that, as Rachel said, "almost nobody understands this. In fact, this misery is not allowed to exist. However, it does." At this point, Rachel revealed that she experienced herself to be composed of 10 persons.

Having received this, Rachel and I turned our attention back to the two painted figures. Rachel explained that they hated each other. "They both don't know what to do. Sometimes there is some space in between, but they are absolutely stuck." One of the two female figures symbolized a network of alters that Rachel experienced inside herself; the other symbolized her self. By explicating her self-hatred, Rachel had taken a last step toward enabling herself to experience the difference between her "self," a self desperately trying to reveal what she was going through, and many self-fragments once created by her self to avert awareness. The stepwise unfolding of her experiencing in the focusing process had enabled this clarification of the state of dissociation that had kept Rachel stuck for many years. By allowing this process of unfolding, Rachel facilitated the gradual recovery of her self: her memories, her hate, her fears. The small, still voice of her self had begun to breathe underneath her suffocating whisperings.

SUMMARY AND CONCLUSION

The focusing technique can augment various methods and modalities of child psychotherapy when children are stuck. It can help children to find their way back to organismic knowing and internal evaluating.

The therapist who teaches focusing searches for entrances that may contribute to children's ability to express themselves. He or she enables children to develop the acceptance, the pace, and the emotional distance—separate from the child's feeling but still in relation to it—that children need to resolve their structure-bound manner of experiencing. In this way, the therapist can help children contain and process their fearful and painful experiences. Each of the three cases presented shows that this is possible, but also that this cannot happen unless the child (1) is able to draw on some kernel of hope that change is possible, and (2) is willing and able to learn his or her inner critic—his or her most frightened part—to allow and bear unpredictable threatening experiences. Children's ability to mobilize this hope and willingness inside themselves will be promoted if the therapist shows sincere dedication to children's own capacity to heal their wounds from the inside.

Children must learn a new relationship with their anxiety. Structure-boundness signals the detrimental effects of anxiety on their functioning. Anxiety is in the way of their ability to fully know, feel, think, observe. To unlock this grip, children need to develop a new distance from their fears as they are manifest in children's circular habitual patterns and harsh inner criticism. They are helped to truly get to the contents of all that needs to be said. "What has been understood exactly need no longer struggle to be heard. Now it can just be here. It can breathe" (Gendlin, 1977, p. 11). The child's feeling process can regain its self-propelling quality.

REFERENCES

Barba, D. (1985). Single case study of a female adolescent firesetter. *The Focusing Folio, 4,* 2.

Bierman, R. (1997). Focusing in therapy with incarcerated domestically violent men. *The Folio, 15,* 2.

Boukydis, Z.F. (1990). Client-centered/experiential practice with parents and infants. In G. Lietaer, J. Rombauts, & R. van Balen (Eds.), *Client-centered and experiential psychotherapy in the nineties.* Leuven: Leuven University Press.

Coyle, M.P. (1987). An experiential perspective on the mother-infant relationship: The first eight months. *The Folio, 6,* 1.

Durak, G.M., Bernstein, R., & Gendlin, E.T. (1997). Effects of focusing training on therapy process and outcome. *The Folio, 15,* 2.

Fuhrmann, E.W. (1992). Some aspects of combining focusing with person-centered therapy in working with psychosomatic clients. *The Folio, 11,* 2.

Gendlin, E.T. (1962). *Experiencing and the creation of meaning.* Toronto: Free Press/Collier-Macmillan.

Gendlin, E.T. (1964). A theory of personality change. In P. Worchel & D. Byrne (Eds.), *Personality change.* New York: Wiley.

Gendlin, E.T. (1974). Client-centered and experiential psychotherapy. In D.A. Wexler & L.N. Rice (Eds.), *Innovations in client-centered therapy.* New York: Wiley.

Gendlin, E.T. (1979). *How I teach focusing.* New York: Focusing Institute.

Gendlin, E.T. (1981). Focusing. New York: Bantam Books.

Gendlin, E.T. (1984). The client's client. In J.M. Shlien & R. Levant (Eds.), *Client-centered therapy and the person-centered approach.* New York: Praeger.

Gendlin, E.T. (1986a). Foreword. In L. Wright, F. Everett & L. Roisman (Eds.), *Experiential psychotherapy with children.* Baltimore: Johns Hopkins University Press.

Gendlin, E.T. (1986b). *Let your body interpret your dreams.* Wilmette: Chiron.

Gendlin, E.T. (1994). Celebrations and problems of humanistic psychology. *The Folio, 13,* 1.

Gendlin, E.T. (1997). *Focusing-oriented psychotherapy: A manual of the experiential method.* New York: Guilford.

Gendlin, E.T., Beebe, J., Cassens, J., Klein, M., & Oberlander, M. (1968). Focusing ability in psychotherapy, personality and creativity. In J.M. Shlien (Ed.), *Research in psychotherapy* (Vol. 3). Washington, DC: American Psychiatric Association.

Grindler, D. (1984). Imagery is more powerful with focusing: Theory and practice. In J.E. Shorr, G.E. Sobel, P. Robin, & J.A. Conella (Eds.), *Imagination and healing.* Amityville, CA: Baywood.

Heintz, F. (1997). Teaching focusing to children 10–14 years old. *The Folio, 16,* 1–2.

Iberg, J.R. (1997). Three phases of focusing: An example from a ten-year-old-boy. *The Folio, 16,* 1–2.

Kafka, F. (1935). *Wedding preparations in the countryside.* New York: Schocken.

Kafka, F. (1985). *Letters to Milena.* New York: Schocken.

Klein, M., Mathieu, P., Kiesler, D.J., & Gendlin, E.T. (1973). The experiencing scale. In D.J. Kiesler (Ed.), *The process of psychotherapy: Empirical foundations and systems of analysis.* Chicago: Aldine.

Lou, N. (1997). Focusing by children. *The Folio, 16,* 1–2.

Marder, D. (1997). Sarah: Focusing and play therapy with a six-year old child. *The Folio, 16,* 1–2.

Meurs, P., & Leijssen, M. (1997). Kindertherapie: Een ontmoeting tussen het psycho-analytische en het cliëntgericht-experiëntiële model [Child psychotherapy: An encounter between the psychanalytic and the client-centered/experiential model]. *Tijdschrift voor Cliëntgerichte Psychotherapie, 35,* 3.

Neagu, G. (1988). The focusing technique with children and adolescents. In C. Schaefer (Ed.), *Innovative interventions in child and adolescent psychotherapy.* New York: Wiley.

Olsen, L., & Gendlin, E.T. (1970). The use of imagery in experiential focusing. *Psychotherapy: Theory, Research and Practice, 7,* 4.

Rappaport Friedman, L. (1988). Focusing and art therapy. *The Focusing Connection, 5,* 3.

Rogers, C.R., Gendlin, E.T., Kiesler, D.J., & Truax, C.B. (Eds.). (1967). *The therapeutic relationship and its impact: A study of psychotherapy with schizophrenics.* Madison: University of Wisconsin Press.

Santen, B. (1988). Focusing with a borderline adolescent. *Person-Centered Review, 3,* 435.

Santen, B. (1990). Beyond good and evil: Focusing with early traumatised children and adolescents. In G. Lietaer, J. Rombauts & R. van Balen (Eds.), *Client-centered and experiential psychotherapy in the nineties.* Leuven: Leuven University Press.

Santen, B. (1993). Focusing with a dissociated adolescent: Tracing and treating multiple personality disorder experienced by a 13-year-old girl. *The Folio, 12,* 2.

Santen, B., & Gendlin, E.T. (1985). Focusing. *Psychologie,* 1–2.

Santen, B., & Koopmans, G., (1980). Some remarks on experiential psychotherapy with children. *Client-Centered/Experiential Discussion Papers, 4,* 1.

Weiser Cornell, A. (1996). *The power of focusing: A practical guide to emotional self-healing.* Oakland: New Harbinger.

Yuba, N., & Murayama, S. (1988). Clearing a space with drawing in play therapy. *The Folio, 7,* 1.

CHAPTER 12

Animal-Assisted Therapy Interventions with Children

THE UTILIZATION of companion animals in the treatment of children's emotional difficulties is a comparatively recent development in psychotherapy (Levinson, 1962, 1969). The concept of utilizing animals as therapeutic adjuncts in work with children is founded not only on the premise that it is easier for a child to project unacceptable feelings on a companion animal, but also on the companion animal's faculty for supplying some of the child's need for cuddling, companionship, and unconditional acceptance (Poresky, 1990; Poresky & Hendrix, 1990).

Although animal-assisted therapy is a relatively novel intervention, there are increasingly more reports in the literature of the value and benefits of contact with companion animals (Beck, 1990; Gonski, 1985; Levinson & Mallon, 1997; Loney, 1971; Ross, 1981, 1983). In a comprehensive review of the literature, Mallon (1992) identified many of them. Several studies (Kidd & Kidd, 1984; Mallon, 1994a, 1994b; Melson, 1990, 1991; Melson, Strimple, & Bustad, 1992; Polt & Hale, 1985) indicate that animals have played an important socializing and humanizing role in the lives of children. Companion animals, particularly dogs and cats—because of their interactive, affectionate, nonjudgmental, and social nature—have been effectively utilized as adjunct therapists in the treatment of children and youth. Other, less traditional companion animals, such as hamsters, ferrets, gerbils, guinea pigs, lizards, snakes, turtles, and birds, have also proven to be useful as adjunctive therapists in the treatment of children.

Utilizing actual case studies from my own clinical practice, this chapter focuses on the useful techniques and strategies utilized for employing companion animals as adjuncts in the treatment of children in psychotherapy.

COMPANION ANIMALS IN THERAPY WITH CHILDREN

It sometimes is forgotten that the same techniques cannot be used with children as with adults. Children ordinarily do not admit there is anything wrong with them or that they need treatment. They usually do not feel an inner urge or need to come for help. They are not aware that whatever discomfort their anxiety causes them can be alleviated by the therapist. By and large, parents initiate the therapy. Clinicians need the parents' cooperation in order to continue. Because the child did not initiate the referral, the child feels that the therapist is the parents' ally and not the child's. This means that there is an extra responsibility placed on the therapist, which is usually nonexistent with the adult patient, when establishing a therapeutic relationship: The therapist must prove his or her usefulness to the child.

This is one of the special issues in child therapy. Because children do not seek out the therapist, they are unlikely to recognize their need for help. Generally, children claim that classmates or teachers or even parents are at fault, but not they. Adults can also be prone to this point of view, except that in seeking help, adults make implicit admission of their own responsibility for their problems.

In this connection, it is worthwhile to remember that although children may tell us that they do not know "what it is all about," actually they are aware, whether consciously or unconsciously, that there is something wrong and may realize that they are not like others. The mere fact of being discussed at home, of parents being unduly concerned about them, of being brought in to a therapist for an evaluation, brings about a qualitative change in children's self-evaluation and feeling of being atypical.

Something reassuring must be done in the first interview to make children feel that the therapist will make living more comfortable, that the therapist understands them and is ready to help. A dog brought in at this point may "break the ice" and be of assistance in developing a relationship with some children. In fact, the therapist who has pet assistance may, through his or her handling of a pet, elicit the young patient's admiration and lead more quickly to patient-therapist rapport.

Child therapists have demonstrated that psychotherapeutic methods used with adults have to be drastically modified when used with children (Boyd-Webb, Boyd-Wilson, & Zigler, 1996). For a variety of reasons, play therapy has been shown to be the best means of communication with the child (Boyd-Webb, 1991). When children's attention is captured by a play object, they temporarily forget their fears of the therapist and relax. Children engaged in a play therapy situation are less likely to censor their replies or disguise their feelings. In addition, the way children relate to and treat the play object can provide important clues for the therapist.

Invaluable as a play session may be, however, its success is problematic to the degree that the child shows interest in and becomes involved with the toy or craft. Even more revealing is the response of a child to the living toy-playmate, a companion animal (Levinson & Mallon, 1997). The use of companion animals gives the therapist an almost ideal way of observing the child in action, fluid in play and without guardedness. On the basis of clinical experience, companion animals are useful in psychodiagnosis and in the play session interview.

Harvey as Co-Therapist

Alberto, a 7-year-old Latino child previously diagnosed with attention deficit disorder, was brought by his grandmother to my office for an interview to evaluate him for placement in a residential treatment center. Although his grandmother claimed that Alberto did not want to come to the interview, they arrived 20 minutes earlier than their scheduled appointment. Harvey, my collie-mix dog, was in the office with me and as they entered, immediately jumped up from his position under my desk to greet both Alberto and his grandmother. Alberto at once sat on the floor with Harvey and began to pet him, asking a rapid series of questions with great urgency: Is the dog a boy or a girl? What is his name? Did he belong to me? How old was he? Did he ever have puppies? Did he have a girlfriend? The grandmother, concerned about the intrusiveness of the questions, made a nonverbal signal for him to stop. I responded by cuing her that his questions were all right and began my evaluation on the spot.

In practice, the procedure for introducing Harvey to the child, or the child to Harvey, automatically standardized itself. Generally, the child plays with the dog, asks Harvey to shake hands and dance. A cookie may be offered to the dog as an incentive. One child said to me, "I am also Harvey—I also want to dance." This child got down on his knees, started to bark like a dog, and asked me to give him a cookie. In great joy and glee, he then picked up the waste basket, scattered its contents, put it on his head, and started howling like a wolf. This apparently relieved him and he went on with his play as usual. He then asked me, "Why can't you have two dogs, and why can't you take me as one of them?"

Interspersed with his requests were questions about me: Did I have a wife? How many children did I have, and how big were they? It was clear that the child wanted to become part of my family. If the human complement was full, perhaps the dog complement was not, and he would like to be considered if a vacancy existed.

There are certain obvious advantages to the use of companion animals in therapy procedures. The speed of making the connection with the client is one of the primary advantages. Utilizing a companion animal in assessment and treatment can become part of a standard approach, and informal norms can evolve as to what behavior is to be expected.

Reliable indicators, not only of children's thinking but also of their pattern of behavior and the roles they play in the family constellation, may also be obtained in this fashion. Children of all ages find playing with a dog or cat reassuring and relaxing because the therapist seems to have brought in the animal just for "the pleasure of it." The threatening fact that the child is under "examination" is forgotten by the child and tensions are dispelled. The presence of a companion animal is particularly helpful when children are not cooperative, either because they are afraid of the interviewer or because they are carrying out a behavior pattern learned at home.

Through the "playing with a pet" interview, the therapist can expect to find answers to such basic questions as: Can the child relate to the therapist? On what level? What seem to be the underlying conflicts that the child observed at home? Are there firm ego boundaries? What is the child's frustration tolerance? Does he or she erupt in a sudden rage at the companion animal or at his or her own inability to master the companion animal? Does he or she tend to withdraw into sullen, almost autistic silence? Does the play itself have neurotic or psychotic overtones? How does the child handle his or her instinctual drives?

Some clues concerning the role aggression and passivity play in the economy of the child's organism can be obtained from observing the kind of activities in which the child chooses to engage with the animal. Children who perceive a dog as an aggressive animal or who misperceive the dog's stance as threatening may do so because they feel aggressive tendencies stirring within themselves that they find difficult to control. It may also indicate that the child perceives the world as a dangerous place.

How children perceive and react to the dog's untidiness, loss of hair, and shedding all over the room is highly significant. Does the child like to observe it, or is he or she revolted by it? One child whose mother had difficulties in his toilet training was afraid of dirt and was overly clean. This child, in particular, liked to feed the dog little tidbits in her dish, played with the dog's shed hair, and then would repeatedly wash the dishes.

COMPANION ANIMALS IN THE CLINICAL ASSESSMENT AND TREATMENT OF YOUNG CHILDREN

Young children, especially at the fantasying age of 3 or 4, love to be "interviewed" by a dog and very readily enter into the spirit of the game, forgetting that they are being examined. Important information is received in this manner that might not otherwise have been obtainable. Generally speaking, the more acquiescent the examiner, the more spontaneous will be the reaction of the child. If the clinician has to interfere and becomes active, this will alter the psychodynamics of the situation and consequently alter the play.

A technique for successfully employing a dog as an interview "tool" with preschool children generally begins by sitting in a casual threesome around a table. A flexible "ritual" is followed. First, the dog "shakes hands" with the child in introduction. Then the dog "whispers" in the clinician's ear that most children have secrets that they usually share with it (the dog). Guilt over the disclosure of family secrets may thus be averted. The therapist tells the child what the dog wishes to know, and the child tells the dog the information requested. In each case, the therapist acts only as agent or intermediary, relaying the message to the dog or the child, carefully stating that "Harvey says . . ."

Many questions can be asked of the child in this manner. I generally begin by asking the child whether he or she has a companion animal. If so, what kind? Who wanted it? How was it obtained? Who cares for it? How do members of family, and particularly the child, feel about it? If the child does not have a companion animal, I ask whether he or she ever had one, and, if so, what happened to it? If the child never had a companion animal, I ask what kind of companion animal he or she would like to have.

Putting together the facts obtained from this questioning, the therapist can profitably introduce at this point the story completion game (Lansky, 1968). The therapist should advise the children that they are going to hear a story and then proceed to tell a story based as much as possible on the case situation. If the facts obtained or thus far known are scant, the clinician will have to invent them "intuitively." At some point, the therapist should stop and ask the children to complete the story. Most children enter into this game willingly and consider it fun. From the endings they provide, one can often reconstruct an important family relationship or situation as well as gauge the child's expectations.

More often than not, children will complete the story with details from an incident or incidents in their own life.

One particularly revealing occasion comes to mind. It was the second visit to my office of a 6-year-old girl whom I shall call Paula. Paula was so frightened of cats that my cat had to be removed from the office on her first visit and before Paula would come into my office on this day, she wanted to know whether the cat was present and if so, would I please take the cat away. I reassured Paula that the cat was not only not in my office but had left the house to go for a long walk in the park behind my office. That afternoon I tried the story completion exercise with Paula. I told her a story about a little girl who was an only child and wanted very much to have a kitten as a companion animal but her father wouldn't permit it. (Paula had said in the previous interview that her parents would permit her to have a companion animal, but she didn't want one.)

Paula's Story

One day, Barbara (the little girl in the story) was visiting with some friends in the neighborhood who had a big, beautiful orange and white cat, just like Dr. Mallon's cat. This big mother cat had a litter of five little butterball kittens who all looked just like their mother. They wandered all over the house, played with almost anything they found on the floor, licked your hand, stumbled all over themselves, and usually found their way back to their mother, where they purred softly, drank some milk, and fell sound asleep. Barbara fell in love with the littlest one of the kittens. Eager to find homes for the kittens, this friend offered Barbara the kitten if Barbara would promise to take good care of it. Barbara was so excited she forgot that she should ask her mother's permission. She took the kitten, carrying it under her jacket gently and warmly. When she arrived at home with the kitten, her mother was waiting anxiously for her because she was a little late and it was almost dark.

At this point, I stopped. Paula had been fully engrossed. I asked if she would finish the story and tell me what happened when Barbara's mother found out about the kitten. Paula picked up the thread and wove a tale that was quite remarkable:

Barbara's mother was very angry when she saw the kitten and said she would have to take it back. Barbara cried very hard. She asked her mother over and over why she couldn't keep the kitten; it was so cute, and so sweet, and it wouldn't hurt anything, and she would take care of it. Barbara's mother told her that she could keep the kitten overnight but she would have to take it back in the morning because kittens are very dirty and they have fleas. When Barbara asked her mother what fleas were, she said they were bugs—like the bugs they sometimes saw in the kitchen and that everyone could get sick from having bugs around.

Paula paused at this point, but when I asked her whether the kitten was returned the next morning, she said very sadly, "No! No! No!" Paula began to cry. I asked her why she was crying, and she said, "Because Barbara killed the kitten; Barbara killed the kitten." Paula explained:

Barbara decided to get rid of the kitten's fleas so that her mother would let her keep it. Barbara took the can of spray that her mother used to kill the bugs in the kitchen. Barbara sprayed and sprayed the kitten because she wanted to make sure that it was very clean and had no more bugs. Then the kitten stopped moving. She couldn't get it to move any more. It was dead. Barbara killed the kitten.

I asked Paula what Barbara did then, and she filled in the remaining details:

Barbara went to her mother to get a doctor but Barbara's mother said it was just as well the kitten had died, it was dirty and it would probably have died of some disease it picked up from digging in garbage cans anyway.

Needless to say, it turned out that Paula had been relating to me most accurately an event from her own experience and one that had shocked this little girl and left her with tremendous feelings of guilt. It also revealed the depth of her mother's dirt phobia and her insensitivity to Paula's urgent needs.

COMPANION ANIMALS IN THE ASSESSMENT AND TREATMENT OF OLDER CHILDREN

The range of clinical techniques involving companion animals broadens rapidly with the advancing age of the patient, although what can be done with a very precocious 6-year-old can sometimes not be used with a rather limited 8-year-old. The applications must depend, as they always do, on the estimate and judgment of the therapist. The classifications are merely organizational conveniences into which the majority of cases I have handled fall. There have been numerous exceptions.

It is frequently important to discover a child's dominant fantasy themes. Both my dog and my cat have provided amazing shortcuts toward this end. By asking my young patients what Harvey dreams about, I have been inundated with stories of dreams, usually the patient's. (There have been noncooperators, too.) From the dream material, however, much has become apparent. Are the dreams aggressive? Is the death theme dominant? One can inquire about the frequency or recurrence of the same dream. One can learn, also, about the occurrence of nightmares and the disturbance of rest and sleep.

Of course, we are more interested in how children feel about their parents and the role parents play in children's fantasies than whether what the children say is true in reality. What do the children think about their parents? Do they feel that their mother is a kind person? Do they believe that they have been adopted? Do they have the foster child fantasy?

One of the most unusual aspects of the use of companion animals in psychotherapy is the development of the "outdoor" therapy session. Weather permitting, I like to go on dog walks with my patients as soon as the situation and the level of rapport indicate. Innumerable aspects of personality are revealed on dog walks. Utilizing animals outside of the therapy office can be a liberating experience for both the professional and the client. The first situation that presents itself, generally, is who shall hold the dog's leash. Harvey is so well trained that I can safely acquiesce when a child asks to hold the leash. How do the children accept this responsibility? Do they retain and maintain it? How quickly do they tire? Do they just drop the leash? What maturities and immaturities show up in this role? How do they react to the dog's urinating? Defecating? How do they react to the swift approach of another dog? Children, who are so constantly "parented" by adults, have little opportunity to practice being a parent or "the masters" themselves. Companion animals provide such opportunities (see Savishinsky, 1974, for an insightful article about the child as the father of the dog).

In my work with children, I often use food as a potent way of approaching and developing relationships with them. (I always obtain a parent's consent in advance.) In a nearby refrigerator, I keep an adequate supply of candy, cake, milk, and eggs. There are various kinds of dog food, also, on a nearby shelf. When a child refuses to accept food, it may be a pathognomonic sign of undue suspiciousness; the refusal may stem from a fear of being harmed or a parental prohibition not to take food from strangers. What an asset Harvey has been here, too! Children who would not themselves take food are often happy to become involved in feeding the dog. Some understanding of the child's family role may be obtained from observing the child's behavior during the preparation of the meal, the meal itself, and the cleaning-up period. If children accept a meal, we can observe whether they are willing to share—with the therapist or with the dog or cat. We can see, also, if they clean up, whether they feel guilty if they make a mess, and possibly whether they project this on the dog. Do the children like to regress and play the role of the infant who has to be fed and cannot assist in the preparation of the meal? Do they eat food that they obviously do not relish and impose the same discipline on the dog (asking it to eat unpleasant food)? Very often, this projective material gives more reliable clues to the child's problems and defense structures than other standardized tests.

How very revealing such techniques can be is indicated in the following excerpt from my records of a session with a 7-year-old patient:

> Ian was glad to be introduced to the dog; he shook hands with
> him and began to play. Ian seemed pleased to have an admiring,

noncompetitive audience, very readily entered into the spirit of the game, and gave the dog the information asked for. He was delighted to share his lunch with the dog, who was presiding over the meal at the head of the table.

Still, throughout the session, Ian gave the distinct impression that it was the novelty of the situation that brought about his favorable response, rather than the fact that he was relating on a lasting level to the therapist as a person. In an unobtrusive way, he was demanding. He had a big lunch and did not volunteer to help. He even expected the clinician to shell his egg, and did not offer to assist with the dishes. He accepted whatever was done for him as if it were his due, thus apparently repeating a pattern he was exhibiting at home. In a sense, he viewed the dog as an extension of himself.

Projective questions may be introduced at this point. Make believe that everyone has to be an animal for twenty-four hours, that you are an animal. Which animal would the children most want to be? Which animal would they least want to be? What are the three best things about this animal? What are the three worst things about this animal? This may give us additional clues concerning the kind of world the child lives in. One must know what the child's previous experiences with companion animals have been to be able to appreciate the meaning and all the nuances that transpire in a companion animal session.

The type of animal children choose to identify with will vary, depending, among other variables, on the children's defensive structure and their problem. However, it frequently helps to clarify the psychodynamics of the core problem. We find that when children select a domestic animal such as a cat, dog, or horse, they are likely to have a mild behavior disorder. However, identification with ferocious and powerful predators is indicative of severe emotional and social disturbance.

PATHOGNOMONIC SIGNS

The companion animal–child play session will give the therapist a chance to observe children in a natural situation, thus, he or she can make a more valid judgment as to how the children function and what their ego defenses may be. Some children are insecure and ask for permission to play with the companion animal; others take the situation in their stride and seem to accept it naturally. It is also important to notice how rapidly children adjust to the companion animals used in an interview and to observe whether they act differently toward different animals.

Do the children get down on all fours, imitating the dog in a deadpan fashion? This is not unusual behavior in very young children, who often pretend to be an animal in their play, speak to their own companion animal, and regard it as of equal status with themselves. In an older child, such posturing could point to emotional conflicts and disorientation.

Whether children touch the animal and which parts of the companion animal's body they touch can be highly significant. Do they reach for or touch the dog's phallus? Clues to the children's conflicts may be shown by their avoidance of the dog. Not touching Harvey may indicate not only the fear of an unknown animal, but also the worry that their hands may become aggressive instruments that could hurt the dog. Sometimes, a sudden cessation of play, when the children are unable to continue the game or involvement, points to diagnostic factors. Did the children unwittingly express aggression toward the companion animal or the therapist? Did they feel guilty? What have they done to undo the situation? On the other hand, overt aggression toward companion animals also spells pathology. A child who insists on kicking the dog or pulling the cat's tail or trying unobtrusively to kill some of the fish in the aquarium presents an aberrant picture. Sometimes, pathognomonic signs of severe maladjustment and even childhood psychosis become evident.

Sometimes, my cat sneaks surreptitiously into the office and jumps on the desk while the examination is proceeding. When the cat snuggles next to the patient, stretches its neck out, languidly lies on its back, and is obviously asking to be petted, the child's response or lack of response may be symptomatic of a personality disorder.

PROGNOSTIC CLUES

Children's behavior when they see a companion animal and their response to a companion animal's friendly overtures may give early clues about recoverability and the likelihood of success in treatment. Generally speaking, children who identify with the dog, even though they may be afraid of it, are better therapy risks. Children who do not hesitate to pet the dog may indicate a need for affection, and thus often present a more promising therapy subject. On the other hand, withdrawal from an obviously inoffensive, friendly animal indicates, in a sense, a withdrawal from environmental stimulation, portraying the child's view of the world as inimical. Such behavior generally presages poor or long-drawn-out therapeutic results.

ANIMAL COMPANIONS IN THE HOME

Companion animals may play an important role in the diagnosis of family relationships (Paul & Serpell, 1992). The presence of animal companion animals in the home is often advantageous in forming a relationship with a withdrawn, psychotic family member, or diagnostically in understanding the family relationships. Companion animals display behavioral reactions that are extensions of the behavioral reactions of the family members. Companion animals are very sensitive to emotionally charged affective states within the family. In addition, companion animals in the home can teach valuable lessons about life. Pregnancy, birth, illness, death—all part of the life cycle—are mirrored in caring for a companion animal.

Children who own companion animals should be permitted if they ask or encouraged if they do not suggest it themselves to bring their companion animals to the therapy sessions. The companion animal should always be welcomed and made part of the session. Often, additional diagnostic material may be elicited. Pearson (1968) reports the case of an enuretic child patient who thought urine was poisonous. Nevertheless, the bird that he brought to the therapy sessions had been named Pee Wee, the term the child used for urine.

The cases cited above indicate how the skilled analyst can make use of the human-animal relationship in obtaining swifter and keener insights into patients. References to companion animals must be treated as having great import. Eventually, it is to be hoped, a more systematic knowledge and understanding of the symbolism involved in human-animal relationships will make all those who work in the mental hygiene field much more alert and sensitive to the contributions companion animals can make to the therapeutic endeavor.

PSYCHOTHERAPEUTIC IMPLICATION

The use of a companion animal as a tool brings new dimensions to child psychotherapy and of necessity helps to crystallize new concepts. To begin with, a completely different relationship is required when a therapeutic situation is structured to include a pet. It is no longer the one-to-one relationship of ordinary play therapy, but comes closer to working as a group situation. It is an advantage both for the therapist who can observe the child's behavior with the companion animal and for the child who has a relaxed opportunity to identify, project, empathize, and patronize.

As long as childhood disorders were considered specific disease entities, emphasis on the use of companion animals in psychotherapy appeared esoteric and far-fetched. However, as soon as such disorders are looked on as maladaptive response patterns, utilizing companion animals to modify these patterns and aid children in reorganizing their "phase of life" by shedding maladaptive patterns of behavior appears reasonable (Condoret, 1983).

The utilization of animals in child therapy is not advocated as a general procedure, but rather to encourage child therapists to venture out and use whatever potentialities exist among their life experiences, interests, and hobbies to enrich the play therapy experience and as aids in reaching the withdrawn child. For maximum effectiveness, companion animals must be planfully introduced into the therapy hours, and in certain cases, they must become part of the written treatment plan. Furthermore, companion animals must be trained for the part they will take in the treatment, and therapists should be oriented to the use of companion animals.

Because companion animals are so active, another implication of their use is that the main locus of therapy need no longer be in the playroom or the office, but can be in the wider world, in the street or playground or wherever the child and the companion animal go. The companion animal can literally lead the child into a larger world in which the child can eventually function. Therefore, to refer to the use of companion animals in therapy as play therapy is a misnomer. The word play connotes a self-chosen activity that is largely absent in the structured setting of a clinic or a private therapist's office, where the purpose of the activities is predetermined and the time set beforehand. What we are actually doing in play therapy is engaging in directed make-believe. It is well-known that through play, children may rehearse and try to resolve some of their life problems. Therefore, it is more accurate to call therapy that involves the planned use of companion animals animal-assisted therapy.

Adults ascribe human attributes to animals; children reverse the process and attribute animal qualities to human beings. Contrary to the widely held impression, it is easier for a child to identify with a human being than with an animal. However, it is difficult for children to project life into and identify with an inanimate object. The great virtue of animal-assisted therapy is that it permits this identification with a living object as a transitional or intermediate level. Experienced child therapists know that dolls, clay, finger paints, and other accessories of the playroom cannot be truly loved. They are not alive; they do not grow, digest, and respond. Children intuitively know that these objects cannot share feelings with them. Animals have certain attributes that furnish the human mind with an excellent medium for displacement of repressed drives. Unlike children's reaction to a doll, children can conceive of the companion animal as being part of themselves and their family and sharing their experiences.

Further, emotionally disturbed children who have experienced difficulty in their relations with people relate more easily and quickly to animals. There are many examples of the unique value of the companion animal (e.g., Blue, 1986; Bryant, 1990). Abused children, for instance, are often resistant in therapy and do not want to confide in the therapist. Such children think they are bad, otherwise they would not have been abused. With the aid of the companion animal, it is possible to break through this resistance so that the children can develop a good relationship with the therapist.

A Better Mom than Mine

Nancy was an 8-year-old child, physically abused by her mother to the point of multiple hospitalizations. She was court-placed at Green Chimneys Children's Services in their residential treatment center, a 150-acre farm, and met with her therapist twice a week for individual sessions. Nancy was essentially nonverbal and never opened up to discuss any of the issues pertaining to her abuse. The worker tried everything: dolls, clay, art; nothing seemed to work for her. One afternoon, the therapist decided to "take the therapy outdoors" and, knowing that some baby animals had recently been born, suggested a walk up to the farm. Nancy agreed to go for a walk. When Nancy saw a group of baby rabbits with their mother in a pen, she panicked and told the therapist, "You better get those babies out of there!" When the therapist asked why, Nancy replied, "Because sometimes mothers hurt babies." After the therapist assured her that the mother rabbit would take good care of the babies, she asked if Nancy knew a mother who hurt babies. Nancy nodded, holding her head down and mumbling, "Yeah, my Mom. This rabbit is a better Mom to her babies than my Mom was to me." This event provided the perfect opportunity for the therapist and Nancy to move into a discussion about her own history of abuse. In subsequent sessions, Nancy asked if she could spend time with the rabbits. She and her therapist ended each session with a visit to the rabbits. Nancy seemed soothed by the rabbits and eventually was permitted by the farm staff to adopt a rabbit of her own.

It is often necessary for children with a history of abuse to gratify some of their elementary needs before any attempt can be made to approach their other conflicts. A child who has been sadly deprived of love may find it most difficult to accept the affection of an adult but may be capable of receiving it from a companion animal. The intervention has also been proven to be most useful with nonverbal children and children who exhibit autistic features (Redefer & Goodman, 1989; Smith, 1985).

Thus, the way children handle the companion animal is much more expressive and revealing of their problem and attitude toward the world than their finger-paintings or their play with puppets. Children create their own fantasies and fairy tales revolving around the companion animal. The companion animal provides children with an outlet for their emotions and a way of abreacting to them. The job of the therapist consists in penetrating into this life and trying to help the children use their imaginary resource in self-healing.

A sensitive therapist can utilize the child's play with the companion animal to understand the child. Understanding what the child is trying to convey strengthens the therapeutic relationship with the child. The companion animal can also solve problems of sharing, separation, and formulation of self-image.

However, it bears repeating that merely assigning companion animals to emotionally disturbed children without at the same time making a provision for psychotherapeutic intervention may not only not be useful, but may even be harmful. Children's playing alone with a companion animal may reinforce their regressive withdrawal patterns, make them dependent for companionship solely on the companion animal, and remove him from competitive and therapeutically useful social anxiety produced by interactions with their peers.

CONCLUSION

Psychodiagnosis is an ongoing procedure that becomes fused with treatment. As I have indicated throughout this chapter, and as the various cases cited have shown, psychological assessment is never complete but continually evolving. This is just as true when the companion animal is used as an assessment tool as when companion animals are not introduced. However, the more one is able to observe the patient interacting with a companion animal, the sharper one's conclusions can become. Later observations provide one with data that often compel a modification of earlier assessments and conclusions and can lead to the utilization of the companion animal as a therapeutic intervention. This is true regardless of whether the therapist has the companion animal in his or her office or patients bring their own companion animal to interviews or relate experiences that describe interactions with a companion animal at home.

For the therapist who has become alerted to and sophisticated about the value of companion animals as tools, they can provide a vital source of clues and insights into personality disturbances. Even more startling is the way the changes in a patient's relationship to a companion animal generally coincide with an increasing ability to handle his or her other problems.

REFERENCES

Beck, A. (1990). *The role of animal interaction with children and adolescents: A presentation of studies and practice.* Paper presented at the Center for Applied Ethology and Animal/Human Interaction, West Lafayette, IN.

Blue, G.F. (1986). The value of pets in children's lives. *Childhood Education, 63,* 84–90.

Boyd-Webb, N. (1991). *Play therapy with children in crisis: A casebook for practitioners.* New York: Guilford.

Boyd-Webb, N., Boyd-Wilson, N., & Zigler, E. (1996). *Social work practice with children.* New York: Guilford.

Bryant, B.K. (1990). The richness of the child-pet relationship: A consideration of both benefits and costs to children. *Anthrozoos, 3,* 253–261.

Condoret, A. (1983). Speech and companion animals: Experience with normal and disturbed nursery school children. In A.H. Katcher & A.M. Beck (Eds.), *New perspectives on our lives with companion animals* (pp. 467–471). Philadelphia: University of Pennsylvania Press.

Gonski, Y. (1985). The therapeutic utilization of canines in a child welfare setting. *Child & Adolescent Social Work Journal, 2*(2), 93–105.

Kidd, A.H., & Kidd, R.M. (1984). Pet owner psychology: The human side of the bond. In P. Arkow (Ed.), *Dynamic relationships in practice: Animals in the helping professions* (pp. 68–82). Alameda: Latham Foundation.

Lansky, L.M. (1968). Story completion methods. In A.I. Rabin (Ed.), *Projective techniques in personality assessment* (pp. 290–324). New York: Springer.

Levinson, B. (1962). The dog as co-therapist. *Mental Hygiene, 46,* 59–65.

Levinson, B. (1969). *Pet-oriented child psychotherapy.* Springfield, IL: Thomas.

Levinson, B., & Mallon, G.P. (1997). *Pet-oriented child psychotherapy* (2nd ed.). Springfield, IL: Thomas.

Loney, J. (1971). The canine therapist in a residential children's setting: Qualifications, recruitment, training and related matters. *Journal of the American Academy of Child Psychiatry, 10*(3), 518–523.

Mallon, G.P. (1992). Utilization of animals as therapeutic adjuncts in the treatment of children and youth: A review of the literature. *Child and Youth Care Forum, 21*(1), 53–67.

Mallon, G.P. (1994a). Cow as co-therapist: Utilization of farm animals as therapeutic aides with children in residential treatment. *Child and Adolescent Social Work Journal, 11*(6), 455–474.

Mallon, G.P. (1994b). Some of our best therapists are dogs. *Child and Youth Care Forum, 23*(2), 89–101.

Melson, G.F. (1990). *Fostering inter-connectedness with animals and nature: The developmental benefits for children.* Paper presented to Green Chimneys People, Pets, and Plants Conference, Brewster, NY.

Melson, G.F. (1991). Studying children's attachment to their pets: A conceptual and methodological view. *Anthrozoos, 4,* 91–99.

Melson, G.F., & Fogel, A. (1989). Children's ideas about animal young and their care: A reassessment of gender differences in the development of nurturance. *Anthrozoos, 2,* 265–273.

Melson, G.F., Strimple, E.O., & Bustad, L.K. (1992, April). *The benefits of interactions of children and animals.* Paper presented at the fourth National Health Policy Forum, Washington, DC.

Paul, E.S., & Serpell, J. (1992). Why children keep pets: The influence of child and family characteristics. *Anthrozoos, 5*(4), 231–244.

Pearson, G.H.J. (Ed.). (1968). *A handbook of child psychoanalysis.* New York: Basic Books.

Polt, J.M., & Hale, C. (1985). Using pets as "therapists" for children with developmental disabilities. *Teaching Exceptional Children, 17,* 218–222.

Poresky, R.H. (1990). The young children's empathy measure: reliability, validity, and the effects of companion animal bonding. *Psychological Reports, 66,* 931–936.

Poresky, R.H., & Hendrix, C. (1990). Differential effects of pet presence and pet-bonding on young children. *Psychological Reports, 66,* 931–936.

Redefer, L.A., & Goodman, J.F. (1989). Brief report: Pet-facilitated therapy with autistic children. *Journal of Autism and Developmental Disorders, 19,* 461–467.

Ross, S.B. (1981). Children and companion animals. *Ross Timesaver Feelings, 23*(4), 13–16.

Ross, S.B. (1983). The therapeutic use of animals with the handicapped. *International Child Welfare Review, 3*(56), 26–39.

Savishinsky, J.S. (1974). The child is the father of the dog: Canines and personality processes in an Arctic community. *Human Development, 17,* 460–466.

Smith, B. (1985). Project In-Reach: A program to explore the ability of Atlantic bottle-nose dolphins to elicit communication responses from autistic children. In A.H. Katcher & A.M. Beck (Eds.), *New perspectives on our lives with companion animals* (pp. 460–466). Philadelphia: University of Pennsylvania Press.

CHAPTER 13

Touch Therapy for Infants, Children, and Adolescents

MARIA HERNANDEZ-REIF and TIFFANY FIELD

TOUCH THERAPIES

MASSAGE IS believed to be the oldest form of touch therapy. Physicians from ancient Greece, Rome, and Arabia prescribed massage for numerous physical as well as mental conditions. In India, oil massage is over 3,000 years old, and still today infants are massaged three times a day. Infant massage is also practiced in Asia and the Pacific Islands to promote development, improve sleep, and relieve colic and irritability. Maoris and Hawaiians also use massage to correct clubfoot, to mold their children's physical features, and to facilitate dancing skills (see Knaster, 1996, for a comprehensive review on body therapies). For centuries, only anecdotal accounts existed on the effectiveness of these therapies.

For the past 20 years, Field and colleagues have been studying the effects of massage therapy for a variety of physical and mental

This research was supported by an NIMH Research Scientist Award (#MH00331) and NIMH Research Grant (#MH40779) to Tiffany Field and funds from Johnson and Johnson. Correspondence and requests for reprints should be sent to Dr. Maria Hernandez-Reif, Touch Research Institute, University of Miami School of Medicine, Department of Pediatrics, PO Box 016820 (D-820), Miami, FL 33101.

health conditions. The resulting body of empirical data documents that massage therapy benefits many conditions. This chapter discusses massage therapy techniques and presents research findings for conditions from birth to adolescence.

MASSAGE THERAPY TECHNIQUES

PRETERM MASSAGE

Preterm infants who are medically stable may be administered massage therapy between feedings. These infants may experience stress from their hospitalization, medical procedures, and even from simple heelsticks for bloodwork. A 15-minute combination of massage therapy and kinesthetics has been found to be effective in helping the preterm infant gain weight and improve in orientation and motor development.

The preterm massage begins with infants on their stomach. Applying moderate pressure and using the palms of the hands, six strokes are delivered slowly to each of the following body parts: (1) head—from the crown to the neck and back to the crown; (2) shoulder—from the middle of the back to the arms and return to middle; (3) back—from the neck to the waist and return to the neck (make sure this is done on either side of the spine and not directly on the spine); (4) legs—one leg at a time, from the ankle to the top of the thigh and back to the ankle, and (5) arms—one arm at a time, from the wrist up to the shoulder and back to the wrist. Subsequently, infants are placed on their back, and kinesthetic movements (six movements for each section) are conducted in the following order: (1) arms—one arm at a time, holding arm at wrist and bending at elbow; (2) legs—one leg at a time, holding leg at ankle and bending at knee; and (3) legs—both legs together, holding at ankles and bending at knee.

INFANT MASSAGE

Infants up to 33 months can be administered the following 15-minute massage between feedings to promote relaxation. A few drops of oil applied to the therapist's hands will help deliver smoother strokes. The massage may be conducted on a small mat or towel placed on the floor with the therapist sitting facing the infant. Starting with the lying infant face up, the following sequence can be followed: (1) face—stroke along both sides of the face and make eye contact with the infant; (2) legs—forming your hands into a C and wrapping your hand around the infant's leg, conduct long strokes from the hip to the foot; squeeze and twist, in a wringing motion, from the foot to the hip (no pressure should be applied to any joints); (3) foot—massage the entire bottom of the foot using your thumbs to make gliding motions from the toes to the heel (a light stroke may tickle the infant and lead to squirming, therefore moderate pressure is recommended); make criss-cross strokes using the thumb and then use thumbs to press into the bottom of the foot; squeeze each toe gently and finish with a gentle pull; make small circles on the ankles, using moderate pressure; (4) Repeat 2 and 3; (5) stomach—hand over hand in paddlewheel fashion (never over ribs or tip of rib cage), use a circular motion with fingers in a clockwise direction starting at the appendix; (6) chest—stroke on both sides of the chest with the flats of fingers going from the middle outward (never pressing down on rib cage); cross strokes from center of chest and going over the shoulders; (7) arms—using oil, make long strokes from shoulders to hand (one arm at a time); follow same procedure as for legs; (8) face—stroke along both sides of the face; flats of fingers across forehead; circular strokes over temples and hinge of jaw; flats of fingers over nose, cheeks, jaw, and chin; massage from top to bottom of ears; (9) turn the infant face down and apply the following strokes to the back—long downward strokes using flats of hands from the upper back to the hips; hand-over-hand strokes from hips to and over shoulders; circular motion with fingertips from head over the long muscles on either side of the spine (never massage the spine directly); circular strokes to the infant's neck and shoulders; long gliding strokes along the length of the back and down to the feet and up.

CHILD AND ADOLESCENT MASSAGE

The child and adolescent massage is similar to the infant massage except that it can be extended to 20 minutes, and wringing motions to legs and arms can be replaced with longer strokes using moderate pressure. In addition, the back of the legs can be added to the massage therapy routine after the back is completed (with child lying on stomach), including firm pressure from ankle to hip, using flats of hands and sliding hands to the outside of legs; small and large circular strokes using thumbs to calves; continuous circles around the ankles; and strokes with flats of fingers from ankle to hip. If the adolescent feels uncomfortable with full-body massage therapy, seated massages can be conducted using special chairs.

MASSAGE THERAPY RESEARCH FINDINGS

EFFECTS ON PRETERMS AND NEWBORN INFANTS AT RISK

In one study conducted at our Neonatal Intermediate Care Unit (NICU), 40 preterm infants were assigned to receive massage therapy or standard care (control group) (Field et al., 1986). Those in the massage therapy group received the 15-minute preterm massage (outlined above) three times a day over a 10-day period.

Infants who received the rhythmic 15-minute massage (1) gained 47% more weight, (2) were alert and more active, (3) received higher scores on orientation and habituation on the Brazelton neonatal examination, (4) showed more mature motor responses, (5) were better able to regulate their state, and (6) were discharged six days earlier at hospital cost savings of $3,000 per infant (in 1986 dollars) (Field et al., 1986). A recent study conducted in the same NICU 12 years later using the same massage therapy procedure on 30 preterm infants revealed that just five days of massage was sufficient to produce an average of 47% weight gain (Dieter, Field, Hernandez-Reif, & Emory, 1998).

Cocaine-Exposed Preterms

Cocaine-exposed infants face premature births, respiratory and urinary problems, risk of developing Sudden Infant Death Syndrome, and attention and motor deficits (Alessandri, Sullivan, Imaizumi, & Lewis, 1993; Mayes, Granger, Frank, Schottenfeld, & Bornstein, 1993). In another study conducted by Field and colleagues, at the same NICU, cocaine-exposed premature infants were once again assigned to 10 days of massage therapy or to a control group (Wheeden et al., 1993). The massaged cocaine preterms displayed (1) 28% greater weight gain per day, (2) fewer stress behaviors, (3) more mature motor behaviors, and (4) fewer postnatal complications than the nontreatment control group.

HIV-Exposed Infants

Infants exposed to the HIV virus during birth are at risk of developing HIV and AIDS. Moreover, HIV-exposed infants show inferior performance on the Brazelton Neonatal Behavior Assessment (Scafidi & Field, 1997). In another NICU study, 28 infants who were HIV-exposed were assigned to a massage therapy or a control group (Scafidi & Field, 1996). As in the other studies, the massaged group receive a 15-minute massage three times a day for 10 days. The control group showed declining performance on the Brazelton Neonatal Assessment over the study period. In contrast, the massaged infants showed an increase in weight and improvements in (1) habituation, (2) motor responses, (3) state regulation, (4) autonomic stability, and (5) displayed fewer stress and excitable behaviors.

Infants of Depressed Mothers

Physically, infants born to depressed mothers often appear normal (e.g., full term and average birth weight). However, research reveals that these infants are at risk for a multitude of delays. For example, studies show that they have less positive affect (Cohn, Matias, Tronick, Connell, & Lyons-Ruth, 1986; Field, 1984). Moreover, recent research from our laboratory revealed that these infants have brain electrical activity (electroencephalogram; EEG) similar to inhibited children or chronically depressed adults (Field, Fox, Pickens, & Nawrocki, 1995; Jones et al., 1998), display poor orientation on the Brazelton Neonatal Scale (Abrams, Field, Scafidi, & Prodromidis, 1995; Lundy, Field, & Pickens, 1996), are less attentive and expressive as neonates when faces are modeled for them (Lundy, Field, Pickens, Cigales, & Cuadra, 1997), show less oral exploration (Hernandez-Reif, Field, Del Pino, Diego, 1998), and have higher stress hormones (Lundy et al., in press).

In a study conducted at a nursery school, 40 full-term infants (1 to 3 months of age) of depressed mothers were assigned to receive infant massage twice a week for six weeks or to a rocking control group (Field, Grizzle, Scafidi, Abrams, et al., 1996). The massaged infants had lower salivary cortisol (stress hormone) levels and urinary catecholamines (norepinephrine, epinephrine), suggesting that they were less stressed. They also had higher serotonin levels by the end of the study, suggesting they were less depressed. In addition, they cried less, were more alert and active when awake, and, were less active during sleep. They were also rated by their teachers as improved in emotionality and soothability and were more sociable than the infants in the rocking control group.

MASSAGE THERAPY EFFECTS FOR INFANTS AND CHILDREN

The effects of sleeplessness, overstimulation, and separation from parents are stressors for healthy infants and young children. In a series of studies, massage therapy effects were evaluated for reducing ordinary stress experienced by normal full-term infants in preschools. Two additional studies examined massage therapy effects on infants' and preschoolers' cognitive and motor performance.

Infant Massage Therapy Effects with Oil

In one study, 60 1-month-old full-term infants were assigned to receive either massage with oil or massage without oil (Field, Schanberg, Davalos, & Malphurs, 1996). Infants who received the oil massage (1) were less active (fewer limb movements), (2) showed fewer stress behaviors (less mouthing and clenching of fists), (3) displayed fewer withdrawing behaviors (less head turning), (4) had lower salivary cortisol levels, and (5) had a larger increase in vagal tone (an indication of increased attention) during massage. These findings reveal that massage therapy reduces stress levels and promotes relaxation for normal infants especially when oil is used.

Sleeplessness

In another study, parents were instructed to give their infants or toddlers with sleep problems a nightly 15-minute infant massage or to read a 15-minute bedtime story (Field & Hernandez-Reif, in press). After one month, the massaged infants fell asleep faster and awoke less often during the night when compared to the infants who were read bedtime stories. Observations at the infants' nursery schools revealed that the massaged infants were more alert, took shorter naps, and had more positive affect than those who were read bedtime stories.

Cognitive and Motor Functioning

In one study, 4-month-olds were assigned to receive an eight-minute massage, eight minutes of play stimulation with a rattle or to a control group prior to habituation and test of two different color-tempo stimuli (red versus blue hammer beating a fast versus slow tempo) (Cigales, Field, Lundy, Cuadra, & Hart, 1997). Only the massaged infants showed evidence of discriminating the color-tempo stimuli, suggesting that massage therapy may enhance infants' perception.

In a nursery school study, preschoolers ($M = 4.4$ years) were given cognitive and perceptual-motor tests (Weschler Preschool and Primary Scale of Intelligence–Revised) before and after a 15-minute massage or a 15-minute storybook reading period (Hart, Field, & Hernandez-Reif, in press). Teachers were also asked to rate the children on a temperament checklist (e.g., calm, difficult, easygoing). Results revealed heightened perception and better motor performance for children in the massage therapy group, particularly for the more temperamental children.

Social Functioning

In a separate study, preschool children received 20-minute massages at their nursery school twice a week for five weeks (Field, Kilmer, Hernandez-Reif, & Burman, 1996). When compared to children in a wait-list control group, independent observers (blind to the children's condition) gave the massaged children better scores on behavior, activity level, vocalization, and cooperation. Teachers also rated the massaged children more optimally, and their parents rated them as less touch-aversive and more extroverted. Sleep observations also revealed that the massaged children fell asleep faster for their daytime nap.

MASSAGE THERAPY FOR CHILDREN WITH
VARIOUS CONDITIONS

In this section, the effects of massage therapy for children with varying conditions are discussed. The conditions are presented in an arbitrary, alphabetical order. Whenever possible, parents were trained to massage their children for these studies. Using parents as therapists has the potential for providing the child with a daily dose of massage therapy; has therapeutic value for the parent, including reducing parental anxiety and stress hormones; can facilitate the parent-child relationship; and is cost-effective.

Asthmatic Children

Parents were instructed to give 20-minute nightly massages or, for the control group, to conduct progressive muscle relaxation exercises with their asthmatic children for one month (Field, Henteleff, et al., 1998). At the end of the study, the children who were massaged showed less anxious behaviors and had lower stress hormone (cortisol) levels. In addition, they had a better attitude about their asthmatic condition. More important, their peak air flow and pulmonary functions improved over the study period, suggesting that a daily massage may improve the airway caliber of asthmatic children.

Autistic Children

In this study, massage therapy was examined for its effects on the classroom behavior and sociability of children with autism (Field, Lasko, et al., 1997). Twenty-two children were recruited and assigned to receive 15-minute child massages or to sit and play on the lap of a volunteer for 15 minutes. The sessions were conducted at the same time of day, with the child fully clothed, except for the removal of shoes. After eight massage therapy sessions, the children displayed (1) less touch aversion, (2) less orienting to sounds and fewer other stereotypic behaviors, and (3) improved scores on social relating. Children in the touch control group also improved on touch aversion and off-task behavior, suggesting that massage and physical touch are therapeutic interventions for autistic children.

Burns in Children

Infants and young children (ages birth to 5 years) who had severe burns that required hospitalization were assigned, immediately prior to dressing changes, to a control group or to receive a

10-minute massage to unaffected body parts (Hernandez-Reif, Field, Redzepi, & Niremberg, 1998, preliminary data). Those in the massage therapy group showed fewer negative behaviors during dressing change, including fewer distress behaviors (e.g., reaching out), and less gross body movement.

Cancer

Children hospitalized with various forms of cancer were randomly assigned to a massage therapy or a control group (Field, Hernandez-Reif, et al., 1999 ongoing study). Parents were trained to massage their children nightly for one month. Preliminary data reveal that parents conducting massage therapy and their children improved in mood by the end of the one-month study period. Moreover, children in the massage therapy group displayed fewer negative behaviors during the IV placement procedure. Massage therapy is also expected to enhance immune function, as it has for other immune-compromised conditions in adults, including HIV (Ironson et al., 1996) and breast cancer (Hernandez-Reif, Ironson, et al., 1999). In those studies, the number of Natural Killer cell number and Natural Killer cell activity increased, suggesting that massage contributes to an increase in the cells that fight tumors and viruses.

Cerebral Palsy

Young children diagnosed with spastic cerebral palsy (3 to 5 years of age) are currently being evaluated at their nursery schools for children with disabilities (Hernandez-Reif, Field, Bornstein, & Fewell, 1999a). Massage therapy is expected to reduce spasticity (rigidity of muscles), improve fine motor (e.g., hand functioning) and gross motor (stance, trunk flexion, walking) functioning, and enhance daily living skills (e.g., self-feeding) and social development (e.g., interacting with others during play).

Cystic Fibrosis

For one month, 20 children (5 to 12 years old) with cystic fibrosis were massaged or read to by their parents for 20 minutes nightly (Hernandez-Reif, Field, Krasnegor, et al., 1998). Parents and children in the massage therapy group reported reduced anxiety. In addition, their mood and peak air flow readings also improved.

Dermatitis

Skin disorders can be stressful and a cause of embarrassment for children. Psychological stress has been shown to heighten eczema outbreaks and severely affect the course of the disease (McMenamy, Katz, & Gipson, 1988). In this study, 10 children received daily massages from their parents for one month (Schachner, Field, Hernandez-Reif, Duarte, & Krasnegor, 1998) and were compared to 10 control children who received only standard medical care. The massaged children showed a reduction in anxiety, and the clinical course of their skin disorder improved, including a reduction in redness, scaling, itching, skin scraping, and thickening. Parents who massaged their children also reported reduced anxiety.

Diabetes

The negative impact of stress on metabolic control and regulation of blood glucose levels is well established (Chan et al., 1996; Surwit, Ross, & Feingloss, 1991). In this study of 24 children with Type I diabetes, nightly 20-minute massages (conducted by parents) over one month decreased the children's anxiety, fidgeting, and depressed affect (Field, Hernandez-Reif, LaGreca, et al., 1997). More important, the massaged children were more compliant with their insulin intake and food regulation, and their glucose levels significantly decreased from a high value (159 mg/dl) to a value within normal range (118 mg/dl). Because massage stimulates the vagus nerve, and vagal activity regulates gastrointestinal functioning and the release of insulin, it was not surprising that massage therapy was effective in regulating blood glucose levels.

Down Syndrome

In this study, 20 (M age = 3.5 years) toddlers diagnosed with Down syndrome received massage therapy or had a reading session twice weekly for 12 weeks at their nursery schools (Hernandez-Reif, Field, Bornstein, & Fewell, 1999b). The children who received massage therapy improved in fine and gross motor skills.

Juvenile Rheumatoid Arthritis

Juvenile rheumatoid arthritis (JRA) is one of the most common and painful chronic diseases of childhood (Cassidy & Petty, 1995). In this study, 20 children with JRA were randomly assigned to a control group or to receive daily massages from their parents for one month (Field, Hernandez-Reif, Seligman, et al., 1997). Data revealed that children assigned to the massage therapy group showed fewer stress behaviors, had lower stress hormone (cortisol) levels, and reported less pain, and their physician's assessment of pain and pain-limiting activities was more optimal by the end of the study.

Posttraumatic Stress Disorder

Sixty grade-school children meeting diagnostic criteria for posttraumatic stress disorder (PTSD) following Hurricane Andrew received massages twice a week for one month or were assigned to watch a children's video on the same time schedule (Field, Seligman, Scafidi, & Schanberg, 1996). Following the one-month therapy, those receiving massage reported being happier and less anxious and had lower salivary cortisol stress levels. In addition, the massage group had lower scores on depression and PTSD reaction following the one-month intervention.

ADOLESCENT MASSAGE THERAPY EFFECTS

Aggressive Adolescents

In an ongoing study, adolescents ($M = 14$ years) diagnosed with oppositional defiant disorder or conduct disorder are receiving massage therapy or progressive muscle relaxation sessions in addition to individual and/or group therapy they are receiving at an adolescent psychiatric clinic (Diego, Field, Hernandez-Reif, & Shaw, 1999). The adolescents receive two massage or relaxation sessions per week over eight weeks. The massages are conducted with the adolescent fully clothed and sitting in a special massage chair. Pilot data reveal the following benefits for the massage therapy group: (1) reduced aggression as measured on an Overt Aggression Scale, (2) parental reports of reduced adolescent aggression, and (3) self-reports of decreased anxiety and improved mood. Testosterone and cortisol stress hormone levels are showing a declining trend for the massage therapy group.

Attention-Deficit/Hyperactivity Disorder

Drug therapy for adolescents diagnosed with ADHD is often difficult because of noncompliance and negative side effects such as motor tics, insomnia, headaches, and social withdrawal (Schachar & Tannock, 1993; Swanson, McBurnett, Christian, & Wigal, 1995). One hypothesis underlying the pathology of ADHD proposes that it is a deficiency in regulating the physiological processes necessary for attention, including slowing motor, respiratory, and heart rate (Porges, 1984). Because, as discussed in previous sections, massage therapy has been shown to reduce anxiety and stress hormones, decrease off-task behavior, and increase vagal tone, we examined massage therapy effects on adolescents with ADHD.

Twenty-eight male adolescents (*M* age = 14.6) diagnosed with ADHD were recruited from self-contained classrooms for children with emotional problems. Half of the group received 15-minute massages or progressive muscle relaxation sessions after school for 10 consecutive school days (Field, Quintino, Hernandez-Reif, & Koslovsky, 1998). The massage therapy group rated themselves as happier, and observers rated them as fidgeting less. Teachers who were unaware of the adolescents' group assignment reported more time on-task and assigned lower Conners hyperactivity scores to those in the massage therapy group.

Bulimia

In a study conducted at an inpatient center for eating disorders, female adolescents diagnosed with bulimia nervosa were assessed on depression and body image (Field, Schanberg, et al., in press). Subsequently, the adolescents (N=24) with eating disorders were assigned to receive two massages per week for five weeks or to a control group. By the end of the study, the massaged group had (1) fewer depressive symptoms, (2) reduced anxiety, (3) improved body image, and (4) lower urinary cortisol stress levels and increased dopamine levels. Moreover, they received better scores on an eating disorder attitude scale. These findings suggest that treating the body of individuals with eating disorders may improve the biochemistry and effectively reduce psychological symptoms associated with the disorder.

Depressed Teenage Mothers

Thirty-two depressed adolescent mothers who had recently given birth at the county hospital were recruited and randomly assigned to a massage therapy or relaxation therapy group (Field, Grizzle, Scafidi, & Schanberg, 1996). The adolescents in the massage therapy group received 30-minute massages on two consecutive days of the week for five weeks. Those in the relaxation group attended 30-minute relaxation therapy sessions on the same time schedule. Both groups reported lower anxiety levels after the first session. However, only the massage therapy group had lower urinary and salivary cortisol levels and showed fewer anxious behaviors and less depressed mood by the end of the study.

Adolescents with HIV

In this study, adolescents with HIV are receiving massage therapy or relaxation sessions twice a week for three months at a pediatric HIV clinic (Diego, Hernandez-Reif, Field, & Shaw, 1998). Preliminary data favoring the massage therapy group reveal (1) improved mood, (2) lower scores for anxiety and depression, (3) increased Natural Killer cell number (CD56 and CD56:CD3), (4) increased CD4 number, a marker of disease progression, and (5) better scores on "confidence." These findings support those from an HIV men's (Ironson et al., 1996) and a breast cancer massage therapy study (Hernandez-Reif, Ironson, et al., 1998) showing a reduction in anxiety and depression and an improvement in immune function (Natural Killer cell number and activity) following massage therapy. That massage therapy boosts the immune system is not surprising given that massage has been shown in numerous studies to reduce cortisol and stress-related hormones (e.g., norepinephrine and epinephrine). Research reveals a negative correlation between cortisol (stress hormones) and the immune system (Lutgendorf, Antoni, Schneiderman, & Fletcher, 1994; Zorrilla, Redei, & DeRubeis, 1994). That massage therapy reduces cortisol levels may underlie the positive effects of massage on diseases affecting the immune system.

Psychiatric Patients

Children and adolescents hospitalized for depression and adjustment disorder were given a 30-minute massage or a relaxing video to watch on five separate days (Field et al., 1992). Anxiety, depression, and salivary cortisol levels were reduced for those in the massage therapy group. Those patients also spent more time sleeping (fewer night wakings and less activity). In addition, nurses rated the children receiving massage as being less anxious and more cooperative and having less trouble sleeping. Only the depressed children who received massage therapy were found to have lower catecholamine levels by the end of the study.

SUMMARY AND CONCLUSIONS

Stress in infancy and childhood may arise from physiological responses to chronic illness, such as prematurity, colic, or diabetes. Stress may also emerge because of a hostile environment, such as crowding, rearing by a depressed mother, or sensory deprivation (Field, 1995; Turkewitz, 1994) or from mental illness or sleep difficulty. In adolescence, stress-related experiences can be rooted in biological development, such as in pubertal changes that involve internal endocrine changes, outer physical changes, weight maintenance, peer pressure to try new experiences, parental expectations, and facing occupational choices (Peterson & Spiga, 1982). Chronic stress has been associated with negative affect, including depression, anxiety, elevated stress hormones, suppressed immune function, and chronic illness (Nair & Schwartz, 1995; Zorilla et al., 1994). Therefore, interventions that reduce stress should have a positive impact on physical and psychological well-being.

In this chapter, data were presented from pediatric studies revealing that massage therapy (1) reduces stress and stress hormones, anxiety levels, and depression; (2) brings about quiescence and alertness during awake states; (3) promotes better sleep patterns; (4) enhances growth and motor development in preterm infants and children with Down Syndrome; (5) enhances immune function; and (6) ameliorates disease markers for diabetes, pulmonary conditions, and skin disorders.

One mechanism underlying many of the observed massage therapy effects is the stimulation of the pressure receptors that activate vagal activity. The vagus nerve branches to the gastrointestinal tract, lungs, and heart and helps slow down physiological functions and regulate digestion, respiration, and heart rate (Porges, 1984). Evidence for vagal activity includes data showing that following massage therapy, there is an increase of vagal tone and insulin levels (Field, 1994) and better glucose control (Field, Hernandez-Reif, LaGreca, et al., 1997); preterm infants gain weight (Dieter et al., 1999; Field et al., 1986; Wheeden et al., 1993); respiration improves in pulmonary conditions (Field, Henteleff, et al., 1998; Hernandez-Reif, Field, Krasnegor, et al., 1998); and attentional performance is enhanced (Cigales et al., 1997; Field, Quintino, et al., 1998; Hart et al., 1998).

Massage therapy has also been shown to reduce cortisol levels, and this is believed to be the mechanism underlying the improved immune functions (increased Natural Killer cells) in our immune studies. This hypothesis is supported by data showing a negative relationship between cortisol and Natural Killer cells (Nair & Schwartz, 1995).

Taken together, massage therapy research findings provide compelling support for massage as a therapeutic intervention. In conjunction with psychotherapy and/or standard medical care, massage therapy may facilitate more optimal mental and physical health status for pediatric cases. The general application of massage therapy for enhancing the mental and physical well-being of infants, children, and adolescents is an important next step.

REFERENCES

Abrams, S., Field, T., Scafidi, F., & Prodromidis, M. (1995). Newborns of depressed mothers. *Infant Mental Health Journal, 16,* 231–237.

Alessandri, S., Sullivan, M., Imaizumi, S., & Lewis, M. (1993). Learning and emotional responsivity in cocaine-exposed infants. *Developmental Psychology, 29,* 989–997.

Cassidy, J., & Petty, R. (1995). *Textbook of pediatric rheumatology* (3rd ed.). Philadelphia: Saunders.

Chan, R., Huey, E., Maecker, H., Cortopassi, K., Howard, S., Iyer, A., McIntosh, L., Ajilore, O., Brooke, S., & Sapolsky, R. (1996). Endocrine modulators of necrotic neuron death. *Brain Pathology, 6,* 481–491.

Cigales, M., Field, T., Lundy, B., Cuadra, A., & Hart, S. (1997). Massage enhances recovery from habituation in normal infants. *Infant Behavior and Development, 20*, 29–34.

Cohn, J., Matias, R., Tronick, E., Connell, D., & Lyons-Ruth, K. (1986). Face-to-face interactions of depressed mothers and their infants. In E. Tronick & T. Field (Eds.), *Maternal depression and infant disturbance*. San Francisco: Jossey-Bass.

Diego, M., Field, T., Hernandez-Reif, M., & Shaw, J. (1999). *Adolescents with conduct disorder and oppositional defiant disorder show lower levels of testosterone and salivary cortisol and improved mood with massage therapy.* (ongoing study).

Diego, M., Hernandez-Reif, M., Field, T., & Shaw, K. (1999). *Adolescents with HIV have improved immune function after massage therapy.* (ongoing study).

Dieter, J., Field, T., Hernandez-Reif, M., & Emory, G. (1999). *Preterm infants gain more weight following 5 days of massage therapy.* (in review).

Field, T. (1984). Early interactions between infants and their postpartum depressed mothers. *Infant Behavior and Development, 7*, 527–532.

Field, T. (1994). Massage therapy for infants and children. *Journal of Developmental and Behavioral Pediatrics, 16*, 105–111.

Field, T. (1995). Psychologically depressed parents. *Handbook of Parenting: Applied and Practical Parenting, 4*, 85–89.

Field, T., Fox, N., Pickens, J., & Nawrocki, T. (1995). Relative right frontal EEG activation in 3- to 6-month-old infants of "depressed" mothers. *Developmental Psychology, 31*, 358–363.

Field, T., Grizzle, N., Scafidi, F., Abrams, S., Richardson, S., Kuhn, C., & Schanberg, S. (1996). Massage therapy for infants of depressed mothers. *Infant Behavior and Development, 19*, 107–112.

Field, T., Grizzle, N., Scafidi, F., & Schanberg, S. (1996). Massage and relaxation therapies' effects on depressed adolescent mothers. *Adolescence, 31*, 903–911.

Field, T., Henteleff, T., Hernandez-Reif, M., Martinez, E., Mavunda, K., Kuhn, C., & Schanberg, S. (1998). Children with asthma have improved pulmonary functions after massage therapy. *Journal of Pediatrics, 132*, 854–858.

Field, T., & Hernandez-Reif, M. (in press). Sleep problems in infants decrease following massage therapy. *Early Child Development and Care.*

Field, T., Hernandez-Reif, M., Field, T., Cullen, C., Kissel, B., Bango-Sanchez, V., & Sprinz, P. (1999). *Pediatric oncology benefits from massage therapy.* (ongoing study)

Field, T., Hernandez-Reif, M., LaGreca, A., Shaw, K., Schanberg, S., & Kuhn, C. (1997). Massage therapy lowers blood glucose levels in children with diabetes. *Diabetes Spectrum, 10,* 28–30.

Field, T., Hernandez-Reif, M., Seligman, S., Krasnegor, J., Sunshine, W., Rivas-Chacon, R., Schanberg, S., & Kuhn, C. (1997). Juvenile rheumatoid arthritis benefits from massage therapy. *Journal of Pediatric Psychology, 22,* 607–617.

Field, T., Kilmer, T., Hernandez-Reif, M., & Burman, I. (1996). Preschool children's sleep and wake behavior: Effects of massage therapy. *Early Child Development and Care, 120,* 39–41.

Field, T., Lasko, D., Mundy, P., Henteleff, T., Kabat, S., Talpins, S., & Dowling, M. (1997). Brief report: Autistic children's attentiveness and responsivity improve after touch therapy. *Journal of Autism and Developmental Disorders, 27,* 333–338.

Field, T., Morrow, C., Valdeon, C., Larson, S., Kuhn, C., & Schanberg, S. (1992). Massage reduces anxiety in child and adolescent psychiatric patients. *Journal of the American Academy of Child and Adolescent Psychiatry, 31,* 125–131.

Field, T., Quintino, O., Hernandez-Reif, M., & Koslovsky, O. (1998). Attention-deficit/hyperactivity disorder adolescents benefit from massage therapy. *Adolescence, 33,* 103–108.

Field, T., Schanberg, S., Davalos, M., & Malphurs, J. (1996). Massage with oil has more positive effects on normal infants. *Pre- and Perinatal Psychology Journal, 11,* 75–80.

Field, T., Schanberg, S., Kuhn, C., Field, T., Fierro, K., Henteleff, T., Mueller, C., Yando, R., Shaw, S., & Burman, I. (1998). Bulimic adolescents benefit from massage therapy. *Adolescence, 33,* 555–563.

Field, T., Schanberg, S., Scafidi, F., Bauer, C., Vega-Lahr, N., Garcia, R., Nystrom, J., & Kuhn, C. (1986). Tactile/kinesthetic stimulation effects on preterm neonates. *Pediatrics, 77,* 654–658.

Field, T., Seligman, S., Scafidi, F., & Schanberg, S. (1996). Alleviating posttraumatic stress in children following Hurricane Andrew. *Journal of Applied Developmental Psychology, 17,* 37–50.

Hart, S., Field, T., & Hernandez-Reif, M. (in press). Preschoolers' cognitive performance improves following massage. *Early Child Development and Care.*

Hernandez-Reif, M., Field, T., Bornstein, J., & Fewell, R. (1999a). *Children with Cerebral Palsy improve with massage therapy.* (ongoing study)

Hernandez-Reif, M., Field, T., Bornstein, J., & Fewell, R. (1999b). *Down Syndrome children show improvement in fine and gross motor skills with massage therapy.* (ongoing study)

Hernandez-Reif, M., Field, T., Del Pino, N., & Diego, M. (1998). *Exploration by mouth differs for neonates of depressed mothers.* (in review)

Hernandez-Reif, M., Field, T., Krasnegor, J., Martinez, E., Schwartzman, M., & Mavunda, K. (1999). Children with cystic fibrosis benefit from massage therapy. *Journal of Pediatric Psychology, 24,* 175–181.

Hernandez-Reif, M., Field, T., Redzepi, M., Niremberg, B., & Peck, M. (1998). *Burn treatments for infants and young children are less stressful following massage therapy.* (in review)

Hernandez-Reif, M., Ironson, G., Field, T., Weiss, S., Katz, G., & Fletcher, M. (1998). *Breast cancer patients have enhanced immune function and lower stress hormones following massage therapy.* (ongoing study)

Ironson, G., Field, T., Scafidi, F., Hashimoto, M., Kumar, M., Kumar, A., Price, A., Goncalves, A., Burman, I., Tetenman, C., Patarca, R., & Fletcher, M. (1996). Massage therapy is associated with enhancement of the immune system's cytotoxic capacity. *International Journal of Neuroscience, 84,* 205–217.

Jones, N.A., Field, T., Fox, N.A., Davalos, M., Lundy, B., & Hart, S. (1998). Newborns of mothers with depressive symptoms are physiologically less developed. *Infant Behavior and Development, 21,* 537–541.

Knaster, M. (1996). *Discovering the body's wisdom.* New York: Bantam Books.

Lundy, B., Field, T., & Pickens, J. (1996). Newborns of mothers with depressive symptoms are less expressive. *Infant Behavior and Development, 19,* 419–424.

Lundy, B., Field, T., Pickens, J., Cigales, M., & Cuadra, A. (1997). Vocal and facial expression matching in infants of mothers with depressive symptoms. *Infant Mental Health Journal, 18,* 265–273.

Lundy, B., Jones, N., Field, T., Pietro, P., Nearing, G., Davalos, M., Schanberg, S., & Kuhn, C. (in press). Prenatal effects on neonates. *Infant Behavior and Development.*

Lutgendorf, S., Antoni, M., Schneiderman, N., & Fletcher, M. (1994). Psycho-social counseling to improve quality of life in HIV infection. *Patient Education and Counseling, 24,* 217–235.

Mayes, L., Granger, R., Frank, M., Schottenfeld, J. & Bornstein, M. (1993). Neurobehavioral profiles of neonates exposed to cocaine prenatally. *Pediatrics, 91,* 778–783.

McMenamy, C., Katz, R., & Gipson, M. (1988). Treatment of eczema by EMG biofeedback and relaxation training: A multiple baseline analysis. *Journal of Behavioral Therapy and Experimental Psychiatry, 19,* 221–227.

Nair, M., & Schwartz, S. (1995). Synergistic effect of cortisol and HIV-1 envelope peptide on the NK activities of normal lymphocytes. *Brain, Behavior and Immunity, 9,* 20–30.

Peterson, A., & Spiga, R. (1982). Adolescence and stress. In L. Goldberger & S. Breznitz (Eds.), *Handbook of stress: Theoretical and clinical aspects.* New York: Free Press.

Porges, S. (1984). Physiologic correlates of attention: A core process underlying learning disorders. *Pediatric Clinics of North America, 31,* 371–385.

Scafidi, F., & Field, T. (1996). Massage therapy improves behaviors in neonates born to HIV-positive mothers. *Journal of Pediatric Psychology, 21,* 889–897.

Scafidi, F., & Field, T. (1997). Brief report: HIV-exposed newborns show inferior orienting and abnormal reflexes on the Brazelton scale. *Journal of Pediatric Psychology, 22,* 105–112.

Schachar, R., & Tannock, R. (1993). Childhood hyperactivity and psychostimulants: A review of extended treatment studies. *Journal of the American Medical Association, 260,* 2256–2258.

Schachner, L., Field, T., Hernandez-Reif, M., Duarte, A., & Krasnegor, J. (1998). Atopic dermatitis symptoms decreased in children following massage therapy. *Pediatric Dermatology, 15,* 390–395.

Surwit, R., Ross, S., & Feingloss, M. (1991). Stress, behavior, and glucose control in diabetes mellitus. In P. McCabe, N. Schneidermann, T. Field, & J. Skyler (Eds.), *Stress, coping and disease.* Hillsdale, NJ: Erlbaum.

Swanson, J., McBurnett, K., Christian, D., & Wigal, T. (1995). Stimulant medication and treatment of children with ADHD. In T.H. Ollendick & R.Z. Prinz (Eds.), *Advances in Clinical Child Psychology, 17,* 265–322.

Turkewitz, G. (1994). Sources of order for intersensory functioning. In D. Lewkowicz & R. Lickliter (Eds.), *The development of intersensory functioning.* Hillsdale, NJ: Erlbaum.

Wheeden, A., Scafidi, F., Field, T., Ironson, G., Valdeon, C., & Bandsta, E. (1993). Massage effects on cocaine-exposed preterm neonates. *Developmental and Behavioral Pediatrics, 14,* 318–322.

Zorrilla, E., Redei, E., & DeRubeis, R. (1994). Reduced cytokine levels and T-cell function in healthy males: Relation to individual differences in subclinical anxiety. *Brain, Behavior and Immunity, 8,* 293–312.

CHAPTER 14

Bibliotherapy: The Use of Children's Literature as a Therapeutic Tool

DEANNE GINNS-GRUENBERG and ARYE ZACKS

HISTORICAL BACKGROUND

THE CONCEPT of using books as a healing device has been around for more than 2500 years. The library in ancient Alexandria, Egypt, had "The Nourishment for the Soul" inscribed over the entranceway. "The Healing of the Soul," read an inscription at the Thebes library, and "The Medicine for the Soul" was inscribed in the walls of the library at an ancient Swiss abbey. Realizing that reading stimulates emotional arousal, Aristotle claimed that reading could heal the mind. The Romans would read religious teachings to the mentally ill, and reading to prisoners and mental patients was common practice throughout the Middle Ages.

In the early 1800s, Benjamin Rush recommended reading for the sick and the mentally ill. In 1846, Dr. John Minson Galt II wrote a seminal article on bibliotherapy, although he is better known for his 1853 essay, entitled "On Reading, Recreation, and Amusement for the Insane."

In a 1916 article for the *Atlantic Monthly*, Samuel McChord Crothers initialed the use of the term *bibliotherapy*. Rooted in the

Latin *biblion* (book) and *oepatteid* (healing), it was defined in 1941, in *Dorland's Illustrated Medical Dictionary* as the "employment of books and the reading of them in the treatment of nervous disease" (Dorland, 1941).

Today bibliotherapy is used to help a wide range of people suffering from a number of different emotional and behavioral problems—from preschool children lacking self-esteem to drug addicts recovering from addiction. Bibliotherapy is also helpful to parents trying to gain insight into the behavior of their children. For example, in *Nugget and Darling* (Joosse, 1997), a story about a dog and cat living in the same home, parents can understand what their children go through when a new baby enters into the family. Bibliotherapists often prescribe or utilize movies, music, newspapers, poetry, and works of art to maximize the benefit for clients. Additionally, they use puppets, dolls, and other expressive techniques.

To maximize the benefit and impact of a book for a client, a trained therapist is critical to increase the focus and facilitate expression of feelings and discussion of issues divulged by the characters.

A modern definition of bibliotherapy is "The use of literature by a therapist to help children resolve problems." With this definition, a triangle is formed between the therapist, the client, and the literature, which facilitates dialog and expression of issues (see Figure 14.1).

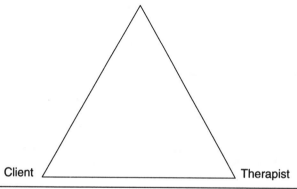

Figure 14.1   The Literature Relationship.

The client reads the literature, or has it read to him, and the therapist uses the literary piece to help the client examine issues. The therapist must have a strong knowledge of the literary content, the developmental level of the child, and the psychological needs of the client. The literature must be age appropriate, culturally accurate, and selected for the specific client (see Figure 14.2). It is not just the reading that facilitates the healing in the client. Rather, it is the therapeutic discussion or expression of feelings following the reading that leads to resolution for the client.

RATIONALE FOR BIBLIOTHERAPY

Although there are many therapeutic change agents in bibliotherapy, the four primary ones are identification, catharsis, insight, and universalization.

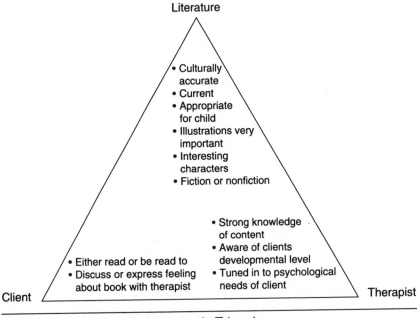

Figure 14.2   The Bibliotherapeutic Triangle.

IDENTIFICATION

The identification process begins with a relationship between the client and a character in the story. This relationship expands the client's self-concept, as the reader comes to understand that his situation is not unique, and he is not alone. For example, young children with limited experience may not recognize their situation is the exception rather than the rule (e.g., physical abuse, child with a mentally ill parent). Also, children (who recognize that their situation is not the norm) learn they are not alone in their situation, and consequently feel less isolated. Seeing their own feelings, expressed by others, in print, affirms to children that others have felt similarly.

CATHARSIS

After identification takes place, readers begin to feel emotional ties to the character, as they relate to the situation or plight of the character. As clients become emotionally involved with the character, they may experience a catharsis, that is, a purging and purifying of their own emotions.

INSIGHT

At this stage, readers learn that their problem doesn't have to be crippling, since characters resolve their crisis by the end of the story, and become positive role models for children. As readers position themselves in the characters' circumstance, they, with the help of the therapist, begin to realize that they, too, have control of their own life situation. This insight allows the client to move from hopelessness to hopefulness.

UNIVERSALIZATION

The client comes to understand, through discussion and/or creative expression with the therapist, that his problems are not his alone. While this stage is touched on during the identification stage, it is more complete here, with the combination of what has been read, along with the dialog and experience between the group members and the therapist.

RESEARCH FINDINGS

A 1986 survey of 487 practitioners in the Portland, Oregon, area showed that 88% of psychologists, 59% of psychiatrists, and 86% of internists use self-help books in their treatment of clients. A national survey taken in 1988 found that 96% of psychologists prescribe books at least occasionally. With so many therapists recommending books to their clients, the question "Do they work?" needs to be asked. Despite the popularity of prescribing books these days, research on the effectiveness of Bibliotherapy is limited.

Stevens and Pfost (1982) reviewed the experimental studies of bibliotherapy from 1965 to 1982. They concluded that bibliotherapy was an effective tool for changing attitudes of clients. These results agreed with those of Schrank and Engels (1981) who found considerable empirical support for the effectiveness of bibliotherapy in changing client attitudes, assertiveness, and self-development. Craighead, McNamara, and Horan (1984) evaluated several self-help approaches. They found bibliotherapy to be an effective intervention for problem drinking, obesity, career indecision, and fear reduction. Other studies have found bibliotherapy to be effective in reducing children's nail biting, treating insomnia, and in changing adolescents' inappropriate behavior.

THERAPEUTIC GOALS
OF BIBLIOTHERAPY

As with other therapies, the overriding goal of bibliotherapy is to provide hope for the client and to empower the client to resolve presenting issues. Bibliotherapy has four specific goals that the therapist tries to help the client achieve:

1. Improve capacity to respond.
2. Increase self-understanding.

3. Increase awareness of interpersonal relationships.
4. Improve reality orientation.

IMPROVING CAPACITY TO RESPOND

When morale is low, clients tend to narrow their view of the world to their own personal worry cycle. They have trouble recognizing anything else. By its very nature, bibliotherapy assists the client in breaking out of this vicious cycle, eliciting concentration on and conversation about the literature. Once the cycle is broken, the client can then attend to things outside the worry cycle.

INCREASING SELF-UNDERSTANDING

Bibliotherapy offers a unique mirror for the people to understand themselves. There are three ways clients gain new self-understanding. First, clients can respond freely, as they express how they feel toward characters and situations in the literature. Ultimately, the simple give-and-take about what transpired can illuminate the path toward a stronger self-understanding. Second, clients gain insight to themselves through remembering the past. The literature can jog their memory, triggering repressed and forgotten memories, which can explain why they are acting the way they are, and give them an appreciation and understanding for the choices that they are currently making in their lives. Third, opinions are the most authentic part of the individual, and what makes each individual unique. Giving opinions about the choices that characters make empower the clients to realize that their opinions matter. It can then lead to better understanding of one's own personal crisis.

INCREASE AWARENESS OF INTERPERSONAL RELATIONSHIPS

Man is a social animal and has a strong need to affiliate with others. Using bibliotherapy, clients learn to interact more with others. First, they develop an awareness of feelings as being universal. Anxiety and other stressful emotions leave people feeling as if they are all alone. Children, especially, haven't learned or don't understand the universality of their suffering. It is only when confronted by a character who understands their feelings and knows exactly what they are thinking, that they begin to comprehend that they are not alone. At the very least, the author of the story knows what they are going through. Moreover, they can accept more fully that they have feelings for others. Regardless of whether those feelings are negative, such as a disagreement with a character's decision; or positive, as in an agreement with a character's decision, the client is forced to acknowledge a sense of feelings for others.

ENLARGING REALITY ORIENTATION

Through literature, the client begins to have a better grip on reality, understanding some of the basic facts of life, such as:

- Life is often times unfair.
- Life is full of challenging ups and downs.
- One must be responsible for the way one lives.
- One cannot always be in control.
- One cannot change how others think, feel, or behave.

The literature used in bibliotherapy is a powerful vehicle for examining these issues. While these four goals are the primary goals when conducting a bibliotherapy session, there are other, more concrete goals, such as:

- Teaching constructive and positive thinking.
- Encouraging free expression.
- Looking at alternative solutions.
- Sensitizing children to others' life situations.
- Examining new coping skills.
- Trying on new behaviors.

APPLICATIONS

Bibliotherapy can be successfully implemented in various situations, including working with children with emotional problems, dealing with minor adjustment problems in children, helping young clients deal with developmental concerns, fostering sensitivity and understanding for other children. It can work well in both group and individual settings. Bibliotherapy can also be used with adolescent and adult clients.

PRINCIPLES OF BIBLIOTHERAPY

There are six basic principles that guide the therapist in making the bibliotherapy session effective for children:

1. Use reading materials that the child is familiar with.
2. Be aware of the length of the reading material.
3. The reading material should be applicable to the child's problem.
4. The therapist must know the child's reading level. If the child is unable to read (or has a learning disability) reading aloud or using audiovisual materials can be used.
5. The child's emotional and developmental age must be considered when choosing reading material.
6. Reading preferences should be considered:
   - Ages 3 to 7 stories of familiar events.
   - Ages 8 to 11, fantasy stories.
   - Ages 12 to 15, animal, adventure, mystery, and sports stories.
   - Ages 15 to 18, romance, war, and adolescent life stories.
   - Ages 18 to 21, personal value, social significance, transitional adult stories.

CHOOSING MATERIALS

The therapist must carefully screen reading materials. All material should be reviewed before being assigned to the child, and the therapist should ask the following questions to determine its appropriateness:

- Can the child identify with the plot, setting, dialog, and characters?
- Does the book reflect an appreciation for individuality?

- Does the story present the crisis as surmountable?
- Are there good coping strategies for the child to learn?
- Is the story culturally accurate?

Additionally, a book may be considered appropriate if it can help the child with the following:

- Acquire information and knowledge of human behavior.
- Discover oneself.
- Find another interest.
- Relieve conscious problems in a controlled manner.
- Utilize an opportunity for identification.
- Illuminate difficulties and get insight into one's behavior.

Many bibliotherapists are hesitant to use books with animals as the main character. They are concerned that the child will not recognize himself in an animal character. This concern is unfounded with preschool and primary grade children. These children often find it easier to express themselves through an animal character. The animal adds an additional level of distance, making it easier for the child to talk about what is truly on his mind.

Books have been published that can help children in many areas, including conflict, guilt, embarrassment, divorce, grief, fear, anger, parental alcoholism, sexual abuse, denial, step-families, peer pressure, and violence. At the end of this chapter is a list of excellent books that can be implemented in bibliotherapy.

THE TECHNIQUE OF BIBLIOTHERAPY

The following is a step-by-step guide for running a bibliotherapy session. The first step applies primarily to school counselors, while the following steps apply to anyone facilitating a session.

STEP 1 FOR SCHOOL COUNSELORS

For bibliotherapy to be effectively implemented in a school, school counselors must begin by explaining the process, what bibliotherapy is, and how it will be used. For example, the therapist might say, "I will be using books to help me assist children who are having difficulty coping with their parents' divorce." The school counselor should be careful to avoid the term bibliotherapy. Many parents are put off by any terminology involving therapy. Rather, they should refer to it as a "Books to Grow With" program, or a similar creative term.

Counselors will also find it helpful to enlist the support of librarians and English teachers who can help select the material. The counselor must be clear about the goals for bibliotherapy for a particular child. They might be to assist the child in improving his capacity to respond, to increase his understanding of self, to clarify his personal relationships, or to enlarge his reality orientation.

STEP 2 LOCATION

Reading is generally associated with relaxation and comfort, so the therapist should try to find a nonthreatening, relaxing area to work. Libraries, outdoors on a nice day, or sitting on a rug on the floor of the therapist's office are just a few of the places a therapist might consider.

STEP 3 LENGTH

The length of the session will vary depending on how many children are involved, the age of the children, and their personality. Generally, for children less than 10, a small group of 4 to 6 children meeting for 30 to 45 minutes, would be appropriate. For children aged 10 to 13, a 50 to 90 minute session with 5 to 8 children is ideal. For a therapist working one on one, where books are only a part of the therapy, the therapist may choose to spend only 10 or 15 minutes on books, and the rest of the time utilizing other modalities. The reading may take place at the beginning, middle, or near the end of the session.

STEP 4 SEATING

In a group setting, the therapist arranges seating in a circle, making everybody equal, and giving everybody a chance to speak out. In individual or group therapy, everyone, including the therapist, should be at eye level, even if this means sitting on a "kiddy chair."

STEP 5 BEFORE THE SESSION BEGINS

With younger children, the therapist should select the reading material that will be read during the group. With adolescents, the therapist often assigns material to be read before the session.

STEP 6 THE SESSION

Before going over the material, you might ask each child in the group to choose a puppet or stuffed animal. During the reading, the puppet may be a comfortable companion for the client to hold. Later, the puppet will allow the child to project his or her feelings. These nonverbal actions often lend insight to what is going on inside the mind of the child.

After everyone is seated, the therapist begins reading the material to the children. The story does not need to be told in its entirety, or read exactly as the author wrote it. The counselor adjusts the story to match the group of children, leaving out material that may be inappropriate or unnecessarily complex, and repeating or emphasizing phrases with powerful messages. When reading, the therapist should pause so the children can look at the pictures, and allow them the opportunity to comment on them. The importance of illustrations cannot be overemphasized, as some children identify more strongly with pictures than the written word.

After completing the story, the therapist opens the discussion of the story. However, the therapist may want to avoid asking direct or confrontational questions. One of the principle benefits of bibliotherapy is that it allows distance for the child. By asking direct, confrontational questions, the therapist may sabotage the bibliotherapeutic process. Rather, the therapist makes open-ended comments, such as "I wonder what Rabbit was thinking." These ambiguous and inviting remarks allow children the necessary distance they need. Children can then project their feelings onto Rabbit. Using the puppets and stuffed animals, children can also have the puppets answer questions, providing another level of distance for the child. Throughout the session, the therapist pays attention to the nonverbal cues the children give, both during the reading and the discussion, such as tone, pitch, rate, intensity, nervous mannerisms, flushing, or tensing.

The therapist encourages everyone's participation, since it is the give and take of the session that allows growth to occur, and leads to the true discovery of self. However, some children will participate more then others, some children will participate nonverbally by using the puppet or drawing a picture, and some will gain merely by watching and observing the rest of the group.

STEP 7 ELICITING PARTICIPATION

In addition to the discussion, and especially for young children who lack language skills, therapists can use other tools and methods to elicit responses. Children can be encouraged to draw pictures. Filtered through their own experiences, these drawings give insight about what is going on inside each child. Puppets are another popular method for getting children to articulate what is going on inside. The natural love children have for puppets and books make this blend a powerful intervention. Many therapists use creative writing exercises to maximize the benefits for their clients. Exercises such as writing a letter from one character to another or rewriting the final chapter, encourage the child to express how he feels about what happened in the story, and can lead to insight and growth.

STEP 8 ENDING A SESSION

Before ending a session, the therapist may encourage everyone in the group to write a sentence or paragraph about what the session meant to them. This allows the therapist to follow growth and detect patterns in the clients. Sharing these comments with the group is an additional option. It is helpful to end the session with an upbeat, fun activity.

SPECIAL CONSIDERATIONS FOR ONE-ON-ONE BIBLIOTHERAPY

With sensitive topics, sometimes it is helpful to just leave several books on a table and allow the child to gravitate to the books that fit his or her needs. For example you might leave several books, such as *Young, Gay, and Proud* (Romesburg, 1995), *Sometimes My Mom Drinks Too Much* (Kenny & Krull, 1992), and *I Told My Secret*

(Gil, 1986), easily accessible to the client. This strategy tells the client that you are comfortable with the topics; it has proven effective with many children.

The therapist can also involve the parent or family members. She may script the parent on what to read and emphasize to the child. For example, at the initial meeting with a client's parent or caretaker, the adult is advised to read at home with the child, *A Child's First Book About Play Therapy* (Nemiroff & Annunziata, 1990), to prepare the child for the upcoming therapy sessions.

SPECIAL CONSIDERATIONS FOR OLDER CHILDREN

Very often, there is a hesitancy to prescribe or read "babyish" books for older children. The child may feel insulted, and not want to read the book, even though the book may help clear up issues for the child. There are several approaches a therapist can use to encourage the older child to read the book. First, be honest with the client. Explain that while the book may look babyish, many children of the client's age and older have found the book to be helpful. Usually the child will read the book, since the therapist has already told him it is a babyish book. A second strategy is to tell the client that you need his help. You have a younger client with similar issues and want to know if he thinks this book will help. Explain to the child that you value her opinion, and since she is closer in age to the client, she may have a better idea about what parts will be most helpful, and what parts can be skipped. A third procedure is the younger sibling/student approach. Ask the child to read the book to a younger sibling or younger student. Explain that while the book might seem babyish to him, it is important so that the younger child can understand it. This method is mutually beneficial to both parties, as it encourages the older child to read the book and gives the younger child a sense of importance, as an older kid is taking the time to read with him.

BARRIERS TO BIBLIOTHERAPY

There are three main pitfalls to bibliotherapy (see Table 14.1). The first is the personality of the client. At times, clients don't identify with the character in the story. Moreover, they may lack an

Table 14.1
Limitations and Overcoming Them

Barriers	Limitation	How to Overcome
Personality	• Feels story doesn't apply. • Doesn't see oneself in story. • Adds to their own burden.	• Role play. • Puppet play. • Rewrite story. • Group dialog. • Write letter. • Alternative plan. • End bibliotherapy.
Therapist	• Lack of understanding of child development. • Failure to review literature in advance. • Use same books for all problems.	• Take child development courses. • Read books carefully. • Attend play therapy workshops. • Take note of what books work for which problems. • Consult with colleagues. • Consult with children about book content.
Interactive	• Client doesn't read material. • Lacks language skills. • Learning disability. • Discussion of surface issues. • Therapist puts down client.	• Alternate modality. • Use play therapy to communicate. • Revisit issues later. • Tape sessions for self-assessment and additional observation.

interest in reading, resist being read to, and refuse to participate. They may feel the lesson doesn't apply, or they don't recognize themselves in the character. To overcome these issues, the therapist can implement a role-playing game, to show the client that he really does have much in common with the character. Other ways to overcome these issues include group discussion, clear explanations of what is going on, or the creation of a related metaphor by the therapist.

A second major difficulty is the therapist's limited knowledge of the developmental stages, and the problems that are associated with moving from one stage to the next. Some therapists are not willing to adapt to the needs of the child, and come to the session with a preplanned agenda. Therapists also must have full understanding of the reading material, and avoid assigning material that preaches.

By enrolling in child development courses, the therapist may develop a clearer appreciation for the ages and stages of child development. The therapist should maintain a database of children's books, including what issues are addressed, best ages for the book, populations addressed, and activities that compliment the book. Finally, the therapist must be flexible to the changing needs and emerging issues that come out in the discussion with the child.

A third pitfall involves interactive process barriers. The failing here can come from several places. If the client doesn't read or pay attention to the material, bibliotherapy won't be very effective. Some children lack the verbal ability to articulate what they would like to say. Another limiting dimension is the discussion of surface issues, while avoiding the core issues. A fourth limitation occurs when the therapist insists on making points at the clients' expense, putting down the child in the process.

Just because children cannot verbally articulate what they have gained from the book, does not exclude them from participating in the process. If the child lacks the verbal skills to communicate what she is feeling, it is a good time to let the child play with toys. Through play therapy, the child will communicate whatever emerges from the reading. As for overcoming the avoidance of serious issues, the therapist will return to those issues, perhaps in a later session, and go over the issues that were glossed over superficially. This may be done metaphorically.

Videotaping sessions offers the opportunity for personal assessment and additional observation of the interactive relationship between client and therapist. The therapist should remember that books might serve a purpose at a later time, even if it is not currently effective.

CASE ILLUSTRATIONS

Jenny

Jenny was a 9-year-old, white female. Her presenting problem was an increasing number of nightmares involving her deceased father murdering family members. She suffered from numerous symptoms including fear of being left alone, refusal to sleep in own bed, increased clinginess to mom and increased anxiety. When Jenny was 7 years old, her father died of emphysema at the age of 40. Jenny felt that she was to blame for his death, since she had often awakened him in the middle of the night while in kindergarten. Recently, Jenny had been dealing with multiple losses. Both her grandparents died within one month of each other. A week after the loss of her second grandparent, she visited her uncle for Christmas, who died of an aneurysm immediately following her stay with him.

At night, Jenny would have terrifying recurring nightmares. In her dreams, her father would come into her mother's room, but her mother would not be in bed. He would then go into the living room, where her mother, sister, brother, and pets were all nailed to the wall.

Jenny's therapy consisted of bibliotherapy, storytelling, puppet play, drawings, and using a sandtray. She loved being read to and guessing how the characters would resolve their problems and surmount their challenges. Additionally, she would take books home to review for her therapist. Role-playing and puppet play were also frequent activities after the stories were read, and Jenny enjoyed recreating the stories in the sandtray.

Jenny's nightmare resolution came subsequent to her therapist selecting *Dear Bear* (Harrison, 1994), the story of a little girl who is scared of a bear that she's convinced lives under the stairway. The girl decides to write a letter to the bear, the bear writes back, and they end up becoming friends. In the story, the girl is empowered and desensitized as the illustrations clearly depict. Jenny was able to identify with the fear of the mysterious bear, the little girl, and identified herself in the pictures throughout the story.

During one session, the therapist asked Jenny to take *Dear Bear* home to review for her. The following session, while doing the sandtray, Jenny asked if she and the therapist could write a letter to her dad, just like the girl in *Dear Bear*. In her letter, she asked her father to come visit her in a dream. After writing the letter, she and her therapist wrote a response from him. In it she absolved herself from responsibility for his death.

Next to the letter, Jenny drew a sequence of pictures, starting with her saying goodnight to her mother, getting into bed with her stuffed animals, and then of her nightmare with Dad in a wheelchair, wielding a knife:

Dear Dad,

Please stop coming and scaring me in my dreams. Be *NICE* in my dreams, and make *SURE* nothing gets me.

Love,

Jenny

Dad's Response

Dear Jenny,

I am so sorry that I have been scaring you. I know you like scary movies, but I would *NEVER* want to hurt you. I want to keep you safe and I want to watch you grow up and be happy and never believe I would hurt you. Jenny, I am sorry if I made you think you caused me to get sick. A person could not make me get my disease. Jenny, I love you and I will come into your next dream and I will be smiling. I will leave my knife in heaven. In fact, I do not need my knife anymore. I will give it to Jesus, and he will break it and throw it away. I would never ever hurt you or your mom or sister or Brian [brother], or Shawn [pet] or Snowy [pet] and Puffy [pet] because I love them too and I especially love you and I would *NEVER EVER LET ANE* [sic] *ONE HURT YOU!!!!!!!!!!!!!!!!!!!!!!!!*

Love,

Dad

The letter had a huge cathartic effect on Jenny. After composing the letter, she read it for the video camera.

The nightmares ceased after that session. Within three weeks, Jenny had returned to sleep in her own bedroom.

Tammy

Tammy is a 4½-year-old female. Her parents divorced when she was 3. Since the divorce, Tammy has become increasingly tyrannical. Her symptoms, always present but especially virulent upon returning from her father's home include frequent tantrums, aggressiveness, mean comments toward her mother, reverting to baby talk, bedwetting, bossing her friends, and physical aggression toward other children.

In addition, Tammy was convinced that her mother would leave her at day care, and that her mother would not return whenever she left the house.

Tammy's therapist invited Tammy and her mother to read the book *Charlie Anderson* (Abercrombie, 1990). Charlie Anderson is a cat happily living in two homes, spending evenings in one home and days in his second home. Tammy reenacted the story with puppets, and her mother reported that Tammy's behavior had drastically improved. It was the mother reading *Charlie Anderson* with her daughter that gave Tammy permission to be happy in two homes. She was subsequently able to live in harmony in both homes. There were other issues that did not go away with the reading of *Charlie Anderson*. However, the issue of the transition from her father's home to her mother's home was reconciled.

Toby

After his parents divorced, 8-year-old Toby, didn't want to go out to play with his friends. He was afraid that other children would tease him for having only one parent living at home. Besieged by sadness and loss, Toby felt shame over his parents' divorce, and believed that he was the one to blame for their divorce. He feared that his parents would stop loving him and divorce him as well. He worried that if he left the house, no one would be there to take care of him when he returned.

Toby's therapist read the book *Dinosaurs Divorce* (Brown & Brown, 1986) with him, and then discussed the characters' issues with Toby. Toby came to understand that others had indeed survived a parent's divorce, and that there was nothing for him to feel ashamed of. Furthermore, he understood that regardless of how his parents felt about each other, they would always feel love toward him. Subsequently, for the first time since his parents' divorce, he was able to arrange a play date at a friend's house.

CONCLUSION

Books provide a voice for the fears, the concerns, the behaviors, and the hopes of the children we work with. Through books, we enter the child's world and let them lead us where they need to go. Books should be used as an adjunct to therapy—not as therapy itself. Bibliotherapy is not a panacea. Rather, it is an effective weapon for the therapist to use.

RECOMMENDED BOOKS FOR PARTICULAR CHILDHOOD PROBLEMS

ABANDONMENT

Great Gilly Hopkins. K. Paterson. Harper (1978). Ages 9 to 15.

Gilly idealizes her absent mother as she is shifted among foster care placements.

Issues include foster care, lying, attachment, and loss.

If Daddy Only Knew Me. L. McGinnis. Whitman (1993). Ages 4 to 8.

Kate's daddy deserted her family and lives a few blocks away with his new family.

Issues include family relationships, loss, and loneliness.

ADD/ADHD

Eagle Eyes. J. Gehret. Verbal Images (1996). Ages 6 to 11.

Ben's life improves after he is diagnosed with ADD and learns how to organize his life.

Issues include self-esteem, forgetfulness, stress management, self expression, family relationships, and seeking professional help.

Help Is on the Way. M. Nemiroff & J. Annunziata. Magination Press (1998). Ages 5 to 9.

Childrens' feelings and concerns about having ADD are normalized.

Issues include effects of ADD, self blame, and getting help.

Learning to Slow Down and Pay Attention. K. Nadeau & E. Dixon. Magination Press (1997). Ages 6 to 11.

This guidebook of checklists, cartoons, and activities offers a wealth of information for children with ADD.

Issues include making friends, school-related problems, anger, organization, seeking professional help, and self-expression.

Putting on the Brakes. P. Quinn & J. Stern. Magination Press (1991). Ages 8 to 12.

Children learn what ADHD is and methods for dealing with it. Activity workbook also available.

Issues include self-control, making friends, time management, and seeking help.

Shelley the Hyperactive Turtle. D. Moss. Woodbine (1989). Ages 4 to 8.

After being diagnosed with ADHD, Shelley feels better about herself.

Issues include hyperactivity, medication, self-esteem, and seeking professional help.

ADOPTION

Adoption Is for Always. L. W. Girard. Whitman (1986). Ages 5 to 8.

Celia acts out after discovering what it means to be adopted.

Issues include common emotions and parent child-communication. Coping techniques are offered by characters.

A Koala for Katie. J. London. Whitman (1993). Ages 3 to 6.

After adopting a baby koala bear, Katie understands why she was adopted.

Issues include family relationships and love.

Tell Me Again about the Night I Was Born. J.L. Curtis. HarperCollins (1996). Ages 3 to 7.

An adopted child asks about the night she was born.

Issues include reassurance and family relationships.

How It Feels to Be Adopted. J. Krementz. Knopf (1988). Ages 10 to 15.

Nineteen children, ages 8–16, talk about what it feels like to be adopted.

Issues include a wide range of experiences and emotions.

ALCOHOL

Banana Beer. C. Carrick. Whitman (1995). Ages 3 to 7.

Charlie discovers that even though his father drinks too much, his Dad will always love him.

Issues include dysfunctional families and friendship.

Dear Kids of Alcoholics. L. Hall & L. Cohn. Gurze Books (1988). Ages 9 to 15.

Jason explains alcoholism to children, describing his family's battle with the disease.

Issues include dealing with an alcoholic parent, destructive behavior, and the recovery process.

Sometimes My Mom Drinks Too Much. K. Kenny & H. Krull. Raintree (1980). Ages 5 to 9.

Maureen struggles with her Mom's alcoholism.

Issues include embarrassment, fear, and anger as well as hopefulness when a parent begins treatment.

ANGER

Don't Rant and Rave on Wednesdays. A. Moser. Landmark (1994). Ages 7 to 11.

Children understand what anger is and learn methods for dealing with their anger.

Issues include anger triggers, emotions, behaviors, and coping strategies.

Hot Stuff to Help Kids Chill. J. Wilde. LGR Publishing (1997). Ages 10 to 14.

Children learn to understand their feelings of anger, and how to calm down.

Issues include the relationship between thoughts and behavior.

I'm Mad. E. Crary. Parenting Press (1992). Ages 6 to 8.

Children learn strategies to deal with anger, in this "choose the next page" book. (Part of a series)

Issues include anger and father-daughter relationship.

Mean Soup. B. Everitt. Harcourt Brace (1992). Ages 2 to 7.

Throwing angry thoughts into a pot, Horace and his mom create a "mean soup" and diminish Horace's angry feelings.

Issues include parent child interaction and expressing feelings.

BEREAVEMENT

Don't Despair on Thursdays. A. Moser. Landmark (1996). Ages 6 to 10.

Children learn about grief and ways of dealing with loss.

Issues include grief feelings, death of someone special, death of a pet, divorce, moving, seeking help, and self-expression.

Help for the Hard Times. E. Hipp. Hazelden (1995). Ages 10 to 15.

A guide for coping with and growing from the loss of a loved one.

Issues include grief feelings, suicide, self-acceptance, peer support, and coping techniques.

Someone Special Died. J. Prestine. Paramount (1991). Ages 3 to 7.

Wonderfully illustrated, a young girl goes through the emotions of loss.

Issues include grief feelings including anger, sadness, loneliness, and memories.

Tough Boris. M. Fox. Voyager Books (1992). Ages 3 to 8.

Boris is a tough pirate, who cries when his parrot dies.

Issues include being tough, belonging, and expressing sadness.

When a Friend Dies. M. Gootman. Free Spirit (1994). Ages 10 and up.

Teens who experience loss are guided through their grief in this easy to read book.

Issues include emotional and physical pain, connecting to others, self-blame, and seeking help.

When Dinosaurs Die. L.K. Brown & M. Brown. Little, Brown (1996). Ages 3 to 10.

This colorful guide explains death and answers questions kids have.

Issues include causes of death, concerns about death, customs, grief feelings, and family relationships.

BULLYING

Being Bullied. K. Perry & C. Firmin. Barron's (1991). Ages 3 to 7.

Rita gets bullied by Bella, until she discovers how to make Bella stop.

Issues include friendship and communicating with parents and teachers.

How to Handle Teasers, Bullies, and Other Meanies. K. Cohen-Posey. Rainbow (1995). Ages 9 to 12.

Children learn creative verbal tactics to deal with bullies.

Issues include cruelty, social skills, and self-esteem.

King of the Playground. P. Naylor. Aladdin (1994). Ages 3 to 7.

Kevin's father teaches him to stand up to the playground bully.

Issues include fear, avoidance, problem solving, and assertiveness.

CHRONIC ILLNESS

The Lion Who Had Asthma. J. London. Whitman (1992). Ages 3 to 6.

Sean uses his imagination to deal with his asthma.

Issues include self-acceptance and stress management.

Taking Diabetes to School. K. Gosselin. Jayjo Books (1998). Ages 5 to 10.

Jayson explains what diabetes is and what it means to live with the disease.

Issues include self-acceptance, peer acceptance, and perseverance.

What About Me? A. Peterkin. Magination Press (1992). Ages 4 to 8.

Laura feels ignored, when her parents spend most of their time with her hospitalized brother.

Issues include jealousy, fear, guilt, and family relationships.

Young People and Chronic Illness. K. Huegel. Free Spirit (1998). Ages 10 to 15.

Nine children tell of their battle with chronic medical problems.

Issues include fear of dying, friendship, education, coping, and lost childhood. Specific diseases include hemophilia, diabetes, epilepsy, asthma, cancer, inflammatory bowel disease, arthritis, lupus, and congenital heart defect.

DIVORCE

Dinosaurs Divorce. L.K. Brown & M. Brown. Little, Brown (1986). Ages 3 to 8.

Dinosaurs explain what divorce is, and capture feelings kids have about divorce.

Issues include blended families, sibling relationships, family dynamics, loss, anger, and fear.

Mama and Daddy Bear's Divorce. C. M. Spelman. Whitman (1998). Ages 3 to 6.

Divorce is explained in the simplest terms, as Dinah Bear's parents divorce.

Issues include emotions related to divorce.

Mom and Dad Don't Live Together Anymore. K. Stinson. Firefly (1984). Ages 3 to 7.

Questions, fears, hopes and dreams a child has during divorce are explored in the voice of the child.

Issues include parent-child relationship and reassurance.

My Parents Are Divorced, Too. J. Blackstone-Ford. Magination Press (1997). Ages 10 to 14.

One family talks about their divorce and provides answers for other kids.

Issues include emotions and loss.

Will Dad Ever Move Back Home? P. Hogan. SteckVaughn (1992). Ages 5 to 8.

Laura is convinced that her parents don't love her anymore, and decides to run away.

Issues include loss, love, and acting-out behavior.

DOMESTIC VIOLENCE

A Family That Fights. S. C. Bernstein. Whitman (1991). Ages 6 to 10.

When dad hits mom, Henry experiences a wide array of emotions.

Issues include physical violence, helplessness, avoidance, and coping techniques.

Bruises. A.D. Vries. Bantam (1992). Ages 12 and up.

With her new friend Michael, Judith overcomes the beatings from her mother.

Issues include physical violence, peer support, and shame.

Don't Hurt Me Mama. M. Stanek. Whitman (1983). Ages 6 to 9.

A young child and her mother receive help after a teacher and school nurse are alerted to signs of physical abuse.

Issues include absent father, alcohol, verbal and physical abuse, and getting help.

Something Is Wrong at My House. D. Davis. Parenting Press (1984). Ages 3 to 10.

A child talks about his feelings, and learns how to cope when his parents fight.

Format for older and younger children.

Issues include fear, anger, hopelessness, and seeking help.

FEAR

Dear Bear. J. Harrison. CarolRhoda (1994). Ages 4 to 9.

Katie learns how to deal with her fear of the imaginary bear under the stairwell.

Issues include anxiety, empowerment, and family relationships.

Don't Be Afraid Tommy. K. Burmgart. Magi (1998). Ages 3 to 7.

While teaching his toy dog to overcome fear, Tommy overcomes his own fears.

Issue includes generalized fear.

Franklin in the Dark. P. Bourgeois. Scholastic (1986). Ages 3 to 7.

Franklin learns how to cope with his fear of dark, after talking to the other animals in the forest.

Issues include bedtime fears, peer support, and parent-child relationships.

FEELINGS

Double-Dip Feelings. B. Cain. Magination Press (1990). Ages 3 to 7.

Children learn that it is normal to have ambivalent feelings.

Issues include contrasting feelings at the same time.

Glad Monster Sad Monster. E. Emberley & A. Miranda. Little, Brown (1997). Ages 3 to 7.

Readers try on masks as they learn about feelings.

Issues include fear, love, sadness, and joy.

Life's Not Always Fair. S. Scott. HRD (1997). Ages 8 to 12.

Based on the life of Nicholas and his animal friends, children learn to identify their feelings and healthy ways to manage them.

Issues include anger, fear, joy, and confusion.

Today I Feel Silly and Other Moods That Make My Day. J.L. Curtis. HarperCollins (1998). Ages 3 to 7.

Silly. Confused. Grumpy. These are just some of the moods rhymed about in this delightful story. Includes a mood indicator chart.

Issues include universal feelings of children.

FOSTER CARE

The Dog Who Had Kittens. P. Robertus. Holiday House (1988). Ages 4 to 8.

Baxter nurtures neglected kittens and develops a relationship with their mother, after the kittens are given away.

Issues include jealousy, neglect, loss, and peer relationships.

Therapeutic Stories for Children in Foster Care. K. Lanners & K. Schwartzenberger. TM Renderings (1992). Ages 5 to 9.

The story of Casey the pig parallels emotions and behaviors of children in foster care.

Issues include rejection, hurt, anger, and anxiety of being abandoned, adjustment to placement (shelter, foster home, adoptive home) reunification, and adoption.

Threadbear. C. Gallaz. Creative Editions (1993). Ages 6 to 11.

Threadbear is taken in by an old man, who is trying to correct his violent past.

Issues include friendship, forgiveness, helping others, and moving on.

FRIENDSHIP

Cap It Off with a Smile. R. Inwald. Hilson Press (1994). Ages 6 to 11.

Children learn how to make and keep friends.

Issues include social skills and rejection.

Charlie the Caterpillar. D. Deluise. Aladdin (1990). Ages 4 to 8.

No one wants to play with Charlie, until he blooms into a beautiful butterfly. Charlie learns he doesn't need those kinds of friends.

Issues include rejection, loneliness, self-esteem, and fair-weather friends.

How to Be a Friend. L. Brown & M. Brown. Little Brown (1998). Ages 5 to 10.

Dinosaurs explain friendship and answer questions kids have in this colorful guide.

Issues include making friends, shyness, bullies, peer support, mediation, and resolving differences.

I'm Terrific. M. Sharmat. Holiday House (1977). Ages 4 to 7.

Jason Bear finds bragging and acting mean don't bring him friends.

Issues include narcissism, rejection, acting-out behavior, and self-esteem.

Roses Are Pink, Your Feet Really Stink. D. de Groat. Mulberry (1998). Ages 3 to 7.

Gilbert writes mean Valentine's Day cards to several of his classmates.

Issues include cruelty, rejection, peer support, and apologizing.

GAY AND LESBIAN

The Duke Who Outlawed Jelly Beans. J. Valentine. Alyson (1991). Ages 5 to 12.

These original fairy tales include children with homosexual parents.

Issues include tolerance, self-acceptance, and courage.

Daddy's Roommate. M Willhoite. Alyson (1990). Ages 4 to 8.

Nick lives with his dad and dad's partner Frank, doing everyday activities.

Issues include love and family relationships.

Saturday Is Pattyday. L. Newman. New Victoria Publishers (1993). Ages 3 to 7.

Frankie misses Patty, after she separates from his Mom.

Issues include separation and visitation.

Young, Gay, and Proud. D. Romesburg, Alyson (1995). Ages 12 to 16.

Teens address common concerns that other gay teens face.

Issues include confusion, loneliness, self-image, myths, coming out, bisexuality, health concerns, and getting help.

HONESTY

The Empty Pot. Demi. Henry Holt (1990). Ages 5 to 9.

After giving 100 percent effort, a young boy is rewarded for acting honestly.

Issues include cheating, shame, despair, decision making, and determination.

Milo and the Magical Stones. M. Pfister. North-South Books (1997). Ages 4 to 8.

Milo discovers magical rocks, which provide light and warmth. Readers choose whether this discovery will be used for good or bad.

Issues include peer relationships, greed, decision making, and loss.

PARENT IN PRISON

Nine Candles. M. Testa. CarolRhoda (1996). Ages 6 to 10.

Raymond visits his mother in prison on his birthday.

Issues include separation from mother, hopefulness, and father's compassion.

When Andy's Father Went to Prison. M. W. Hickman. Whitman (1990). Ages 6 to 11.

Andy, ashamed that his father is in prison, finds solace when he befriends a boy whose father is also unavailable.

Issues include school adjustment, anxiety, stealing, rejection, separation from parent, moving, and friendship.

Self-Esteem

Alexandra Keeper of Dreams. M. Baumgardner. Rocky River (1993). Ages 4 to 8.

Alexandra the duck perseveres to reach her dreams.

Issues include body image, accepting limitations, and setting goals.

Don't Feed the Monster on Tuesdays. A. Moser. Landmark (1991). Ages 6 to 11.

Children learn about self-esteem and get a self-esteem boost.

Issues include put-downs, self-talk, friendship, and self-worth.

I Like Me. N. Carlson. Puffin Books (1988). Ages 3 to 6.

Pig feels good about her body, her faults, and her personality.

Issues include positive self-awareness, body image, and making mistakes.

If I Ran the Family. L. Johnson & S.K. Johnson. Free Spirit (1992). Ages 5 to 8.

Debbie Dundee explains how things would be, if she were in charge of her family.

Issues include family relationships and opening discussions on sensitive topics.

The Lovables in the Kingdom of Self-Esteem. D. Loomans. Starseed (1991). Ages 3 to 7.

All the animals in the kingdom describe what makes them special.

Issues include courage, bravery, pride, and strength.

Separation Anxiety

Cat Got Your Tongue? C. E. Schaefer. Magination Press (1992). Ages 4 to 7.

With the help of her therapist, kindergartner Anna overcomes her anxiety and learns to make new friends.

Issues include school adjustment, stranger anxiety, shyness, making new friends, elective mutism, and seeking help.

The Kissing Hand. A. Penn. Child and Family Press (1993). Ages 3 to 7.

Chester is scared to leave his mother to go to school, until she tells him about the kissing hand.

Issues include parent-child relationship fear, anxiety, empowerment, and ritual.

Owl Babies. M. Waddell. Candlewick (1992). Ages 3 to 6.

Baby owls worry that their mother won't return when she goes out for a hunt.

Issues include fear, anxiety, and family relationships.

SEXUAL ABUSE

I Told My Secret. E. Gil. Launch Press (1986). Ages 3 to 8.

This book answers the questions kids have after they are abused.

Issues include self-blame, secrets, telling, rejection, trust, removal from home, going to court, and seeking help.

Laurie Tells. L. Lowery. First Avenue (1994). Ages 9 to 15.

After enduring abuse by her father, Laurie finally turns to her aunt for help.

Issues include parental denial, emotions after not being believed, courage to tell, and seeking help.

NoNo and the Secret Touch. S. Patterson. NSERDC (1993). Ages 3 to 8.

NoNo the Seal is molested. Includes audio cassette.

Issues include self-blame, tattling versus telling, seeking help, and friendship.

Someone in My Family has Molested Children. E. Gil & J. Turner. Launch Press (1997). Ages 5 to 10.

Questions and concerns children have about being molested are answered in this easy-to-read format.

Issues include feelings and fears after being molested, removal from home, jail, and seeking help.

Something Happened and I'm Scared to Tell. P. Kehoe. Parenting Press (1987). Ages 3 to 7.

After discussing it with a friendly lion, the child tells a grown up about being molested.

Issues include feelings of isolation and worthlessness, disclosure, and seeking help.

SIBLING RIVALRY

Darcy and Gran Don't Like Babies. J. Cutler. Scholastic (1993). Ages 3 to 6.

Darcy's grandmother helps Darcy accept her new baby brother.

Issues include intergenerational relationship, jealousy, expressing feelings, and acceptance.

Nugget and Darling. B. Joosse. Clarion (1997). Ages 3 to 7.

When Darling, a cat enters the family, Nugget, the family dog, gets jealous.

Issues include parent-child relationship, jealousy, new baby, and acting-out behavior.

Will You Mind the Baby, Davy? B. Weninger. North-South (1997). Ages 3 to 6.

Davy doesn't want a new sister, until he holds her in his arms.

Issues include friendship, responsibility, and love.

SPECIAL NEEDS

Andy and His Yellow Frisbee. M. Thompson. Woodbine (1996). Ages 6 to 10.

Andy, an autistic child, is befriended by the new girl at school, while his sister keeps an eye on him.

Issues include sibling relationships, friendship, and transitions.

Talking to Angels. E. Watson. Harcourt (1996). Ages 4 and up.

Christa is a very special girl.

Issues include autism, love, and acceptance of sister.

Very Special Critter. G. Mayer & M. Mayer. Golden (1992). Ages 3 to 6.

Little Critter learns that Alex can be one of the gang, even though he is in a wheelchair.

Issues include fear, acceptance at school, parental support, and friendship.

STEPPARENT

Changing Families. D. Fassler, M. Lash, & S. Ives. Waterfront (1996). Ages 4 to 12.

This workbook gives advice on coping with a changing family.

Issues include separation, divorce, and stepfamilies.

Room for a Stepdaddy. J. T. Cook. Whitman (1995). Ages 4 to 8.

Joey finds that there is a place in his life for his parents and his stepfather.

Issues include accepting two families.

STRESS

Cool Cats Calm Kids. M. Williams. Impact Publishers (1996). Ages 3 to 9.

Cats show children nine relaxation techniques.

Issues include stress management.

Don't Pop Your Cork on Mondays. A. Moser. Landmark (1988). Ages 6 to 10.

Children understand what stress is, and learn methods for dealing with their stress.

Issues include stress management and positive self-talk.

Relax. C. O'Neill. Child's Play (1993). Ages 5 to 10.

Children learn about stress triggers and new coping techniques to manage stressful situations.

Issues include childhood stresses, fears, and coping.

TERMINAL ILLNESS

Kathy's Hats. T. Krisher. Whitman (1992). Ages 6 to 11.

Kathy has cancer and has to wear a hat to cover her bald head.

Issues include peer acceptance at school, reframing, chemotherapy, and overcoming odds.

Little Tree. J. Mills. Magination (1992). Ages 5 to 12.

When little tree loses its branches to lightening, he thinks his life is over, until the wizards come and heal his broken branches.

Issues include body image, grief and loss, self-worth, accepting limitations, and discovering strengths.

TRAUMA

Brave Bart. C. Sheppard. TLC (1998). Ages 4 to 10.

Bart the Cat learns his thoughts, feelings and behavior after the trauma are common and normal.

Issues include PTSD triggers, peer relationships, getting professional help, trust, reassurance, group support, and hopefulness.

A Trauma Is Like No Other Experience. B. Steele. TLC (1997). All Ages.

You're Not Alone. B. Steele. TLC (1997). All ages.

What Parents Need to Know. B. Steele. TLC (1997). Parents.

These three books normalize feelings common in people experiencing post-traumatic stress disorder.

Issues include trauma experience, fear, hypervigilance, avoidance, and intrusive symptoms.

REFERENCES

Abercrombie, B. (1990). *Charlie Anderson*. New York: McElderry.

Afolayan, J. (1992). Documentary perspective of bibliotherapy in education. *Reading Horizons, 33,* 137–148.

Aiex, N.K. (1993). Bibliotherapy *Eric Digest, EDO-CS-93-05,* 2–3.

Brown, L.K., & Brown, M. (1986). *Dinosaurs divorce: A guide for changing families.* Boston: Little, Brown.

Cianciolo, P.J. (1965). Children's literature can affect coping behavior. *Personnel and Guidance Journal,* 897–903.

Craighead, L.W., McNamara, K., & Horan, J.J. (1984). Perspectives on self-help and bibliotherapy: You are what you read. *Handbook of counseling psychology.* New York: Wiley.

Dorland, W.A. (1941). *The American Illustrated Medical Dictionary: A complete dictionary of the terms used in medicine, surgery, dentistry, pharmacy, chemistry, nursing, veterinary science, biology, medical biography, etc., with the pronunciation and definitions.* Philadelphia: Saunders.

Gil, E. (1986). *I told my secret: A book for kids who were abused.* Rockville, MD: Launch.

Gladding, S.T., & Gladding, C. (1991). The ABCs of bibliotherapy for school counselors. *The School Counselor, 39,* 7–13.

Harrison, J. (1994). *Dear bear.* Minneapolis: CarolRhoda.

Hynes, A.M., & Hynes-Berry, M. (1986). *Bibliotherapy the interactive process: A handbook.* Boulder: Westview.

Jeon, K.W. (1992, November–December). Bibliotherapy for gifted children. *Gifted Child Today,* 16–19.

Joosse, B. (1997). *Nugget & Darling.* New York: Clarion.

Kenny, K., & Krull, H. (1992). *Sometimes my mom drinks too much.* Austin, TX: Steck-Vaughn.

Koberstein, J., & Shepherd, T. (1989). Books, puppets, and sharing: Teaching preschool children to share. *Psychology in the Schools, 26,* 7–89, 311–313.

Mills, J., & Crowley, R. (1986). *Therapeutic metaphors and the child within.* New York: Brunner/Mazel.

Nemiroff, M., & Annunziata, J. (1990). *A child's first book about play things.* Washington, DC: American Psychological Association Press.

Ouzis, D. (1991). The emergence of bibliotherapy as a discipline. *Reading Horizons, 31,* 199–205.

Pardeck, J. (1994). Using literature to help adolescents cope with problems. *Adolescence, 29,* 421–427.

Riordan, J.R., & Wilson, L. (1989). Bibliotherapy: Does it work? *Journal of Counseling and Development, 67,* 506–507.

Romesburg, D. (1995). *Young, gay & proud*. Boston: Alyson.

Rubin, R.J. (1978). *Bibliotherapy sourcebook*. Phoenix: Oryx.

Schaefer, C., & Millman, H. (1981). *How to help children with common problems*. St Louis: Mosby.

Schrank, F.A., & Engels, D.W. (1981). Bibliotherapy as a counseling adjunct: Research findings. *Personnel & Guidance Journal, 60,* 143–147.

Stevens, M.J., & Pfost, K.S. (1982). Bibliotherapy: Medicine for the soul. *Psychology: A Quarterly Journal of Human Behavior, 19,* 21–25.

Author Index

Subject Index